ISSUES AND TRENDS IN LITERACY EDUCATION

THIRD EDITION

RICHARD D. ROBINSON
University of Missouri, Columbia

MICHAEL C. McKENNA
Georgia Southern University

JUDY M. WEDMAN
University of Missouri, Columbia

Boston   New York   San Francisco
Mexico City   Montreal   Toronto   London   Madrid   Munich   Paris
Hong Kong   Singapore   Tokyo   Cape Town   Sydney

Series editor: *Aurora Martínez Ramos*
Editorial assistant: *Katie Freddoso*
Senior marketing manager: *Elizabeth Fogarty*
Manufacturing buyer: *Andrew Turso*
Cover designer: *Jill Winitzer*
Production coordinator: *Pat Torelli Publishing Services*
Editorial-production service: *Chestnut Hill Enterprises, Inc.*
Electronic composition: *Stratford Publishing Services, Inc.*

For related titles and support materials, visit our online catalog at www.ablongman.com.

Library of Congress Cataloging-in-Publication Data
Issues and trends in literacy education / [edited by] Richard D. Robinson, Michael C. McKenna, Judy M. Wedman.—3rd ed.
    p. cm.
  Includes bibliographical references and index.
  ISBN 0-205-36110-2
    1. Language arts.   2. Reading.   3. English language—Composition and exercises.
  4. Literacy.   I. Robinson, Richard David   II. McKenna, Michael C.   III. Wedman, Judy M.

LB1576.I87 2004
372.6'044—dc21   2003040315

Whosoever therefore acknowledges himself
to be a zealous follower of truth, of happiness,
of wisdom, of science, or even of faith, must
of necessity make himself a lover of books.
—Richard de Bury (1473)

This book is dedicated to those teachers
who have inspired in their students
an undying love for reading and writing.

CONTENTS

PREFACE

Reading is the sole means by which we slip, involuntarily, helplessly, into another's skin, another's voice, another's soul.

—Joyce Carol Oates

The primary purpose of this book is to help you better study and understand the field of literacy education. What was once a rather limited discipline is today a vast and complicated body of knowledge and field of inquiry, frequently drawing on information from many diverse areas such as psychology, sociology, and linguistics. The individual wishing to investigate a question or topic in literacy today may find the experience a daunting one.

For example, a recent computer search on the subject "reading comprehension" identified over 12,000 references to this one topic. Ranging across a broad spectrum of subtopics, the results of this search clearly showed the diversity that is typical of the literacy field. These results included data-based research studies, classroom observational inquiries, theoretical research papers, as well as personal opinion articles. These references represented the work of university faculty, classroom teachers, commercial publishers, and private individuals. Complicating the situation is the fact that there is not only a great deal of information currently available, but many different opinions and perspectives as well. These viewpoints often range between a single individual's position on a topic and a national movement reflecting the philosophies and attitudes of many thousands of people.

It is with these circumstances in mind that this book was written. We have attempted to identify the most significant issues and trends facing literacy educators today and to locate sources that explain principal viewpoints on these issues. Beyond selecting sources and providing textual aids to promote comprehension and engagement, our contribution has been minimal. We prefer to let the authors speak for themselves.

We have assumed that most readers of this book have had at least some introduction to the study of literacy education. The book has been developed with practicing teachers in mind—practitioners interested in extending their own thinking about the important issues they face in classrooms. We have not attempted to produce an introductory text, but assume that the foundations of literacy instruction—its purposes, concepts, and methods—have already been laid by means of prior coursework and teaching experience.

ORGANIZATION OF THE TEXT

Each chapter is made up of four parts: (1) a brief introduction to the topic, (2) the articles themselves, (3) an annotated bibliography, and (4) suggestions for further involvement.

Chapter Introductions

Each topic is first summarized in a brief section designed both to provide necessary background and to help stimulate thinking related to the topic. Many readers of this book will have—either through previous education classes or classroom teaching experiences—ideas and feelings about the topics discussed in this book. We challenge you to keep an open mind about what you currently believe concerning literacy instruction. In many literacy areas, either because of recent research or relevant classroom experiences, instructional strategies that were once considered appropriate are now being challenged by new ideas and pedagogy.

Each chapter introduction concludes with a list of important questions designed to guide your reading and organize your thinking. Actively considering them should give you a better understanding of your current knowledge, beliefs, and feelings about a particular literacy issue.

Articles

Following the introduction are the selections. Our intent is that this section will help familiarize you with important, though sometimes incompatible, views on the chapter topic. Of particular note is the presentation of differing points of view. For some topics, where there is little disagreement or controversy, you will find a general discussion of the literacy trend. You should understand that the selections are never intended to be all-inclusive but rather to introduce the topic and encourage you to pursue further study on your own.

Following the articles are two sections called **Integrating Sources** and **Classroom Implications.** As the headings indicate, the intent is to help you resolve differences between the articles and to consider possible implications for classroom literacy instruction. These sections are purposely designed to be open-ended.

Annotated Bibliographies

Although every article has its own reference section, we have attempted to supplement these with a careful selection of sources useful for further reading. In some cases, the material is divided into a historical and a current listing of literacy sources. In these cases, the reader can see the development and changes in thinking on a literacy topic, noting how historical issues and trends have influenced current opinions and practices.

You Become Involved

The final section of each chapter is designed to help you formulate your own views by engaging in activities that encourage independent thought. For each chapter, a range of possibilities is presented. The ideas can be approached individually or in groups and are meant to be undertaken selectively.

FOR THE UNIVERSITY TEACHER

Today, colleges of education are increasingly faced with issues of accountability related to their preparation of teachers. Whereas some standards, such as those of the National Council for the Accreditation of Teacher Education (NCATE), apply across the general field of education, subject matter organizations have developed guidelines for more specialized teacher preparation. In this respect, the International Reading Association (IRA) has long been involved in the development of standards for the preparation of literacy educators at all levels. The IRA publication, *Standards for Reading Professionals* (Lunsford & Pauls, 1992), was written to guide the preparation and professional development of literacy educators. Emphasized as a fundamental principle throughout this publication is the fact that all educators, whether at the preservice or inservice level, need an extensive conceptual framework related to the field of literacy instruction.

The following specific guidelines are only part of those listed by which university and college programs of teacher education in the field of literacy will be evaluated. They include the following student outcomes:

- Has knowledge of current and historical perspectives about the nature and purposes of reading and about widely used approaches to reading instruction
- Pursues knowledge of reading and learning processes by reading professional journals and publications and participating in conferences and other professional activities
- Employs inquiry and makes thoughtful decisions during teaching and assessment
- Interprets and communicates research findings related to the improvement of instruction to colleagues and the wider community
- Initiates, participates in, or applies research on reading
- Reads or conducts research with a range of methodologies (e.g., ethnographic, descriptive, experimental, or historical)
- Promotes and facilitates teacher-based and classroom-based research

The primary purpose of this book is to assist you in helping your students meet these wide and diverse guidelines for literacy education. Chapter content is designed to encourage further exploration of certain selected topics in literacy education through the effective use of a wide variety of resources and materials. We would hope that the end product of this book and your instruction is an educator who has been made more aware of the prominent issues and trends in the field of literacy education today and who appreciates their implications for practice.

We wish to take this opportunity to thank the following reviewers for their helpful comments: Tom Caron, Marshall University, Graduate College; Patricia Douville, University of North Carolina, Charlotte; Lois Fisch, Utica College of Syracuse University; and Barbara O'Byrne, Marshall University, Graduate College.

INTRODUCTION TO THE FIELD OF LITERACY EDUCATION

Books are yours,
Within whose silent chambers treasure lies
Preserved from age to age; more precious far
Than that accumulated store of gold
And orient gems which, for a day of need,
The sultan hides deep in ancestral tombs.
These hoards of truth you can unlock at will
—William Wordsworth, 1802

The study of literacy today is a vast and often complicated enterprise. In many fields, information is concentrated in a limited number of journals or produced by relatively few individuals; this is certainly not the case in literacy education, however. For example, important literacy research and writing are currently being done by individuals in fields as diverse as linguistics, cognitive psychology, sociology, computer science, anthropology, and education. Even within the general field of education, literacy materials are often indexed under a broad range of descriptors, such as emergent literacy, assessment, materials, teacher training, and so on. This information is frequently reported in a wide variety of outlets—including journals, books, and search reports—and has recently been lodged in huge computer databases. For the literacy educator, this wide spectrum of knowledge and available resources often presents a daunting challenge.

The purpose of this chapter is to facilitate your further study of literacy education. The intent here is to provide specific information that will help you learn more about the most prominent resources and current thinking in the field. You may already be familiar with some of the sources mentioned.

AS YOU READ

Your study of this chapter should prepare you to examine the issues that follow. As you read, keep the following objectives in mind:

1. Describe some effective strategies for literacy research and study.
2. Identify some of the current trends in literacy education.
3. Identify the major national organizations in the field of literacy study.
4. Describe some of the important journals and references in the field of literacy.

INTRODUCTION

Edmund Huey, writing early in the twentieth century about the study of the reading process, noted that "to completely analyze what we do when we read would almost be the acme of a psychologist's achievements, for it would be to describe very many of the most intricate workings of the human mind, as well as to unravel the tangled story of the most remarkable specific performance that civilization has learned in all its history" (Huey, 1908, p. 6). This single statement, in many respects, epitomizes even today the ongoing search for a better understanding of the reading process. Although it is true that much has been done in the study of fundamental processes related to literacy as well as in the development of new instructional programs in literacy since Huey wrote, many important questions remain unanswered at the present time.

CURRENT TRENDS IN LITERACY EDUCATION

Today, as in the past, the literacy community often finds itself split according to philosophies, theories, and/or practical applications. Although terms may have changed, much of what is debated today is often strikingly similar to the substance of past disputes. Issues such as the most appropriate methods and materials to use in the teaching of literacy as well as how to effectively assess what is learned are, after extended controversy, still the center of much of the literacy debate today.

As you continue your study of literacy issues, it is important to be aware that you must inevitably confront divergent viewpoints and opinions. For almost any of these issues, there is a wide range of opinions and feelings. These differences are clearly evident in the available literature on most topics. Expecting them should make you better at identifying and appraising the various viewpoints on each literacy topic.

A preview of some of the most prominent issues facing literacy educators today may well convince you of the range of problems involved. A major issue is that of whole language versus more conventional philosophies to instruction. Related to it is the role of phonics instruction, spelling, and basal readers. The nature of emerging literacy in early childhood has challenged older notions of "readiness," just as research into vocabulary instruction may surprise you with its implications for day-to-day practice. In content area classrooms, new conceptualizations have arisen as to how literacy activities can help students learn. In the larger arena of education, debate over the proper approaches to assessment and the desirability of national standards has spilled over into literacy. Finally, new advances in technology challenge educators to make the best uses of it in developing literate behavior in students. Each of these topics will be covered later in this book, though their interrelatedness will frequently compel you to cross-reference your thinking!

ORGANIZATIONS IN LITERACY EDUCATION

Many professional organizations address literacy issues as part of their programs, but the following are the most prominent:

- *International Reading Association.* The IRA is the largest organization in the literacy field, with a widespread membership that includes teachers at all levels from college and university faculty through elementary teachers. This organization is noted for its many quality literacy publications as well as a structure that invites participation at local, state, regional, national, and global levels. Its periodicals include *The Reading Teacher, Journal of Adolescent and Adult Literacy, Reading Research Quarterly*, and *Lecutra y Vida* (Spanish language).

- *National Council of Teachers of English.* The NCTE is a large organization representing teachers interested in language arts instruction. Like the IRA, the NCTE is noted for a variety of publications, including its two principal journals, *Language Arts* and *English Journal*.

- *National Reading Conference.* This organization is primarily comprised of college and university faculty interested in all types of literacy research. Its periodical is the *Journal of Literacy Research*, and its yearbook also presents research on a wide variety of literacy-related topics.

- *College Reading Association.* Members of this organization are primarily college and university faculty. CRA publishes a journal, *Reading Research and Instruction*, as well as a yearbook.

LEADING JOURNALS IN THE FIELD OF LITERACY

The following journals are among the most prominent:

- *The Reading Teacher.* This journal, published by the International Reading Association, includes articles primarily related to the teaching of literacy in the elementary school.

- *Journal of Adolescent and Adult Literacy.* This journal, formerly titled *Journal of Reading,* is published by the International Reading Association with emphasis on literacy education in the content areas as well as on middle, high school, and adult education.

- *Reading Research and Instruction.* Formerly *Reading World,* this journal combines research reports with articles that suggest ideas. It is published by the College Reading Association.

- *Reading Research Quarterly.* This is the leading journal of literacy research. The articles published in this journal consistently represent important contributions to the field of literacy research. Often, the articles published in the *Reading Research Quarterly* include extensive bibliographies of related materials and thus are excellent sources for further study. This journal is a publication of the International Reading Association.

- *Reading Horizons.* This journal is intended primarily for classroom teachers and typically publishes articles related to classroom applications of new literacy research.

- *Journal of Literacy Research.* Primarily a literacy research journal published by the National Reading Conference, this publication also presents position papers and issues-oriented commentary.

- *Reading Psychology.* This journal contains a wide variety of literacy articles, including research, opinion pieces, and suggestions for practice.

- *Language Arts.* This journal is published by the National Council of Teachers of English. Although areas of the language arts curriculum are included, there is a substantial number directly related to literacy concerns. The primary orientation of the journal is toward elementary instruction.

- *English Journal.* Published by the National Council of Teachers of English, this journal addresses the concerns of teachers serving adolescent and older populations.

REFERENCES IN THE STUDY OF LITERACY EDUCATION

Although a seemingly endless flow of new titles enters the field of literacy education, the following books have been selected as important sources for further study. They have been chosen on the basis of their importance to the field and should be excellent starting points for further study.

REFERENCE MATERIALS

Adams, M. J. (1990). *Beginning to read: Thinking and learning about print.* Cambridge, Massachusetts: MIT Press.

This important and scholarly reference reflects the continuing interest in the study of the sound/symbol relationships related to word analysis. Comprehensive synthesis of research in the areas of cognitive and developmental psychology, instructional methodology, and related areas is included.

Farstrup, A., & Samuels, S. J. (2002). *What research has to say about reading instruction.* Newark, Delaware: International Reading Association.

This is a valuable reference on current reading research, reflecting important work in the areas of theory and classroom practices that are supported by reliable studies. Chapters include balanced reading, phonemic awareness, and comprehension.

Flood, J., et al. (Eds.). (1991). *Handbook of research on teaching the English language arts.* New York: Macmillan.

This collection of research reviews focuses on topics broadly ranging across the language arts.

Goodman, K. (1986). *What's whole in whole language?* Portsmouth, New Hampshire: Heinemann.

A thorough discussion of the philosophical foundations of the whole language movement is provided.

Kamil, M., & Langer, J. A. (1985). *Understanding research in reading and writing.* Boston: Allyn and Bacon.

This book is a discussion of the uses of various research methodologies and their specific application to the study of literacy. For those interested in the development of a research design related to literacy, this is an excellent reference.

Pearson, P. D., et al. (1984). *Handbook of reading research.* White Plains, New York: Longman.

Barr, R., et al. (1991). *Handbook of reading research: Volume II.* White Plains, New York: Longman.

Kamil, M. L., et al. (2000). *Handbook of reading research, Volume III.* Mahwah, New Jersey: Earlbaum.

Each of these three volumes is an important resource in the study of literacy education. They contain inclusive reviews of important issues in the field as well as extensive bibliographies of related materials. They should be excellent starting points for most studies in the field of literacy education.

Robinson, R. D. (2001). *Historical Sources in U.S. Reading Education 1900–1970.* Newark, Delaware: International Reading Association.

This volume reviews the principle reading research studies completed by past authorities in the field of literacy education.

Robinson, R. D. (2002). *Classics in literacy education: Historical perspectives for today's teachers.* Newark, Delaware: International Reading Association.

This book brings together excerpts from eight classic writers in the field of literacy education whose works address topics facing today's reading teachers.

Samuels, J., & Farstrup, A. (1992). *What reading research has to say about reading instruction.* Newark, Delaware: International Reading Association.

This is a series of articles written by noted literacy authorities on how current research informs several important issues in the field.

HISTORICAL MATERIALS

The following references have been selected to provide a historical perspective on the research and teaching of literacy. They should provide you with information on important past work done by noted authorities in the field.

Altick, R. D. (1963). *The art of literacy research.* New York: W. W. Norton.

This cornerstone work on the research methods in literacy anticipates many of the present-day concerns of qualitative researchers.

Anderson, I. H., & Dearborn, W. F. (1952). *The psychology of reading.* New York: Roland Press.

This is an important reference in the early study of the psychology of literacy processes.

Betts, E. A. (1946). *Foundations of reading instruction.* New York: American Book Company.
    Written for preservice teachers on the teaching of literacy in the elementary grades, this important reference is excellent for comparison with current methods texts.
Dolch, E. W. (1939). *A manual for remedial reading.* Champaign, Illinois: Garrard Press.
    This is one of the first references written on the topic of the remediation of reading difficulties.
Gates, A. I. (1929). *The improvement of reading.* New York: Macmillan.
    This is one of the first textbooks in elementary literacy instruction.
Gray, W. S. (1948). *On their own in reading.* Chicago: Scott Foresman.
    Written by one of the early leaders in the study of literacy, this important reference focuses on the study and classroom use of the sound/symbol relationships.
Huey, E. B. (1908). *The psychology and pedagogy of reading.* Cambridge, Massachusetts: MIT Press.
    This is an early exploration of cognitive processes that underlie reading. It is famed for the later substantiation through research of many of the author's premises.
National Society for the Study of Education Yearbooks. Chicago: University of Chicago Press.
    This series of landmark books deals with important issues in the field of education. These books contain important articles that were often instrumental in the development of later reading policies and research. The following editions deal with the study of literacy: 20th (1921), 24th (1925), 36th (1937), 47th (1948), 48th (1949), 55th (1956), 60th (1961), 67th (1968), 83rd (1984).
Robinson, H. M. (1946). *Why pupils fail in reading.* Chicago: University of Chicago Press.
    This is a foundation report in the clinical approach to the study of reading disabilities in children.
Smith, N. B. (1934). *American reading instruction.* New York: Silver, Burdett.
    This is a classic in the study of the historical foundations of the study of literacy and of reading instruction from colonial times forward.

STRATEGIES FOR LITERACY RESEARCH

For most readers of this book, a literacy study will begin with a question about a particular concern or interest in this area. This question may arise in response to an assignment in a graduate class in literacy education or as the result of a personal interest in a literacy topic. It also might be initiated by a need to solve a classroom problem related to literacy, such as finding out more about a specific teaching technique or the background related to new commercial materials. For whatever reason, the formation of a question is a very important first step in any literacy study (Altick, 1963).

Unfortunately, it is at this point that many individuals begin to have varying degrees of difficulty. Frequently, initial questions are far too general to be answered in a realistic and effective manner. For example, questions such as the following are almost unanswerable:

- What causes literacy problems?
- What are effective literacy materials?
- What is the best method of teaching literacy skills?

These examples could be improved considerably by narrowing their scope:

- Does the home environment of a child have a lasting effect on literacy development?

- What is the influence of library books on the development of literacy skills?
- Has the use of language experience been shown to be superior to the use of the basal reader in first-grade literacy development?

The degree of specificity of any question will largely be determined by the background knowledge and purposes of each individual.

Once the question has been formulated, the investigator needs to propose a possible answer, sometimes with limited information, but always on the basis of theory. Continuing with the previous examples, the projected answers might look like these:

- The home environment of a child, especially parents reading to their children, does have a positive and long-term effect on literacy development.
- Library books are best used under the direction of a professional librarian rather than the classroom teacher.
- First-grade teachers find language experience instruction to be better suited to disadvantaged students than the use of the basal reader.

Each of these statements may or may not be true. It then becomes the goal of the investigator to find information either to support or to refute these tentative conclusions. In accomplishing this objective, the literacy researcher needs to be aware of a number of potential difficulties. The first is the typically large amount of information available on almost every aspect of literacy education. In the area of literacy education, the question frequently is not "Can I find information on my topic?" but rather "How can I select from the voluminous material available?" The second problem is the wide diversity of sources. Not only are there prominent journals and references in the field, there are also many other resources that publish literacy-related information. These sources include journals, books, research and development reports, newspaper articles, and so forth. Finally, one must consider the fact that for many issues in literacy education, there are widely differing opinions. Thus, for many literacy issues, you should expect to find various personal opinions as well as research results—and differing opinions on what the results mean!

With these obstacles in mind, it may seem an almost impossible task to find an answer to any literacy question. Yet the careful and thorough process of investigation should, in most cases, prove to be successful. Altick (1963), in summarizing this approach to scholarship, noted a pair of elementary principles: "(1) collect all the evidence, internal and external, that has any connection with your hypothesis, and (2) give as much consideration to evidence that weighs against the hypothesis, or that tends to support an alternative one, as to the substantiating kind. And maintain the critical attitude to the very end; the collapsible premise and the spurious fact are always lurking in the path of the unwary" (p. 122). Hopefully, with these thoughts in mind, you should be able to successfully begin, work through, and produce an effective literacy study into a topic of particular interest to you.

REFERENCES

Altick, R. D. (1963). *The art of literacy research*. New York: W. W. Norton.

Huey, E. B. (1908). *The psychology and pedagogy of reading*. Cambridge, MA: MIT Press.

Wordsworth, W. (1994). *The excursion: Book 4. Despondency corrected. The works of William Wordsworth.* Ware, Hertfordshire, England: Wordsworth Editions, Ltd.

CHAPTER ONE

TEACHER EDUCATION IN LITERACY

Let the tutor demand an account not only of the words of his lesson, but of their meaning and substance, and let him estimate the profit he has gained, not by the testimony of his memory, but of his life. Let him show what he has just learned from a hundred points of view, and adapt it to as many different subjects, to see if he has rightly taken it in and made it his own.
—Michel de Montaigne (1580)

[There is] growing agreement that there is no one and only orthodox way of teaching and learning this greatest and hardest of all arts [reading], in which ear, mouth, eye, and hand must in turn train the others to automatic perfection.
—G. Stanley Hall (1887)

Becoming a thoughtfully adaptive [reading] teacher is a career-long endeavor.
—Gerald Duffy (2002)

For decades, literacy educators have struggled to determine the most effective ways to prepare preservice teachers to teach literacy in K-12 schools. Some of the struggles are influenced by research that informs and alters literacy paradigms about teacher preparation. Within the past three decades, teacher preparation programs have shifted from paradigms that primarily consisted of course work (with student teaching at the end) to paradigms that focus heavily on field-based learning. For example, it is not unusual for programs to include:

- student teaching experiences that occur in a single classroom for 16 weeks;
- observations that are completed in a variety of schools so preservice teachers can examine teaching practices, classroom/school environments, and diversity among students;

- collaboration between university faculty, classroom teachers, and preservice teachers to link theory and practice; and
- field experiences that occur throughout a teacher preparation program.

Some of the paradigm shifts in programs that educate preservice teachers have been influenced by the way in which teacher preparation programs answer the question, "How do preservice teachers gain knowledge of content and pedagogy?" This question will provide the basis for issues included in this chapter on Teacher Education in Literacy.

MODELS OF TEACHER EDUCATION

Historically, many preparation programs answered the above question by providing content knowledge throughout a pedagogy course and by placing preservice teachers in classrooms where they "apprenticed" under the tutelage of an experienced teacher. The preservice teachers were "practicing to teach," using methods similar to those of the experienced teacher's methods.

More recently, many teacher preparation programs have abandoned the "apprenticeship" model for teacher preparation in favor of the "reflective practice" model (Schon, 1983). Reflective practice places the preservice teacher in the role of an inquiring teacher who questions traditional teaching practice, thinks about the consequences of decisions and practice, and assumes the responsibility of lifelong learning in order to meet the diverse needs of students.

Reflective practice as a goal for teacher preparation encourages preservice teachers to examine classroom, teaching, or learning problems from more than one perspective. That is, consideration should be given to the complexities of school environments as well as social/political situations that may influence classroom teaching and learning.

Unfortunately, through decades of research, many findings report that "teachers tend to teach the way they were taught" (Clark, 1988; Kagan, 1992; Lortie, 1975) and that teacher preparation is "washed out" by the classroom experiences and the socialization effects that preservice teachers encounter in schools (Zeichner & Tabachnick, 1981).

RESEARCH IN TEACHER EDUCATION

Currently, the question of improved teacher education in literacy is an issue coming to the forefront of literacy research. Anders, Hoffman, and Duffy (2000) emphasized the need for examining the effectiveness of preservice teachers' learning to be literacy teachers in the *Handbook of Reading Research:*

The question "How should teachers be taught to teach reading?" has received little attention from the reading research community. Reading researchers have attended to the reading process . . . and tested their theories. Relatively few researchers have asked questions about the processes that teachers go through as they learn and continue to learn to teach reading. We sense, however, that reading researchers are beginning to turn their attention to this critical question (p. 719).

A few studies indicate that important factors in preservice programs may include university experiences that directly impact preconceived ideas about literacy instruction (Wolf, Carey, & Mieras, 1996). That is, learning experiences included in teacher preparation must go beyond descriptions and models of the most effective literacy practices (Hiebert & Stigler, 2000). The experiences should include intense and authentic opportunities for teaching and reflection along with guidance from experienced mentors. In addition, university experiences should explore and build on preservice teachers' personal and professional knowledge to help them grow as reflective practitioners and to develop the perspectives necessary for meeting the challenge of a diverse literacy classroom (Duffy & Atkinson, 2001).

As teacher educators in literacy continue to examine questions of "how to prepare preservice teachers to teach literacy," issues of quantity and quality will continue to surround teacher preparation programs. Political leaders question the necessity of traditional teacher preparation requirements, and alternative teacher certification is now acceptable to some school districts and available from many teacher preparation institutions.

Potential teachers are being recruited from among citizens who have retired early and who already hold a college degree. In addition, a teacher shortage is imminent and schools are scrambling to fill vacant positions. The issue of teacher supply and demand as well as quality programs may have a profound effect on teacher education in literacy and the question of "how to prepare teacher educators to teach literacy," becomes even more fraught with issues that extend beyond traditional teacher preparation programs.

AS YOU READ

The article in this section presents a comprehensive discussion of the history, difficulties, and need for future research related to teacher education in literacy. "Teacher Education in the Next Millennium: What Your Grandmother's Teacher Didn't Know That Your Granddaughter's Teacher Should" (2002) discusses some of the changes that must be addressed by teacher educators that include changes in literacy, students, schools, and society. You might consider some of the following questions as you read this important article.

1. What do you believe should be the primary role of literacy education in preparing preservice teachers to teach literacy?
2. What role do you believe schools and teachers should have with preservice teachers in literacy preparation programs?

REFERENCES

Anders, P. L., Hoffman, J. V., & Duffy, G. G. (2000). Teaching teachers to teach reading: Paradigm shifts, persistent problems, and challenges. In M. L. Kamil, P. B. Mosenthal, P. D. Pearson, & R. Barr (Eds.), *Handbook of Research on Reading Research* (Vol. 3, pp. 719–742). Mahwah, NJ: Erlbaum.

Clark, C. M. (1988). Asking the right questions about teacher preparation; Contributions of research on teacher thinking. *Educational Researcher, 17* (2), 5–12.

Duffy, A. M., & Atkinson, T. S. (2001). Learning to teach struggling (and non-struggling) elementary school readers: An analysis of preservice teachers' knowledge. *Reading Research and Instruction, 41,* 83–102.

Hiebert, J., & Stigler, J. W. (2000). A proposal for improving classroom teaching: Lessons from the TIMMS video study. *Elementary School Journal, 101,* 3–20.

Hoffman, J., & Pearson, P. D. (2000). Reading teacher education in the next millennium: What your grandmother's teacher didn't know that your granddaughter's teacher should. *Reading Research Quarterly, 35* (1), 28–44.

Kagan, D. M. (1992). Professional growth among preservice and beginning teachers. *Review of Educational Research, 62* (2), 129–169.

Lortie, D. (1975). *Schoolteacher: A sociological study.* Chicago: University of Chicago Press.

Schon, D. (1983). *The reflective practitioner.* New York: Basic Books.

Wolf, S. A., Carey, A. A., & Mieras, E. L. (1996). What is this "literachurch" stuff anyway? Preservice teachers' growth in understanding children's literary response. *Reading Research Quarterly, 31* (2), 130–157.

Zeichner, K., & Tabachnick, B. R. (1981). Are the effects of teacher education washed out by school experience? *Journal of Teacher Education, 32* (3), 7–11.

Reading Teacher Education in the Next Millennium:

What your Grandmother's teacher didn't know that your granddaughter's teacher should

JAMES HOFFMAN

P. DAVID PEARSON

INTRODUCTION

It is likely that your grandparents were taught to read in school by teachers who had no more than two years' preparation beyond their high school diploma. In their normal school studies, or the equivalent, your grandparents' teachers probably didn't take any specific courses on how to teach reading. Instead, they took one or two general courses in pedagogical methods and a series of content area courses on topics related directly to the subject areas of the elementary curriculum (Monroe, 1952). From our perspective today, and with our knowledge of the remarkable economic progress that has been made over the past 50 years, we can judge the efforts of these teachers as heroic in the context of limited resources. But the context for teaching has changed as our society has changed, just as the context for literacy practices has changed. Yesterday's standards for teaching and teacher education will not support the kinds of

First published in *Reading Research Quarterly*, *35* (2000): 28–44. Reprinted with permission of the authors.

5

learning that tomorrow's teachers must nurture among students who will be asked, in the next millennium, to meet literacy demands that our grandparents could not fathom.

Who will teach your grandchildren to read? How will their teachers be prepared? What will they know? What will they do? We can only speculate on the answers to these important questions. The possibilities are endless, and the reality will be shaped by many factors, some of which are broadly societal, and outside the realm of reading education and reading research. Consider the following projections for the start of the 21st century:

1. The children of the baby-boom generation are already filling our elementary schools to capacity, and their numbers will continue to escalate over the next three decades. Between 1996 and 2006, total public and private school enrollment will rise from a record 51.7 million to 54.6 million (U.S. Department of Education, 1996).

2. The proportion of children from poverty and second language backgrounds will continue to grow. For example, it is projected that between 2000 and 2020 there will be 47% more Hispanic children aged 5–13 in schools than there are today (National Center for Educational Statistics, 1997). These children have not been served well by our educational system in the past. With increasing numbers, the challenge is likely to continue to grow.

3. The teaching force is aging rapidly. Retirements, coupled with teacher attrition rates (nearly 30% quitting teaching during their first three years), could lead to a tremendous teacher shortage by the year 2010. "Over the next decade we will hire more than 2 million teachers for America's schools. More than half the teachers who will be teaching ten years from now will be hired during the next decade" (Darling-Hammond, 1996, p. 5). By the year 2006, we will need 190,000 additional teachers (U.S. Department of Education, 1996).

4. The profession struggles to attract and retain teachers (Archer, 1999), especially teachers who represent the diversity of the students we serve and the goals we embrace. At the elementary levels, we continue to be mostly white, mostly female, and mostly middle-class in background (Grant & Secada, 1990). We express a value for diverse thinking and creativity, and yet the teaching force is largely conservative and socialized toward traditional thinking and values (Zeichner, 1989; Zeichner & Tabachnick, 1985).

5. The literacy demands on the work force of the next millennium, in particular the use of electronic texts, will far outstrip anything we have known in the past (Reinking, 1995). It is quite possible that many people regarded as functionally literate today will live to see themselves become functionally illiterate.

Each of these projections presents a stark challenge to the future of reading teacher education. Collectively, they present a daunting scenario.

Some of the factors that will shape the future of teacher education lie within our purview as a reading research community. We contend that the reality that lies 15–25 years ahead in reading teacher education will be shaped substantially by the research agenda we enact today. It is our goal in this article to make recommendations regarding this research agenda based on a consideration of where we have traveled in the past and where we find ourselves located in the present. We will go beyond a traditional retrospective synthesis of the findings from existing research to a prospective envisionment of the challenges the future holds and the critical role that research must play in setting a productive course of action. We structure our look-ahead around five basic questions.

1. Is teacher preparation effective?
2. What do we know about training teachers of reading?
3. What do we know about teaching teachers of reading?
4. What will it be—training or teaching teachers of reading?
5. What should our research agenda for reading teacher education look like?

We have not selected these questions because they are the ones for which we have answers. We have posed them because we believe that they embody the issues that will make our conversations regarding future research efforts most productive.

IS TEACHER PREPARATION EFFECTIVE?

There is no simple, direct answer to this question. Rather, we must assume a number of different perspectives on the goals and processes of teacher education to gather converging evidence regarding the effectiveness of teacher education programs. In examining the issues related to this question, we will begin with a look at the general teacher education literature and later return to focus specifically on the issues of reading teacher education. We have identified five perspectives that contribute to our understanding of the effects of teacher preparation programs.

Adopting a service model, we can address the question of effectiveness by looking at the satisfaction levels of those who participate in these programs (i.e., the clients). Here we find generally high levels of satisfaction with the patterns suggesting program improvements over the past decade. For example, the National Center for Educational Statistics (1995) reported on a survey of teacher satisfaction that compares perceived quality between all teachers and those with less than five years' experience. For 1984, they reported that 46% of the teachers expressed a very high level of satisfaction with their preservice programs as compared with 58% in 1995. They found that 64% of those teachers with less than five years' experience expressed a very high level of satisfaction. In another study, they reported on teacher satisfaction with their teacher preparation program with respect to teaching students from a variety of ethnic backgrounds. These data were collected on the same group of teachers before and after their first year of teaching. In the preservice phase of their development, they found that 81% of the teachers gave a positive response to the question. After the first year of teaching, the number dropped to 70% in the affirmative. The findings from these studies and others suggest a generally positive regard for teacher preparation.

Adopting a product perspective on teacher preparation, we can examine the data from teacher examinations, licensing procedures, and performance-based assessments. The vast majority of students completing teacher education programs pass the initial certification examinations, either meeting or exceeding the standards set by their states. Similarly, the studies of first-year teacher induction programs suggest that the vast majority complete these programs with high ratings on performance assessments while they are teaching. Principal ratings on the qualities of new teachers entering the teaching force are high (Hoffman, Edwards, O'Neal, Barnes, & Paulissen, 1986).

Adopting an evaluation perspective on teacher preparation, we can examine the data on program evaluations conducted by several major teacher education programs across the country (e.g., Ayers, 1986). These studies have typically examined not just the quality of the graduates as they enter the teaching force; they have also attempted to map the features and emphases within preservice programs onto specific teaching practices in their first year of teaching. Although the vast majority of teacher education programs in the country do not collect follow-up or longitudinal data on their graduates, those that do have documented program impact on teaching qualities.

Adopting a productivity perspective on teacher preparation, we can examine the data from studies that have examined the impact of teacher education on student learning. The studies that fall into this perspective tend to be large-scale gross analyses of relationships between student test scores and resource allocations (including the level of teaching experience, teacher education levels, etc.). Ferguson (1991) examined the relationship between student scores on a state-mandated skills test in Texas and a number of resource allocation variables, including the scores of the teachers on another state-mandated test. He found that the variation in teacher test scores accounted for a statistically significant portion of the variance in student achievement. This analysis included complete data on teachers and students in 900 school districts (over 80% of the school districts in the state). He also reported similar positive effects on pupil test scores for teaching experience, advanced studies (i.e., positive effects for master's degrees in grades one through seven), and class size (i.e., larger class sizes leading to decreases in student scores). Greenwald, Hedges, and Lane (1996) explored similar issues in a meta-analysis of input–output studies relating educational resource allocation to variation in pupil test scores. Positive effects were found for levels of teacher education and experience. In one analysis, they reported that increased allocations of resources will reap the greatest rewards if the money is invested in teacher education. After reviewing the literature comparing nontraditional with traditional programs, Evertson, Hawley, and Zlotnik (1985) concluded that traditional programs look favorable, for the most part, in terms of outcome variables considered.

Finally, adopting an experimental design perspective, we find more evidence on the positive effects of teacher education. We are not aware of any pure experiments in teacher education, where, for example, teacher education was withheld from one group while provided to another; however, a number of studies have compared the teaching performance of graduates from traditional programs with teachers certified through alternate or emergency certification procedures. These studies suggest that the teaching performance, teacher satisfaction levels, and students' learning in the classroom are inferior for the nontraditional students (Ashton & Crocker, 1987).

While most of these studies, regardless of perspective, fall short in identifying the qualities of effective teacher education practices or programs, they are encouraging in documenting the broad positive impact of teacher preparation. While most of the studies fail to offer specific information or guidance in matters of reading teacher education, they do suggest that a careful inspection of the reading teacher education literature has the potential to reveal similar patterns of excellence and impact.

WHAT DO WE KNOW ABOUT TEACHING TEACHERS OF READING?

In this section and the one that follows, we will make some critical distinctions between the terms training and teaching teachers. We will argue that the differences are not just superficial, semantic labeling issues, but rather cut to the very heart of understanding the complexity of teacher education and achieving excellence in our profession.

We will use training to refer to those direct actions of a teacher that are designed to enhance a learner's ability to do something fluently and efficiently. In a very direct sense, we can map the construct of training onto the notion of skill. Skills are behavioral routines that operate, when internalized, with automaticity and a minimum amount of cognitive attention or inspection. While there is a tendency to locate skill learning at a very simple level of operation, many would argue that the concept of skills, and thus skills training, can extend up to complex cognitive processes (e.g., higher-level thinking skills, problem solving skills, and even attitudes). Behavioral psychology, which reached its high point of influence in educational psychology during the 60s and 70s, became the theoretical basis for framing this view of learning onto the training of teachers. In many ways, the training perspective is aligned with a technological perspective on teaching. By contrast, as we argue later in this essay, we regard teaching as the intentional actions of a teacher to promote personal control over and responsibility for learning within those who are taught.

Competency-Based/Performance-Based Teacher Education

Training models depend on the identification of specific behavioral and psychological routines that become the target of interventions. The earliest iterations of teacher training following this perspective were found in the competency-based teacher education movement. The most notable effort within this conception was represented in the U.S. Office of Education's effort to improve preservice teacher education using a skills/training model (Cruickshank, 1970). Successful bidders in this grant competition were required to describe the teacher preparation program in terms of teacher competencies (see Houston & Howsam, 1972, for a description of the early work in the CBTE movement). Numerous lists of competencies were produced as a result of this initiative. The 1,119 competencies (i.e., behaviors), for example, in the Florida Catalog of Teacher Competencies (Dodl et al., 1972), are organized under the headings of assessing and evaluating student behavior, planning instruction, conducting and implementing instruction, performing administrative duties, communicating, developing personal skills, and developing pupil-self.

Sartain and Stanton (1974) described the efforts of the International Reading Association (IRA) in the development of a set of modules for the preparation of reading teachers that drew heavily on a competency-based perspective. The IRA Commission on High Quality Teacher Education identified 17 essential components of a professional development program:

1. Understanding the English Language as a Communication System
2. Interaction with Parents and Community
3. Instructional Planning: Curriculum and Approaches
4. Developing Language Fluency and Perceptual Abilities in Early Childhood
5. Continued Language Development in Social Settings
6. Teaching Word-Attack Skills
7. Developing Comprehension: Analysis of Meaning
8. Developing Comprehension: Synthesis and Generalization
9. Developing Comprehension: Information Acquisition
10. Developing Literary Appreciation: Young Children
11. Developing Literary Appreciation: Latency Years
12. Developing Literary Appreciation: Young Adults
13. Diagnostic Evaluation of Reading Progress
14. School and Classroom Organization for Diagnostic Teaching
15. Adapting Instruction to Varied Linguistic Backgrounds
16. Treatment of Special Reading Difficulties
17. Initiating Improvements in School Programs.

Instructional modules were developed in each of these areas. The modules contained a list of "teacher competencies to be attained—a precise, behavioral statement of the expected outcomes . . ." (Sartain, 1974, p. 35). In addition, each of the modules specifies criterion behaviors to specify learning outcomes, suggested learning experiences, and a continuing assessment plan. Other than the description of their development and the contents of these modules, we could not locate any published evaluation of their use in teacher education programs.

The competency-based movement peaked in the late 1970s. Roth's (1976) review of CBTE programs in 56 colleges and universities was inconclusive regarding changes in teacher education. What had been heralded by many within the profession as the future of teacher education all but vanished in less than a decade. Explanations regarding the demise of the competency-based movement ranged from institutionalized resistance at the college/university level, to fears of a dehumanization of teacher education, to a questioning of the sparse research literature supporting such an initiative, to a growing distrust of anything in teaching remotely associated with a behaviorist view.

The Teaching Effectiveness Movement

Certainly the emergence of the research in the teaching movement must be considered as another contributing factor in the demise of the competency-based teacher education movement (see Tom, 1984, for an enlightening discussion of the relationship between the Performance-Based Teacher Education movement and the teacher effectiveness movement). Research in teacher effectiveness—in particular, the research within the process–product paradigm—offered teacher educators a potential curriculum for training that was more defensible than the skills listed in the competency modules, even though there was considerable overlap at times. The compelling feature of this knowledge base was its grounding in teaching practices that were directly related to growth in student achievement. The fact that these effective practices were typically represented as specific teaching behaviors fit perfectly into a training model. The paradigm and the related findings have been described in detail in other sources both with respect to general teaching practices (Brophy & Good, 1986; Dunkin & Biddle, 1974) and reading in particular (Duffy, 1981; Hoffman, 1986; Rupley, Wise, & Logan, 1986). We focus our consideration here on the findings from this research as a basis for a new direction in teacher education.

Rosenshine and Furst (1973) made an impassioned call for a descriptive–correlational–experimental feedback loop in research in teaching. The science of teaching could best be advanced by taking the findings on effective teaching behaviors uncovered through correlational studies and putting them to the test in true experimental studies where the causal relationships are fully revealed. This became the focus for much of the research in the teaching movement during the late 70s and early 80s. Since this research typically involved the training of teachers in particular teaching practices, the lines between research in teaching and research in teacher education began to blur. Studies of this type proliferated and ranged across content areas (e.g., Good & Grouws, 1977, in mathematics), teaching processes (e.g., Emmer, Evertson, & Anderson, 1980, in classroom management), and age levels (e.g., Stallings & Kaskowitz, 1974, in early childhood, and Stallings, Needels, & Stayrook, 1979, with high school–aged students).

Anderson, Evertson, and Brophy's (1979) study of first-grade reading group instruction is instructive regarding this line of research. These researchers extrapolated a set of 22 research-based principles from their earlier process–product correlation studies. These principles ranged across a variety of areas from turn-taking practices in oral reading recitations to teacher feedback to inappropriate responses. Experimental teachers were trained in the principles, and control teachers were not. Implementation of the principles was systematically monitored and pupil achievement measured. The analysis focused on the degree to which the principles were successfully implemented under the experimental training conditions as well as an analysis of the relationship between the implementation of each particular principle and student achievement growth. The findings were interpreted as corroboration for the causal relationship of a number of the principles as influential on achievement. They were also interpreted in terms of a demonstration of the potential connection between research in teaching and teacher education.

Griffin and Barnes (1986) combined the research on effective staff development with the findings from the research in teaching literature. Teachers and staff developers in the experimental group were trained in effective practices. Implementation was monitored through direct observations of teachers and analysis of the logs/journals of the staff developers. Positive effects for the training were observed for both the teachers and the staff developers. This study provided for a valuable linking of training at two levels: the teachers and the teacher trainer.

The findings from the process–product literature also entered into teacher education through the teacher evaluation and certification standards route. During the mid-1980s, many states began to develop and implement induction/evaluation programs for beginning teachers that would delay full certification until the demonstration of competence in actual classroom teaching. These programs were intended both to screen out the incompetent and to provide support for those struggling though their first year of teaching (Defino & Hoffman, 1984). The evaluation instruments used for these programs drew heavily on the process–product research literature. In turn, the induction programs to support first-year teachers focused on training in the specific skills and strategies that had been identified. In a study of two state-mandated programs of this type, Hoffman and his colleagues found some positive effects for such programs in supporting teachers through their first year of teaching, but they found little evidence that the programs or the criteria were effective in screening out incompetent teachers (Hoffman et al., 1986).

While much of the work just described tended to focus on specific behaviors or routines drawn out of the process–product literature, other efforts tended to focus on the efficacy of larger constructs that might become the basis for teacher training. The work in the development of a direct instruction model is illustrative here. The roots of direct instruction, as it is connected to the research in teaching movement, are to be found in the Follow-Through studies (Stallings & Kaskowitz, 1974), the Beginning Teacher Evaluation Studies (BTES, Fisher et al., 1978), and the syntheses of Barak Rosenshine (Rosenshine, 1971; Rosenshine & Stevens, 1984). The direct instruction (DI) model proved to be eminently trainable to teachers under experimental conditions, effective in promoting student engagement in classroom tasks as demonstrated through classroom observations, and statistically significantly related to growth in pupil achievement as measured on standardized tests (Myer, 1988).

Paralleling this emerging conception of direct instruction in the process–product literature, we also find the writings of Madeline Hunter (Hunter, 1985, 1993) and Joyce and Showers (1988) influential in the staff development arena. Models of teaching and the direct instruction model itself began to coalesce in the late 1980s and on into the 1990s as a favorite teacher training model. As we point out later, the influence of these models has gradually atrophied since the mid-1980s, although the models appear to be resurfacing recently as more and more scholars return to the study of effective teaching and schooling, especially for students at-risk for failure to learn to read, write, and compute effectively (e.g., Puma et al., 1997; Stringfield, Millsap, & Herman, 1997; Wharton-MacDonald, Pressley, & Hampston, 1998).

Programmatic Models for Reading Teacher Training

The focus on specific effective teaching behaviors as the basis for teacher training, and even the focus on a generic direct instruction model of teaching, has given way in recent years to packaged programs. These programs can be characterized as more content-specific, more age-specific, and more organizationally complex than their forerunners. Reading Recovery, as a specific intervention program, is probably the most notable example in the field of reading, but it is not alone in this regard. The Success for All program has its roots firmly planted in a series of studies exploring effective reading instruction. There are other examples. It is not our intent here to review the full range of these programs or their effectiveness. We will simply point out that the conception of teaching effectiveness and teacher training has expanded to include consideration of the context in which teachers work (i.e., the context is also a target for the interventions, not just the teacher), the refinement of teacher training into trainer of trainer models with strict control over and monitoring of performance, ongoing data gathering for program validation and program improvement purposes, and the protection of proprietary rights to the materials and processes used.

Reading Recovery.   The Reading Recovery program was developed in New Zealand by Marie Clay. The program was formally introduced into the United States through a collaborative arrangement with Ohio State University (Lyons, Pinnell, & DeFord, 1993). The program offers intensive instruction at the first-grade level to struggling readers in need of acceleration. Students enrolled in the program are tutored intensively for 30 minutes daily. In theory, the students being tutored are reading well enough to be discontinued after 12 to 14 weeks of remedial help.

Studies in New Zealand and in the United States suggest that this program has been highly effective in accelerating the development of reading skills (Clay, 1990a, 1990b; Lyons et al., 1993). In a comprehensive review of the studies examining the effectiveness of Reading Recovery, Shanahan and Barr (1995) reported favorably on the findings from studies showing positive effects, concluding that many of the students served by Reading Recovery are brought up to the level of their average-achieving peers. However, they express some concerns over methodological issues (e.g., the exclusion of certain students who were not responding well to the program from the data analysis in some evaluation studies), program costs, and professional development.

Of most interest to us is the model of teacher training/education implicit in the implementation of Reading Recovery (see Gaffney & Anderson, 1991). The training is intensive, long-term, and universal (everyone at every level participates). Reading Recovery teachers are enrolled in over a year of intensive training in the strategies and routines to be followed in the tutorial. "While training is delivered during two hour inservice sessions at one or two weekly intervals over the period of a year, teachers are working with children and carrying out other teaching duties throughout the period they are in training" (Clay, 1987, p. 45). The training involves a great deal of on-line reflection about teaching. This is facilitated by a one-way mirror set-up. One trainee conducts a live lesson with an individual child behind the glass, while the rest of the class looks on and, with the prompting and probing of the trainer, conducts an on-line critique of the lesson, trying to ferret out the bases of her/his decisions and alternative practices he or she might have tried at key points. Afterward, the behind-the-glass teacher joins the rest of the class for a recapitulation of the lesson and the critique. This type of reflective but focused critique helps to ensure the high levels of fidelity to the program elements and philosophy that are demanded both during the initial training and in the follow-up phases. And there is some evidence (Gaffney & Anderson, 1991) to suggest that the reflection teachers engage in during these training sessions shows up as changes in their classroom teaching repertoire; that is, they work differently with groups in their classrooms because they possess new knowledge about learning to read. While containing aspects of an educative (what we are calling teaching teachers) model of teacher learning, the model in Reading Recovery must, in the final analysis, be regarded as either a training model, because of its emphasis on the mastery of a specific set of teaching procedures, or as an example of training set in the context of teaching, a topic to which we will return as we speculate about the future of this line of research.

Success for All. Robert Slavin and colleagues have developed a program designed to ensure that every child in a school is reading on grade level by the end of the third grade (Slavin, Madden, Karweit, Livermon & Dolan, 1990). The program, Success for All (SFA), is designed as a schoolwide intervention and includes components focused at the preschool and kindergarten levels up through the intermediate grades. The literacy program is intensive and varied and is centered in a daily period of reading instructional time. The content and processes of the reading period are based on classroom research into the CIRC model (Cooperative Integrated Reading and Composition) conducted at Johns Hopkins (Stevens, Madden, Slavin, & Farnish, 1987). Students are grouped for instruction (cross-aged) based on skill level for this block. Instructional group size is reduced to 15 students per teacher for the reading block. Tutoring support is also available to students in an additional 20-minute daily period.

Monitoring of student progress is a critical part of the SFA model. Children's progress is assessed four times a year. Training for teachers is intensive, and the implementation of the program elements is carefully monitored. The adoption of the SFA model in a school requires a formal commitment by the faculty and staff to the effort. The initial reports regarding the effectiveness of the SFA program have been positive (Slavin, Madden, Karweit, Dolan, & Wasik, 1992). However, some recent reports raise questions regarding effectiveness (e.g., Jones, Gottfredson, & Gottfredson, 1997). SFA proponents argue that the degree of success of the program is directly tied to the fidelity of implementation. Fully implemented programs are required for success to result in challenging settings (Nunnery et al., 1997), and, of course, full implementation is highly dependent upon the fidelity of the staff development program to the goals and procedures of SFA. Staff development is a key feature of the model; each site, in fact, has a full-time coordinator whose major responsibility is to conduct staff development sessions that initiate teachers into the SFA routines and sustain their continued use throughout the duration of the program.

We feature these two programs in our discussion because of the high levels of popularity they enjoy. While there are important differences in their philosophical underpinnings regarding reading, reading acquisition, and intervention, there are strong similarities with respect to a view of teacher development. They share a commitment to the systematic training of teachers as a critical element to improvement. Both programs are school-based, and both programs are connected to broadly conceived reform initiatives (Clay, 1990a, 1990b; Cooper, Slavin, & Madden, 1996). And, when all is said and done, with their emphasis on learning an explicit set of procedures and routines, they bring a training, not a teaching, model to the question of how best to promote teacher learning.

The Critical Elements of Teacher Training

The findings related to teacher training are compelling. We know how to train teachers. The elements of effective training can be described with some confidence (Sparks & Loucks-Horsley, 1990; Cruickshank and Metcalf, 1990) summarized the findings from the literature on training in terms of the following elements:

1. Establish clear performance goals and communicate them to learners.
2. Ensure that learners are aware of the requisite skill level of mastery.
3. Determine learners' present skill level.
4. Introduce only a few basic rules during early learning stages.
5. Build upon learners' present skill level during early learning stages.
6. Ensure, during the initial acquisition stage, a basic, essential, conceptual understanding of the skill to be learned and when and why it is used.
7. Demonstrate during the initial stage what skill performance should look like.
8. Provide opportunities for the learners to discuss demonstrations.
9. Provide sufficient, spaced skill practice after understanding has been developed.
10. See that practice of the skill is followed by knowledge of the results.
11. Provide frequent knowledge of the results early in the learning process.
12. Provide knowledge of results after incorrect performance.
13. Delay knowledge of results when the learner is beyond the initial stage of learning.
14. Provide for transfer of training that is enhanced by maximized similarity between the training and the natural environment, overlearning salient features of the skills, providing for extensive and varied practice, using delayed feedback, and inducing reflection and occasional testing.
15. Provide full support and reinforcement for the use of skills in natural settings.

Variations in the labeling, ordering, and emphasis of some of these aspects of skill teaching abound, but the essential elements are represented in these 15 points.

We find value in Green's (1971) distinctions related to teaching and training. He argues for teaching as a more general, overarching construct focused on planful actions designed to promote learning. Training sits alongside a set of other interactive approaches, such as conditioning, instructing, and indoctrinating, all of which share the attribute of situating knowledge and authority within the teacher rather than the learner. We argue, using this view, that training is an incomplete and insufficient construct on which to base our models of teacher preparation. It may get teachers through some of the basic routines and procedures they need for classroom survival, but it will not help teachers develop the personal and professional commitment to life-long learning required by those teachers who want to confront the complexities and contradictions of teaching. Reading is a complex and ill-structured domain; it cries out for the sorts of multiple models and metaphors documented as necessary in other ill-structured domains such as medicine and film criticism (Spiro & Jehng, 1990). By analogy, we argue that training is equally insufficient and incomplete as a model for preparing readers. There are aspects of reading (and writing) that most certainly can and should be trained. But there are also complexities to reading that can only be fostered in the context of a balanced approach that is considerate of the relationship between learning goals and teaching strategies. The same holds true for reading teacher education. Our teaching of teachers must take a broad approach in selecting the strategies that are employed to nurture excellence. Nothing in what we will present here should be interpreted as pejorative regarding the elements of teacher training described in the previous section. Our goal is not to reject training as a useful heuristic for helping teachers acquire a part of their teaching repertoire but to situate training within a broader vision of teaching and teacher learning.

We base this argument on the findings from research in teaching that have revealed the qualities of expertise that go beyond the level of teaching behaviors. Process–product research did not help us to understand the nature of teacher knowledge or offer us insight into the reflective, adaptive, and responsive aspects of teaching. These elusive but important entities, which seemed so important even from a prima facie analysis, just could not be characterized using skill level analyses and interpretations. Interestingly, the impetus for this line of work parallels the evolution of the impetus for the process–product movement itself. The fundamental advances in research in teaching emerged as researchers moved into classrooms to understand teaching. Similarly, fundamental advances in teacher education are emerging as researchers have begun to study directly the processes and contexts of teacher learning, including both the college classroom and the classrooms in our schools.

And so, we begin this section with an answer of no to the question of, "Do we know how to teach teachers of reading?" But we hasten to add that we are learning a great deal from ongoing research, much of it in the area of reading education. We will inspect, in this section, some of the promising programs of research in reading teacher education for what they might reveal.

First, though, we present some conceptual preliminaries. New theoretical insights have made this sort of analysis more accessible than ever before. Recently, both Richardson and Placier (in press) and Cochran-Smith & Lytle (in press) have provided useful heuristics for understanding the essence of teaching teachers. Cochran-Smith and Lytle distinguish three approaches to understanding teacher learning: knowledge-for-practice, knowledge-in-practice, and knowledge-of-practice. In the knowledge-for-practice tradition of teacher learning, teachers are provided—

usually, though not necessarily, by being told—the knowledge they will need to be effective teachers by more knowledgeable others, usually university professors. In the knowledge-in-practice approach, teachers discover the knowledge they need in the field as they reflect on and critique their own practice, either individually or in some collaborative arrangement. In the knowledge-of-practice approach, teachers, invariably in community settings, construct their own knowledge of practice through deliberate inquiry, which may well involve ideas and experiences that emerge from their own practice as well as those codified as formal knowledge within the profession. Cochran-Smith and Lytle value the knowledge-of-practice conception of teacher learning because of their conviction that knowledge thus constructed is the only truly professional knowledge—the only knowledge that will sustain teachers through the exigencies of daily practice.

Richardson and Placier, because their topic is teacher change, focus on learning in school settings. A major distinction in their treatment of teacher change is between empirical–rational and normative–re-educative approaches (after Chin & Benne, 1969). In the former, when an innovation is deemed desirable, someone (other than a teacher) initiates professional development; "teachers are told about it, it is demonstrated to them, and, as rational human beings, they are expected to implement it in their classrooms" (Richardson & Placier, in press, p. 2). In this view, teacher change (and teacher learning) is a necessary evil—externally imposed, difficult, and painful, but needed for improvement in student learning. This is very much in the classic dissemination/technology transfer tradition spawned by the Enlightenment and the modernist research tradition emanating from it (Gallagher, Goudvis, & Pearson, 1988): give people new information (i.e., the truth) and it (the truth) will make them free. This is very much like Cochran-Smith and Lytle's knowledge-for-practice conception of teacher learning. Prototypic examples of the rational–empirical approach are the teacher education reforms emanating from the effective teaching movement discussed earlier. By contrast, in the normative–re-educative approach, control is exercised by teachers who have voluntarily decided that change is required; they set the agenda, engage in the inquiry, and determine the topics and resources needed. Outsiders, such as administrators or university facilitators, might be involved, but only in facilitative or advisory capacities. Richardson and Placier's normative–re-educative approach appears to embrace both the knowledge-in-practice and the knowledge-of-practice conceptions of teacher learning detailed by Cochran-Smith and Lytle, though with a clear bias for the knowledge-of-practice approach, with its emphasis on teachers constructing knowledge through deliberate inquiry in response to a variety of experiences and information sources.

Within reading education, an interesting illustration of the movement toward this tradition is represented in the work of Gerald Duffy and his colleagues. Duffy (1991), in his presidential address to the National Reading Conference, described his intellectual growth from an implanting of effective skills and strategies view of teacher education to more teacher-centered, deliberative models. He argued that our reading teacher education models must be directed toward the development of empowered teachers who are in control of their own thinking and actions. He cautioned against a wide range of disempowering practices that exist, not only within our teacher education programs, but also within the practices of reading teacher education researchers themselves. He argued:

> We must make a fundamental shift from faith in simple answers, from trying to find simple solutions, simple procedures, simple packages of materials teachers can be directed to follow. Instead, we must take a more realistic view, one which Roehler (1990) calls "embracing the complexities" (p. 15).

One of the more ambitious studies within this emerging tradition was carried out by Richardson and her colleagues (see Anders & Richardson, 1991; Placier & Hamilton, 1994; Richardson & Anders, 1994; Richardson & Hamilton, 1994). The researchers worked with 39 intermediate grade (3–6) teachers over a period of three years, examining changes in their beliefs and practices in response to readings and discussions about improving students' reading comprehension. A major focus of their research was the development of a theory about the relationship between teacher beliefs and practices. Indeed, a major breakthrough was the finding that in their naturalistic (under local teacher control) change setting, teachers often changed their beliefs prior to changing their practices (or changed beliefs interactively with changes in practice), thus contradicting the more common finding, especially in studies of mandated change, of changes in practice preceding changes in beliefs.

Over the three-year period of the study, they found that both beliefs and practices changed in ways that were consistent with the ideas (dubbed practical arguments, after Fenstermacher, 1986, 1994) arising from dyadic and larger group discussions. It appeared that teachers were, in a manner consistent with Cochran-Smith and Lytle's knowledge-of-practice approach, constructing new knowledge of teaching in response to both external (the readings brought in by the university partners) and local ideas and experiences. It is worth noting that this group of researchers was able to document increased learning among students of the teachers engaged in the staff development (Bos & Anders, 1994), as well as a disposition among these teachers to continue to reflect on and change their practices well after formal conclusion of the research study (Valdez, 1992). The Valdez study is classic in its embodiment of the principles underlying the normative–re-educative approach and, in our view, the knowledge-for-practice conception. As Richardson and Placier (in press) noted:

> The teachers had become confident in their decision-making abilities and took responsibility for what was happening in their classrooms. Thus they had developed a strong sense of individual autonomy and felt empowered to make deliberate and thoughtful changes in their classrooms (p. 28).

In the Metcalf Project, Tierney and his colleagues (1988) conducted a two-year study cut from the same cloth. Using the model of teacher as researcher (Goswami & Stillman, 1987; Lytle, in press; Lytle & Cochran-Smith, 1992), they documented the teacher learning, curriculum change, and student learning that occurs when individual teachers take charge of their own professional development within a collaborative setting. The approach to teacher research within a collegial study group involved several steps/activities. Teachers found their own problems and questions, designed their own approaches to studying them, shared their work with colleagues, supported colleagues in similar endeavors by critiquing their work, and participated in public dissemination about the project. Moll (1992), as a part of his larger funds of knowledge project, engaged teachers in a different model of research. He involved them as community ethnographers to encourage them to learn more about the Latino community in which their children and their children's families lived and worked. The net result was substantial learning on the part of the teachers leading to a documented increase in their culturally relevant pedagogy.

The model "teacher as researcher" is but one of many collaborative models in place in today's schools. Other models of collaboration have an equally long and illustrious history (see Cochran-Smith & Lytle, in press, for a full treatment of teacher learning communities). We have been involved (separately, not jointly) in learning communities organized to address dilemmas around the problems of classroom assessment. In addition to attempting to improve assessment practices, these collaborations provided opportunities to examine teacher learning when it is focused on highly specific goals. While not directly germane to this agenda, it is worth noting that in all of these efforts, as well as others not directly related to teacher learning (see Pearson, Spalding, & Myers, 1998), discussions of assessment tools lead almost inevitably to discussions of curriculum and teaching. Teachers want to know what sorts of teaching led to the artifacts in question; thus, discussions of better ways to assess student learning appear to be useful catalysts for discussions of practice.

In a series of studies, Pearson and his collaborators (Sarroub, Lycke & Pearson, 1997; Sarroub, Pearson, Dykema & Lloyd, 1997) have examined teacher learning, teacher practice, and student response to new assessment initiatives. In a junior high school setting (Sarroub et al., 1997a, 1997b), they found that the activities, which focused on building a consequential English language arts portfolio based upon new state standards, and the school–university collaboration itself influenced teacher learning and the evolution of roles played by the teachers in the effort. In the case of one teacher, the collaboration became a site for reconstructing her entire English curriculum. In the case of a second, the portfolio became a way of engaging students in reflections on their own growth as readers and writers. Most significant in the elementary English as a Second Language (ESL) setting was the evolution of roles played by university and school members of the collaborative (see McVee, Pearson, McLellan, Svoboda, & Roehler, 1997), from the more traditional division of labor in which university folks do the research and school folks implement the practices to a model of shared responsibility for all roles. In Vygotskian terms (after Gavelek & Raphael, 1996), the teachers literally appropriated the discourse, tools, and roles of researchers as the collaboration played itself out. The impact on student learning in both the junior high setting and the elementary ESL setting was evident in increased student capacity to reflect on and evaluate their own progress as readers, writers, and speakers.

Hoffman and his colleagues worked with a group of first-grade teachers who had become concerned about the pernicious influence that standardized assessments were having on their students and their own teaching of early reading and mathematics (Hoffman, Roser, & Worthy, 1998). They petitioned for and were granted a waiver from standardized testing in their classrooms. In its place they worked to develop a performance-based assessment plan that would provide data useful to teachers for making classroom and to administration for making macrolevel decisions. The PALM (Performance Assessment in Language Arts and Mathematics) system was implemented and evaluated in a yearlong study. The study yielded compelling findings regarding the potential for this assessment plan to provide data that was useful to both audiences. In addition, the conceptualization, planning, implementation, and evaluation processes proved to have a powerful impact on the participating teachers' professional development.

It is important, we believe, that all of the examples we selected to document teaching teachers come from inservice settings in schools rather than preservice settings in universities. While some scholars have documented attempts to create undergraduate classroom communities in literacy education (e.g., Florio-Ruane, 1994) there are surprisingly few efforts of this sort reported in the literature. We are not sure why this discontinuity exists. It could be that we have a naive view that novices require more direction from us, thus we feel virtually compelled to adopt a knowledge-for-teaching stance toward them as we introduce them into the profession, with the clear but implicit promise to bring them into full partnership later on. It could be that preservice training is so massive in scope, at least in comparison to the inservice settings in which we find ourselves working (e.g., we tend to hook up with small collectives of teachers, not the entire elementary force of a large district). That the discontinuity, both in our research and in our practice, exists should be of such concern to us that we are compelled to address it in a timely and energetic fashion.

It is also true that we have privileged, highly situated, decidedly local, and intensely personal models of teacher learning in this section on teaching teachers. It is our position that such models challenge us to think differently than traditional change and staff development models (Hoffman, 1998). We could have taken a more critical stance on these efforts, as have some of our colleagues in professional development (e.g., Hargreaves & Fullan, 1992), and cited their idiosyncratic, ". . . self-indulgent, slow, time-consuming, costly, and unpredictable" (pp. 12–13) character. Indeed, many leading scholars (e.g., Fullan, 1993; Lieberman, 1996; Little, 1981, 1992; Nelson & Hammerman, 1996) insist that the school is the appropriate unit of teacher learning, that teacher learning is school learning. Even so, we are equally suspicious of the bureaucratization of learning that can occur when individual needs and interests are overlooked in favor of the common good. Both Little (1992) and Richardson and Placier (in press) provide a way of coping with the individual–collective dilemma. What we need, according to Richardson and Placier, is some "sense of autonomy and responsibility that goes beyond the individual classroom . . . to the school and community levels" (p. 62). Little's (1992) solution to the tension between individual liberty and civic responsibility is to find joint work that provides an occasion for teachers to leave their autonomy in the classroom in the service of schoolwide issues and goals.

We would also comment on the range of research methodologies represented in the examples we have selected. Classical, experimental designs are absent, but they are not limited to qualitative/interpretive studies. In every case, the studies have involved highly interactive models of inquiry that position the researchers in close contact, if not identification, with the participants. Many of the studies involved quantitative measures and a statistical analysis of outcomes, but always along with rich descriptions of contexts and cases. Mixed-methods tend to dominate. It is our view that the adoption of a wide range of research methodologies, both within and across studies, offers greater opportunity to fathom the complexities of learning to teach and the effects of various forms of support on both teacher and student learning.

We said, in the beginning of this section, that we did not know how to teach teachers. We hope, however, that we have convinced you that we have many promising models to emulate and study with greater care and precision. The truth is that serious attempts to teach teachers, to engage them in educative practice and inquiry rather than provide them with a set of bureaucratically endorsed recipes, is a relatively new phenomenon. The concept has been around for a long time (Dewey, 1904), but it has been a serious matter of scholarship and enactment for only a few decades at most. It needs our nurture and our scrutiny.

TRAINING VS. TEACHING TEACHERS OF READING: DO WE HAVE TO CHOOSE?

The training perspective is rooted in a technological perspective for teaching (Feiman-Nemser, 1990). As long as the outcomes can be specified and the context controlled, training serves our needs. But the reality of teaching is one of constantly changing conditions with fairly abstract and even ambiguous learning outcomes. It should be obvious from our presentation up to this point that we endorse a teaching teachers perspective on reading teacher education. This is not, to be clear, a teaching vs. training of teachers dichotomy; rather, we support a nesting of training within a broader construct of teaching. We know that training will be an important part of what we do in our teacher preparation programs, especially for those aspects of teaching that are more skill-like in their conception, but there are many other important aspects of teaching that can only be nurtured through the kinds of reflective, discursive, and dialogical strategies and experiences described in the previous section.

We pose the "What will it be . . . ?" question in recognition of the fact that there are tremendous pressures surrounding teacher education that favor a training model, and that these forces can, if not acknowledged and addressed, push the teaching of teachers into the background of preparation programs. The pressure to adopt a training model comes from a number of different directions and a number of different considerations. It is tempting to adopt a training preference for a host of reasons:

■ We know how to train. We have evidence that training works on teachers and translates directly into student learning. We have some evidence that a teaching model may be more powerful in the long run, but the empirical data are not entirely compelling at this point in time.

- We can train efficiently and cheaply. This is a time and resource allocation issue. We can calculate, target, and budget the cost of training in relation to our needs and goals. The investment required in teaching teachers is much more substantial.
- We can communicate clearly with the public regarding what we do and why we do it in a training model. Teaching teachers is, like teaching itself, filled with ambiguity and uncertainty. To the outsider, this ambiguity can translate into confusion or inefficiency.
- Training in teacher preparation makes few assumptions about the learner's motivations, background knowledge, prior beliefs, or current levels of expertise. Teaching is designed to build on the known.
- Training creates conformity in practice. Teaching teachers is more likely to lead to diversity in practice at a surface level of examination.
- Teacher shortages and teacher turnover require an increasing supply. A training model can supply more teachers faster. Teaching teachers takes time, must be continuous, and costs more.
- Supervisors and those who must evaluate teachers don't need much expertise beyond an understanding of the features of the training model itself. Teachers of teachers must understand the processes of teacher learning and the contexts and strategies that promote growth.

The pressures toward a training model for teacher preparation are not derived solely from practical arguments. There are those who would argue at a conceptual level that training can become the path to more complex levels of thinking in teaching. According to Showers, Joyce, and Bennett (1987):

> The purpose of providing training in any practice is not simply to generate the external visible teaching moves that bring that practice to bear in the instruction setting but to generate the conditions that enable the practice to be selected and used appropriately and integratively . . . a major, perhaps the major, dimension of teaching skill is cognitive in nature (pp. 85–86).

Cruickshank (1987) has designed and studied a teacher education model to promote reflective teaching. According to his view, training in reflective teaching is a consistent and powerful strategy for teacher preparation.

We are cautious in accepting this representation of teaching and training. While we are comfortable with the notion that some level of technical training can scaffold a developing teacher to higher levels of thinking, we are skeptical regarding the broad application of training principles to all of teacher education. Training as a strategy, nested in a larger construct of teaching and learning to teach as reflective practice (Schon, 1983, 1987), is a more powerful and compelling vision for a future in which teachers are more likely to encounter change, not routine.

The debate over the direction we will follow will involve a substantial commitment of resources and will therefore be a highly political struggle. In the absence of any compelling data that would document the value added from a broader perspective than just training teachers, we are left with a course chartered for the next millennium. The responsibility within the reading research community is clear: plan for a program of research that informs the practice of teacher education but also informs the public regarding the benefits of such a deliberative, reflective approach.

WHAT SHOULD OUR RESEARCH AGENDA FOR READING TEACHER EDUCATION LOOK LIKE?

We have projected that the next millennium promises increasing challenges to the teaching of reading. We have argued that an increased focus on research in reading teacher education offers our best opportunity to meet these challenges. Our goal in this section will be to speak directly to the reading teacher education community regarding an agenda for future research that is considerate of our history and the conditions and the challenges we currently face. Our goal is not to prescribe specific studies but to share some thoughts about how we might better adjust the contexts, set goals, and establish priorities for our work. Here is our list of actions we need to take, both collectively, as a profession, and individually, in our roles as scholars and teacher educators within our institutional settings:

1. Take a leadership role in building a research agenda for teacher preparation in reading. The paucity of research in the area of reading teacher education is disturbing given the large numbers of reading researchers who spend a good portion of their daily lives immersed in teacher preparation. It is becoming increasingly clear that, if reading teacher educators don't take initiative and responsibility for setting a research agenda, someone else will.

2. Create critical spaces for dialogue, deliberation, discussion, and debates regarding reading teacher education research. This is not a call for a new organization as much as it is a challenge for those in the reading teacher education community to become more visible and more active in research within existing structures such as IRA, NCTE, NRC, AERA, and AACTE.

3. Get started on a database for reading teacher education. As a profession of reading educators, we know too little about the range of programs operating nationally and around the world—their characteristics, course work patterns, course content, instruction, internship experiences, and enrollments in reading education courses. Without accurate, up-to-date information about the nature and impact of our programs, we have difficulty countering high profile claims made by individuals pushing a particular policy agenda. With these data, we can begin to establish the benchmarks for our reform efforts.

4. Develop better tools to assess the impact of teacher education. We have made great progress in expanding the repertoire of measures available to examine reading acquisition, and we can credit much of that progress to better conceptual frameworks for understanding the acquisition process. We need similar development in reading teacher education—both better conceptual frameworks and better measures. Surely our search for better measures will include indices of student learning, but it will also include indicators for the knowledge, skills, and

dispositions teachers need to promote student learning. And our search for better frameworks must include an account of how teacher learning improves student learning.

5. Encourage rapprochement between the traditions of teacher training and teacher education. Instead of using the other tradition as a straw person useful only for establishing the worth of one's own perspective, we should be asking what each tradition has to contribute to research on teacher learning and what we can learn about our own work from the work of others. It would be even more compelling if we were to document empirically the ways in which training and teaching can complement one another.

6. Listen carefully and respond to the concerns of the public and policymakers. As scholars of reading education, we certainly need to take the lead in setting our own research agenda, but ours is not the only voice in this conversation. The public wants better schools, and they see teacher education as an important lever for school improvement. Any hesitancy on our part in studying this critical linkage will (and should) be viewed with suspicion by a public uncertain about our capacity to contribute solutions to our educational problems.

7. Make electronic texts a viable part of our curriculum and pedagogy in reading teacher education. We cannot expect in our elementary classrooms what we fail to use in our own work. Research on how reading teacher education can be enhanced through the use of electronic media and texts must accompany our program development efforts.

8. Place issues of diversity at the top of our priority list for research. We put this at the end of our list because it may be the most challenging issue we face, but it is also the most important. It is simply unacceptable that a vastly disproportionate number of minority students fail to learn to read. It is unacceptable that we have so few teachers of color in our schools. It is even more unacceptable that so many majority teachers possess so little knowledge about cultural and linguistic diversity. We may not be the sole source of the problem, but we can and must become part of the solution.

CONCLUSION

What should your granddaughter's teacher know about teaching reading that your grandmother's teacher didn't? Your grandmother's teacher was prepared to teach in a classroom very much like the one she attended as a student. The plan for preparation was quite straightforward. Your granddaughter's teacher will teach in a classroom quite different from the one she attended. There are few assumptions about that classroom of the future that we can use to extract a training model. We subscribe to van Manen's standard that "to be fit for teaching is to be able to handle change" (1996, p. 29). Change, and rapid change, will characterize the next millennium. Whether the conduit for these changes will be research or politics is up to us. To become the conduit for change, it may be necessary for the research community to abandon some of the research traditions that have served our scholarship in the past (e.g., criticizing practice, chronicling change) and become active participants in change. Van Manen's standard applies not only to classroom teachers but to teacher educators and researchers of teaching as well. The dispassionate, distant, objective scientist metaphor for studying teaching and teacher education has taken us about as far as it can in understanding the complexities of teaching and learning to teach. The research community must become participants in the change if we are to influence the outcomes.

REFERENCES

Anders, P., & Richardson, V. (1991). Research directions: Staff development that empowers teachers' reflection and enhances instruction. *Language Arts, 68*, 316–321.

Anderson, L., Evertson, C., & Brophy, J. (1979). An experimental study of effective teaching in first-grade reading groups. *Elementary School Journal, 79*, 193–223.

Archer, J. (1999, March 17). New teachers abandon the field at high rate. *Education Week 18* (27), 1.

Ashton, P., & Crocker, L. (1987). Systematic study of planned variations: The essential focus of teacher education reform. *Journal of Teacher Education, 38*, 32–38.

Ayers, J. B. (1986). *Teacher education program evaluation: A case-study past and future.* (ERIC Document Reproduction Service No. ED 275 669).

Bos, C. S., & Anders, P. L. (1994). The study of student change. In V. Richardson (Ed.), *Teacher change and the staff development process: A case in reading instruction* (pp. 181–198). New York: Teachers College Press.

Brophy, J. E., & Good, T. G. (1986). Teacher behavior and student achievement. In M. Wittrock (Ed.), *Handbook of research in teaching, 3rd ed.* (pp. 328–375). New York: Macmillan.

Chin, R., & Benne, E. (1969). General strategies for effecting changes in human systems. In W. Bennis, K. Benne, & R. Chin (Eds.), *The planning of change, 2nd ed.* (pp. 32–59). New York: Holt, Rinehart and Winston.

Clay, M. M. (1987). Implementing Reading Recovery: Systematic adaptations to an educational innovation. *New Zealand Journal of Educational Studies, 22*, 35–58.

Clay, M. M. (1990a, April). *Reading Recovery in the United States: Its successes and challenges.* Paper presented at the annual meeting of the American Educational Research Association, Boston.

Clay, M. M. (1990b). The Reading Recovery programme, 1984–1988: Coverage, outcomes and Education Board district figures. *New Zealand Journal of Educational Studies, 25*, 61–70.

Cochran-Smith, M., & Lytle, S. L. (in press). Relationships of knowledge and practice: Teacher learning in communities. In A. Iran-Nejad & P. D. Pearson (Eds.), *Review of research in education*, Vol. 24. Washington, DC: American Educational Research Association.

Cooper, R., Slavin, R., & Madden, N. A. (1996). *Success for All: Improving the quality of implementation of whole-school change through the use of a national reform network.* (ERIC Document Reproduction Service No. ED 420 107).

Cruickshank, D. R. (1970). *Blueprints for teacher education: A review of phase II proposals for the U.S.O.E. comprehensive elementary teacher education program models program.* Washington, DC: US Department of Health, Education and Welfare. (ERIC Document Reproduction Service No. ED 013 371).

Cruickshank, D. R. (1987). *Reflective teaching: The preparation of students of teaching.* Reston, VA: Association of Teacher Educators.

Cruickshank, D. R., & Metcalf, K. K. (1990). Training within teacher preparation. In W. R. Houston (Ed.), *Handbook for research in teacher education* (pp. 469–497). New York: Macmillan.

Darling-Hammond, L. (1996). *What matters most: Teaching for America's future.* New York: National Commission on Teaching & America's Future.

Defino, M., & Hoffman, J. V. (1984). *A status report and content analysis of state mandated teacher induction programs* (Technical Report No. 9057). Austin, TX: The University of Texas at Austin, Research and Development Center for Teacher Education.

Dewey, J. (1904). The relation of theory to practice in education. In C. A. McMurray (Ed.), *The relation of theory to practice in the education of teachers* (pp. 9–30). The third NSSE yearbook, Part I. Chicago, IL: University of Chicago Press.

Dodl, N., Elfner, E., Becker, J., Halstead, J., Jung, H., Nelson, P., Purinton, S., & Wegele, P. (1972). *Florida catalog of teacher competencies.* Tallahassee, FL: Florida State University.

Duffy, G. G. (1981). Teacher effectiveness research: Implications for the reading profession. In M. L. Kamil (Ed.), *Directions in reading: Research and instruction* (pp. 113–136). Thirtieth yearbook of the National Reading Conference. Chicago: National Reading Conference.

Duffy, G. G. (1991). What counts in teacher education? Dilemmas in educating empowered teachers. In J. Zutell & S. McCormick (Eds.), *Learner factors/teacher factors: Issues in literacy research and instruction* (pp. 1–18). Fortieth Yearbook of the National Reading Conference. Chicago: National Reading Conference.

Dunkin, M., & Biddle, B. (1974). *The study of teaching.* New York: Holt, Rinehart & Winston.

Emmer, E. T., Evertson, C., & Anderson, L. (1980). Effective classroom management at the beginning of the school year. *Elementary School Journal, 80,* 219–231.

Evertson, C., Hawley, W., & Zlotnik, M. (1985). Making a difference in educational quality through teacher education. *Journal of Teacher Education, 36*(3) 2–12.

Feiman-Nemser, S. (1990). Teacher preparation: Structural and conceptual alternatives. In W. R. Houston (Ed.), *Handbook for research in teacher education* (pp. 212–233). New York: Macmillan.

Fenstermacher, G. D. (1986). Philosophy of research on teaching: Three aspects. In M. Wittrock (Ed.), *Handbook of research on teaching, 3rd ed.* (pp. 37–49). New York: Macmillan.

Fenstermacher, G. D. (1994). The knower and the known: The nature of knowledge in research on teaching. *Review of Research in Education, 20,* 1–54.

Ferguson, R. (1991). Paying for public education: New evidence on how and why money matters. *Harvard Journal of Legislation, 28,* 465–498.

Fisher, C. W., Filby, N. N., Marliave, R., Cahen, L. S., Dishaw, M. M., Moore, J. E., & Berliner, D. C. (1978). *Teaching behaviors, academic learning time, and student achievement: Final report of phase III-B, beginning teacher evaluation study.* San Francisco: Far West Educational Laboratory for Educational Research and Development.

Florio-Ruane, S. (1994). Future teachers' autobiography club: Preparing educators to support literacy learning in culturally diverse classrooms. *English Education, 26*(1), 52–66.

Fullan, M. (1993). *Change forces: Probing the depths of educational reform.* London: Falmer Press.

Gaffney, J., & Anderson, R. C. (1991). Two-tiered scaffolding: Congruent processes of teaching and learning. In E. H. Hiebert (Ed.), *Literacy for a diverse society: Perspectives, programs, and policies* (pp. 184–198). New York: Teachers College Press.

Gallagher, M., Goudvis, A., & Pearson, P. D. (1988). Principles of organizational change. In S. J. Samuels & P. D. Pearson (Eds.), *Changing school reading programs* (pp. 11–39). Newark, DE: International Reading Association.

Gavelek, J. R., & Raphael, T. E. (1996). Changing talk about text: New roles for teachers and students. *Language Arts, 73,* 182–193.

Good, T., & Grouws, D. (1977). Teaching effects: A process-product study in fourth grade mathematics classrooms. *Journal of Teacher Education, 28,* 49–54.

Goswami, P., & Stillman, P. (1987). *Reclaiming the classroom: Teacher research as an agency for change.* Upper Montclair, NJ: Boynton/Cook.

Grant, C. A., & Secada, W. G. (1990). Preparing teachers for diversity. In W. R. Houston (Ed.), *Handbook for research in teacher education* (pp. 403–422). New York: Macmillan.

Green, T. F. (1971). *The activities of teaching.* New York: McGraw-Hill.

Greenwald, R., Hedges, L., & Lane, R. D. (1996). The effect of school resources on student achievement. *Review of Educational Research, 66,* 361–396.

Griffin, G., & Barnes, S. (1986). Using research findings to change school and classroom practices: Results of an experimental study. *American Educational Research Journal, 23,* 572–586.

Hargreaves, A., & Fullan, M. (1992). Introduction. In A. Hargreaves & M. Fullan (Eds.), *Teacher development and educational change* (pp. 1–19). New York: Teachers College Press.

Hoffman, J. V. (1986). Process-product research on effective teaching: A primer for a paradigm. In J. V. Hoffman (Ed.), *Effective teaching of reading: Research and practice* (pp. 39–52). Newark, DE: International Reading Association.

Hoffman, J. V. (1998). When bad things happen to good ideas in literacy education: Professional dilemmas, personal decisions, and political traps. *Reading Teacher, 52,* 102–113.

Hoffman, J. V., Edwards, S. A., O'Neal, S. H., Barnes, S., & Paulissen, M. (1986). A study of state-mandated beginning teacher programs. *Journal of Teacher Education, 37*(1), 16–21.

Hoffman, J. V., Roser, N., & Worthy, J. (1998). Challenging the assessment context for literacy instruction in first grade classrooms. In C. Harrison & T. Salinger (Eds.), *Assessing reading 1: Theory and practice* (pp. 166–181). London: Routledge.

Houston, W. R., & Howsam, R. B. (Eds.). (1972). *Competency-based teacher education: Progress, problems and prospects.* Chicago: Science Research Associates.

Hunter, M. (1985). What's wrong with Madeline Hunter? *Educational Leadership, 42*(5), 57–60.

Hunter, M. (1993). Education as a profession. *Journal of Staff Development, 14*(3), 42–44.

Jones, E. M., Gottfredson, G. D., & Gottfredson, D. C. (1997). Success for some: An evaluation of a Success for All program. *Evaluation Review, 21,* 643–670.

Joyce, B., & Showers, B. (1988). *Student achievement through staff development.* New York: Longman.

Lieberman, A. (1996). Practices that support teacher development: Transforming conceptions of professional learning. In M. W. McLaughlin & I. Oberman (Eds.), *Teacher learning: New policies, new practices* (pp. 185–201). New York: Teachers College Press.

Little, J. W. (1981, April). *The power of organizational setting: School norms and staff development.* Paper presented at the annual meeting of the American Educational Research Association, Los Angeles. (ERIC Document Reproduction Service No. ED 221 918).

Little, J. W. (1992). Teacher development and educational policy. In M. Fullan & A. Hargreaves (Eds.), *Teacher development and educational change* (pp. 170–193). London: Falmer Press.

Lyons, C. A., Pinnell, G. S., & DeFord, D. (1993). *Partners in learning: Teachers and children in Reading Recovery.* New York: Teachers College Press.

Lytle, S. (in press). Teacher inquiry and the cultures of teaching. In M. Kamil, P. Mosenthal, P. D. Pearson, & R. Barr (Eds.), *Handbook of reading research.* Mahwah, NJ: Erlbaum.

Lytle, S., & Cochran-Smith, M. (1992). Teacher research as a way of knowing. *Harvard Educational Review, 62,* 447–474.

McVee, M., & Pearson, P. D. (1997, December). *Exploring alternative assessment in an ESL setting: Researchers, teachers, and students learning to use portfolios.* Paper presented at the annual meeting of the National Reading Conference, Scottsdale, AZ.

McVee, M., Pearson, P. D., McLellan, M., Svoboda, N., & Roehler, L. (1997). What counts? Perspectives on assessment in an ESL classroom. In C. Kinzer, K. Hinchman, & D. Leu (Eds.), *Inquiries into literacy: Theory and practice* (pp. 156–165). Forty-sixth Yearbook of the National Reading Conference. Chicago: National Reading Conference.

Moll, L. (1992). Literacy research in community and classrooms: A sociocultural context approach. In R. Beach, J. Green, M. Kamil, & T. Shanalas (Eds.), *Multidisciplinary perspectives on literacy research* (pp. 211–244). Urbana, IL: National Council of Teachers of English.

Monroe, W. (1952). *Teaching-learning theory and teacher education 1890–1950.* Urbana: University of Illinois Press.

Myer, L. (1988). Research on implementation: What seems to work. In S. J. Samuels & P. D. Pearson (Eds.), *Changing school reading programs: Principles and case studies* (pp. 41–57). Newark, DE: International Reading Association.

National Center for Educational Statistics. (1995). *Pocket projections: Projections of education statistics to 2005.* Washington, DC: U.S. Office of Education.

National Center for Educational Statistics. (1997). *The condition of education, 1997.* Washington, DC: U.S. Department of Education.

Nelson, B., & Hammerman, J. (1996). Reconceptualizing teaching: Moving toward the creation of intellectual communities of students, teachers and teacher education. In M. McLaughlin & I. Oberman (Eds.), *Teacher learning: New policies, new practices* (pp. 3–21). New York: Teachers College Press.

Nunnery, J. et al. (1997). *Effects of full and partial implementations of Success for All on student reading achievement in English and Spanish.* (ERIC Document Reproduction Service No. ED 408 558).

Pearson, P. D., Spalding, E., & Myers, M. (1998). Literacy assessment in the New Standards Project. In M. Coles & R. Jenkins (Eds.), *Assessing reading 2: Changing practice in classrooms* (pp. 54–97). London: Routledge.

Placier, P., & Hamilton, M. L. (1994). Schools as contexts: A complex relationship. In V. Richardson (Ed.), *Teacher change and the staff development process: A case of reading instruction* (pp. 135–159). New York: Teachers College Press.

Puma, M. J., Karweit, N., Price, C., Ricciuitti, A., Thompson, W., & Vaden-Kiernan, M. (1997). *Prospects: Final report on student outcomes.* Washington, DC: Planning and Evaluation Service, U.S. Department of Education.

Reinking, D. (1995). Reading and writing with computers: Literacy research in a post-typographic world. In K. Hinchman, D. Leu, & C. Kinzer (Eds.), *Perspectives on literacy research and practice* (pp. 17–33). Forty-fourth Yearbook of the National Reading Conference. Chicago: National Reading Conference.

Richardson, V., & Anders, P. (1994). A theory of change. In V. Richardson (Ed.), *Teacher change and the staff development process: A case of reading instruction* (pp. 199–216). New York: Teachers College Press.

Richardson, V. & Hamilton, M. L. (1994). The practical-argument staff development process. In V. Richardson (Ed.), *Teacher change and the staff development process: A case of reading instruction* (pp. 109–134). New York: Teachers College Press.

Richardson, V., & Placier, P. (in press). Teacher change. In Richardson, V. (Ed.), *Handbook of research on teaching (4th ed.).* Washington, DC: American Educational Research Association.

Roehler, L. (1990, May). *Embracing the complexities.* Paper presented at the University of Maryland Conference on Cognitive Research and Instructional Innovation, College Park, MD.

Rosenshine, B. (1971). *Teaching behaviors and student achievement.* Windsor, England: National Foundation for Educational Research in England and Wales.

Rosenshine, B., & Furst, N. (1973). The use of direct observation to study teaching. In R. M. W. Travers (Ed.), *Second handbook of research on teaching* (pp. 122–183). Chicago: Rand McNally.

Rosenshine, B., & Stevens, R. (1984). Classroom instruction in reading. In P. D. Pearson (Ed.), *Handbook of reading research* (pp. 745–798). New York: Longman.

Roth, R. A. (1976). *A study of competency based teacher education: Philosophy, research, issues, models.* Lansing, MI: Department of Education, Teacher Preparation and Professional Development Services.

Rupley, W. H., Wise, B. S., & Logan, J. W. (1986). Research in effective teaching: An overview of its development. In J. V. Hoffman (Ed.), *Effective teaching of reading: Research and practice* (pp. 3–36). Newark, DE: International Reading Association.

Sarroub, L. K., Lycke, K., & Pearson, P. D. (1997 December). *How new assessments impact student learning, curriculum, and professional development: A case study in a junior high setting.* Paper presented at the annual meeting of the National Reading Conference, Scottsdale, AZ.

Sarroub, L. K., Pearson, P. D., Dykema, C., & Lloyd, R. (1997). When portfolios become part of the grading process: A case study in a junior high setting. In C. Kinzer, K. Hinchman, & D. Leu (Eds.), *Inquiries into literacy: Theory and practice* (pp. 101–113). Forty-sixth Yearbook of the National Reading Conference. Chicago: National Reading Conference.

Sartain, H. W. (1974). The modular content of the professional program. In H. Sartain & P. Stanton, (Eds.), *Modular preparation for teaching reading* (pp. 31–59). Newark, DE: International Reading Association.

Sartain, H. W., & Stanton, P. E. (1974). A flexible model for preparing teachers of reading. In H. Sartain & P. Stanton, (Eds.), *Modular preparation for teaching reading* (pp. 3–11). Newark, DE: International Reading Association.

Schon, D. (1983). *The reflective practitioner: How professionals think in action.* New York: Basic Books.

Schon, D. (1987). *Educating the reflective practitioner.* San Francisco: Jossey-Bass.

Shanahan, T., & Barr, B. (1995). Reading Recovery: An independent evaluation of the effects of an early instructional intervention for at-risk learners. *Reading Research Quarterly, 30, 958–996.*

Showers, J., Joyce, B., & Bennett, B. (1987). Synthesis of research on staff development: A framework for future study and a state-of-art analysis. *Educational Leadership, 45*(3), 77–87.

Shulman, L. S. (1985). Paradigms and research programs in the study of teaching: A contemporary perspective. In M. C. Wittrock (Ed.), *Handbook of research on teaching* (pp. 3–36). New York: Macmillan.

Slavin, R. E., Madden, N. A., Karweit, N. L., Dolan, L., & Wasik, B. A. (1992). *Success for All: A relentless approach to prevention and early intervention in elementary schools.* Arlington, VA: Educational Research Service.

Slavin, R. E., Madden, N. A., Karweit, N. L., Livermon, B. J., & Dolan, L. (1990). Success for All: First-year outcomes of a comprehensive plan for reforming urban education. *American Educational Research Journal, 27, 255–278.*

Sparks, D., & Loucks-Horsley, S. (1990). Models of staff development. In R. Houston (Ed.), *Handbook of research in teacher education,* (pp. 234–250). New York: Macmillan.

Spiro, R., & Jehng, J. (1990). Cognitive flexibility and hypertext: Theory and technology for the linear and nonlinear multidimensional traversal of complex subject matter. In D. Nix & R. Spiro (Eds.), *Cognition, education, and multimedia: Exploring ideas in high technology* (pp. 163–205). Hillsdale, NJ: Erlbaum.

Stallings, J., & Kaskowitz, D. (1974). *Follow-through classroom observation evaluation 1972–1973* (SRI Project URU-7370). Stanford, CA: Stanford Research Institute.

Stallings, J., Needels, M., & Stayrook, N. (1979). *The teaching of basic reading skills in secondary schools, Phase I and Phase II.* Menlo Park, CA: Stanford Research Institute.

Stevens, R. J., Madden, N. A., Slavin, R. E., & Farnish, A. M. (1987). Cooperative and integrated reading and composition: Two field experiments. *Reading Research Quarterly, 22, 433–454.*

Stringfield, S., Millsap, M. A., & Herman, R. (1997). *Urban and suburban/rural special strategies for educating disadvantaged children: Findings and policy implications of a longitudinal study.* Washington, DC: U.S. Department of Education.

Tierney, R., Tucker, D., Gallagher, M., Crismore, A., & Pearson, P. D. (1988). The Metcalf Project: A teacher-researcher collaboration. In S. J. Samuels & P. D. Pearson (Eds.), *Changing school reading programs* (pp. 207–226). Newark, DE: International Reading Association.

Tom, A. (1984). *Teaching as a moral craft.* New York: Longman.

U.S. Department of Education. (1996). *A back to school special report. The baby boom echo.* Washington, DC: Author.

Valdez, A. (1992). *Changes in teachers' beliefs, understandings, and practices concerning reading comprehension through the use of practical arguments: A follow-up study.* Unpublished doctoral dissertation, College of Education, University of Arizona, Tucson.

van Manen, M. (1996). Fit for teaching. In W. Hare & J. P. Portelli (Eds.), *Philosophy of education: Introductory readings.* Calgary, Alberta: Detselig.

Wharton-MacDonald, R., Pressley, M., & Hampston, J. M. (1998). Literacy instruction in nine first-grade classrooms: Teacher characteristics and student achievement. *Elementary School Journal, 99,* 101–128.

Zeichner, K. (1989). Preparing teachers for democratic schools. *Action in Teacher Education, 11*(1), 5–10.

Zeichner, K., & Tabachnick, B. R. (1985). The development of teacher perspectives. Social strategies and institutional control in the socialization of beginning teachers. *Journal of Education for Teaching, 11,* 1–25.

INTEGRATING SOURCES

Two areas discussed by the authors of this article were models for teacher preparation evident during the 1970s, 1980s, and the 1990s and research about teacher preparation. Identify the issues that literacy preparation faced during the years that each of the models was in place. Identify parallel issues or responses to issues that underlie the research presented. What relationship might exist between the issues you identified and the agenda for future research?

CLASSROOM IMPLICATIONS

1. How can classroom teachers' professional development and literacy practices keep pace with the important issues in literacy teaching?

2. Based on the information presented in this article, what kind of conversation would you have with a teacher who has been teaching for twenty years that would describe the importance of literacy education? What conversation might you have with a building administrator?

ANNOTATED BIBLIOGRAPHY

Bartlett, A. (2001). "Call it courage": A first-year teacher learns to teach reading with children's literature. *Journal of Reading Education, 26,* 9–13.
Describes a first-year teacher's experiences teaching literature to a fourth-grade classroom, emphasizing the need for evaluating various approaches to reading instruction.

Commeyras, M. (2001). Pondering the ubiquity of reading: What can we learn? *Journal of Adolescent and Adult Literacy, 44,* 520–524.
Discusses the teaching value of creating a personal anthology of reading experiences for both preservice teachers as well as their literacy instructor.

Davis, B. H., Resta, V., Davis, L., & Camacho, A. (2001). Novice teachers learn about literature through collaborative action research. *Journal of Reading Education, 26,* 1–6.
Suggests that the extended use of literature circles can often provide both important reasons for enjoying reading as well as a method for improving student literacy performance in the classroom setting.

Dwyer, E. J. (2001). My life as a reader: Gaining insights through writing about learning to read. (ERIC Reproduction Service No. ED449476).
Notes that teachers can gain valuable information on their literacy instruction as they reflect on how they themselves became readers as young people. Specific suggestions include information on how to write a personal autobiographical essay relating their personal history as a reader and how teachers and parents helped in this process.

Flippo, R. (2001). Researchers in search of common ground. Newark, DE: International Reading Association.
Reports on the different reading philosophies of eleven leading reading authorities and, while they differed on various instructional points, there were many similarities among these literacy experts as well.

Knudson, R. E., & Maxson, S. (2001). How students learn to teach beginning reading. *Reading Improvement, 38,* 125–131.
Discusses student progress in a preservice literacy class based on both their university class experiences as well as their field experience.

Mather, N., Bos, C., & Babur, N. (2001). Perceptions and knowledge of preservice and inservice teachers about early literacy instruction. *Journal of Learning Disabilities, 34,* 472–482.
Examines the ideas and knowledge of both preservice and inservice teachers concerning early literacy instruction for those students identified as high-risk individuals.

Miller, R. (2001). A 20-year update on reading instruction and primary school education: Mexican teachers' viewpoints. *Reading Teacher, 54,* 704–716.
Compares the results of a 1998/1999 survey of Mexican teachers' views of various aspects of literacy education with those collected in the period 1978/1979.

Roller, C. (2001). *Learning to teach reading: Setting the research agenda.* Newark, DE: International Reading Association.
Describes the results of the International Reading Association's 2000 Research Conference, with particular emphasis on the importance of the role of the classroom teacher in an effective literacy program.

Wham, M. A., Cook, G., & Lenski, S. D. (2001). A comparison of teachers whose literacy orientations reflect constructivist or traditional principles. *Journal of Reading Education, 26,* 1–8.
Presents information on the teaching of reading as viewed by teachers who believe in the constructivist view of the literacy process compared to more traditional approaches to reading instruction.

Wolf, S. A. (2001). "Wax on/wax off." Helping preservice teachers 'read' themselves, children, and literature. *Theory Into Practice, 40,* 205–211.
Discusses the experiences of one preservice teacher when she taught a single child and how this instruction challenged her perceptions of the reading process.

YOU BECOME INVOLVED

1. Interview a teacher who graduated from a teacher preparation program fifteen to twenty years ago. Interview a second teacher who graduated within the past one to five years. Construct an interview that would explore issues related to their literacy preparation program such as:

   ■ Describe the effectiveness of your preparation for teaching literacy.

   ■ How could your preparation for teaching literacy have been improved?

   ■ Recall the problems you had during your first and second years of teaching related to literacy.

   ■ How have you continued to learn about literacy teaching?

   ■ How have your literacy beliefs and practices changed over the course of your career? What has influenced those changes?

2. Compare the interview responses to explore likeness, differences, common influences, common perceptions, and so on. Write a summary that illustrates your findings. Do you notice any similarities to the models or research described by the authors of the article?

CHAPTER TWO

EARLY LITERACY INTERVENTION

*I observe that betwixt three and four years of age
a child hath great propensity to peep into a book and then
is the most reasonable time for him to begin to learn to read.*
—C. Hoole (1660)

*When a child can talk, 'tis time he should learn to read. And when he reads, put
into his hands some very pleasant book suited to his capacity, wherein the
entertainment he finds may draw him on, and rewards his pains in reading.*
—J. Waugh (1752)

*. . . children who are ultimately most likely to be successful comprehenders of
reading are those who acquire the strongest literacy foundations during the early
childhood years.*
—Diane Tracy & Lesley Morrow (2002)

NATIONAL ISSUES

First Lady Laura Bush's educational initiatives are directed toward parents, teachers, and others who can help children become successful in life. The First Lady comments:

> Some children enter school without even knowing the basics. . . . For these children, reading and learning can often be a struggle . . . that affects every American because if our children are not able to read, they are not able to learn.
>
> As first lady, I will work tirelessly to make sure that every child gains the basic skills to be successful in school and life . . . I want to recruit more teachers, shine the spotlight on successful early childhood pre-reading and vocabulary programs, and help parents get access to information that will help them help their children learn.

Each of us has a duty to help our children achieve their full potential. By working together, we can shape the destiny of America's children with our hands and hearts. Children who are able to read will be ready to learn. . . .

The First Lady actively supports programs that aim to improve the educational opportunities for children and to increase the number of teachers in schools. Through the Reach Out and Read program, parents are taught the importance of reading to their very young children by pediatricians and volunteers working in clinical settings. During each clinical visit, the pediatricians prescribe that the parents read to their children and volunteers demonstrate creative ways that books can be used. At the end of each visit, the child receives a book.

Other projects supported by Ms. Bush include Teach for America, a program that involves college students in tutoring children in reading; The New Teacher Project, a teacher-recruitment program for inner-city and rural schools; and Troops to Teachers, an invitation to retired military servicemen and -women to enter the teaching profession (U.S. Department of Education, 2001).

Clearly, early intervention is an issue at the national level. However, the emphasis is not new. During the past thirty years the federal government has established a system of early intervention services through mandates, regulations, funding programs, and incentives. In addition, there have been court cases and parent efforts that have combined to have a wide-ranging impact on children's lives at home, preschool, and school (Bailey, 2000).

STATE ISSUES

Many states support early intervention programs that support "at-risk" children's learning. The programs focus on a variety of factors that range from increased parent education to improved teacher-preparation programs. For example, Missouri implements a successful Parents as First Teachers' program. The program employs staff who make regular at-home visits to help parents learn parenting skills and ways that literacy experiences can help their young children.

Alabama targets student's reading performance through the Alabama Reading Initiative, which focuses on retooling existing teachers in three areas: beginning reading instruction, expanding reading power in grades 2–12, and intensive intervention for students in grades K–12. Principals and teachers participate in intensive training sessions with certified trainers who emphasize research-based practices. The training also includes demonstration sites in local classrooms. Initially, the initiative was funded by community, businesses, private organizations, and government agencies. The state now funds expansion of the initiative throughout the state's school districts.

Some states focus on improving the preparation for teaching reading in undergraduate teacher-education programs. For example, preservice teachers majoring in elementary education are commonly required to complete two or three courses in the teaching of reading. Middle and secondary preservice teachers may be required to complete one reading course. In addition, while there is growing research evidence about what it takes to teach children to read, inconsistencies exist about what is taught both in reading courses across universities as well as among professors who teach different sections of the same course within one university. In response, some states are changing the number of reading courses required for initial teacher certification. For example, Maryland, North Carolina, Georgia, Mississippi, Kentucky, and Texas have increased the course requirements in reading for teacher preparation. Other states require that literacy instruction be consistent with current scientific research about children's literacy learning.

SCHOOL ISSUES

For decades, school districts have focused on remediating reading difficulties (e.g., Title 1, Special Education, ability grouping, class-within-a-class, etc.). However, there is a growing body of evidence that suggests that reading failure can be prevented in the majority of cases (Hall, Prevatte, & Cunningham, 1993; Hiebert & Taylor, 1994; Lin, 2001; Reynolds, 1991). Conversely, there is little empirical evidence supporting the success of programs designed to correct children's reading problems after the second grade (Kennedy, Birman, & Demaline, 1986).

Early intervention programs have historically referred to preschool programs such as Head Start. While researchers indicate that preschool programs effectively contribute to children's learning to read, schools question whether or not early intervention programs should be extended into first grade. There are many programs available for first-grade intervention, and most of them require extensive teacher training. The issue faced by school districts and teachers becomes whether to invest time and money into continuing existing remediation programs or committing to early intervention programs in first grade, and, if so, which one? Reading Recovery? Success for All? Early Intervention in Reading? What should an early intervention program provide to children? Consider these issues:

- Quality instruction should be provided along with additional instructional time.
- Individual or very small group (four to five) instruction should be provided.
- Intervention should be focused at first grade (some children will need special instruction beyond first grade).
- Texts should be simple so that children can successfully read them (predictable text, literature with natural language).
- Text should be reread so that fluency is developed.
- Children should construct meaning about the text.
- Attention should focus on words, letters, phonemic awareness, phonics, and word patterns.
- Daily writing activities should be short, with instructional focus on letter and word features.
- Students' progress should be monitored.
- Communication between school and home should be frequent.
- Materials should be sent home daily for the children to read.

■ Training and support should be provided for teachers so that instruction will be effective (Pikulski, 1994; Edwards, McMillon, Turner, & Laier, 2001).

Failure in learning to read has a devastating effect on children. The resulting frustration, humiliation, and suffering that follows them through life is well documented. Yet the issues remain: should the large amounts of dollars continue to be spent on marginally effective remediation-type reading programs, or redirected toward prevention of young children's failure to learn to read?

AS YOU READ

It is clearly evident from both research and practice that when young children appear to be "at-risk" of unsuccessfully developing literacy abilities, intervention programs and practices must be available. Ideally, the intervention would occur early in the child's life, both at home and at school. Juel & Minden-Cupp (2001) indicate that differences in the type of classroom literacy instruction makes a difference in children's literacy development. They further indicate that, once children can read independently, they profit from vocabulary instruction, book discussions, and reading from a variety of texts. In the second article, Denton (2000/2001) discusses the role of assessment and phonic instruction. In the third article, Daniel, Clarke, and Ouellette (2001) address policy issues related to early intervention that resulted from the National Governor's Association. You might consider some of the following questions as you read these different viewpoints.

1. Who should assume the responsibility for ensuring that children successfully develop literacy abilities?
2. To what extent can communities, schools, and policymakers work together to help children develop literacy?
3. Given that research has identified environmental conditions and instructional practices that are effective in helping "at-risk" children develop literacy, what could be done to increase the prevalence of those factors in homes and schools?

REFERENCES

Bailey, D. B. (2000). The federal role in early intervention: Prospects for the future. *Topics in Early Childhood Special Education, 20(2)*, 71–78.

Daniel, J., Clarke, T., & Ouellette, M. (2001). Developing and supporting literacy-rich environments for children. Washington, DC: National Governors Association. ERIC Reproduction Service No. 459 912.

Denton, D. R. (2000/2001) Teaching all children to read. Atlanta, GA: Southern Regional Education Board. ERIC Reproduction Board Service No. 440 364.

Edwards, P. A., McMillon, G. T., Turner, J. D., & Laier, B. (2001). Who are you teaching?: Coordinating instructional networks around the students and parents you serve. *Reading Teacher, 55(2)*, 146–150.

Hall, D. P., Prevatte, C., & Cunningham, P. M. (1993). Elementary ability grouping and failure in the primary grades. Unpublished manuscript.

Hiebert, E., & Taylor, B. (Eds.). (1994). *Getting reading right from the start: Effective early literacy interventions.* Boston, MA: Allyn & Bacon.

Juel, C., & Minden-Cupp, C. (1999–2002). One down and 80,000 to go: Word recognition instruction in the primary grades. On-line. Available at: http://www.ciera.org/library/archive/1999-02/abs-online-99-02.html

Kennedy, M. M., Birman, B. F., & Demaline, R. E. (1986). The effectiveness of Chapter 1 services. Washington, DC: U. S. Department of Education, Office of Educational Research and Improvement.

Lin, C. H. (2001). Early literacy instruction: Research applications in the classroom. ERIC Reproduction Service No. ED459424.

Pikulski, J. J. (1994). Preventing reading failure: A review of five effective programs. *Reading Teacher, 48*(1), 30–39.

Reynolds, A. J. (1991). Early schooling of children at risk. *American Educational Research Journal, 28,* 392–422.

U.S. Department of Education. (2001). Ready to read, ready to learn: First Lady Laura Bush's educational initiatives. Washington, DC: Author. ERIC Reproduction Service No. ED 450 342.

Teaching All Children to Read

DAVID R. DENTON

Reading is fundamental. This message is not new, but in the last decade research clearly has shown that our schools should be able to teach every child to read. Achieving that goal will require changes in reading instruction at many levels.

WHAT DOES IT TAKE TO TEACH ALL CHILDREN TO READ?

WHAT DOES COMPREHENSIVE READING REFORM LOOK LIKE?

To teach all children to read, six key areas must be addressed:

- early assessment to identify each child's individual needs and detect problems early
- classroom reading instruction that meets the needs of all children
- early intervention to help children who are at risk of not learning to read
- intervention for older children who are not reading at grade level
- teacher education that prepares new teachers to meet every child's reading needs and
- professional development that helps teachers continually improve their skills in teaching reading

Each area requires individual attention just as children do, but it also is important to recognize that they are all closely linked and that the last two—teacher education and professional development—are central to each of the others.

U.S. Department of Education, Educational Resources Center.

EARLY ASSESSMENT TO IDENTIFY
READING PROBLEMS

Research on how children learn to read clearly shows that effective reading instruction needs to address certain basic issues. In particular, all children need to understand the relationship between sounds and letters (phonemic awareness) and must know how to use phonics to sound out unfamiliar words. They also must learn to recognize words automatically, including a core vocabulary of irregular words that cannot be sounded out. The best way to become a fluent reader is to read a lot—to practice reading quality texts that match each student's reading level but also challenge him or her to learn new vocabulary and new forms of language.

But children are different, and no one lock-step curriculum can produce the same results for all of them. Some will master word-recognition skills quickly and easily; these children will be ready to progress quickly to reading higher-level material. Others will require more—sometimes much more—intensive instruction in phonics before they can read effectively for meaning. To teach every child effectively, teachers need to provide a balance of learning experiences that is consistent with each child's needs. Achieving the appropriate balance will be possible only if teachers have reliable, meaningful ways of assessing children's reading needs and can use these results in deciding how to teach each child.

States have taken various approaches to early assessment in reading. Alabama has developed a single reading assessment that will be used by every school in the state. North Carolina developed a reading assessment but gives each local district permission to select an alternative assessment that meets the same objectives. Texas developed a reading assessment that many districts have adopted but also allows them to choose from a list of approved alternative assessments. Mississippi does not specify which assessments schools must use but instead provides detailed *Reading Instructional Supplements* to guide both instruction and assessment.

While their approaches to identifying acceptable assessments differ, these and other states share a commitment to two key principles for effective assessment. They recognize that assessment must be a continual process until children reach and remain at grade level in reading. They also recognize that consistently reliable results for individual children cannot be expected before the second half of kindergarten and that early intervention will be most effective if it begins no later than the middle of first grade.

While some assessments could provide results that are useful both for decision making about individual children's needs and for school accountability purposes, the importance of flexibility in how and when children are assessed makes such a dual use problematic. So far no SREB state has made reading assessment prior to third grade a part of its statewide school-accountability program.

EVERY CLASSROOM TEACHER NEEDS
A FULL TOOLBOX

Even the best assessment will be useful only if classroom teachers are able to use the information to meet all children's needs. This task requires them to possess a broad range of skills and knowledge about the structure of language, the process of learning to read and the teaching strategies that are effective for different children.

> **Question:**   What percentage of elementary school teachers have all the skills and knowledge they need to teach all children to read?
>
> **Moats:**   Perhaps 20 percent of new teachers are very well-prepared.

Providing students with individualized instruction does not mean that teaching must be one-on-one, although some children with serious reading problems may require one-on-one instruction. Teachers do need to be attentive to each child's rate of progress and should have an individual instructional plan for every child who has problems reading. One of the most effective ways to meet individual needs is through flexible grouping of children based on regular evaluation of each child's progress. Flexible grouping should not be confused with tracking. With flexible grouping children may be in different groups for instruction in different areas of reading, and the groups should change as children progress at different rates.

Teachers also need to recognize that reading instruction needs to be taught as a system. While children learn at different rates and require emphasis in different areas, all of them need teachers who understand the relationship between speech sounds and written language and who are able to communicate that understanding to their students. Unlike speech, reading does not develop naturally but must be learned, even though it may appear natural for some children.

EARLY INTERVENTION PREVENTS
LATER FAILURE

Early intervention for children with reading difficulties is essential to prevent them from falling far behind their classmates. Intervention can take a variety of forms— from intensive one-on-one tutoring to activities in small groups. It can be offered in the regular classroom or outside of it. Most important, even more than with everyday classroom instruction, the intervention must be designed specifically to meet the individual child's needs and must be provided by a teacher who truly understands those needs.

Question: How much phonics instruction is enough?

Moats: The minimum is what it takes to teach the child to read any new word quickly and accurately.

Morris: While they are learning phonics, it is essential that they be provided with as many opportunities to read at their own levels as possible. Phonics is an essential skill but the only way to become an expert reader is to do lots of reading.

Many states have made ending social promotion a high priority. While this goal is worthwhile, it is important to recognize that repeating the same instruction that failed the first time dooms children to continued failure as surely as does promoting them when they have not achieved grade-level objectives. In many cases, early intervention during the school year in first or second grade and/or appropriate summer programs can eliminate the need for retention. When retention is unavoidable, it is essential that children's experiences during the repeated year be designed to correct what did not work the first time.

The Oklahoma Legislature clearly recognized the relationship between early intervention and an end to social promotion in its 1997 Reading Sufficiency Act. The act requires that each student who does not read at grade level be provided with a plan for intensive instruction to remedy reading deficiencies. This intervention program is to continue until the student reads at or above grade level, and the student may continue to progress from grade to grade while working within the plan. Several states have passed similar legislation in recent years.

INTERVENTION FOR STUDENTS IN THE MIDDLE GRADES AND HIGH SCHOOL

Improving classroom instruction in reading and providing effective early intervention to children who need it ultimately should reduce dramatically the number of students in the middle grades and in high school who cannot read adequately. Unfortunately, many poor readers already have reached these high grades, and more will do so before meaningful change comes to all elementary classrooms.

Question: Can we expect classroom teachers to correct students' reading problems in the middle grades and high school?

Moats: Teachers in those higher grades need to be better trained in reading, but students who are many grades behind in reading will need intensive one-on-one help from expert reading teachers.

The longer a reading problem persists, the more difficult it is to correct. Years of reading difficulties not only make grade-level material far too difficult but also leave students with significant gaps in the basic knowledge needed to comprehend advanced content. Although it is difficult to overcome the cumulative deficit from years of reading below grade level, research has proved that it is possible to help older students correct serious reading problems. To do so requires a correct diagnosis of the problems and appropriate intervention measures.

Developing and Supporting Literacy-Rich Environments for Children

JERLEAN DANIEL, THERESA CLARKE,

AND MARK OUELLETTE

SUMMARY

Early reading success is a strong predictor of academic success in later grades, and the early childhood years (birth through age eight) are critical ones for literacy development. After grade three, demands on the student change from "learning to read" to "reading to learn," as reading becomes a fundamental means to acquire new knowledge about all subjects.

According to current research, literacy development begins long before children begin formal instruction in elementary school.[1] It proceeds along a continuum, with children acquiring literacy skills in a variety of ways and at different ages. Early behaviors such as "reading" from pictures and "writing" scribbles are an important part of children's literacy development. Social interactions with caring adults and exposure to literacy materials (e.g., storybooks) nourish literacy development. "Literacy-rich environments" offer daily, extended conversations with adults about interesting topics.

Policymakers that want to develop and support literacy-rich environments in their states can take these actions:

- **Raise public awareness.** Policymakers should make parents and caregivers aware of the importance of their being a child's first teacher. A literacy campaign can bring adults and children together to read and discuss books daily.

- **Provide resources and information.** States may want to provide free materials that explain cognitive research to help parents and caregivers understand how to enhance a child's vocabulary and establish a literacy-rich environment.

- **Improve professional development.** High-quality reading instruction in child care settings, preschool, and the primary grades requires teachers who are well prepared and trained in teaching reading.

■ **Increase access to literacy-rich environments.** Policymakers can increase the number of spaces in approved child-care programs for low-income families and designate funding streams to support these programs.

WHAT IS THE PROBLEM?

Of every three kindergartners, one comes to school unprepared to learn. Moreover, parents routinely read to only 50 percent of infants and toddlers. For children to be successful in school, they must have early experiences with language. The latest research in literacy development shows that a child's experiences with oral language development and literacy, as early as the first months of life, begin a foundation for later reading success.

Children need three skills to become good readers.[2] Good readers have an understanding of how the alphabet works, an awareness that reading is about meaning, and sufficient fluency in reading. Some children obtain these three skills quickly. Other children need to be taught about the relationship among letters, that letters represent small sounds in words, and about the relationship of specific letters to specific sounds. Often, parents, caregivers, and teachers need to help children understand that the reason they read is to uncover a message. The most effective way to convey this is to provide children with a literacy-rich environment.

WHAT IS A LITERACY-RICH ENVIRONMENT?

In a literacy-rich environment, parents, teachers, and caregivers ensure that children engage in one-on-one conversations about everyday life—activities, people, or events the *children* find interesting. Literacy-rich environments include daily reading, extended discourse (talking or writing), experimentation with reading materials, book talk (discussion of characters, action, and plot), and dramatic play. In this environment, children have many opportunities to see how printed words are used for many purposes. They become familiar with print and language, and these are both integrated into everyday activities.

Literacy-rich environments have the following characteristics.[3]

■ Children are surrounded by oral language, books, and print. Various reading and writing materials are available throughout the home for children and adults.

■ Adults share their ideas and feelings with children and encourage them to express themselves.

■ Children see adults reading for pleasure and for practical and specific purposes, such as paying bills or learning about the news.

- Families consider children's emergent reading and writing to be real, valuable experiences. They accept children's efforts without correcting mistakes or providing direct instruction.

- Families talk with children about the print they see around them and explain how it provides information (e.g., signs on buses and streets, labels on food packages, and coupons).

- Teachers provide the experience of group learning and design their classrooms to encourage reading and writing.

In literacy-rich environments, children learn about the world through talking and reading, refining these skills along the way. Children's knowledge of language is built on their own investigative skills applied to interesting topics, coupled with the finely honed skills of a talented teacher and a well thought out curriculum. Young children in the United States spend their days in a variety of places—homes, child care centers, preschools, and elementary schools. Each of these places should be a literacy-rich environment, so parents, child-care providers, and teachers must all understand how to provide such environments for children.

WHAT CAN POLICYMAKERS DO TO DEVELOP AND SUPPORT LITERACY-RICH ENVIRONMENTS?

Instruction in the early primary grades (grades one through three) is most effective when children arrive at school motivated to learn how to read.[1] Children who arrive at school with the necessary linguistic, cognitive, and early literacy skills are better able to succeed in reading.[2] State policymakers can support literacy readiness by helping parents and caregivers improve the quality of literacy environments before children enter school and in the crucial first years of school. Policymakers can develop and support literacy-rich environments through these actions.

Raise Public Awareness

Policymakers can help parents and caregivers provide literacy-rich environments by increasing their awareness of the importance of their being a child's first teacher.[3] A statewide literacy campaign is one strategy to increase awareness and provide information. A campaign can bring adults and children together in families, schools, and communities to read and discuss books daily. Reading aloud to children exposes them to vocabulary and concepts beyond their reading capacity, but not beyond their understanding with the help of context clues and the knowledge of more advanced readers.[4] Early collaborative involvement of a state's nonprofit literacy programs, early childhood teachers, book vendors, and book clubs can offer a wealth of creative ideas and implementation strategies. In Maine First Lady Mary Herman collaborated with the state commissioner of education to release a new report to spell out six key elements in early childhood literacy education.[5]

Provide Resources and Information

Policymakers can also support parents and caregivers in their important roles as first teachers by providing free books and other materials that explain current cognitive research, such as *Open Young Minds: Read to Children*, a brochure published by the National Governors Association Center for Best Practices. These materials should discuss literacy-promoting and vocabulary-enhancing techniques parents, teachers, and caregivers can use. Some of these activities include discussing a child's drawings, reading books on topics in which a child has expressed an interest, and describing to children the difference between newspaper text and poetry. Providing useful literacy resources to parents and caregivers is a powerful tool to help them create literacy-rich environments for children.

Improve Professional Development

State policymakers can help improve the quality of teaching by improving professional development. Optimal environments and excellent instruction in child care settings, preschool, and the primary grades require teachers who are well prepared and highly knowledgeable in teaching reading. Governors and other state policymakers can also develop policies to ensure the appropriate licensing of providers and teachers. States require elementary school teachers to be licensed to teach, but most states do not require licenses to teach in child care or preschool settings. Students of teachers who hold teaching certificates in their fields—early childhood education or elementary education in this case—perform better academically than students whose teachers are not certified. High-quality child care programs require stricter licensing requirements for staff and smaller staff-child ratios. Such high-quality programs result in enhanced language outcomes for children, especially those from low-income homes.

Increase Access to Literacy-Rich Environments

State policymakers can also promote literacy-rich environments for children by increasing access to quality early education. Support for early care and education in Early Head Start programs, Head Start programs, preschool programs, child care centers, and schools can come from a variety of federal, state, and local funding sources, including federal education funds, Temporary Assistance for Needy Families (TANF), and Child Care Block Grant monies, child care funds, state general education funds, and local dollars. States can increase the number of spaces in approved child care programs and help communities provide literacy-rich environments in child care and education settings by designating innovative funding streams to develop and sustain them.

WHAT ARE SOME STATE STRATEGIES FOR SUPPORTING LITERACY-RICH ENVIRONMENTS?

Connecticut's 1999 Act Concerning School Readiness and Child Day Care allows its department of education to administer grants to high-need school districts and programs to provide school readiness services, including preliteracy and literacy activities, to three-, four-, and five-year-olds. In addition, this legislation called on the nonprofit organization, Connecticut Charts-A-Course, to implement the state's career development plan for early education and school-age care providers. Charts-A-Course provides quality training and career support to professionals teaching young children. The legislation also requires each local and regional board of education to develop and implement a three-year plan to improve the reading skills of students in kindergarten through grade three. In-service training programs must provide information on teaching language arts, reading, and reading readiness to teachers of students in kindergarten through grade three. Finally, the legislation requires that continuing education completed by early childhood through grade three teachers include at least 15 hours of training in the teaching of reading and reading readiness and the assessment of reading performance.

Delaware First Lady Martina S. Carper launched the Delaware Reading Is Fundamental (RIF) initiative in 1998 to stimulate family literacy by bringing literacy services and free books to young children and their families. The preschool program provides reading readiness activities for the home, read-aloud strategies for parents and caregivers, and children's books to take home. Mrs. Carper also co-chaired the Delaware Commission for Reading Success, which produced a comprehensive report for addressing the state's literacy needs. Two other state-supported early childhood programs are the Early Childhood Assistance Program and the Parents as Teachers program for first-born children at-risk for later learning challenges.

With strong involvement from First Lady Mary Herman, Maine is pursuing a wide range of creative strategies and partnerships focused on early and family literacy, building on a long history of success on standardized tests of early literacy performance. A new report from the Maine Department of Education on early literacy education, *A Solid Foundation*, together with the Department's newly established Center of Inquiry on Early Literacy, is catalyzing conversations and professional development for teachers and parents, as well as follow-up research. Maine is leveraging available federal grants including Title 1 and a Reading Excellence Act grant for ongoing professional development in early literacy and establishment of family literacy programs. Maine is also using creative private-sector partnerships to reach young children and parents with books and support in early reading. The Read With Me program, sponsored by the Verizon Foundation, provides books and reading support materials to nearly all kindergarten students and their families across Maine when they enter school in September; the Raising Readers program supported by Maine's Libra Foundation will distribute a dozen books to each child born in Maine, based on a "prescription to read" approach that gives each newborn two books at birth with additional books at each pediatric checkup through age five.

Michigan Governor John Engler first outlined READY (Read, Educate, and Develop Youth), a parent information effort on the importance of reading and early learning, in his 1998 state-of-the-state address. READY seeks to strengthen parent involvement in the early childhood years so children develop the language and pre-reading skills they need to enter school ready to read and succeed. A READY kit containing written, audio, and visual information and materials was developed, and the Governor formally unveiled the kit in August 1998. Three levels of READY kits in Spanish and English have been created for parents of infants, toddlers, and preschoolers. Since inception in 1998, more than 300,000 READY kits have been distributed to parents through a network of READY county coordinators comprised of early childhood education programs, human service coordinating bodies, hospitals, agricultural extension offices, and intermediate school districts. Funding has been appropriated to permit the distribution of an additional 350,000 READY kits in 2000.

Missouri's Parents as Teachers (PAT) program is a home-school-community partnership supporting parents in their role as first teachers. The Early Childhood Development Act that established PAT provides funds to public school districts to implement developmental screenings and parent education services. Children are screened in the areas of language, motor, health and physical development, and sensory functioning. Parent education services are delivered through small group meetings with parents of similarly aged children and personalized private visits. PAT programs collaborate with federal and state agencies and programs, including Head Start, Even Start, Title 1, First Steps, Missouri Caring Communities, county health departments, and the Missouri Division of Family Services.

North Carolina Governor James B. Hunt Jr. launched Smart Start, an early childhood initiative, in 1993 to address the concern that many children arrive at school unprepared for school success. Smart Start uses early childhood education to enhance the literacy skills of young children before they enter kindergarten. The family literacy programs of Smart Start help family members learn to read and encourage them to read to their young children. Smart Start's success is based on local control, community planning and collaboration, and a comprehensive approach to reach all children. In its 1999–2000 budget, the legislature funded Smart Start at $220 million. State statute requires a 10-percent match from the private sector each year, and the initiative has garnered more than $50 million in private funds and contributions since it began.

Ohio's Ready to Learn initiative seeks to help parents and home caregivers expose children to an expanded set of learning opportunities by producing public service announcements and conducting workshops for adults who care for children in their homes. One of the four workshops, "Help Me Learn," uses brain development research to teach parents and caregivers about how children learn. The U.S. Department of Education funds Ready to Learn with an annual allocation of $7 million. Ohio added $1.3 million from the Child Care and Development Fund to produce the public service announcements and to design and implement the workshops.

South Carolina's Office of Family Independence in the department of social services and the National Center for Family Literacy (NCFL) initiated a pilot project in 1996 to combine Head Start activities with family literacy and employment services for parents. The project's goal was to develop a more comprehensive approach to assisting welfare families by promoting parent and child literacy. In fiscal 1998–99, South Carolina used funding from three sources to pilot this initiative. The state allocated $36,000 in TANF block grant funds to provide parents with employment and life-skills training at Head Start centers ($6,000 per site); $90,000 from the U.S. Department of Education's Rural Initiative Grant ($15,000 per site); and $300,000 over three years from the federal Head Start Bureau to the NCFL for training and technical assistance.

In his 1999–2001 biennial budget, Wisconsin Governor Tommy G. Thompson earmarked $10.5 million from the Federal Child Care Development Fund to create 18 innovative, state-of-the-art Early Childhood Excellence Centers for low-income children age birth to five. Each center provides innovative, high-quality programs that enhance children's physical, social, emotional, cognitive, and language development. These centers also provide parent education services and deliver training to child-care providers. All programs provide an environment that is rich in visual, auditory, tactile, and other sensory experiences that are guided by research on the development of the brain and are provided through positive interactions with consistent caregivers. These centers strive to ensure that children under the age of five, primarily from low-income families, reach their full potential.

WHAT CAN STATES DO?

Governors and other state leaders are aware that children's language skills are fundamental to success in school and in everyday life. In designing policies to promote literacy, policymakers may want to consider raising public awareness, providing information and resources, improving professional development, and increasing access to high-quality care and education.

Policymakers understand that the earlier children are exposed to books the better. The next step is to ensure adult constituents have the ability and opportunity to develop and sustain literacy-rich environments at home and in the schools.

ENDNOTES

1. North Central Regional Educational Laboratory, *Critical Issue: Addressing the Literacy Needs of Emergent and Early Readers* (Oak Brook, Ill.: North Central Regional Educational Laboratory, 1999), at <http://www.ncrel.org/sdrs/areas/issues/content/entareas/reading/li100.htm>.
2. Pediatric Services, "Catherine Snow on Helping Your Child Develop Language," at <http://www.pediatricservices.com/answers/009-language.htm>.

3. Kidsource, "Language and Literacy Environments in Preschools," at <http://www.kidsource.com/education/lang.lit.preschool.html>.
4. Jim Trelease, *The Read-Aloud Handbook* (New York, N.Y.: Penguin Books, 1995).
5. "Report Lists Best Methods to Teach Young Reader," *Bangor Daily News*, 22 November 2000.

One Down and 80,000 to Go:
Word Recognition Instruction in the Primary Grades

CONNIE JUEL & CECILIA MINDEN-CUPP

INTRODUCTION

In the focus groups conducted in preparation for the CIERA grant, teachers and administrators raised more questions about how to teach children to read words than any other issue in early reading. They expressed concern over which, and how many, strategies for word recognition teachers should model for first-grade children. Should teachers, for example, ask children to "sound out" words, focus on the visual array of letters by spelling the word, try to make an analogy to a key word on the word wall, emphasize what makes sense, or some combination of such strategies? What word unit should receive the most emphasis—the word (e.g., *hat*); the onset and rime (e.g., /h/ and *at*); or individual letter–sounds in words (e.g., /h/, /a/, /t/)? How much emphasis should word recognition activities receive in the their total language arts programs? They wanted answers to both the nitty-gritty issues involved in word recognition instruction and to questions of how to balance such instruction in the broader picture of literacy.

We expect much of children and their teachers in the early grades. Learning to read is difficult. It depends upon both learning to read words and having the background knowledge of concepts and the world to understand text. The sheer volume of words that children are expected to read quickly and accurately is daunting. According to Carroll, Davies, and Richman (1971) and Adams (1990), children will be expected to recognize and know well over 80,000 different words by the end of third grade. This means that they must be able to recognize these words and know their meanings.

Juel, Connie, & Minden-Cupp, Cecilia (Dec. 1999/Jan. 2000). One down and 80,000 to go: Word recognition instruction in the primary grades. *The Reading Teacher*, 53 *(4)*, 332–335.

While the emphasis is squarely on developing word recognition skill in the very early grades, we must also prepare children for the avalanche of concepts and information they will be expected to understand. Research indicates that early school development of vocabulary and world knowledge is especially critical for children who come from impoverished homes (Snow, 1999).

We know that one route to learning vocabulary and world knowledge is through reading: Children who learn to read early on read considerably more than their peers who are still struggling to decode, and through reading they learn things that increase their text comprehension (Juel, 1994; Stanovich, 1986). Reading itself helps students gain both world knowledge and word recognition skill. Once a child can read enough words to independently enter the world of books, additional words are learned as a consequence of seeing them several times in print (Reitsma, 1990: Share, 1995). Thus, the critical question is how teachers can help children gain enough skill to successfully enter this world so that, in a sense, children can read enough to become their own teachers.

Word recognition must become something children can do on their own, because they will quickly be expected to read words they have never before seen in print. Only a few thousand words usually receive direct instruction in the primary grades. It would be impossible to directly teach children all the words they will encounter in print. It is also impossible to directly teach children all the letter–sound correspondences that they will need to be able to "sound out" novel words. Even the most comprehensive phonics programs rarely provide direct instruction for more than about 90 phonics "rules." Yet, over 500 different spelling–sound "rules" are needed to read (Gough & Juel, 1990: Juel, 1994).

The focus of this first year of a five-year CIERA study was to closely examine language arts instruction as it naturally occurred in four classrooms. We were especially interested in the form of word recognition instruction and how different types of instruction appeared to affect students with different early literacy foundations. Our goal in this first-year study was to identify specific instructional practices that appear to best foster learning to read words for particular profiles of children. We also wanted to see how this instruction was embedded in the language arts curriculum.

METHOD

We began by identifying four first-grade teachers who had considerable classroom experience, were considered good teachers by their principals, and taught at schools with similar demographics. The two schools were located in nearby neighborhoods in a city in the southeastern United States. In each school, approximately 70% of the children qualify for subsidized lunch, 60% of the children are African-American, 36% are Caucasian, and 4% are from other ethnic groups. We observed the language arts instruction in each of these four classrooms each week for at least one hour. We used laptop computers to write running narratives of what was going on in the classroom during language arts. Observers focused on the activities, reading materials, strategies teachers taught students for identifying words, and units of word instruction (e.g., whole words, phonograms). These observations were later analyzed in various ways. We coded and tallied, for example, the frequency of occurrence of specific activities, and looked qualitatively at the form of teacher–child interactions.

To try to determine how instruction affected children's growth in reading, we assessed the children in September, December, and May on several measures. We assessed the children on factors that influence word learning, including phonemic awareness, alphabet knowledge, concept of word, and letter–sound knowledge. We assessed the children on their ability to read both words on a standardized measure and words on which they had received direct instruction in the classroom. We assessed the children on their ability to read and understand passages. And, in December and May, we used a think-aloud procedure to help determine what strategies children actually applied as they identified words in isolation and in passages.

RESULTS

Each classroom held no more than 17 students and had three reading groups. However, considerable variation was found in instructional practices among the four classrooms.

Classroom 1 was the most traditional of the classrooms. Reading groups frequently were conducted in a round robin fashion and, especially during the second semester, the reading material was an old basal reading series. Compared to the other three classrooms, there was a lot of similarity in what children did in their reading groups. While they did not read the same materials, they often followed similar styles of reading (e.g., round robin reading) and were often assigned the same writing tasks.

Word recognition instruction in classroom 1 occurred primarily through a whole-class word wall activity. The letters in the new words were chanted and each word was written several times by each child. In all three reading groups, there was relatively little attention paid to word units other than initial consonants and whole words. The teacher was never observed modeling sounding and blending units within words. Primary word recognition strategies were to consider meaning, to predict, to reread, to spell the word, and to look on the word wall. If a child struggled to read a word, the teacher frequently told the child the word.

The teacher in classroom 2 made up for the relatively small number of books for very beginning readers—a problem all teachers in the study faced—by creating many charts and individual little books. Typically, a poem appeared on a chart, and after a reading group read the chart, each child was provided a copy of the poem in the form of a little book. Classroom teacher 2 made considerable use of manipulable materials in phonemic awareness and phonics instruction. Children in the low and middle groups frequently sorted word cards into categories based on spelling patterns or sorted picture cards on the basis of sounds. Instruction in the three reading groups, however, was tailored to the specific needs of children in the group. Children in the low group in classroom 2 were provided considerable modeling by their teacher as to how to chunk words into their component units. In general, these units were onsets and rimes. Such units were natural ones, given the extensive use of poetry in the classroom. This teacher was also fairly insistent that children finger point to words as they read.

Classroom 3 was packed with trade books. We saw considerably more discussion of texts and the meaning of what was read in classroom 3 than we did in classrooms 1 or 2. Children in all reading groups spent considerable time writing both individual texts and journals. Children in the low group also engaged in several language experience writing activities. Classroom teacher 3 relied heavily on peer coaching to facilitate word recognition. When a child in a reading group could not identify a word, other children in the group were encouraged to provide a clue. There were suggested clues (e.g., reread, sound it out, see if it makes sense, look at the word wall). But the children were encouraged to provide any clues they thought would help. There was relatively little direct phonics instruction in classroom 3. What phonics there was came as it fell out of the trade books. In other words, there wasn't a preset curriculum; rather, the teacher took advantage of a word in a book to highlight a spelling pattern.

Classroom teacher 4 was clearly the most phonics oriented of the four teachers. She was also the most adamant about the behavior of her students. Instruction differed considerably between her reading groups. During the fall semester, the low group engaged in many phonics activities, especially sorting word cards into categories based on spelling patterns. In contrast, the high group spent very little time on phonics activities and a lot of time reading text. Classroom teacher 4 showed the most change in her instructional practices between the fall and spring semester in all three of her reading groups. In the spring semester, the children in each group were considerably more involved in discussions of both vocabulary and the texts they read than they had been during the fall.

While classroom teacher 4 spent considerable time in phonics with her low reading group, this activity was nearly finished by the end of February. Her phonics curriculum was highly sequenced. She spent considerable time on consonants and phonograms in the fall. She spent considerable time in the winter contrasting short and long vowel phonogram patterns (e.g., "an" versus "ain" words). Classroom teacher 4 helped children segment words into chunks, modeled sounding and blending phonemes, and modeled combining what made sense with known letter–sounds. Like classroom teacher 2, she was especially insistent during the fall semester that children finger-point to words as they read.

The differences in instructional practices among the four classrooms appeared to be related to growth in reading on all our measures. An analysis of covariance (adjusting for preexisting literacy differences in September), for example, indicated significant classroom differences on passage reading in May. Follow-up pairwise contrasts indicated that children's reading achievement in every classroom was significantly different from that in every other classroom: On average, children in classroom 1 were reading at a primer level; children in classroom 2 were reading at an end-of-first grade level; children in classroom 3 were reading on a mid second-grade level; and children in classroom 4 were reading on a late second-grade level.

When looking at how reading groups fared within and across classrooms, however, there was an interesting interaction. Children in the low groups across the four classrooms showed no significant differences on measures in September, but their reading achievement in May was quite different. All the children in the low reading group in classroom 4 were reading at or near an end-of-first grade level in May. In second place were the children in classroom 2. In last place, and barely able to read, were the children in classroom 3. In contrast, a child in the middle or high group—a child who entered first grade with at least "middle" range literacy skills (e.g., alphabet knowledge, phonemic awareness)—was likely to make exceptional growth in reading during the year if he or she was in classroom 3! Nine children who entered classroom 3 with literacy skills in the middle range exited with reading skill one standard deviation above the mean.

CONCLUSIONS

Children who entered first grade with the weakest knowledge of the alphabet, phonemic awareness, and other early literacy foundations were most likely to be on-grade-level readers at the end of first grade if they were in a reading group which had a structured phonics format until February and in which a "no nonsense" approach to discipline was taken. They benefited from teacher-modeled strategies of segmenting words into chunks (e.g., onset and rime) and, going a step further, sounding and blending the individual phonemes in those chunks. After they knew many letter–sound relationships, they benefited from instruction that modeled how to combine known letter–sounds with what makes sense to identify an unknown word in text. Peer coaching in word recognition strategies proved a disaster for children with few incoming literacy skills. Once children reached a beginning primer reading level, however, they benefited from the same extensive reading, discussion of the vocabulary in the texts, and discussion about the meaning of the texts that was successful with children who entered first grade with higher literacy levels.

Children who entered first grade with minimal reading skill seemed to have greatest success with the following classroom practices:

1. Teachers modeled word recognition strategies by:
   a) chunking of words into component units such as syllables, onset/rimes, or finding little words in big ones;
   b) sound and blending individual phonemes;
   c) considering known letter–sounds and what makes contextual sense.
2. The children were encouraged to finger-point to words as text was read.
3. Children used manipulable materials to actively compare and contrast words (e.g., pocket charts for sorting of picture cards by sound and word cards by spelling pattern).
4. Instruction groups were small with lesson plans designed to meet the specific needs of each child within that group.

While our first-year study is suggestive of what instructional practices facilitate children's word recognition skill, we are currently following up with a larger-scale longitudinal study. Concurrent with the study reported here, we collected a wide range of data on over 200 preschool children (e.g., oral vocabulary, visual memory). These children went on to attend kindergarten at three elementary schools which have quite different curricula. We have regularly observed the children in their classrooms and will continue to do so until they exit third grade. We are hopeful that this broad-scale picture will enable us to see how early characteristics of children and their classrooms combine with their later reading skills and instructional experiences to create accomplished readers.

REFERENCES

Adams, M. J. (1990). *Beginning to read: Thinking and learning about print.* Cambridge, MA: MIT Press.

Carroll, J. B., Davies, P., & Richman, B. (1971). *Word frequency book.* New York: American Heritage.

Gough, P. B. & Juel, C. (1990, April). *Does phonics teach the cipher?* Paper presented at the annual meeting of the American Educational Research Association, Boston.

Juel, C. (1994). *Learning to read and write in one elementary school.* New York: Springer-Verlag.

Reitsma, P. (1990). Development of orthographic knowledge. In P. Reitsma & L. Verhoeven (Eds.), *Acquisition of reading in Dutch* (pp. 43–64). Dordrecht: Foris.

Share, D. L. (1995). Phonological recoding and self-teaching: Sine qua non of reading acquisition. *Cognition, 55,* 151–218.

Snow, C. E. (1999, May). *Why the home is so important in learning to read.* Paper presented at the George Graham Lecture in Reading, Charlottesville, VA.

Stanovich, K. E. (1986). Matthew effects in reading: Some consequences of individual differences in the development of reading fluency. *Reading Research Quarterly, 21,* 360–406.

INTEGRATING SOURCES

1. Compare the issues and conclusions described by Juel & Minden-Cupp to those described by Denton. How are the issues similar? Different?

2. To what extent would Juel & Minden-Cupp and Denton agree or disagree with the policy and practices put forth by the National Governors Association?

CLASSROOM IMPLICATIONS

1. If you identified improving your relationship with students' parents or caretakers as an area for professional improvement, what changes would you make in your classroom literacy practice? What would you need to be successful?

2. What changes should you make in your classroom environment, assessment, and instruction that would maximize the literacy development of all children?

3. What issues do classroom teachers face that serve as barriers to meeting all children's literacy development needs?

ANNOTATED BIBLIOGRAPHY

Ezell, H. K., & Gonzales, M. D. (2000). Emergent literacy skills in migrant Mexican American preschoolers. *Communication Disorders Quarterly*, 21, 147–153.

Emphasizes that, while the importance of both the home and the Head Start program are important for the literacy skills of students, the home tends to be the dominant influence.

MacKenzie, K. K. (2001). Using literacy booster groups to maintain and extend reading. *Reading Teacher*, 55, 222–234.

Suggests that students who have participated in Reading Recovery can benefit from extra instruction once they are returned to the regular classroom setting.

Neuman, S. B., & Dickinson, D. K. (Eds.). (2001). *Handbook of early literacy research*. New York: Guilford.

This comprehensive handbook discusses the field of early literacy research, reviewing the most current knowledge in this area.

Riggins, C. G. (2002). Closing the performance gap. *Principal*, 81, 47–49.

Describes a plan to help improve both reading and mathematics achievement through a variety of early intervention strategies.

Smith, S. B., Baker, S., & Oudeans, M. K. (2001). Making a difference in the classroom with early literacy instruction. *Teaching Exceptional Children*, 33, 8–14.

Discusses the link between teachers' various views of the reading process and specific student literacy performance as measured on a basic skill assessment procedure.

Torgeson, J. K. (2000). Individual differences in response to early intervention in reading. *Learning Disabilities Research and Practice*, 15, 55–64.

Reports on the importance of early evaluation and related intervention in reading and the educational implications of these educational procedures.

Wood, M. (2001). Projects story boost: Read-alouds for students at risk. *Reading Teacher*, 55, 76–83.

Encourages the use of various types of read-alouds for kindergartners who lack exposure to fundamental literacy skills.

YOU BECOME INVOLVED

1. Visit a preschool and first-grade classroom. Compare the environment for similarities and differences as described in this chapter.

2. Interview a parent and first-grade teacher to find out what is done to maximize children's initial literacy development.

3. Interview a remedial reading teacher (i.e., Title I or special education) and a preventative reading teacher (i.e., Reading Recovery) to examine differences in their training and programs. Chart the similarities and differences.

CHAPTER THREE

. . . . .

FAMILY LITERACY

Some one . . . may be able to teach it [reading] to all the rest of the house, even while their hands may be otherwise well occupied in working for a living, or otherwise being idle or sitting by the fire, without any further let or cost.

—John Hart (1574)

Children who grow up in a reasonably articulate family with books and habitual reading going on are at an enormous advantage, because the important thing is not what you read, but the desire to read.

—Northrop Frye (1987)

When [parents] can spend quality time reading with their children, helping them with homework and reinforcing the importance of reading, they're able to pass on a priceless legacy.

—Editorial, Denver Post (2002)

Long before a child begins formal instruction in school, (Amstutz, 2000; Steinthrop & Hughes, 2000) the first, and perhaps most important, training begins in the home. The family, especially the parents, often plays a critical role in this learning process. Of particular importance are beginning experiences in the area of language and literacy development. For instance, research has clearly shown that children who are read to from an early age are much more likely to be better readers later in life than those who have only limited exposure to print (Manzo & Manzo, 1995; McGee & Richgels, 2000).

Goal One of the National Educational Goals Panel states that "All children in America will start school ready to learn." (National Goals for Education, 1990). Unfortunately, despite this worthy objective, many students have not entered school with the necessary background experiences needed for positive academic achievement (National Goals, 1990; Promising Practices, 2000; Raising Achievement, 2001). In

response to this continuing educational problem, the current emphasis on family literacy is one effort to provide all students with the skills they need to be successful in the
classroom.

HOME/SCHOOL RELATIONSHIPS

Because of the importance of family literacy, schools and teachers have long been
interested in how to build effective ways for the development of better home/school
communication (Bevans, Furnish, Ramsey, & Talsma, 2001; Rasinske, et al., 2001).
Whether it be parent/teacher conferences, home visits, or newsletters, effective communication between parents and teachers regarding literacy development in students
is critical.

PARENT INVOLVEMENT IN LITERACY ACTIVITIES

The establishment of an atmosphere that encourages positive and effective literacy
development in the home is very important (Klassen-Endrizzi, 2000; Yarosz & Barnett, 2001). While most parents are interested in family literacy, they frequently do
not know in a practical way how to accomplish these goals. Often, it then becomes the
responsibility of the classroom teacher to provide the needed information to parents
on how they can best help their children with language development.

AS YOU READ

The following selections provide a variety of viewpoints on the field of family literacy.
While each article individually discusses a particular aspect of family literacy, in total,
they give a comprehensive picture of this important aspect of literacy education. The
first selection is a position statement on family literacy from the International Reading
Association (2002). Fillmore (2000) discusses the loss of family languages and the need
for literacy educators to be aware of this language problem.

REFERENCES

Amstutz, D. D. (2000). Family literacy: Implications for public school practice. *Education and Urban
    Society, 32*, 207–220.
Bevans, B., Furnish, B., Ramsey, A., & Talsma, S. (2001). *Effective strategies for home-school partnerships
    in reading.* (ERIC Reproduction Service No. ED453522).
*Family-school partnerships: Essential elements of literacy instruction in the United States. A position state-
    ment of the International Reading Association.* (2002). Newark, DE: International Reading
    Association.
Fillmore, L. W. (2000). Loss of family languages: Should educators be concerned? *Theory Into Practice,
    39*, 203–210.
Klassen-Endrizzi, C. (2000). Exploring our beliefs with families. *Language Arts, 78*, 62–70.

Manzo, A. V., & Manzo, U. C. (1995). *Teaching children to be literate: A reflective approach.* Fort Worth, TX: Harcourt Brace.

McGee, L. M., & Richgels, D. J. (2000). *Literacy's beginnings: Supporting young readers and writers* (3d ed.). Boston: Allyn & Bacon.

National goals for education. (1990). (ERIC Reproduction Service No. ED319143).

Promising practices: Progress towards the goals, 2000. Lessons from the states. (2000). (ERIC Reproduction Service No. ED455590).

Raising achievement and reducing gaps: Reporting progress toward goals for academic achievement. A report to the National Educational Goals Panel. Lessons from the states. (2001). (ERIC Reproduction Service No. ED453594).

Rasinski, T. V., et al. (Eds.) (2001). *Motivating recreational reading and promoting home-school connections; Strategies from "The Reading Teacher."* Newark, DE: International Reading Association.

Steinthorp, R., & Hughes, D. (2000). Family literacy activities in the homes of successful young readers. *Journal of Research in Reading, 23,* 41–54.

Yarosz, D. J., & Barnett, W. S. (2001). Who reads to young children: Identifying predictors of family reading activities. *Reading Psychology, 22,* 67–81.

Family–School Partnerships:

Essential Elements of Literacy Instruction in the United States

INTERNATIONAL READING ASSOCIATION

Despite widespread endorsement of family–school partnerships to support student learning, most educators in the United States have received little or no training in working effectively with families. Surveys of teacher educators, teachers, and administrators (Shartrand, Kreider, & Erickson-Warfield, 1994), evaluations of current professional education programs (Powell, 1991), and content analysis of state certification tests (Radcliffe, Malone, & Nathan, 1994) all support the conclusion that programs for prospective teachers neither provide student teachers with information about and supervised experiences in working with families, nor expect them to demonstrate relevant competencies and skills for certification.

Because family involvement is a potentially powerful element of effective literacy instruction, the International Reading Association believes parents, family and community members, teachers, school administrators, researchers, and policymakers must be aware of its importance and must receive information and training that allows them to effectively execute their respective roles in establishing family involvement in literacy learning. Teachers and school personnel especially must receive appropriate training.

There is extensive evidence that family involvement in the education of children is critical to effective schooling. Research such as that reviewed by Swap (1993), Henderson (1981, 1987), and Henderson and Berla (1994) shows that family involvement improves student achievement, attitudes toward learning, and self-esteem. Schools that undertake and support strong comprehensive family involvement efforts and have strong linkages with the communities they serve are more likely to produce students

International Reading Association. (2002). *Family–school partnerships: Essential elements of literacy instruction in the United States.* (A position statement of the International Reading Association.) Reprinted with permission. All rights reserved. Available at: www.reading.org

who perform better than identical schools that do not involve families. Children from low-income and culturally and racially diverse families experience greater success when schools involve families, enlist them as allies, and build on their strengths. Family involvement in a child's education is a more important factor in student success than family income or education.

Although it is important to have data about the particular kind of family involvement program being implemented, collaborative partnerships with parents have been shown to benefit families, schools, and teachers in addition to students. As a result of such partnerships, for example, families better understand the work of schools, have more confidence in schools, and often enroll in continuing education to advance their own learning. The teachers with whom parents work have higher opinions of such families and higher expectations for their students, which leads to increased achievement. Schools that work well with families have better teacher morale, higher ratings of teachers by parents, and better reputations and linkages to resources in the community (Epstein & Dauber, 1991; Henderson & Berla, 1994; Swap, 1993).

In addition, there is specific research related to positive effects of family involvement on literacy. For example, Morrow and Young (1997) attempted to bridge home and school literacy contexts by involving families in literacy activities with their children. Results indicated a significant difference in favor of children involved in the family program. Bevans, Furnish, Ramsey, and Talsma (2001) also focused on literacy development and found that the parent involvement intervention led to an increase in at-home reading, as well as improvement in home–school communication and an increase in parents' knowledge about reading. Both children's and parents' attitudes toward reading improved. Paratore, Melzi, and Krol-Sinclair (1999) found similar positive effects in a study that focused on Latino children and their families' involvement in a literacy project. Leslie and Allen (1999) found that parent involvement in recreational reading was a predictor of children's reading growth.

Family literacy programs also support the notion that parent involvement is a powerful component of effective literacy programs. Padak and Rasinski (1997) reviewed the literature related to family literacy and found that children, parents, families as units, and the larger society all benefited from family literacy programs.

TEACHER PREPARATION AND PROFESSIONAL DEVELOPMENT ARE ESSENTIAL

No amount of programs to "bring the school to the community" and no amount of investment in supportive materials and equipment can bring about family–school partnerships if educators are not prepared to initiate and support those partnerships. Educators, parents, and other stakeholders need to be effectively prepared to carry out this broader range of collaborative roles. This position on family involvement is consistent with other Association positions that emphasize the central importance of well-prepared teachers to achieving desired outcomes.

Teacher preparation programs at the elementary, middle, and secondary levels must focus on broader definitions of family involvement and must view family involvement as a collaboration between educators and families. We believe that these partnerships should be established in preprimary school settings and enhanced throughout the elementary, middle, and high school levels.

There are no formulas for creating effective programs; rather, educators must be prepared to ask questions about the particular situation and build family–school partnerships based on the answers they receive. Some critical questions include, Who are the family members and what roles should they assume? What kinds of involvement are advantageous for our school? What terms should be used to accurately portray the kind of balanced family involvement we want? Are there areas in which families have expressed interest or need to be involved? In addition, the classroom-level questions and school-level questions that follow will help as family–school partnerships develop.

Over the years, many schools and teachers have puzzled over questions such as

- To represent the school's philosophy of parental involvement, should teachers and administrators formulate a singular definition or multiple definitions of parental involvement?
- Should schools develop specific policies about the roles parents may or should assume?

These kinds of questions are important for administrators, particularly because they set school policy. Principals and other school administrators might organize family nights or other types of events, but it is important that these officials have thought about deeper and broader definitions of parent involvement.

Further, schools have puzzled over a question raised by Berger (1983):

- Does the thought that parents could be involved as education policymakers in conjunction with the school interest or threaten you? (p. 1).

This question is crucial because school administrators can view more parent involvement as a blessing or a curse.

Still further, schools have puzzled over questions like those posed by Greenwood and Hickman (1991):

- What types of parent involvement have the strongest impact on different types of student achievement (e.g., higher order and lower order)?
- What types of parent involvement have the strongest effects on parent and student attitudes and behaviors?

- What parent and family characteristics influence student performance and parent involvement?

- What types of parent involvement work best with families of different socioeconomic status and ethnic backgrounds? (p. 287)

In addition to the preceding school-level questions, many teachers have puzzled over questions that directly affect their individual practices of parent involvement:

- What should I do? How can I do more in my classroom to promote meaningful parent involvement?

- How should I reorganize my classroom instruction based on what I know about my students' home situations and their parents' abilities to help them?

- What do I need to know so I will not offend parents—particularly parents of minority students?

- How should I interact with parents who have an ideology of parental involvement that conflicts with my own expectations?

- Should I only expect the parents of my students to be involved in their education? When the parents of my students choose not to be involved, should I seek out other family or community members to serve as advocates for these children?

- Should I begin to think about parent-involvement initiatives in terms of my students' social, emotional, physical, and academic environment? Based on the families of the children I teach, are my expectations for parent involvement unrealistic?

- How can I begin to rethink, in my classroom, the taken-for-granted, institutionally sanctioned means for teachers and parents to communicate (i.e., parent-teacher association meetings, open house rituals at the beginning of the school year, writing and telephoning parents, etc.)?

All the preceding school- and classroom-level questions relate to various stages in individual educators' thinking about family involvement, and these questions are an important part of the process of conceptualizing and understanding family involvement. Furthermore, these questions help teachers target the kinds of parent involvement they need in their particular classrooms (Edwards, 1999; Edwards, Pleasants, & Franklin, 1999), and teachers can ask these questions to begin generating specific ideas of parent involvement. More important, these questions can and should be included as part of staff-development workshops to challenge teachers to reflect on a wide range of questions that need to be addressed when thinking about parent involvement initiatives. Answering these questions will help to foster in all relevant participants the attitudes, knowledge, and skills necessary for successful collaboration among teachers, school staff, and families.

Activities to develop family–school partnerships also need to look different at the elementary, middle, and high school levels. Not only do adolescents' needs and abilities differ from those of younger students, their relationships with family members and educators change as they mature. The failure to include older students in family–school activities may partially account for the dramatic decline in working partnerships as students move through the grades.

Educators need to view partnerships with families as an integral part of good teaching and student success. Family involvement in the education of children is in part an issue of access and equity. Children whose families know how to "navigate the system" and advocate effectively on their behalf tend to experience more success in their education than children whose families do not. However, most families need help learning how to be productively involved in their children's education at each grade level, especially at transition points between elementary, middle, and high school. School programs and educator practices to organize family–school connections are equalizers to help families who would not become involved on their own (Epstein & Dauber, 1991). The benefits of developing collaborative relationships with all families are many, and they accrue to educators, families, and students.

An outcomes-based approach to educator preparation reflects what we know, as an Association, about the interconnected roles of the school, family, and community in children's learning and development; about the necessity for taking account of the values and attitudes of educators, students, and the community served; and about the need for educators to acquire knowledge about direct practice with families and communities. The underlying goal of this approach is to encourage the implementation of innovative, responsive, and flexible programs that can prepare educators for family–school partnerships in a changing world.

The International Reading Association believes that because family involvement is a potentially powerful element of effective literacy instruction, it is an essential component of any effort to promote literacy instruction. If schools are to implement partnerships with families and communities so that all students can succeed, the Association makes the following recommendations to teacher educators, classroom teachers, and school administrators:

- Be aware of the importance of family–school connections and be committed to the concept of partnerships with the families of all children.

- Be able to think systematically about your family-involvement attitudes and practices and learn from your experiences.

- Understand the goals and benefits of different types of family involvement, as well as the barriers to their implementation.

- Be aware of the way cultural assumptions and life experiences influence interpretation of events, and respect the beliefs, values, opinions, lifestyles, and childrearing practices of all families.

- Be able to build on family diversity in the classroom, at the school site, and in the home.

- Be able to work collaboratively with each other, with other professionals, and with families and students to develop a common vision of partnership.

- Be willing to assume responsibility for initiating, supporting, rewarding and monitoring various types of partnership activities, ensuring access for all parents, and respecting all types and levels of participation.

REFERENCES

Berger, E. H. (1983). *Beyond the classroom: Parents as partners in education* (Rev. ed.). St. Louis, MO: Mosby.

Bevans, B., Furnish, B., Ramsey, A., & Talsma, S. (2001). *Effective strategies for home–school partnerships in reading.* Unpublished masters thesis. Saint Xavier University, Chicago.

Edwards, P. A. (1999). School–family connections: Why are they so difficult to create? In W. D. Hammond & T. E. Raphael (Eds.). *Early literacy instruction for the new millennium* (pp. 73–91). Grand Rapids, MI, & Ann Arbor, MI: Michigan Reading Association & Center for the Improvement of Early Reading Achievement.

Edwards, P. A., Pleasants, H. M., & Franklin, S. H. (1999). *A path to follow: Learning to listen to parents.* Portsmouth, NH: Heinemann.

Epstein, J. L. (1995). School/family/community partnerships: Caring for the children we share. *Phi Delta Kappan, 76,* 701–712.

Epstein, J. L., & Dauber, S. L. (1991). School programs and teacher practices of parent involvement in inner-city elementary and middle schools. *The Elementary School Journal, 91,* 289–305.

Greenwood, G. E., & Hickman, C. W. (1991). Research and practice in parent involvement: Implications for teacher education. *The Elementary School Journal, 91*(3), 279–288.

Henderson, A. T. (1981). *Parent participation—student achievement: The evidence grows (an annotated bibliography).* Columbia, MD: National Committee for Citizens in Education.

Henderson, A. T. (1987). *The evidence continues to grow: Parent involvement improves student achievement.* Columbia, MD: National Committee for Citizens in Education.

Henderson, A. T., & Berla, N. (1994). *A new generation of evidence: The family is critical to student achievement.* Columbia, MD: National Committee for Citizens in Education.

Leslie, L., & Allen, L. (1999). Factors that predict success in an early literacy intervention. *Reading Research Quarterly, 34,* 404–424.

Morrow, L. M., & Young, J. (1997). A collaborative family literacy program: The effects on children's motivation and literacy achievement. *Early Child Development and Care, 127–128,* 13–25.

Padak, N., & Rasinski, T. (1997). *Family literacy programs: Who benefits?* Kent, OH: Ohio Literacy Resource Center. (ERIC Document Reproduction Service No. ED407568)

Paratore, J. R., Melzi, G., & Krol-Sinclair, B. (1999). *What should we expect of family literacy? Experiences of Latino children whose parents participate in an intergenerational literacy project.* Newark, DE: International Reading Association.

Powell, D. (1991). Parents and programs: Early childhood as a pioneer in parent involvement and support. In S. L. Kagan (Ed.), *The care and education of America's young children: Obstacles and opportunities* (90th Yearbook of the National Society of the Study of Education). Chicago: The National Society of the Study of Education.

Radcliffe, B., Malone, M., & Nathan, J. (1994). *Training for parent partnership: Much more should be done*. Minneapolis, MN: Center for School Change, Hubert H. Humphrey Institute of Public Affairs, University of Minnesota.

Shartrand, A., Kreider, H., & Erickson-Warfield, M. (1994). *Preparing teachers to involve parents: A national survey of teacher education programs* (Working paper). Cambridge, MA: Harvard Family Research Project.

Swap, S. M. (1993). *Developing home–school partnerships: From concepts to practice*. New York: Teachers College Press.

Loss of Family Languages:
Should Educators Be Concerned?

LILY WONG FILLMORE

By conservative estimates, 3.5 million children in U.S. schools are identified as limited in English proficiency (LEP) (Macias, 1998). Their knowledge of English is so limited that without linguistic help they are excluded "from effective participation in the educational program offered" by the schools they attend (*Lau v. Nichols*, 1974). The Supreme Court's ruling in *Lau v. Nichols* held that these children must be provided instructional help to overcome the linguistic barrier to the school's instructional programs. The Court did not specify a particular programmatic remedy, but suggested that bilingual education was one possible approach, while instruction in English as a second language (ESL) was another. Since then, both bilingual and ESL programs have been established in many states to help children learn English and gain access to the curriculum.

The dilemma facing immigrant children, however, may be viewed as less a problem of learning English than of primary language loss. While virtually all children who attend American schools learn English, most of them are at risk of losing their primary languages as they do so.

In one sense, primary language loss as children acquire English is not a new problem. Few immigrant groups have successfully maintained their ethnic languages as they became assimilated into American life.[1] As they learned English, they used it more and more until English became their dominant language.

The outcome in earlier times was nonetheless bilingualism. The second generation could speak the ethnic language and English, although few people were equally proficient in both languages. The loss of the ethnic language occurred between the second and the third generations because second generation immigrants rarely used the ethnic language enough to impart it to their own children. Thus, the process of language loss used to take place over two generations. (Fishman & Hofman, 1966; Portes & Rumbault, 1990).

The picture has changed dramatically in the case of present day immigrants. Few current second generation immigrants can be described as bilinguals (López, 1982). Ordinarily, we assume that when children acquire a second language, they add it to their primary language, and the result is bilingualism. But in the case of most present-day immigrant children, the learning of English is a subtractive process (Lambert, 1977), with English quickly displacing and replacing the primary language in young first generation immigrants. The result is that few immigrant children become bilinguals today by learning English. Over the past 25 years, this process of accelerated language loss in immigrant children and families has been documented repeatedly (Fillmore, 1991a, 1991b; Hinton, 1999; Kouritzin, 1999; Portes & Hao, 1998). The following is an account of the experiences of one such family.

A CASE OF LANGUAGE SHIFT AND LOSS

The Chen[2] family is like many Chinese immigrants who have come to the United States over the past several decades. The family came from China's Canton province via Hong Kong, where they had spent nearly a decade waiting for a visa to immigrate to the United States. The Chens arrived in the United States in 1989: Mother, Father, Uncle (Father's brother), Grandmother (Father's mother), and the children, Kai-Fong, age 5 at the time of arrival (now 16); and Chu-Mei, age 4 (now 15). Once settled, the family quickly added two more children—the "ABC" ("American born Chinese") members of the Chen family, both girls, Chu-wa (now 10); and Allison (now 9 years old). A consideration of how the members of this family fared in their first decade in America is revealing. Sadly, it is a story that many immigrant families have experienced firsthand.

Contrasting experiences

The Chens settled in a suburban town in the San Francisco Bay area where Father, Mother, and Uncle had jobs waiting for them in a restaurant owned by a relative. They went to work in the restaurant's kitchen, and because the kitchen workers were all Chinese, their lack of English was not a handicap. They worked long hours each day, leaving home early in the morning and returning close to midnight. Grandmother stayed at home with the children, and everything was fine at first. She got the children ready for school and was at home to care for them when they were out of school.

School was difficult for the children initially, but they did not complain much. The elementary school that Kai-fong and Chu-mei attended had many minority group students. Some, although not many, were LEP students like themselves. The school had no bilingual or ESL classes, so non-English speakers like Kai-fong and Chu-mei were simply placed in regular classes where it was assumed they would learn English. Both began kindergarten at the same time and were placed in the same classroom. The teacher spoke English only, but she gave the several non-English speakers in her class extra attention whenever she could.

Chu-mei soon made friends with classmates and learned some English from them and from the teacher. Her adjustment, after the first year in school, was excellent. She had learned enough English in kindergarten to make reading in the first grade more or less possible. She was neat, agreeable, and sociable. She fit into the social world of the classroom without difficulty.

Kai-fong had quite a different experience in school. He was not as outgoing as his sister, and from the start, had difficulty establishing himself socially with his classmates. Some of the boys in the class teased him mercilessly. After Grandmother had cut his hair, it stuck straight out and would not lie flat. They called him "Chi, chi, chi, Chia-pet," after a then popular gift that was advertised frequently on television—a pig-shaped vase that grew spikey grass hair when watered. Kai-fong probably did not know what a "chia-pet" was, but he knew his classmates were making fun of his appearance. He wore homemade trousers that Grandmother had made from some polyester stretch yardage for him and for Chu-mei. The fabric worked well for Chu-mei, but not for Kai-fong. The boys in his class teased him about his "flower pants."

One day at school, there was a rock throwing incident involving Kai-fong and some other boys. It was unclear who started throwing rocks at whom, but they were all caught with rocks in their hands. The other children could tell their side of the story to the teacher on yard duty; Kai-fong could not. When the incident was reported to Father and Mother, they did not understand what had happened. They knew only that Kai-fong had gotten into trouble at school. Kai-fong was severely reprimanded by Father, Mother, and Grandmother, and he gradually began to withdraw.

In time, Kai-fong learned enough English to get by, and his wardrobe and hair became less distinctive. But he remained an outsider. In class, he was an indifferent student and rarely said anything spontaneously. He had a small group of friends with whom he played on the playground—other Asian immigrant boys who, like himself, were not finding it easy to fit into the social world of the school. Several boys were Vietnamese, one was Filipino, the others were Thai. The English they spoke had many dialect features that were picked up from the African-American children in the school, although they had little interaction with them. Kai-fong and his friends seemed to admire the African-American boys, and copied their dress, musical taste, and speech. The African-American boys were also outsiders at school, but they were the "cool guys," and they operated within their own social sphere both in and out of school.

Increasing separation

At home, Kai-fong became increasingly an outsider. Once he learned a little English, he stopped speaking Cantonese altogether. When Grandmother spoke to him, he either ignored her or would mutter a response in English that she did not understand. When pushed, he would simply stop speaking. Grandmother's complaints to Mother and Father resulted in frequent scoldings, and increasingly severe reprimands and sanctions. The more the adults scolded, the more sullen and angry Kai-fong became.

By the age of 10, Kai-fong, who was now known as Ken, was spending most of his time away from home, hanging out with his buddies, away from the scolding and haranguing. He and his friends spoke English only, and although some of them may have retained their primary languages, Kai-fong/Ken did not. He no longer understood Cantonese well and rarely said anything in that language.

Over time, Grandmother became withdrawn too. She had chronic headaches, which often immobilized her. Whether the headaches were caused by the tension in the home or not, it certainly did not help. The headaches made it hard for her to care for the younger children, and this was often left to Chu-mei. Each day, while her sisters were young, she hurried home from school and would play with them and teach them things she was learning. From her they learned English, the language she spoke at school and the language she could express herself in most easily.

Neither Chu-wa nor Allison (named after Chu-mei's best friend at school) speak Cantonese. They call Grandmother "Ah Yin-Yin" (the address term for paternal grandmother in Cantonese), but they do not know how to say much else in Cantonese to their grandmother or their parents. In fact, the only child in this family who can still communicate with the adults in Cantonese is Chu-mei, or Sondra, as she prefers to be called. She interprets for her family members when they need to communicate with one another.

But although Chu-mei/Sondra still speaks Cantonese, she is not as fluent as she should be. She is unable to express herself completely in Cantonese, and occasionally slips English words and phrases into her speech as she attempts to communicate with the adults in the family. This could be evidence of language loss or an indication that her primary language has not continued to develop as she has grown more mature. Either way, she is not as proficient in Cantonese as Chinese children her age ordinarily are.

Deteriorating family relations

Accelerated language loss is a common occurrence these days among immigrant families, with the younger members losing the ethnic language after a short time in school. In the Chen family, the adult members have not learned much English after a decade of residence in the United States. Mother, Father, and Uncle would like to study English, but their long work days do not allow them to take English as a second language classes at the adult education center in town. Father and Uncle have begun to pick up a little English from coworkers and from the Americans they see occasionally, but Mother and Grandmother have not learned much at all, although Grandmother spends most of her time at home with her English speaking grandchildren.

Clearly, the Chen family was deeply affected by the ways in which the children adjusted to life in their new society. The shift from Cantonese to English in this family and the loss of the family language by the children have had a great impact on communication between the adults and the children and ultimately on family relations. There is tension in this home: The adults do not understand the children, and the children do not understand the adults. Father, Mother, and Grandmother do not feel they know the children, and they do not know what is happening in their lives.

This is most obvious in the case of Kai-fong/Ken, who spends little time at home these days. He dropped out of school over a year ago and is out with his friends most of the time. His father says he does not know what Kai-fong is doing, but he does not think he has a job.

WHAT IS LOST WHEN A LANGUAGE IS LOST?

From a strictly pragmatic perspective, what happened to this immigrant family appears unfortunate but hardly tragic. From the school's point of view, this could even be seen as a relative success story. Of the four children in the Chen family, three are doing well in school. Only one has gotten lost, but that can happen in any family. But is it an acceptable loss? The questions that must be asked are these: What does school success mean, and can we afford to lose one child in four in the process of educating them? The three Chen children who can be described as successful students are so because they have learned English quickly and have made progress at school. They are acquiring the skills and information they need for educational advancement and participation in the work world. But is that all that is important? Can school provide children with everything they need to learn through the formal educational process?

I contend that the school cannot provide children what is most fundamental to success in life. The family plays a crucial role in providing the basic elements for successful functioning. These include: a sense of belonging; knowledge of who one is and where one comes from; an understanding of how one is connected to the important others and events in one's life; the ability to deal with adversity; and knowing one's responsibility to self, family, community. Other elements could be added to the list, but the point is that these are things the family must provide children at home while they are growing up. They cannot be taught at school. The content differs from family to family, but this is the curriculum of the home—what parents and other family members teach and inculcate in children in the socialization process.

The curriculum of the home is taught by word and example, by the way adults relate to the children of the family, beginning at birth and not ending until the children are mature and on their own. When parents send their children to school for formal education, they understand that their job of socializing their children is far from done. They continue to teach their children what they need to know as they mature. The school can take what the family has provided and augment or modify it even, but the foundation must be laid by the family.

What happens in families where parents cannot communicate easily with the children? What happens when the major means of socializing children into the beliefs, values, and knowledge base of the family and cultural group is lost? If the parents know any English, often they switch to that language and, while their capacity to socialize the children might be diminished, they are nonetheless able to teach their children some of what they need to learn. But it is not easy to socialize children in a language one does not know well. It takes thorough competence in a language to communicate the nuances of a culture to another.

In his autobiography, *Hunger of Memory* (1982), Rodriguez describes what happens in families when parents try to socialize their children in a language they do not know well. He recalls what happened as he and his siblings moved from Spanish to English after the parents were advised to stop using Spanish at home with the children:

> My mother and father, for their part, responded differently as their children spoke to them less. She grew restless, seemed anxious at the scarcity of words exchanged in the

house. It was she who would question me when I came home from school. She smiled at the small talk. She pried at the edges of my sentences to get me to say something more. (What?) She'd join conversations she overheard, but her intrusions often stopped her children's talking. By contrast, my father seemed reconciled to the new quiet. Though his English improved somewhat, he retired into silence. At dinner he spoke very little. One night his children and even his wife helplessly giggled at his garbled English pronunciation of the Catholic Grace before Meals. Thereafter he made his wife recite the prayer at the start of each meal, even on formal occasions, when guests were in the house. Hers became the public voice of the family. On official business, it was she, not my father, one would usually hear on the phone or in stores, talking to strangers. His children grew so accustomed to his silence that, years later, they would speak routinely of his shyness. But my father was not shy, I realized, when I'd watch him speaking Spanish with relatives. Using Spanish, he was quickly effusive. Especially when talking with other men, his voice would spark, flicker, flare alive with sounds. In Spanish, he expressed ideas and feelings he rarely revealed in English. With firm Spanish sounds, he conveyed confidence and authority English would never allow him (pp. 24–25).

Can parents keep informed of what is happening to their children? Can they stay connected with them when the children no longer understand the family language? Can parents maintain their roles as authority figures, teachers, and moral guides if they are not listened to? We discern in Rodriguez's poignant description a family that has lost its intimacy—the closeness between parents and children. Children learn what it means to be parents by observing their own parents. In this family, the children saw shadows only and not true pictures of who their parents were and what they were like as persons. Rodriguez reveals how greatly the loss of language and intimacy in the family changed the very structure of the family as well. The loss of language in this family severed the spiritual bond between parents and children:

> The silence at home, however, was finally more than a literal silence. Fewer words passed between parent and child, but more profound was the silence that resulted from my inattention to sounds (p. 25).

That is the dilemma. That is what is lost. One might argue that despite all of this, Rodriguez has been a success. He is a talented writer; he is thoughtful and sensitive; and he has accomplished a great deal in his life. But what his writings reveal to this reader is a deeply conflicted and lonely man who is trying to figure out who he is, where he belongs, and what his culture means. Does it matter that children lose their family language as they learn English as long as it does not interfere with their educational development and success in school? I think it does.

For immigrant children, learning English as a second language and dealing with school successfully are just one set of problems to be faced. Hanging on to their first language as they learn English is an equally great problem. Hanging on to their sense of worth, their cultural identities, and their family connections as they become assimilated into the school and society is a tremendous problem for all immigrant children. What is at stake in becoming assimilated into the society is not only their educational development but their psychological and emotional well being as individuals as well (Cummins, 1996).

The questions we educators need to consider are these: How and why do children give up and lose their primary languages as they learn English? What is involved, and what role are the schools playing in the process?

HOW IS A LANGUAGE LOST?

Language loss is not a necessary or inevitable outcome when children acquire second languages. Otherwise the world would have no bilinguals. In many places around the world, bilingualism and even multilingualism are commonplace. In the United States, however, and in other societies like it, powerful social and political forces operate against the retention of minority languages. To many and perhaps most Americans, English is more than a societal language; it is an ideology. The ideological stance is this: To be American, one must speak English.

English gives access to participation in the life of the society, but it is also proof of an individual's acceptance of and loyalty to the American ideal. Conversely, the inability to speak English is a sign that a person has not accepted the conditions of being American. These sentiments are powerful forces in how people see and deal with one another, especially in places like California, which have heavy concentrations of recent immigrants.[3] How do these forces affect the children discussed in this article?

The inability to speak English in school is a handicapping condition in many communities, particularly in places that have no programs designed to help children who are limited in English proficiency. Children in such situations, irrespective of background or age, are quick to see that language is a social barrier, and the only way to gain access to the social world of the school is to learn English. The problem is that they also come to believe that the language they already know, the one spoken at home by their families, is the cause of the barrier to participation, inclusion. and social acceptance. They quickly discover that in the social world of the school, English is the only language that is acceptable. The message they get is this: "The home language is nothing; it has no value at all." If they want to be fully accepted, children come to believe that they must disavow the low status language spoken at home.

Children often start using English almost exclusively outside of the home just as soon as they have learned barely enough to get by. Before long, they are speaking English at home as well, even with parents who do not understand the language. If the parents do not realize that this shift in language behavior signals a change in the children's language loyalty, English will supplant the family language completely in the children's speech.

Language loss is the result of both internal and external forces operating on children. The internal factors have to do with the desire for social inclusion, conformity, and the need to communicate with others. The external forces are the sociopolitical ones operating in the society against outsiders. against differences, against diversity. They are the forces behind the passage of various public referendums in California against "immigrants" and "outside influences": Proposition 63 in 1986, banning the use of languages other than English in public life; Proposition 187 in 1994, denying undocumented immigrants health, welfare, and educational services provided by public funds[4]; Proposition 209 in 1996, ending affirmative action programs in jobs and education; and finally Proposition 227 in 1998, eliminating bilingual education as the preferred instructional program for LEP students.

Children may not understand what these public actions mean, but they are aware of the underlying sentiment. They interpret it as saying to them: To be different is to be unacceptable. Thus children do what they believe they must to rid themselves of what makes them unacceptable. Language is an obvious difference, so it is the first to go. Names, dress, haircuts—whatever is obviously different is changed: Chu-mei becomes Sondra, Kai-fong becomes Ken, and Allison is Allison from the start. Baggy-legged jeans and oversized T-shirts replace unfashionable homemade garments, and the children are transformed. They are still different from their schoolmates, but not quite as different as before. They are no longer outsiders: They are Americans, not foreigners like their parents.

The processes of language loss and social adaptation may differ across individuals in detail from the picture sketched here, but the broad outline of these processes is general enough so that many immigrants will be able to map their own experiences onto it. They know what happens in families when children abandon the family language, and parents are no longer able to communicate easily with them. They know about the gradual erosion of trust and understanding among family members and about the loss of parental control.

Why do people allow this to happen? Few of those who are involved in the process of language loss realize the consequences it can have on their family or children until it is too late. It is difficult for people to believe that children can actually lose a language. They recognize that their children are changing, becoming "Americanized," as it were, or more independent. But few parents doubt that their children, if required to do so, could switch back to their primary language. And indeed, it might be somewhat true for some children. The loss of a primary language is rarely total. But in most cases, when children are not actively using their primary language in everyday interactions, they do not develop it further, as was the case with Chu-mei, or Sondra. She is still able to speak Cantonese, but not at an appropriate level for a child her age.

SUGGESTIONS FOR EDUCATORS

What can educators do to make the process of learning the school language and adapting to life in American culture easier on immigrant children and their families? What can they do to make English learning less subtractive than it is now? Ideally children would attend schools where the primary language is used along with English, and they would be given opportunities to develop both languages fully. But that may not be possible under current sociopolitical conditions. Whether or not it is, parents and teachers should be working together to find other ways to support children's development and retention of their primary languages, and to make their adjustment to school an easier one for everyone involved.

Such collaborative efforts between educators and parents, although needed, are not easy. The parents who need the most help are unlikely to speak or understand much English. If teachers can speak their language, they can work directly with them.

Otherwise teachers must work through interpreters, and that is never easy. The parents must be convinced that they need to be involved and to find time to work with the school for efforts like this to work.

Many immigrant parents have long workdays and may find it difficult to participate in school activities after work. Others may lack the confidence to work with teachers with whom they are not able to communicate easily. Still others may not understand the need for joint action on the part of the home and school. Undertakings such as the ones I am suggesting require a strong developmental effort on the part of the school. The suggestions that follow are meant to help educators become aware of the need to work with parents to make the situation in their school and community easier on immigrant students.

First, teachers can help parents understand that they must provide children opportunities to attain a mature command of their first language in the home, whether or not it is supported in school. This is done by using more and more mature forms of the language at home in talking with the children as they grow older and expecting more mature speech from them. Parents should be encouraged to find time to talk with their children, read to them (if this is a practice in the culture of the home), and teach them things that interest educated members of their group. Families that come from cultures with a rich oral tradition will have many stories and histories to share with the children. Teachers should encourage them to use these materials and to regard them as equal to written materials that other families might use with their children at home.

Second, teachers and parents should be aware of the traumatic experiences children may be undergoing as they try to fit themselves into the social world of the school. They need to be alert to signs of emotional problems and to treat such problems gently and supportively rather than cause children to withdraw further from family and teachers.

Third, teachers and parents need to work together to neutralize some of the negative forces that operate on children in our society. When children become alienated from parents in the process of becoming Americans, the parents do not always know what is going on in their children's lives. Teachers sometimes see what is happening with children that the parents do not (Olsen, 1997).

Finally, teachers should help parents understand that the only way ethnic languages and cultures can survive in societies like the United States is through community action. Immigrant communities have historically been involved in supporting heritage language and cultural programs. This requires community action, and such action can be taken only by members of the immigrant community. Community action is necessary if the family's language and culture are to survive the process of becoming Americans.

ENDNOTES

1. Some groups are more retentive of their ethnic languages than others, and have managed to maintain them even into the third generation (Fishman & Hofman, 1966; Portes & Hao, 1998).

2. The family name Chen is a pseudonym, as are all the given names used here. Chen is about as common a surname among the Chinese as Smith or Jones is among Americans. I have tried to use both Chinese and American given names that are similar enough to the real names of family members since their names revealed how they were adjusting to the American experience.

3. According to the Immigration and Naturalization Service, one of every four immigrants to the United States eventually resettles in California. When I was recently called for jury duty, I overheard three separate remarks from individuals complaining about "foreigners" who could not speak English well. The young woman who was calling names of prospective jurors on the public address system did so with evidence of Spanish in her pronunciation of English. Her English was nonetheless completely grammatical and intelligible. In the San Francisco Bay area, with its very diverse population, there were many unfamiliar surnames to be called, and she occasionally stumbled over the names she was reading, as anyone might. A woman who was sitting beside me in the jury assembly room complained to those seated around her: "They should not hire people who can't speak English! People who don't speak English properly shouldn't be allowed to deal with the public." That was just one of three such remarks I overheard that day.

4. Proposition 187 was declared to be unconstitutional in 1997 in a legal challenge brought before the federal court in Los Angeles. Invoking the "Personal Responsibility and Work Opportunity Reconciliation Act of 1996," the welfare reform legislation enacted by Congress, Judge M. R. Pfaelzer found in *League of United Latin American Citizens v. Wilson*, that 187 was an effort by the state to regulate immigration by restricting access to welfare and educational services. The regulation of immigration is exclusively a federal responsibility, and the state does not have the power to override federal legislation with its "own legislative scheme to regulate access to public benefits," the judge declared. Former Governor Pete Wilson appealed the decision in the Ninth Circuit Court of Appeals, but he was out of office before the case was heard. It was left to the present governor, Gray Davis, to settle the matter. In 1999, Davis asked the court to submit the case for mediation. The state and the opponents of 187 recently came to terms of agreement, ending any future challenges to the ruling.

REFERENCES

Benjamin, R. (1993). *The maintenance of Spanish by Mexicano children and its function in their school lives.* Unpublished doctoral dissertation, The University of California at Berkeley.

Cummins, J. (1996). *Negotiating identities: Education for empowerment in a diverse society.* Ontario, CA: California Association for Bilingual Education.

Fillmore, L. W. (1991a). Language and cultural issues in early education. In S. Kagan (Ed.), *The care and education of America's young children: Obstacles and opportunities* (The 90th yearbook of the National Society for the Study of Education) (pp. 30–49). Chicago, IL: University of Chicago Press.

Fillmore, L. W. (1991b). When learning a second language means losing the first. *Early Childhood Research Quarterly, 6,* 323–346.

Fishman, J. A. (1996). What do you lose when you lose your language? In G. Cantoni (Ed.), *Stabilizing indigenous languages* (Monograph series, special issue) (pp. 80–91). Flagstaff: Center for Excellence in Education, Northern Arizona University.

Fishman, J. A., & Hofman, J. E. (1966). Mother tongue and nativity in the American population. In J. A. Fishman (Ed.), *Language loyalty in the United States* (pp. 34–50). The Hague, Netherlands: Mouton & Co.

Hinton, L. (1999, December). Involuntary language loss among immigrants: Asian-American linguistic autobiographies. *ERIC Digest,* p. 3. Retrieved July 29, 2000 from the World Wide Web: http://www.cal.org/ericcll/digest/involuntary .html.

Kouritzin, S. G. (1999). *Face(t)s of first language loss.* Mahwah, NJ: Erlbaum.

Lambert, W. E.(1977). The effects of bilingualism on the individual: Cognitive and socio-cultural consequences. In P. Hornby (Ed.), *Bilingualism: Psychological, social and educational implications.* New York: Academic Press.

Lau v. Nichols, 414 U.S. 563, 566-69, 94 S.Ct. 786, 788-90, 39 L.Ed.2d 1 (1974).

López, D. E. (1982). *Language maintenance and shift in the United States today.* Los Alamitos, CA: National Center for Bilingual Research.

Macias, R. F. (1998). *Summary report of the survey of the states' limited English proficient students and available educational programs and services, 1996–97.* Washington, DC: National Clearinghouse for Bilingual Education.

Olsen, L. (1997). *Made in America: Immigrant students in our public schools.* New York: New Press.

Portes, A., & Hao, L. (1998). *E pluribus unum: Bilingualism and language loss in the second generation.* (Economics Working Paper Archive at Washington University, St. Louis). Retrieved July 29, 2000 from the World Wide Web: http://ideas.uqam.ca/ideas/data/Papers/wpawuwpma9805006.html

Portes, A., & Rumbault, R. G. (1990). *Immigrant America: A portrait.* Berkeley: The University of California Press.

Rodriguez, R. (1982). *Hunger of memory: The education of Richard Rodriguez.* Toronto and New York: Bantam Books.

INTEGRATING SOURCES

1. In what specific ways did these articles describe the role of the family unit in the development of literacy?

2. Fillmore describes a number of problems associated with the loss of family languages. Based on what you have read here and your personal experiences, what do you believe are some workable solutions to these difficulties?

CLASSROOM IMPLICATIONS

1. Try to learn as much as you can about each of your students' family literacy situations. For those individuals who have difficult home situations, what are some possible solutions you might try in your classroom?

2. Be aware of cultural and educational differences that may exist between the classroom and the home. What are some effective ways you as the classroom teacher can better encourage cultural awareness in your students?

ANNOTATED BIBLIOGRAPHY

Gelfer, J., Higgins, K., & Perkins, P. (2001). Literacy education and families: A program and its progress. *Early Child Development and Care, 167,* 329–50.

Describes Project Literacy Education and Families (LEAF), which is designed to provide a variety of literacy learning experiences for parents based on four distinct themes or components: adult literacy, early childhood education, parent education and parent–child literacy, and play interaction time.

James, H., & Kermani, H. (2001). Caregivers' story reading to young children in family literacy programs: Pleasure or punishment? *Journal of Adolescent & Adult Literacy, 44,* 458–466.

Notes the different ways in which families from a variety of cultural backgrounds accept and adapt information and teaching techniques related to family literacy.

Jongsma, K. (2001). Literacy links between home and school. *Reading Teacher, 55,* 58–61.

Describes effective materials that can be developed for a variety of literacy centers such as neighborhood community centers, church programs, and home settings.

Langely, L. P., Brady, D., & Starsky, M. (2001). Family literacy in action: The primetime family reading time program. *Public Libraries, 40,* 160–161, 164–165.

Describes the use of public libraries in the development of family literacy, especially as it relates to the extensive use of children's literature.

McKay, R. A., & Kendrick, M. E. (2001). Images of literacy: Young children's drawings about reading and writing. *Canadian Journal of Research in Early Childhood Education, 8,* 7–22.

Describes how a variety of children's drawings in grades 1–3 illustrate themselves in relation to literacy activities both within and without the classroom setting.

Meoli, P. L. (2001). Family stories night: Celebrating culture and community. *Reading Teacher, 54,* 746–747.

Illustrates a home literacy activity in which the entire family shares a story in their native language and then the children provide an English translation.

Quiroa, R. E. (2001). The use and role of multiethnic children's family literacy programs: Realities and possibilities. *New Advocate, 14,* 43–52.

Discusses the important role of multiethnic literature in the development of effective home literacy efforts.

Smith, C. B. (2001). How to talk to your children about books. Bloomington, IN: ERIC Clearinghouse on Reading, English, and Communication.

Provides specific information to parents on how they can help their children become better readers through a variety of home activities. Included are techniques on appropriate book selection, ideas related to book discussion between parents and children, and the use of a variety of motivational techniques in literacy.

Spielman, J. (2001). The family photography project: "We will just read what the pictures tell us." *Reading Teacher, 54,* 762–770.

Illustrates the importance of the use of a variety of family artifacts in developing literacy education in the home.

YOU BECOME INVOLVED

Carefully consider ways in which you can involve families of your students in the development of a variety of positive literacy activities in their homes. Examples might include a parent newsletter describing effective home literacy practices, school meetings on a variety of language activities, and making yourself easily available to parents who might have questions on family literacy issues.

● ● ● ● ●

CHAPTER FOUR

MULTICULTURAL DIVERSITY

For we cannot form our children as we would wish; as God has given us them,
so must we accept and love, educate them as we best may, and rest content.
For each has different gifts; every one is useful, but in his proper way.

—Johann Wolfgang von Goethe (1798)

I have a dream that my four little children will one day live in a nation where
they will not be judged by the color of their skin but the content of their character.
I have a dream today!

—Martin Luther King (1963)

A country as tolerant of inequities as America should
not be surprised at [low educational test] results.

—Michael Casserly, Director of the Council of Greater City Schools,
Philadelphia (2001)

The schools today are truly a multicultural community. Students in the typical classroom community represent a wide variety of countries and cultures. Many bring with them to the school setting a rich and varied background, most notably in their first languages. It is the role of the classroom teacher, while encouraging this diversity in all students, to be an effective language and literacy teacher as well (Blake & Sickle, 2001; Salinas, 2002; Villegas & Lucas, 2002).

Questions abound on how to most effectively meet the educational needs of this diverse community of students. Answers to these many problems are, in today's society, often answered according to political, social, or economic factors as opposed to educational needs (Gonzalez, 2001; Wortham, Murillo, & Hamann, 2002).

1. What language should be used for primary instruction, especially in the area of reading specifically and the language arts generally?

2. For those students who use English as a second language, what are the most appropriate teaching techniques and materials?
3. What types of literacy materials seem to work best to encourage multicultural knowledge in all students?
4. How can a sense of mutual respect and tolerance be created in students that encourages respect by all for the various cultures represented both within and beyond the classroom setting?

REASONS TO ENCOURAGE MULTICULTURAL EDUCATION

There are many reasons for teachers to encourage students to read widely about other cultures and peoples (Schmidt & Mosenthal, 2001; Risko & Bromley, 2001). We live in a world community today that is dramatically impacted by events from many differing locations throughout this group of nations (Crowther, Hamilton, & Tett, 2001). Whereas at one time we could feel comfortable in our isolation, this is not true today and will be even less so in the future. Not only is there better communication among nations and cultural groups, but there is also a dramatic increase in the numbers of international students who are now in our classrooms. It thus becomes the responsibility of the teacher to encourage a wider knowledge of diversity in each student.

The readings in this section were selected to help you carefully consider the many challenges as well as the many rewards in the effective teaching of multicultural education, especially through the extensive use of reading and writing activities.

AS YOU READ

The following selections provide a variety of views and opinions related to various issues in multicultural education, with particular emphasis on the language arts curriculum. Miller (2001) discusses the importance of developing in students, not just basic information and knowledge about multicultural questions but also a "sense of empathy" concerning these issues as well. MacGillivray & Rueda (2001) note the critical importance of inner-city classroom literacy teachers learning as much about the social backgrounds of their students as their educational needs. Peregoy and Boyle (2000) discuss specific classroom instructional recommendations for teaching students who are learning English as a second language. As you read this material on multicultural education, you might consider the following questions:

1. How do these various authors define *multiculturalism*? In what ways is your personal definition of *diversity* similar or different from these articles?
2. What are some of the current multicultural issues that you believe educators need to be aware of and how might they effectively deal with these concerns in their literacy instruction?

REFERENCES

Blake, M. E., & Sickle, M. V. (2001). Helping linguistically diverse students share what they know. *Journal of Adolescent and Adult Literacy, 44,* 468–475.

Crowther, J., Hamilton, M., & Tett, L. (Eds.). (2001). Powerful literacies. (ERIC Reproduction Service No. ED452383).

Gonzalez, R. E. (Ed.). (2001). *Language ideologies: Critical perspectives on the official English movement.* Urbana, IL: National Council of Teachers of English.

MacGillivray, L., & Rueda, R. (2001). *Listening to inner-city teachers of English-language learners: Differentiating literacy instruction.* Ann Arbor, MI: Center for the Improvement of Early Reading Achievement, University of Michigan School of Education.

Miller, H. M. (2000/2001). Teaching and learning about cultural diversity. *Reading Teacher, 54,* 380–381.

Peregoy, S. E., & Boyle, O. E. (2000). English learners reading English: What we know, and what we need to know. *Theory Into Practice, 39,* 337–347.

Risko, V. J., & Bromley, K. (Eds.). (2001). *Collaboration for diverse learners: Viewpoints and practices.* Newark, DE: International Reading Association.

Salinas, J. P. (2002). *The effectiveness of minority teachers on minority student success.* Houston, TX: National Association of African American Studies & National Association of Hispanic and Latino Studies.

Schmidt, P. R., & Mosenthal, P. B. (Eds.). (2001). *Reconceptualizing literacy in the new age of multiculturalism and pluralism.* Greenwich, CT: Information Age.

Villegas, A. M., & Lucas, T. (2002). *Educating culturally responsive teachers: A coherent approach.* Ithaca, NY: State University of New York Press.

Worthham, S., Murillo, E. G., & Hamann, E. T. (Eds.). (2002). *Education in the new Latino diaspora: Policy and politics of identity. Sociocultural studies in educational policy formation and appropriation.* Westport, CT: Greenwood.

Teaching and Learning about Cultural Diversity

A dose of empathy

HOWARD M. MILLER

Item: A 15-month-old boy named Michael responds to the crying of his friend Paul by offering him his own teddy bear. When Paul continues to cry, Michael brings Paul's security blanket to him (Goleman, 1995, p. 98).

Item: A white high school student describes her participation in a multicultural summer program in which she was battered with stories of white racism, oppression, and genocide that left her feeling "like ripping off my White skin" (Howard, 1999, p. 20).

Item: A group of high school students is taken to see the movie *Schindler's List* (1993, Steven Spielberg, Director), and they react to the depiction of the Holocaust not with respect or shock, but "with hilarity" (Beck, 1995).

What do these stories have in common? They are all about empathy—achieved, gone awry, or untapped—the extraordinary capacity for one human being to see things through the eyes of the "other," the source of compassion, tolerance, and understanding that leads us away from egocentrism to a world view that lies at the heart of multicultural education.

Empathy is a powerful force that needs to be carefully titrated; too little or too much can be defeating. The girl in the second story, for example, felt so much empathy with the suffering of the minority groups that she saw herself as shameful as their victimizers. Contrast this with the high school students in the third story who could not connect with the events as they unfolded in *Schindler's List*; instead, they responded to something they could relate to—being with their friends on what they saw as a holiday from school.

Neither of these represents the kind of story we like to hear about when we are discussing cross-cultural understanding. But the first story, revealing the capacity to

Reprinted by permission of the author from *The Reading Teacher, 54* (2000), 380–381.

feel for and reach out to others even at a very young age, does represent something we wish we could bottle and keep close to us, and perhaps spray on our students from time to time.

PREPARE THE MIXTURE

How can we add empathy to a mix that already includes integrity, accuracy, and as much truth as we can gather together to defuse ignorance and prejudice?

One answer lies in helping our students to make connections with the literature we read to and with them, or that they read to themselves or with one another. Louise Rosenblatt (1995), the grande dame of reader response theory, has taught what now amounts to generations of language arts teachers to appreciate the range of reading experiences, from what she calls the "efferent" (reading for information) to the "aesthetic" (reading as a personal, emotional experience). Multicultural education needs to embrace both: information to dispel ignorance and personal engagement to embed the lessons in our hearts.

Teachers have come to value the aesthetic in reading, often encouraging students to share personal responses in their journals. For example, one of my former seventh-grade students wrote about the xenophobic inhabitants of the fictional town of Jenkinsville, Arkansas, in Betty Greene's novel *Summer of My German Soldier* (1973, Dell):

> They are prejudice [sic] towards anyone who is not like them. There used to be a Chinese man running a grocery store. His name was Mr. Lee. The people didn't call him that though they called him something worse. Everybody in the town is prejudice against everyone but themselves. I would hate to live in Jenkinsville!

Analyzing this student's response, we could say that she has shown an intellectual understanding of what prejudice is and recognizes that it is a negative quality. But she has also shown a personal connection by considering her own values and deciding that she would not want to associate with the prejudiced townspeople. She may not fully grasp what Mr. Lee felt as prejudice's victim, but she would rather identify with the victim than with the victimizers.

ADD BENEVOLENT DESIRES

In the video *Not in Our Town* (1995, California Working Group), which tells the uplifting true account of the residents of Billings, Montana, USA, taking a unified stand against an outbreak of hate crimes, one community member speaks of a Native American expression that translates into English as "the benevolent desires of the soul." He tells us we must not allow these "benevolent desires" to remain buried inside us; we must find a way to let them out or we will grow ill.

Surely children's author Patricia Polacco must have heeded the benevolent desires of her soul when she wrote *Pink and Say* (1994, Philomel). The book recounts a family story about Polacco's ancestor who had been a Union soldier in the U.S. Civil War at the age of 15. Nicknamed "Say," the young soldier, who was white, was rescued and carried to safety by an equally young black soldier nicknamed "Pink." Both boys were later captured and taken to the notorious Andersonville Confederate prison. Say survived the ordeal; Pink did not. At the end of the story, in a style that gives it the weight of history the way a family Bible might, Polacco wrote,

> I know this story to be true because Sheldon Russell Curtis ["Say"] told his daughter, Rosa. Rosa Curtis Stowell told it to her daughter, Estella. Estella Stowell Barber, in turn, told it to her son, William. He then told me, his daughter, Patricia.
> This book serves as a written memory of Pinkus Aylee since there are no living descendants to do this for him.
> When you read this, before you put this book down, say his name out loud and vow to remember him always.

Polacco's passion and compassion communicate so effectively that it would take a stony-hearted person indeed to read this book aloud without choking up, and there is no doubt the name of Pinkus Aylee will be remembered for a long time to come. In heeding the message of her own benevolent desires, Polacco has touched ours.

Another story to engage the heart as well as the mind is Ezra Jack Keats's *Louie* (1975, Greenwillow). This book tells of a young boy who is somehow different from the other children in his neighborhood and who has not always been treated with patience or kindness. In this description from a dream Louie has, Keats suggests the situation with just a few well-chosen words:

> There were kids all around. They were making fun of him.
> "Hello, hello!
> "Nah—it's good-bye, good-bye!"
> "Oh, yeah—hello and good-bye, Louie!"

Louie has become enamored of a puppet used in a show put on by some of the other children. During the show, he interrupts in order to talk to the puppet. This is the first time anyone recalls ever hearing him speak. In the end, some of the children, in a demonstration of generosity and compassion, arrange for Louie to find the puppet and have it for himself.

ADJUST THE INGREDIENTS

In Michael Rosen's *Elijah's Angel* (1992, Voyager Books), a young Jewish boy is given the gift of a hand-carved wooden angel by an elderly African American man with whom he is friendly. The boy, Michael, is thrilled with the gift but is embarrassed to show it to his parents because it was offered as a Christmas present, a "Christian guardian angel." In the end, Michael learns a valuable lesson about cultural inter-changes, that empathy does not require the subversion of one's own values and identity in order to honor someone else's. As Michael's parents tell him:

What this angel means to you doesn't have to be what it means to Elijah . . . Elijah cares about you. It's an angel of friendship. And doesn't friendship mean the same thing in every religion?

In her book *I Never Knew Your Name* (1994, Ticknor & Fields), author Sherry Garland reminds us that failing to reach out to others may have dire consequences. The book deals with a teenager's suicide as seen through the eyes of an unnamed narrator, a young neighbor:

That last day, you were up on the roof feeding the pigeons. I grabbed a handful of bread and started to go up there, too, but you looked like you were crying and wanted to be alone, so I went and watched a boring old movie on TV instead.

GIVEN THE RIGHT DOSE

We cannot teach empathy, generosity, and kindness in the same way we show our students how to solve a math problem, but we can help raise awareness of these values and affirm them whenever possible. Each of the picture books cited here presents an opportunity to examine the importance of reaching out to others, and may provide the impetus to do just that. Knowledge may be the key to eroding ignorance, but it takes a good dose of empathy to move our students from intellectual understanding to compassionate action.

REFERENCES

Beck, B. (1995, Spring). The road to Auschwitz: What's so funny about *Schindler's List? Multicultural Education*, pp. 13–15.

Goleman, D. (1995). *Emotional intelligence*. New York: Bantam.

Howard, G. (1999). *We can't teach what we don't know: White teachers, multiracial schools*. New York: Teachers College Press.

Rosenblatt, L. (1995). *Literature as exploration*. New York: Modern Language Association.

Listening to Inner City Teachers of English Language Learners:

Differentiating Literacy Instruction

LAURIE MacGILLIVRAY & ROBERT RUEDA

THE PROBLEM

Too many students are not learning to be successful readers and writers. They are moving into the upper elementary grades as struggling readers. This inability becomes a burden that affects all of their academic learning. Children of color living in poverty and/or learning English are grossly overrepresented in the group of unsuccessful literacy students. There has been important research in the last fifteen years that can help teachers and principals better meet the needs of children often unintentionally neglected by traditional instruction. Differentiated instruction improves children's chances for becoming competent readers and writers.

We have examined literacy learning in the inner city of Los Angeles for several years. Our research has been one of many studies conducted under the auspices of the nationally-funded Center for the Improvement of Early Reading Achievement. Recently we analyzed what we have learned from teachers about high quality instruction for poor second language learners. We preface the discussion with a short description of the notion of responsivity, which subsumes the specific practices and guidelines presented later in the paper.

Used by permission of the Center for the Improvement of Early Reading Achievement, University of Michigan School of Education. ©2001, CIERA. The work reported herein was supported in part under the Education Research and Development Centers Program PR/Award Number R305R70004, as administered by the Office of Educational Research and Improvement, U.S. Department of Education. However, the contents do not necessarily represent the positions or policies of the National Institute on Student Achievement, Curriculum, and Assessment or the National Institute on Early Childhood Development, or the U.S. Department of Education, and you should not assume endorsement by the federal government.

Vygotskian Notion of Responsivity

Sociocultural theory, with roots in Vytogsky's sociocultural theory of mind, emphasizes the social and cultural basis of teaching, learning, and development (Tharp & Gallimore, 1988). In this view, teaching is seen as providing assistance (social mediation) to a learner at a level just above what the learner might accomplish independently. Good instruction, which is responsive, then, falls in that space between what the learner can already do alone and what can be done with assistance. Instruction that ignores what students already know or can do, or that is too difficult, does not represent effective pedagogy. It is therefore important to understand and respond to what children know and to recognize what knowledge they come into the classroom with. It is also important to assure that simple factors such as language differences do not make instruction inappropriately difficult.

Differentiating Instruction

There are many ways to consider differentiating instruction for emergent readers and writers. We strongly believe that problems are situated within specific contexts much more than within specific individuals. Therefore, a single approach to varying instruction will not be appropriate for all schools, all teachers, or all children. Educators must have a repertoire of strategies so that they can vary their interactions and curriculum as needed. Below, we describe seven broad guidelines we have drawn from our research with teachers.

Be Responsible for Knowing about Your Students' Lives

Teachers must learn about their children's lives beyond the school walls. This inquiry can be formal or informal. Teachers can systematically investigate families' worlds. In his work with Latino immigrant families, Moll & Whitmore (1993) used the term "funds of knowledge" to refer to the incredible wealth of typically untapped community wisdom. He involved classroom teachers in examining the highly developed information networks that enabled families to be successful in a variety of areas.

But, there are some less time-consuming steps toward increasing their knowledge of specific communities. They can go for a print walk around the neighborhood, noting the types of public messages (business signs to graffiti), the languages utilized, and the purposes of text. Walking students home or other impromptu acts offer insights into children's lives beyond the schoolyard.

Expect the Most; Avoid the Deficit Model

It is important that we don't confuse differentiating instruction with lowering expectations. All too often this is the case, even with well-intentioned teachers. Allington (1983) captured this in a study on the way teachers' lead leveled reading groups. He found that students in the lower groups focused less on meaning than the "high group" and spent more time focused on phonemes. Frequently with second language learners, English oral proficiency is confounded with cognitive competence. Similarly, children with differing ways of experiencing narrative (such as story telling) are regularly assumed to be lacking intelligence. Children need high expectations and challenges in order to thrive. Educators need to figure out what children do know and use those strengths to move them forward.

Implement Curriculum That Is Meaningful to the Children

Most prepackaged curricula were created with middle-class, native English speakers in mind. Many of the children that fall outside of this group feel alienated when they cannot find images of their own lives in the curriculum. We must find ways to involve them and their worlds in the day-to-day life of the classroom.

One teacher that we recently worked with in a study on reading engagement used issues in the children's lives as the foundation for literacy instruction. For example, during the controversy over bilingual education (instigated by Proposition 227) one of her first graders asked why anyone would want people to know just one language. She set aside her plans and took the time to explore the issue more fully. The little boy came to the front of the class and explained what he had seen and how he felt. The class discussed the advantages of knowing two languages and the disadvantage of knowing just English or Spanish.

In another instance during Social Studies, she asked the children to create 3-D habitats. Many of the children talked about their overcrowded apartments and homes they wished to have in the future. These kinds of activities legitimize the children's lives and concerns that are rarely represented in curriculum materials.

Recognize Knowledge of Two Languages and Cultures

Often students labeled "low" or "struggling" in reading are using language in rich and complex ways outside of school. Specifically, many of these children act as "language brokers," a term coined by McQuillan & Tse (1995). They help monolingual family members interact with the English-dominant environment. This can mean explaining to salespeople what a parent wants, paying bills, and/or translating for doctors and teachers. Literacy brokers learn to be sensitive to cultural and contextual norms when moving between two languages.

Besides carrying the burden of critical interactions, these young English-language learners are figuring out the difficult process of translation, as well as frequently working with a wide variety of genres including bills, receipts, coupons and legal documents. Teachers can tap into this typically ignored resource of knowledge. This knowledge can inform teachers' whole group instruction as well as individualized interventions.

Another benefit to recognizing children's linguistic backgrounds is a better understanding of students' writing and inventive spelling. Although teachers can not be fluent in every language spoken in their classroom, general knowledge about other languages can lead to informative analysis. For example, a rudimentary knowledge of Spanish enables specific knowledge of why some students may be using some spelling patterns, such as "ll" for a "y" sound. Remembering to reflect on the deeper reasons students may be writing or spelling in a certain way can inform differentiated instruction.

Be Aware of Default Curriculum: Content and Structure

There are routines and topics that are viewed by many as "givens." One very common structural pattern of classroom interactions is teacher–lecture, teacher–question, followed by teacher–conclusion. The teacher decides what will be covered, how it will be covered, and students respond within a narrow band of behaviors with a small ratio of talk compared to that of the teachers. Teachers we worked with remember hating this structure, but many are reproducing it in their own classrooms. This default curriculum is what new teachers see practiced in their classrooms, represented in most curriculum guides, expected by teachers and, for most, was dominant in their schooling experience.

Similarly, there is default content. For example, in Los Angeles, many elementary classrooms spend some time focusing on the four seasons. But it is rare to find a tree with orange and yellow leaves in the fall, we only see snow on the peaks of mountains; and rainy season does not fit neatly into winter, fall, spring, or summer. As teachers and principals, we must interrogate our curriculum. We need the structure and content to work for our students. Also, we need to remember to communicate the reasons for our practices to both our students and their parents.

LOOKING BEYOND READING INSTRUCTION

Differentiating instruction can improve the chances for all children to be successful. But there are some larger societal issues that need to be a part of the conversation. Teachers and principals need society's support.

Poverty

Edmund W. Gordon, the first director of Head Start, stated, "I think schools can be much more powerful, but I don't think they can reverse all the ill effects of a starkly disadvantaged status in society" (as quoted in Traub, 2000). The inequities of our society and the pervasiveness of poverty is recognized in many ways in the mass media. Yet schools are often expected to balance out all inequities. As Traub (2000) wrote in a New York Times article, "The idea that school, by itself, cannot cure poverty is hardly astonishing, but it is amazing how much of our political discourse is implicitly predicated on the notion that it can."

As educators, we need to fight outside the school walls as well as inside to increase the chance for success for poor children. Learning about the economic realities of our children's parents and community issues can enable us to see the complexity between economic opportunities and poverty.

Anti-immigrant Sentiment and Anti-bilingualism

Recently there has been an increase in anti-immigrant sentiment as well as a move to discourage bilingualism. One way to examine this issue is to consider the recent initiatives that have been put before the California voters. This state seems to be leading a trend that is moving across the country.

Proposition 187, which focused on illegal immigrants in 1994, was the first major initiative that caught voters' attention. It made illegal aliens ineligible for public social services, public health care services (unless in cases of emergency under federal law), and public school education at elementary, secondary, and post-secondary levels. Various state and local agencies, including schools and specifically teachers, were required to report those who were suspected of being in the country illegally. The measure was described in the official ballot argument as "the first giant stride in ultimately ending the ILLEGAL ALIEN invasion."

Although this proposition was found unconstitutional in the courts, two years later Proposition 209 was passed in California. Commonly known as the "Anti-Affirmative Action Proposition," among other things, it prohibited ". . . the state, local governments, districts, public universities, colleges, and schools, and other government instrumentalities from discriminating against or giving preferential treatment to any individual or group in public employment, public education, or public contracting on the basis of race, sex, color, ethnicity, or national origin."

Perhaps the most controversial initiative of all was Proposition 227, commonly known as the "Antibilingual Initiative." On June 2, 1998, California voters overwhelmingly approved Proposition 227, an initiative that largely eliminates bilingual education from the state's public schools. Under the California initiative, most limited-English-proficient students in that state are now placed in English-immersion programs and then shifted as quickly as possible into regular classrooms.

Parents, students, and bilingual teachers talk about their feelings of shame even though they knew these propositions were wrong. These larger societal and institutional issues impede children's learning. When students do not feel valued and when they are encouraged to disown parts of themselves, they are less likely to engage in school tasks.

Lack of Resources

Most of the schools serving poor children have fewer resources than those in middle- and upper-class neighborhoods. For example, the most recent elementary school where we conducted research on reading engagement did not have a library until last year. When they did get one, it was solely because the principal obtained a grant. The scarcity of written materials is a common problem even though literacy researchers have documented how access to books increases the time children spend reading, and thus improves their literacy competencies.

Even though many children have strong family and community networks and there are advantages to living downtown, the difficulties are numerous. Money for community and police-sponsored programs that once flourished in large cities has shrunk. Drug deals are common in the streets and crime is high. Safe areas to play outside are almost non-existent when living in a downtown apartment, hotel, or shelter. Most importantly, many of the educational opportunities are expensive. We found that many families had not visited the nearby Children's Museum due to high admission fees. The library also was often not used because the parents were afraid of the fines attached to late, damaged, and lost books. Transportation to other areas of town is typically time-consuming and/or cost-prohibitive.

There are solutions to these problems, but they need to be long-term and multifaceted. Many corporations are beginning to make positive differences in downtown living conditions. Creation and support of after-school and weekend programs provides safe places for children. Another way to intervene is to become politically active. Pushing for extra funding for fieldtrips is yet another area in which efforts could fight the disadvantages of living in urban poverty.

Environmental Hazards

Safety and health issues are rarely discussed problems that decrease children's chances for being successful literacy learners. In our conversations with teachers and their principals, we found they spent a great deal of time and energy fighting for the conditions that are a given in suburban schools. For over a year, one teacher requested to have the vents cleaned in her bungalow because of health reports connecting the presence of microorganisms to cancer. Bungalows were also found to lack good circulation, since the only door in the room is closed and many do not have windows that open. Neither of these issues was addressed in the media until they were an issue in the suburban schools.

These classrooms are also supposed to be vacuumed once a month. In many classrooms in other schools it is done once a week. One teacher had to write several letters to the plant manager informing him that she was not being included, and then waited months for action. The plant manager does not report to the principal, so there is not an immediate supervisor on campus.

These problems may arise in all school districts, but they are more numerous and the resolutions seem to take longer in crowded urban schools. Even when parents are involved in academic activities, such as literacy nights, there are deterrents to participation, including long schedules and language issues, that make further involvement difficult. In suburban schools, at least a few vocal parents are more likely to intervene in these kinds of problems. Also, middle- and upper-class parents tend to know more about how to influence the system. For example, they know at what level to complain, whom to write letters to, and the best tone and content for interactions with the schools.

CONCLUSION

Improving the numbers of successful literacy learners requires action on multiple levels: teachers and administrators, academics, community leaders, parents, and politicians. As educators we need to simultaneously look inward at classroom curriculum, and outward at societal issues that impede our students' progress. Practicing the guidelines we have learned from teachers is difficult. Support networks of teachers and administrators are critical for rethinking our curriculum and our role in larger community issues, to best serve the needs of poor, inner-city second language learners.

REFERENCES

Allington, R. (1983). The reading instruction provided readers of differing abilities. *Elementary School Journal, 83*, 548–559.

Heath, S. (1982). *Ways with words*. Cambridge: Cambridge University Press.

McQuillan, J., & Tse, L. (1995). Child language brokering in linguistic minority communities: Effects on cultural interaction, cognition, and literacy. *Language and Education, 9*(3), 195–215.

Moll, L. C., & Whitmore, K. F. (1993). Vygotsky in classroom practice: Moving from individual transmission to social transaction. In E. Forman, N. Minick, & C. A. Stone (Eds.), *Contexts for learning: Sociocultural dynamics in children's development*, pp. 19–42. New York: Oxford University Press.

Morrow, L. (1992). The impact of a literature-based program on literacy achievement, use of literature, and attitudes of children from minority backgrounds. *Journal of Reading Behavior, 22*, 255–275.

Traub, J. (March 13, 2000). What no school can do. *New York Times Supplement.*

Worthy, J. (1996). Removing barriers to voluntary reading for reluctant readers: The role of school and classroom libraries. *Language Arts, 73*, 483–492.

Yaden, D., Tam, A., Madrigal, P., Brassell, D., Massa, J., Altamirano, L. S., & Armandariz, J. (2000). Early literacy for inner-city children: The effects of reading and writing interventions in English and Spanish during the preschool years. *The Reading Teacher 54*(2), 186–189.

English Learners Reading English:
What We Know, What We Need to Know

SUZANNE F. PEREGOY

OWEN F. BOYLE

Of all school learning, success in literacy, especially reading, is certainly among the most important achievements for all students due to its key role in academic learning and consequent social and economic opportunities. In recent years, pressures to prepare a highly literate populace together with concerns over reading achievement have prompted federal and state leaders in the United States to focus attention on ways to teach reading more effectively. Debates over best teaching practices have fueled differences between whole language and phonics advocates.

The result is a highly vocal and polarized rhetoric that fails to capture the reality of today's classrooms: dedicated teachers combining experience, insight, and professional judgment to address the increasingly diverse and changing learning needs of their students. Often missing in the debate are the literacy needs of English learners, though as a group, they score among the lowest in reading achievement nationwide. Finding a place for English learners in the discussion of best practices is thus imperative.

The inadequacy of efforts to define simple guidelines for teaching English learners to read is not due to lack of concern on the part of researchers, educators, or politicians. Rather a combination of factors makes English learners' reading a conceptually difficult topic to encompass. Among these factors are the dynamic, evolving, and sometimes controversial state of reading research in general; a lack of consistent, generalizable research findings on second language reading processes and programs in particular; and the rapid growth and tremendous diversity among English learners themselves (Fitzgerald, 1995).

As we write this article, we enter the arena well aware of these obstacles. Nonetheless, we see this as an opportunity to synthesize research, theory, and practice

From *Theory Into Practice, 39,* 2 (Spring 2000) is reprinted by permission. Copyright 2000 by the College of Education, The Ohio State University. All rights reserved.

in the field of second language reading. We begin by describing English reading processes among native and non-native English speakers. Then, using theory, experience, and research where available for support, we offer a set of recommendations for teaching English learners to read in English.

DIVERSITY AMONG ENGLISH LEARNERS

The most salient feature of English learners as a group is their remarkable diversity. At the very least, these students vary in age, prior educational experiences, cultural heritage, socioeconomic status, country of origin, and levels of both primary language and English language development, including literacy development. Some are immigrants or children of immigrants and represent languages from every continent in the world. Others have roots in U.S. soil that go back for generations, maintaining languages as diverse as Spanish, Navajo, Chippewa, Cherokee, Choctaw, Apache, and Crow. Of course English learners also vary along personal lines, as do all students, in terms of their interests, desires, aptitudes, and potentials.

Just as English learners vary one from another, so do the classrooms and programs that serve them. While some classrooms serve English learners from the same primary language background, often Spanish, other classrooms may include students from over 10 different primary language backgrounds. Some students will receive literacy instruction in the primary language; many will not. Regardless of program type or classroom composition, tremendous diversity will be found in any classroom in terms of students' English proficiency, reading and writing ability, primary language literacy, and literacy practices in the home.

As daunting as the diversity among second language readers may be, one unifying factor in the equation is that the *process* of reading in English is essentially similar for all readers, whether they are native or non-native English speakers (Fitzgerald, 1995; Goodman & Goodman, 1978). This process involves decoding written symbols into the language they represent to arrive at meaning. What differs between native and non-native English readers are the cognitive-linguistic and experiential resources they bring to the reading task, especially in terms of those variables that relate directly to reading comprehension in English, i.e., (a) English language proficiency, (b) background knowledge related to the text, and (c) literacy abilities and experiences, if any, in the first language. We elaborate later on these three differences between native and non-native English readers, but first we briefly describe how native English speakers read in English in order to establish those elements of the reading process shared in common by native and non-native English readers.

GOOD READERS READING IN ENGLISH

How do good readers read? That is, how do native English speakers who are also good readers make sense of a text written in English? First, good readers generally approach a text with a particular purpose in mind. They have enough experience with written language to know its various uses, and they put that understanding into practice when selecting a text to achieve their purpose.

Along with a purpose, good readers may bring at least some prior knowledge of the text topic. The more familiar the topic, the easier it will be for the reader to understand the text. That is, comprehension is affected by the extent to which the reader is familiar with the topics, objects, and events described in a text (Anderson, 1994). Good readers activate prior knowledge of the text topic by imagining what they know and do not know about the topic, predicting what the text will be about, and generating questions the text might answer.

Having set a purpose and activated prior knowledge, the good reader begins reading by visually processing the print from left to right, top to bottom of the page, given that we are talking about reading in English. Processing the print involves decoding the words on the page, i.e., producing a mental or verbal equivalent to access meaning. However, decoding word by word is insufficient, as evidenced by some students who accurately call out every word in a sentence without understanding the meaning.

As they are decoded, the words on the page must also be interpreted, initially in the context of the phrases and sentences of which they are a part, and subsequently across sentences and paragraphs as the larger meaning of the text is constructed. The comprehension process thus depends upon the reader's knowledge of the particular vocabulary and grammatical structures that comprise the sentences of the text and also upon the reader's familiarity with the way the text as a whole is structured.

As the good reader moves across sentences and paragraphs to construct the larger meaning of a text, familiarity with the genre and its text structure comes into play in the comprehension process, helping the reader anticipate and predict the direction and flow of ideas (Kintsch & Van Dijk, 1978). For example, a text that begins, "Once upon a time," signals the beginning of a fairy tale told with a narrative text structure.

Contrast that with a paragraph that begins. "Three key events led to California's rapid rise to statehood." This sentence signals an informational text that will probably be written with an enumeration text structure. Good readers are sufficiently familiar with a variety of genres and text structures to use this knowledge for predicting and confirming meaning across sentences, paragraphs, and passages that comprise a text.

As good readers move through the text, decoding and constructing meaning, they need to hold on to their ongoing textual interpretation in order to elaborate, modify, and further build upon it, thereby keeping their interpretation going and growing. Reading is thus a complex, cognitive-linguistic process that engages background knowledge and taxes both short- and long-term memory. It is also a process that takes place in a social context while serving as a social act of communication between the author and reader. In this interactive view, text comprehension is simultaneously driven by the reader's purpose, prior knowledge, and ongoing interpretation as these interact with decoding to achieve communication (Rumelhart, 1994).

Finally, good readers are strategic readers, meaning they monitor their understanding as they read to check whether their interpretation makes sense and to make sure they are achieving their purpose (Brown, Campione, & Day, 1980). They employ fix-up strategies, such as rereading a confusing part, to assist themselves in comprehending a text and achieving their purpose for reading. In this sense, reading is an active process of constructing and confirming meaning, one that is both linear and sequential as well as recursive and selective in that good readers may preview the text, reread a sentence, or go back to a different section to double check their evolving interpretation.

We have briefly described how good readers set a purpose for reading and bring several knowledge resources to bear upon the comprehension process, among them: decoding ability, language knowledge, background knowledge, written genre knowledge, familiarity with text structures, and comprehension-monitoring abilities. Nonnative English readers engage in a similar reading process, calling into play similar knowledge resources, with certain important differences that we focus on in the next sections: (a) English language proficiency, (b) background knowledge, and (c) literacy knowledge and experience in the primary language.

ENGLISH LANGUAGE PROFICIENCY

English language proficiency stands out as the defining difference between native and non-native English speakers, even though English learners range along a broad continuum from non-English to fully English proficient. In this context, English language proficiency refers to an individual's general knowledge of English, including vocabulary, grammar, and discourse conventions, which may be called upon during any instance of oral or written language use (Canale & Swain, 1980; Peregoy & Boyle, 1991).

To the extent that a reader is limited in English language proficiency, the ability to make sense of a text written in English is likewise hindered. Even second language readers who are proficient in English have been found to read more slowly than native English speakers, attesting to the comprehension difficulties related to English language proficiency during reading (Fitzgerald, 1995). This fact calls into question the validity of standardized reading achievement test results for many English learners.

BACKGROUND KNOWLEDGE: TEXT CONTENT

Interestingly, the comprehension challenges imposed by limited English proficiency are alleviated when the text concerns content with which the second language reader is familiar. For example, in one study, Arab Muslim and Hispanic Catholic college students in the United States were given two passages to read, one with Muslim-oriented content and one with Catholic-oriented content (Carrell, 1987). For both groups, comprehension was better when reading the passage reflecting their own cultural tradition. In similar studies involving culturally familiar and culturally unfamiliar passages of similar linguistic difficulty, comprehension was higher for the culturally familiar text (Fitzgerald, 1995). In other words, familiarity with text content alleviated limitations associated with second-language proficiency in text comprehension.

Background knowledge is a powerful variable for both native and non-native English readers. However, it becomes doubly important in second language reading because it interacts with language proficiency during reading, alleviating the comprehension difficulties stemming from language proficiency limitations. Therefore, building background knowledge on a text topic through first-hand experiences such as science experiments, museum visits, and manipulatives can facilitate success in reading.

BACKGROUND KNOWLEDGE: TEXT STRUCTURE

In addition to familiarity with text content, familiarity with text structure also facilitates reading comprehension (Carrell, 1987, 1992). Because text structure conventions can vary from one language to another, explicit instruction on English text structures is beneficial for English learners, especially those who are literate in their primary language. For example, knowing how a story plot or a cause/effect argument is structured can facilitate reading comprehension in those genres.

Text structure knowledge boosts comprehension by helping readers anticipate and predict the direction of a plot or argument, thereby facilitating attention to the larger meaning of the text. For example, familiarity with problem/solution text structure can assist the reader in anticipating, seeking, and finding the author's proposed solution to the problem posed. Similarly, calling students' attention to headings and subheadings used in content area texts provides them a strategy for previewing text content and creating potential questions to answer when reading.

Familiarity with English text structures results from extensive experience reading a variety of texts in English, especially when explicit discussion of text structure is provided to help students perceive these patterns and use them to understand text. All English learners can benefit from text structure instruction, especially those who are literate in the primary language, given that text structure conventions may vary across languages and cultures. By showing students the elements, organization, and sequencing that make up a "good essay," a "good story," or a "good argument" in English, teachers can immediately boost the quality of their students' reading and writing.

Assisting English learners with expository text structures is especially critical because content area texts become longer, more complex, and more conceptually dense from the third grade and up through high school and college. Text structure knowledge can help students grapple with these challenging texts, promoting reading comprehension and learning in science, social studies, and other content areas.

In summary, to the extent that the reader's background knowledge is reflected in a text, the text is easier to understand. Furthermore, background knowledge and language knowledge *interact* during second-language reading, so that comprehension limitations can be overcome to some extent when the text topic is familiar. Knowledge of text structure conventions also enables readers to predict and confirm the meaning in a passage, enhancing comprehension. By tailoring instruction to students' English proficiency and building background knowledge for particular text content and structure, teachers significantly increase their students' chances for success in reading English.

Success in reading English is a valued outcome in itself, but it has the additional benefit of providing a useful source of linguistic input for English language development. Wide reading not only increases reading ability but also promotes English language development (Elley & Mangubhai, 1983). Furthermore, wide reading increases general background knowledge, which in turn facilitates comprehension when reading texts of all kinds, including content area texts.

PHONEMIC AWARENESS AND PHONICS

Thus far we have highlighted language knowledge and background knowledge as important aspects of the reading process. These factors can only be brought into play, however, if the reader has adequate knowledge of the writing system to access the language encoded in the text, a fact that holds equally true for both first and second language readers. In English and other languages that use alphabetic writing systems, speech sounds are represented by letters and letter sequences, reflecting the nature of the alphabetic principle. In order for beginning readers to make use of the alphabetic principle, they need to be able to (a) hear individual speech sounds in words, i.e., phonemic awareness; and (b) learn the symbols that represent those sounds, i.e., phonics or graphophonics. Without substantial knowledge of these sound/symbol correspondences, readers are deprived of a useful tool for recognizing unfamiliar words.

Phonics is not the only tool readers may use to unlock an unfamiliar word. Good readers also use context to help them predict a word that fits grammatically and makes sense in the context of the sentence and passage. Here again, we see language knowledge, background knowledge, and experience with written texts fueling word recognition, as a passage is read and comprehended. The essential question is not whether students should be taught sound/symbol correspondences but rather how these should be taught.

For English learners, there is very little research either on phonemic awareness (the ability to hear, isolate, and manipulate sounds in spoken words) or phonics instruction (instruction on sound/letter correspondences). However, because both phonemic awareness and phonics are language-based processes, and because English learners vary in their English language proficiency, English language proficiency must be taken into consideration in deciding how and when to emphasize phonemic awareness and phonics instruction, a topic we return to in our instructional recommendations at the end of this article.

EXPERIENCE IN THE PRIMARY LANGUAGE

Another difference English learners bring to their reading is the quantity and kind of literacy knowledge and experience they have in their primary language, if any, a variable that ties in closely with the age of the student, prior educational experiences in the primary language, and the socioeconomic status and educational level of the parents. When a student begins English reading instruction solidly literate in the primary language, even in a language that uses a very different writing system from English such as Russian or Chinese, that student possesses funds of knowledge that go well beyond simply being able to read (Moll, 1994).

For example, students who are literate in their home language have some knowledge of the *functions* of print. While the purposes of literacy in the primary language may differ from those they are learning for English, students literate in their primary language have nonetheless experienced the value, utility, and perhaps pleasures of print. In terms of reading per se, they have exercised the process of making sense from print, and, depending on their reading abilities, they are more or less automatic at decoding and comprehending text in their primary language.

In addition, students literate in the primary language are typically accustomed to the discipline and demands of school, whether educated in the United States or elsewhere. Education in the primary language thus facilitates academic adjustment while providing a solid experiential base for literacy development in English. The power of primary language literacy as a foundation for second language literacy provides the cornerstone for many bilingual education programs in the United States and worldwide.

Types of writing systems

When we make the claim that primary language literacy provides a good foundation for English literacy, we are suggesting that various aspects of reading and writing transfer across languages, including attitudes and expectations about print as well as the general process of decoding, interpreting the language, constructing meaning from text, and monitoring comprehension (Carrell, 1991; Pritchard, 1990; Tragar & Wong, 1984). At a more specific level, transfer of literacy ability from one language to another depends on the similarities and differences between their writing systems, including the unit of speech symbolized by each character.

For example, alphabetic writing systems, such as the three different ones used for English, Greek, and Russian, represent speech sounds or phonemes with letters or letter sequences. In contrast, in logographic writing systems, such as Chinese, each written character represents a meaning unit or morpheme; while in syllabic writing systems, such as kana in Japanese and Sequoyah's Cherokee syllabary, each written symbol represents a syllable.

In addition to differences in the unit of speech represented, directionality and spacing conventions differ across writing systems. For example, Hebrew reads from right to left whereas English and other European languages read from left to right. Chinese traditionally reads right to left. We suggest that specific differences among writing systems must be explicitly addressed when teaching English reading to students who are literate in their primary language. In order to do so, teachers need to learn about the writing systems their students use and the extent to which they are literate in them.

Writing systems similar to English

While providing substantial funds of knowledge upon which to base English literacy, the ability to read (and write) in another language thus poses the challenge of learning the similarities and differences between the ways English and the primary language are portrayed in print. To the extent that the writing systems are similar, positive transfer can occur in decoding.

Take Spanish and English, for example. In our experience (Peregoy, 1989; Peregoy & Boyle, 1991), certain features transfer readily such as the idea that speech sounds are represented by letters and letter sequences and the notion that print is read left-to-right and top-to-bottom. Specific letter-sound correspondences may transfer as well. For example, a native Spanish speaker who is proficient in reading Spanish will encounter a similar alphabet in English, with consonant letters representing similar sounds in the two languages. For example, the letters *b, c, d, f, l, m, n, p, q, s,* and *t* represent sounds that are similar enough in both English and Spanish that they may transfer readily to English reading for many students. Consequently, minimal phonics instruction is needed by many students for these consonants.

In contrast, the vowel letters look the same in Spanish and English but represent sounds very differently. Therefore English vowel sounds and their numerous "unruly" spellings present a challenge to Spanish literate students learning to read English because the one-to-one correspondence between vowel letters and vowel sounds in Spanish does not hold true in English. Moreover, English has a plethora of vowel spellings that often include "silent letters." Consider the "long a" sound as spelled in the following words: *lake, weight, mail.* These spellings present a challenge to native and non-native English speakers alike. For Spanish literate students, explicit instruction on English vowel spelling patterns is often useful, preferably in the context of reading simple texts. At the same time, attention to text comprehension is essential, given that some students learn to decode English so well that they *appear* to be comprehending when in fact they are merely "word calling," i.e., pronouncing words without understanding the meaning.

Writing systems different from English

Clearly, some students may begin English reading instruction accustomed to a writing system that bears little or no resemblance to the one they must learn for English. For example, students who are literate in a logographic system such as Chinese are faced with learning the English convention of representing speech sounds instead of meaning units, and the practice of reading from left to right instead of right to left. These differences may require considerable concentration in the early stages of English reading acquisition as students develop an understanding of the alphabetic principle and begin to learn specific sound/symbol correspondences.

Early on, memorization of whole words and their meanings may prove useful for Chinese literate students, transferring a strategy they may have used to learn Chinese characters. Eventually, though, they need to grasp the alphabetic principle, attend to individual sounds in spoken English words (phonemic awareness), and associate those sounds with certain letters and letter sequences (phonics). As students learn to decode English, they also need to develop the English language knowledge that will allow them to access the meaning of the text, or their decoding will not lead to text comprehension.

In contrast to students with logographic literacy, some English learners may be literate in alphabetic writing systems that nonetheless use letters and print conventions that are very different from English, such as Arabic, Hebrew, and Thai. These students are apt to be well-versed in the alphabetic principle, which they acquired in the process of learning to read in the primary language, and that understanding should transfer easily to English reading. They are also more or less aware of various functions of print and have had considerable experience constructing meaning from text, another source of positive transfer. What will be new for these students are the specific letters and letter/sound correspondences used in English. To learn to read in English, they need to learn the specific conventions of how English is represented in print while at the same time developing English language proficiency to facilitate reading comprehension.

Students with minimal literacy experience

It is important to note that some English learners may come to school at any age with minimal literacy experience or abilities in any language. Before selecting instructional interventions for nonliterate students, teachers need to find out as much as possible about the student's non-literacy. For example, is it due to minimal or interrupted schooling resulting from family mobility or circumstances of immigration? Is it because the family stems from a background without a literate tradition? Or does the child have some sort of visual, auditory, or linguistic processing difficulty that hinders the reading process? Knowing the student's prior experiences helps teachers know where to start.

By and large, students without prior literacy experiences benefit from exposure to the many practical purposes that written language can serve in daily life (Hamayan,

1994). Daily modeling of reading and writing is needed in which meaning and purpose are palpably clear, such as read alouds using texts with reliable picture cues to convey meaning, making and using lists of classroom duties, and reading students' names from a word wall to take roll.

In a language and literacy rich environment, learners will begin to develop English language proficiency while simultaneously gaining a rudimentary sense of how print works, both in form and function. These experiences will also offer opportunities for students to grasp the essence of the alphabetic principle upon which the English writing system is based. From there, students can benefit from word identification strategy instruction, using stories, poems, and songs they already know well due to repeated exposures in which textual meaning and purpose are made clear.

A NOTE OF CAUTION

We have described our view of the reading process of English learners as similar to that of native English speakers, with important differences stemming in particular from variations in English language proficiency, background knowledge, and prior literacy experiences. We based our discussion on current theory and research in reading, including second language reading. Throughout our discussion, we have suggested ways to facilitate English learners' reading success by addressing the particular resources and special needs they bring to the task.

We need to point out here certain critical issues regarding the research base in second language reading. First, most of the research on second language reading has been conducted with older learners in secondary school or college. This is particularly the case for research on background knowledge and language proficiency effects on reading comprehension. Relatively little research addresses elementary school-aged English learners, and when it does, it focuses on students who are already able to read connected text (e.g., Peregoy, 1989; Peregoy & Boyle, 1991).

Beginning English reading acquisition and instruction for English learners, especially among students who are not literate in the primary language, are virtually untouched topics in the research literature, creating a dilemma for those who seek a strong research base to validate instructional practices. Teaching practices for native English speakers cannot simply be applied whole cloth to English learners without modifications that consider, at the very least, students' English language proficiency and primary language literacy. Topics such as phonemic awareness, phonics, decoding, and effective approaches to beginning reading instruction are yet to be adequately researched for English learners.

In terms of phonemic awareness, in particular, research must address several important questions: (a) At what point in non-native English language development does phonemic awareness in English emerge? (b) How difficult is it for beginning English language learners to hear and manipulate speech sounds in English, and do these abilities vary based on the age of the learner? based on the student's primary language (e.g., Spanish vs. Turkish vs. Cantonese vs. Crow)? (c) Does primary language literacy in an alphabetic writing system facilitate phonemic awareness in English? What about primary language literacy in a logographic or syllabic writing system? If English learners do not demonstrate phonemic awareness, what methods of reading instruction will best promote their English literacy development? Virtually no research addresses these issues.

INSTRUCTIONAL IMPLICATIONS

Below we draw a number of instructional implications from our discussion of English learner reading. For our purposes here, we provide only a brief overview of instructional strategies. For more in-depth descriptions, see Boyle and Peregoy (1998), Peregoy and Boyle (1997, in press), and Opitz (1998). In addition, see Meyer (this issue).

Learning about students

Learning as much as possible about individual English learners is essential to planning effective literacy instruction, especially in the broad areas we have discussed in this article: English language proficiency, prior knowledge and life experiences, and literacy in the primary language. This kind of information makes it possible to validate students for what they *do know* and build from there.

Building learning activities upon familiar concepts, for example, not only facilitates literacy and content learning but also helps students feel more comfortable and confident at school. In addition to school records, if they exist, good initial sources of information include the students themselves, their families, and community organizations. It may also be helpful to talk with other teachers who have students from the same family. In addition, school personnel such as community liaisons and paraprofessionals may prove helpful in providing information about students.

English language proficiency

By definition, English learners are still learning English. Classroom instruction often consists of oral language interactions between teachers and students. When using English as the language of instruction, teachers need to use sheltering strategies to assure that students will be able to understand and participate successfully in learning activities. Pairing nonverbal cues (e.g., pictures, demonstrations, and gestures) with verbal instruction helps make lessons comprehensible for students. Paraphrasing and defining important vocabulary in context also aid comprehension. As lessons are made more comprehensible for students, instruction simultaneously promotes language acquisition and content learning. For second language learners, every lesson is a potential language learning opportunity, and must be structured as such (Peregoy & Boyle, 1999).

Sensitivity to the varied language development levels of English learners will determine how much sheltering is needed, how much time it will take for students to process instructional content, and by what means (e.g., oral, written, pictorial, dramatization) they will display their learning. The more experience teachers have working with English learners, the more knowledgeable they become in determining those aspects of English their students are apt to find difficult, including vocabulary; word order; verb forms to express past, present, and future; word formation elements such as prefixes, suffixes, and roots; and function words such as articles, prepositions, and conjunctions.

Beyond these linguistic elements, day-to-day observation allows teachers to gauge how well students use English to accomplish routine learning tasks and social interactions in ways that are appropriate to the classroom context. This knowledge helps teachers plan specific modifications in their own instructional language and guides them as they plan ways to prepare students for reading and understanding specific texts (see Meyer, this issue).

English learners who are beginning English reading instruction may be literate in the primary language due to education in another country or as a result of bilingual instruction in the United States. The benefits of primary language literacy are many, both as a foundation for English literacy and as a vehicle for developing full bilingualism and biliteracy. Although primary language reading instruction is beyond the scope of this article, suffice it to say that primary language development, including literacy, is a valuable educational goal for English learners themselves and for U.S. society as a whole (see Fillmore, this issue). Indeed without instruction in the primary language, oral and written skills are apt to deteriorate or become lost completely. Even so, many English learners find themselves learning oral and written English simultaneously, without the benefit of primary language instruction. The strategies for teaching English reading described below are applicable to English learners with or without primary language literacy abilities. The discussion assumes that English is the language of instruction.

Beginning readers

When English learners are beginning to read in English, attention to meaning is paramount at every step of instruction. In addition to using sheltering strategies to help students understand the *lesson*, teachers need to help students understand the meaning and purpose of the *text*. Texts used for beginning reading instruction should be short, simple pieces such as poems, pattern books, songs, simple directions, or recipes. Student understanding of the meaning and purpose may be developed by reading the text aloud, pointing out and defining or dramatizing important content words, and using other sheltering strategies to help students understand the text. Repetition, perhaps with hand movements like those used in finger plays, is useful for this purpose and can be fun and enjoyable.

This phase of the lesson serves English language development and provides exposure to the forms and functions of print, creating a firm foundation for sight word recognition and subsequent instruction on specific sound/symbol correspondences and other word identification strategies. By using whole texts for which meaning has been developed, students learn the details of print in the context of reading for a purpose.

The above procedures apply for students of different ages. However, for older students care must be taken to assure that text content is age-appropriate. One way to do so is to base early reading instruction on student generated text, such as pattern poems, beginning "I like___." Similarly, texts may be generated in class based on a particular learning experience, such as planting a garden, baking a casserole, or driving a car. The students provide the ideas, perhaps in one or two words, and the teacher writes the ideas down in conventional English sentences. These texts provide initial, meaningful encounters with print on which to base reading instruction.

To help teachers choose materials, many book lists are available on picture books with content appropriate for older students (e.g., Benedict, 1992) and on high interest, easy reading (e.g., Riechel, 1998; Rosow, 1996). (Searching the Internet using keywords, *high interest low vocabulary*, yields a number of good resources including Libraries Unlimited at http://www.lu.com/lu/.) In addition to providing appropriate materials, it is important to learn about the student's primary language and whether the student is literate in it. If so, the teacher can validate the student for this accomplishment and anticipate areas of positive and/or negative transfer to reading in English.

Intermediate readers

English language learners who can read connected text develop as readers by reading longer, more complex texts in a variety of genres. Teachers need to prepare students for any given text by focusing on specific aspects of its genre, vocabulary, grammar, content, and text structure that may be new to them. The strategies described below may be selected before, during, and after reading to facilitate reading comprehension in any genre, including stories, essays, or content area textbook selections.

Before reading.   Students need to know their purpose for reading, and what they will be asked to do with the information after reading. Teachers therefore need to assess students' background knowledge pertinent to the text to be read and build background before students begin to read. It is often helpful to introduce important concepts/vocabulary through visuals, demonstrations, and graphic or pictorial organizers prior to reading. While doing so, teachers can informally assess the extent of their students' knowledge of the topic. Brainstorming and clustering about a topic in small groups is another way to assess and build background information for students who are fairly fluent in English, provided sheltering strategies are used. Teachers may prepare students for unfamiliar text structures by presenting graphics that sketch the structure illustrated with two or three examples of actual text that follow the structure. Recipes and business letters are two easy text structures to display graphically, for example, while story maps offer a useful graphic representation of narrative structure.

Staying with a text.   To help students "get into" and stick with the text, the teacher may read a page or two aloud to the students, asking prediction questions to help them anticipate the direction of the piece. If the piece is especially difficult, the teacher may guide students through it by reading and discussing one paragraph at a time. Other strategies include pairing students to read to each other, with the teacher on hand to assist through rough spots. Additional strategies to help keep students on track during reading include student response logs and story maps or other graphic depictions of text meaning.

After reading.   Strategies used after reading serve to help students process the story or passage more deeply and to organize and remember the information. Some strategies include: mapping, dramatization, creating a mural, and writing a script for a play or a reader's theater. Any of these strategies may be used for in-depth literature study, content area reading, and theme-related projects.

CONCLUSION

In this article, we have discussed the special characteristics English learners bring to the task of reading and learning to read in their new language. We have pointed out the tremendous diversity among second language readers, illustrating the difficulties inherent in making simple generalizations concerning their reading acquisition and instruction. Using theory and research, we have presented a view of reading comprehension to illustrate similarities and differences in reading processes of English learners and native English speakers.

Throughout our discussion we have emphasized the need to consider English language proficiency, prior knowledge and experiences, and primary language literacy as important factors in English learner reading, variables that must be considered by teachers and researchers alike as they go about their work. Not only do we need to learn more about reading development among English learners of varying ages and backgrounds, we also need to learn more about the most effective instruction for particular groups of English learners. Specific programs and materials need to be developed and evaluated in terms of how well they meet the literacy development needs of particular groups of students. There is much to be done as teachers and researchers work together to expand the knowledge base for creating the best instruction for English learners and their literacy development.

REFERENCES

Anderson, R. C. (1994). Role of reader's schemata in comprehension, learning and memory. In R. B. Ruddell, M. R. Ruddell & H. Singer (Eds.), *Theoretical models and processes of reading* (4th ed.; pp. 469–482). Newark, DE: International Reading Association.

Benedict, S. (1992). *Beyond words: Picture books for older readers and writers.* Portsmouth, NH: Heinemann.

Boyle, O., & Peregoy, S. (1998). Literacy scaffolds: Strategies for first- and second-language readers and writers. In M. Opitz (Ed.), *Literacy instruction for culturally and linguistically diverse students* (pp. 150–157). Newark, DE: International Reading Association.

Brown, A., Campione, J. C., & Day, D. J. (1980). *Learning to learn: On training students to learn from texts* (Technical Report No. 189). Urbana: University of Illinois, Center for the Study of Reading.

Canale, M., & Swain, M. (1980). Theoretical bases of communicative approaches to second language teaching and testing. *Applied Linguistics, 1*(1), 1–47.

Carrell, P. L. (1987). Content and formal schemata in ESL reading. *TESOL Quarterly, 21*, 461–481.

Carrell, P. L. (1991). Second language reading: Reading ability or language proficiency? *Applied Linguistics, 12*, 159–179.

Carrell, P. L. (1992). Awareness of text structure: Effects on recall. *Language Learning, 42*, 1–20.

Elley, W., & Mangubhai, F. (1983). The impact of reading on second language readers. *Reading Research Quarterly, 19*, 53–67.

Fitzgerald, J. (1995). English-as-a-second-language learners' cognitive reading processes: A review of research in the United States. *Review of Educational Research, 65*, 145–190.

Goodman, K., & Goodman, Y. (1978). *Reading of American students whose language is a stable rural dialect of English or a language other than English* (Final Report No. c-003-0087). Washington, DC: National Institute of Education.

Hamayan, E. (1994). Language development of low literacy children. In F. Genesee (Ed.), *Educating second language children: The whole child, the whole curriculum, the whole community* (pp. 278–300). Cambridge, UK: Cambridge University Press.

Kintsch, W., & Van Dijk, T. A. (1978). Toward a model of text comprehension and production. *Psychological Review, 85*, 363–394.

Moll, L. C. (1994). Literacy research in community and classrooms: A sociocultural approach. In R. B. Ruddell, M. R. Ruddell, & H. Singer (Eds.), *Theoretical models and processes of reading* (4th ed.; pp. 179–207). Newark, DE: International Reading Association.

Opitz, M. (1998). *Literacy instruction for culturally and linguistically diverse students.* Newark, DE: International Reading Association.

Peregoy, S. (1989, Spring). Relationships between second language oral proficiency and reading comprehension of bilingual students. *Journal of the National Association for Bilingual Education, 13*, 217–234.

Peregoy, S., & Boyle, O. (1991). Second language oral proficiency characteristics of low, intermediate and high second language readers. *Hispanic Journal of Behavioral Sciences, 13*(1), 35–47.

Peregoy, S., & Boyle, O. (1997). *Reading, writing, and learning in ESL: A resource book for K-12 teachers* (2nd ed.). New York: Longman.

Peregoy, S., & Boyle, O. (1999, Spring & Summer). Multiple embedded scaffolds: Support for English speakers in a two-way Spanish immersion kindergarten. *Bilingual Research Journal, 23*(2 & 3), 110–126.

Peregoy, S. & Boyle, O. (in press). *Reading, writing and learning in ESL: A resource book for K-12 teachers* (3rd ed.). New York: Longman.

Pritchard, R. (1990, December). *Reading in Spanish and English: A comparative study of processing strategies.* Paper presented at the annual meeting of the National Reading Conference, Miami, FL.

Riechel, R. (1998). *Children's non-fiction for adult information needs: An annotated bibliography.* North Haven, CT: Linnet Professional Publications.

Rosow, L. (1996). *Light 'n lively reads for ESL, adult and teen readers: A thematic bibliography.* Englewood, CO: Libraries Unlimited.

Rumelhart, D. E. (1994). Toward an interactive model of reading. In R. B. Ruddell, M. R. Ruddell, & H. Singer (Eds.), *Theoretical models and processes of reading* (4th ed.; pp. 864–894). Newark, DE: International Reading Association.

Tragar, B., & Wong, B. K. (1984). The relationship between native and second language reading comprehension and second language oral ability. In C. Rivera (Ed.), *Placement procedures in bilingual education: Education and policy issues* (pp. 152–164). Clevedon, UK: Multilingual Matters.

INTEGRATING SOURCES

1. In what ways might Miller's suggestions for developing empathy for cultural diversity be incorporated into literacy teaching as well as suggestions by Peregoy and Boyle?

2. MacGillivray & Rueda suggest a number of specific ways in which the classroom literacy curriculum can be made more relevant to the students. How do these ideas compare or contrast with those of the writers in this discussion of diversity on literacy education?

CLASSROOM IMPLICATIONS

1. Reexamine your personal views of multicultural education, particularly as it relates to your classroom teaching of the literacy curriculum.

2. Interview the ESL teacher(s) in your district, noting how they approach the many issues in multicultural education.

3. To what extent are you helping prepare your students for life in the new millennium, especially in relation to diversity?

ANNOTATED BIBLIOGRAPHY

Dressman, M., et al. (2001). Linguistic diversity. *New Advocate, 14,* 171–178.

Reviews fourteen trade books for young readers, selected for the diversity of the cultures and languages they include.

Gil-Garcia, A., & Canizales, R. (2001). Commanding strategies by Hispanic students as they think about their own thinking process. (ERIC Reproduction Service No. ED457135).

Discusses the various metacognitive strategies found to be useful by bilingual students in various language activities, including both reading and writing.

Meloi, P. L. (2001). Family stories night: Celebrating culture and community. *Reading Teacher, 54,* 746–747.

Describes a language activity in which a family shares a story in their native tongue and the children provide an English translation.

Reyes, M., & Halcon, J. J. (Eds.). (2001). *The best for our children: Critical perspectives.* Williston, VT: Teachers College Press.

A collection of papers written by some of the leading authorities on the issue of effective literacy instruction for Latino students.

Rosowsky, A. (2001). Decoding as cultural practice and its effects on the reading process of bilingual pupils. *Language and Education, 15,* 56–70.

Discusses the importance of an emphasis on decoding as a significant aspect of the development of reading comprehension in bilingual students.

Senn, R. (2001). Reading in a second language: Factors associated with progress in young children. *Educational Psychology, 21,* 189–203.

Reports on the results of a study dealing with various factors associated with Indian children learning to read English.

Slavin, R. E., & Calderon, M. (Eds.). (2001). *Effective programs for Latino students.* Mahwah, NJ: Lawrence Erlbaum.

This collection of papers discusses educational issues related to Hispanic American students with special emphasis on literacy concerns.

Shore, Kenneth. (2001). Success for ESL students. *Instructor, 110,* 30, 32.

Reviews twelve educational teaching ideas related to effective language instruction for second-language learners.

Smith, K., & Hudelson, S. (2001). The NCTE Reading Initiative: Politics, pedagogy, and possibilities. *Language Arts, 79,* 29–37.

Describes how a bilingual school incorporates the principles of professional development as suggested by the NCTE Reading Initiative.

YOU BECOME INVOLVED

1. Work with your fellow teachers, both in your building as well as in your district, on an assessment of current issues related to multicultural education. What are some of the successes and problems that these faculty identify in this important area of instruction, especially as they relate to literacy education?

2. Develop a plan, as well as an active program of instructional strategies, to address these many issues related to multicultural education.

CHAPTER FIVE

COMPREHENSION

*If a man has read a great number of books, and does
not think things through, he is only a book case.*
—Shu Shuehmou (16th century)

*Unless . . . books are studied and understood, the whole thing is useless. If a man
read only one book all his life, and it made him think, it would be worth more
than having a smattering of a thousand works.*
—Henry Golden (1959)

*. . . there are multiple ways to improve comprehension, with all of them
potentially affected by instruction. Although a good case can be made for teaching
comprehension strategies to elementary students, it is most defensible to do so in
the context of a reading program that includes teaching to promote word
recognition skills, vocabulary knowledge, and extensive reading of books filled
with the world knowledge that young readers need to acquire.*
—Michael Pressley (2002)

Comprehension—the "bottom line" of reading—is arguably the most important dimension of reading instruction. It is also among the most complex, and psychological models of comprehension processes have shed relatively little light on how readers make sense of text. It is little wonder that numerous issues continue to surround this topic. It is important that literacy educators be cognizant of these issues and develop personal stances toward them that will inform their instructional decision making. In this overview section, we will attempt to identify the principal issues, which we state in the form of questions.

Is comprehension the construction or reconstruction of meaning? Constructivist notions maintain that each reader interprets the content of print in a unique way based on prior knowledge, values, purposes for reading, and other factors. This stance has clear implications for assessment: If there is no single meaning for a text, then asking questions that have only one correct answer makes little sense. On the other hand, a reconstructionist view holds that, even though differences exist among readers, a central goal of most reading (especially of nonfiction) is to determine the intended meaning of the author—that is, to mentally *reconstruct* the author's intended message. Although there may be innumerable ways of interpreting a memo from the principal, for example, it is vital to figure out the one meaning that was actually intended.

What is the difference between improving comprehension of a particular selection and improving comprehension ability? This is a distinction worth noting, for it often separates teachers into two camps. A high school biology teacher, for instance, may be concerned about students' comprehension of the textbook but indifferent to their overall growth as readers. A first-grade teacher may have a different perspective because the comprehension of most selections is seen as a means to an end. Of course, some teachers wear both hats, possibly at different times during the school day. Fortunately, many instructional techniques do double duty if they are well applied: They improve comprehension of specific selections and they foster general comprehension ability over time.

Can comprehension be measured? Because it seems so amorphous and vague, comprehension may appear difficult to measure. As Frank Smith once observed, "Comprehension cannot be measured at all, despite constant educational efforts to do so, because it is not a quantity of anything" (1988, p. 53). This view may seem harsh because the traditions of testing and measurement have long involved seeking quantitative indicators of psychological constructs like reading comprehension. Asking questions, for example, may not be a perfect approach, but children's accuracy at answering them yields one widely accepted gauge of their understanding. In recent years, alternative approaches, such as retelling, have been proposed to offset the reliance on questions. Teachers will continue to require evidence of student growth in their ability to comprehend, and this usually means measurement of some kind.

Can comprehension be broken down? Does it make sense to "subdivide" the vague, global concept of comprehension into specific abilities? Doing so certainly makes instructional planning simpler and helps teachers "get a handle" on this elusive area. It may also have led to a superabundance of worksheets devoted to such skills as "inferring the main idea," "identifying explicit sequences of events," and "predicting outcomes." Is this approach to be embraced or avoided? Perhaps the answer depends on the proposed alternative.

Should comprehension be taught as skills or strategies? When comprehension is partitioned into discrete skills, the answer to this question is obvious. A criticism of teaching comprehension skill by skill, however, is that students may find it difficult to coordinate their use of skills taught in such a piecemeal manner. Imagine teaching an individual to use a screwdriver, a hammer, pliers, a table saw, and so forth and then, without further instruction, expecting that same individual to use these tools to make a chair. Even though the person may be proficient in the use of each tool, some strategy is needed to know when to use each one and why. Similarly, comprehension strategies entail the use of one or more skills to achieve a particular purpose. From a teacher's standpoint, it is important that students be able to apply skills purposefully so that they can achieve independence as readers. This does not preclude the need to teach skills, of course, but it does broaden the goal of comprehension instruction.

AS YOU READ

The articles that follow scarcely scratch the surface of the material available on teaching children to comprehend. Our goal is to provide a quick start with respect to current, research-based ideas by presenting principles prepared by the Center for the Improvement of Early Reading Instruction (CIERA). The more detailed article by Michael Pressley then examines the course of strategy instruction in the context of long-term trends. The following questions should guide your thinking:

1. How do the CIERA principles align with your own preexisting notions of effective comprehension instruction? Are there points at which you would take issue with the CIERA researchers?
2. Pressley critiques some prevalent contemporary views and arrives at a number of important points about effective instruction. What are they?

REFERENCE

Smith, F. (1988). *Understanding reading* (4th ed.). Mahwah, NJ: Erlbaum.

Improving the Reading Comprehension of America's Children:

10 Research-Based Principles

PREPARED BY THE CENTER FOR THE IMPROVEMENT OF EARLY READING INSTRUCTION (CIERA)

The purpose of reading is comprehension. How do we teach children to comprehend more difficult and varied texts? Until recently, we had few answers. But research from recent decades has provided a general outline of how to effectively teach reading comprehension.

1. *Effective comprehension requires purposeful and explicit teaching.*

Effective teachers of reading are clear about their purposes. They know what they are trying to help a child achieve and how to accomplish their goal. They provide scaffolded instruction in research-tested strategies (predicting, thinking aloud, attending to text structure, constructing visual representations, generating questions, and summarizing). Scaffolded instruction includes explicit explanation and modeling of a strategy, discussion of why and when it is useful, and coaching in how to apply it to novel texts.

2. *Effective reading instruction requires classroom interactions that support the understanding of specific texts.*

Effective teachers have a repertoire of techniques for enhancing children's comprehension of specific texts, including discussion, writing in response to reading, and multiple encounters with complex texts. They are clear about the purposes of teacher- and student-led discussions of texts, and include a balance of lower and higher-level questions focusing on efferent and aesthetic response. Well-designed writing assignments deepen children's learning from text.

Reische, Jim, et al. Reprinted by permission of CIERA.

3. *Effective reading comprehension instruction starts before children read conventionally.*

Children in preschool and kindergarten develop their comprehension skills through experiences that promote oral and written language skills, such as discussions, play activities, retellings, and emergent readings. Early childhood environments can be made literacy-rich through thoughtful inclusion of appropriate materials and practices. Reading and rereading a wide variety of texts contributes to both phonemic awareness and comprehension.

4. *Effective reading comprehension teaches children the skills and strategies used by expert readers.*

Expert readers are active readers who use text and their own knowledge to build a model of meaning, and then constantly revise that model as new information becomes available. They consider the author's intentions and style when judging a text's validity, and determine the purposes that the text can serve in their lives—how it can further their knowledge, deepen their enjoyment, and expand their ways of examining and communicating with the world. They also vary their reading strategy according to their purpose and the characteristics of the genre, deciding whether to read carefully or impressionistically.

5. *Effective reading comprehension instruction requires careful analysis of text to determine its appropriateness for particular students and strategies.*

Teachers analyze each text to determine its potential challenges and match it with their goals. They consider conceptual and decoding demands and apply strategies to meet those challenges. Interactions with texts requiring minimal teacher support help hold children accountable as independent readers. Scaffolded experiences ensure that all children are exposed to high-level text and interactions.

6. *Effective reading comprehension instruction builds on and results in knowledge, vocabulary, and advanced language development.*

Children are better able to comprehend texts when they are taught to make connections between what they know and what they are reading. Good comprehension instruction helps them make these connections more effectively. Vocabulary knowledge is an important part of reading comprehension, and good vocabulary instruction involves children actively in learning word meanings, as well as relating words to contexts and other known words. Teaching about words (including morphology) improves children's comprehension.

7. *Effective reading comprehension instruction pervades all genres and school subjects.*

Children need to read in a wide variety of genres—not only narrative, but informational, procedural, biographical, persuasive, and poetic. They will only learn to do so through experience and instruction. Each school subject requires the ability to read in specific genres; therefore, comprehension should be taught in all subjects.

8. *Effective reading comprehension instruction actively engages children in text and motivates them to use strategies and skills.*

Effective teachers create an environment in which children are actively involved in the reading process. In such an environment children read more, which in turn improves their comprehension and knowledge. Children need to be motivated to learn and apply skills and strategies during reading.

9. *Good comprehension instruction requires assessments that inform instruction and monitor student progress.*

The use of multiple assessments provides specific and timely feedback to inform instruction and monitor student progress toward research-based benchmarks. Good assessment identifies students' comprehension levels as they develop from preschool to advanced grade levels, and helps the teacher to evaluate each child's need for support in areas such as language development, strategy, and the application of knowledge. Effective assessment also enables teachers to reliably interpret data and communicate results to students, parents, and colleagues.

10. *Effective reading comprehension instruction requires continuous teacher learning about the processes and techniques detailed in the previous nine principles, and ways to use such knowledge to develop the comprehension skills and strategies of all students.*

Working closely with their peers in school-based or interest-based learning communities, effective teachers learn to use assessment data, reflections on their own practice, and moment-by-moment feedback from children to vary the support they provide to students with different levels of expertise and confidence.

REFERENCES

1. Purposeful and Explicit Teaching

Dole, J. A., Duffy, G. G., Roehler, L. R., and Pearson, P. D. (1991). Moving from the old to the new: Research on reading comprehension instruction. *Review of Educational Research, 61,* 239–264.*
Hogan, K., & Pressley, M. (1997). *Scaffolding student learning: Instructional approaches and issues.* Cambridge, MA: Brookline Books.
National Reading Panel. (2000). *Report of the National Reading Panel.* Washington, DC: Government Printing Office.
Taylor, B., Pearson, P. D., Clark, K., & Walpole, S. (1999). *Schools that beat the odds* (CIERA Report 2-008). Ann Arbor: CIERA.*

2. Interactions that Support Understandings of Specific Texts

Beck, I. L., McKeown, M. G., & Wonhy, M. J. (1996). Questioning the author: A yearlong classroom implementation to engage students with text. *Elementary School Journal, 96,* 385–414.
Duke, N. K., & Pearson, P. D. (2002). Effective practices for developing reading comprehension. In A. E. Farstrup & S. J. Samuels (Eds.), *What research has to say about reading instruction* (3rd ed.). Newark, DE: International Reading Association.*

Tierney, R. J., Soter, A., O'Flahaven, J. F., & McGinley, W. (1989). The effects of reading and writing upon thinking critically. *Reading Research Quarterly, 24,* 134–169.

3. Before Children Read Conventionally

Dickinson, D. K., & Tabors, P. O. (2001). *Beginning literacy with language: Young children learning at home & school.* Baltimore: Paul H. Brookes Publishing.

Van Kleeck, A., Stahl, S. A., & Bauer, E. B. (in press). *On reading storybooks to children: Parents and teachers.* Mahwah, NJ: Lawrence Erlbaum Associates.*

Neuman, S. B. (1999). Books make a difference: A study of access to literacy. *Reading Research Quarterly, 34,* 286–311.

Snow, C. E., Burns, M. S., & Griffin, P. (1998). *Preventing reading difficulties in young children.* Washington, DC: National Academy Press.

Yaden, D. B., Jr., Rowe, D. W., & MacGillivray, L. (1999). *Emergent literacy: A polyphony of perspectives* (CIERA Report 1-005). Ann Arbor: CIERA.*

4. Skills and Strategies Used by Expert Readers

Kucan, L., & Beck, I. L. (1997). Thinking aloud and reading comprehension research: Inquiry, instruction and social interaction. *Review of Educational Research, 67,* 271–299.

Kintsch, W. (1998). *Comprehension: A paradigm for cognition.* Cambridge: Cambridge University Press.

5. Careful Analysis of Text

Hiebert, E. H. (1999). *Text matters in learning to read.* (CIERA Report 1-001). Ann Arbor: CIERA.*

Hoffman, J. V., & Schallert, D. L. (in press). *The texts of early reading acquisition.* Mahwah, NJ: Lawrence Erlbaum Associates.*

6. Knowledge, Vocabulary, and Advanced Language Development

Anderson, R. C., & Pearson, P. D. (1984). A schema-theoretic view of basic processes in reading. In P. D. Pearson et al. (Eds.), *Handbook of reading research* (pp. 255–292). White Plains, NY: Longman.*

Stahl, S. A. (1998). *Vocabulary development.* Cambridge, MA: Brookline Press.*

7. All Genres and School Subjects

Duke, N. (2000). 3.6 minutes per day: The scarcity of informational texts in first grade. *Reading Research Quarterly, 35,* 202–224.*

Pearson, P. D., & Duke, N. K. (in press). *Comprehension instruction in the primary grades* (CIERA Archives). Ann Arbor: CIERA.*

8. Actively Engaging Children

Guthrie, J. T., et al. (1996). Growth of literacy engagement: Changes in motivations and strategies during concept-oriented reading instruction. *Reading Research Quarterly, 31,* 306–332.

9. Assessments That Inform Instruction

Pearson, P. D., & Stallman, A. C. (1993). *Approaches to the future of reading assessment: Resistance, complacency, reform* (Tech. Rep. No. 575). Champaign, IL: Center for the Study of Reading.*

10. Continuous Teacher Learning

LeFevre, D., & Richardson, V. (2001). *Staff development in early reading intervention programs: The facilitator* (CIERA Report 3-011). Ann Arbor: CIERA.*

Meisels, S. J., Bickel, D. D., Nicholson, J., Xue, Y., & Atkins-Burnett, S. (2001). Trusting teacher's judgments: A validity study of a curriculum-embedded performance assessment in Kindergarten–Grade 3. *American Educational Research Journal, 38,* 73–95.

Paris, S. G., & Winograd, P. (2001). *The role of self-regulated learning in contextual teaching: Principles and practices for teacher education* (CIERA Archives 01-04). Ann Arbor: CIERA.*

*At least one author is a CIERA researcher.

Contributors:
Deanna Birdyshaw
Nell K. Duke
Scott G. Paris
P. David Pearson
Katherine A. D. Stahl
Steven A. Stahl
Elizabeth Sulzby
Barbara M. Taylor
Elaine Weber

Comprehension Strategies Instruction:

A Turn-of-the-Century Status Report

MICHAEL PRESSLEY

I did my first research on comprehension strategies instruction in the school year 1974–1975 (Pressley, 1976), before many thought it was a good idea to teach comprehension strategies to children. During the quarter century since, a great deal of informative research has been done about comprehension and comprehension strategies instruction. Those of us producing this research should be justifiably proud of these accomplishments. Even so, for someone who had spent much of his career studying comprehension strategies instruction, 1998 was a very bad year—indeed, an absolutely depressing year. There were multiple indications in 1998 that educators were ignoring my work and the work of many of us who had focused on teaching comprehension skills to students.

First, one of the most painful articles I have ever written appeared in print. In the school year 1995–1996, Ruth Wharton-McDonald, Jennifer Mistretta-Hampston, Marissa Echevarria, and I spent a great deal of time observing the language arts instruction in 10 fourth- and fifth-grade classrooms in upstate New York (Pressley, Wharton-McDonald, Mistretta-Hampston, & Echevarria, 1998). The good news was that we observed lots of instructional practices that make very good sense based on research about effective literacy instruction. For example, we saw lots of literature-driven instruction, explicit teaching of vocabulary, one-to-one miniconferences between teachers and students, language arts–content integration, use of the plan–draft–revise model of writing, and cooperative learning. That said, we also saw very little comprehension instruction, very little of teaching students how to process text so that they might understand and remember it, although there was a great deal of testing of comprehension.

Reprinted by permission from *Comprehension Instruction: Research-Based Practices* edited by C. C. Block & M. Pressley (pp. 11–27). New York: Guilford Press, 2002. ©2002 by the Guilford Press.

In the past, when I have related this finding to audiences, those with a historical understanding of reading instruction recall a study by Durkin (1978–1979). When Durkin observed upper elementary-grade classes more than 2 decades ago, she also encountered little teaching of comprehension, although there was much testing of comprehension. What is surprising about the more recent Pressley et al. (1998) observation, however, was that there has been a great deal of research in the past several decades on comprehension instruction. Indeed, the evidence is now overwhelming that upper-grade elementary students can be taught to use comprehension strategies, with substantial improvements in student understanding of text following such instruction (Pearson & Dole, 1987; Pearson & Fielding, 1991; Pressley, Johnson, Symons, McGoldrick, & Kurita, 1989). As one of the individuals who did quite a bit of research on comprehension strategies instruction for elementary students, I found it exceptionally disheartening to confront the reality that little to no comprehension instruction was being given in grades 4 and 5.

The second painful event of 1998 for researchers who had dedicated much of their careers to comprehension instruction came in the form of the National Research Council report *Preventing Reading Difficulties in Young Children* (Snow, Burns, & Griffin, 1998), which was released in the early spring of the year. On the positive side, the message was loud and clear in the volume that word-level processes were critical to comprehension and to making meaning from text, that comprehension depended on fluency in word recognition. Moreover, there was a good deal of acknowledgment that comprehension depends on vocabulary development and development of background knowledge. Unfortunately, much less was said about comprehension strategies. Yes, it was mentioned a few times that elementary students should be taught comprehension strategies, such as prediction, summarization, and monitoring of comprehension, but some well-validated strategies (e.g., construction of mental images) received no mention, and almost nothing was said about how comprehension strategies should be taught. In fact, the only comprehension strategies instruction given explicit endorsement was a very dated approach, reciprocal teaching (Palincsar & Brown, 1984). Although this approach is historically important (Pressley & McCormick, 1995) in that it was the first empirically validated approach to the teaching of a package of comprehension strategies (i.e., prediction, question generation, summarization, and seeking clarification), there has been a great deal of development of more flexible and longer term approaches to development of comprehension strategies in students. In general, I left my reading of the National Research Council volume feeling that comprehension strategies instruction had been very much ignored by the authors of a report who were charged to cover comprehensively the literature on prevention of reading difficulties in elementary students.

The third blow in 1998 came with the publication of my book *Reading Instruction That Works: The Case for Balanced Teaching* (Pressley, 1998). I tried to make the case in the book that effective elementary literacy instruction balances skills instruction, especially word-level skills and higher order competencies (i.e., composition and comprehension). Despite that intention, the reaction to my book centered entirely on its relevance to the debate over phonics versus whole language, with many comments (both pro and con) regarding my stances on beginning word-level instruction. There was hardly a mention in the reactions about comprehension, let alone instruction of comprehension strategies.

The fourth assault came near the end of 1998. On December 1, just as I arrived at the convention hotel for the National Reading Conference, I was confronted by P. David Pearson and Elfrieda Hiebert. They wanted to share with me an important finding from their first year of study at the recently funded Center for Improvement of Early Reading Achievement (CIERA). Researchers at the center had just spent a good deal of time observing grade 4 classrooms, generating quite a bit of data from sites across the nation. What they had observed was what my colleagues and I had seen in upstate New York: very little comprehension strategies instruction. As Pearson put it, "It's as if that whole body of research on teaching of comprehension strategies did not exist; everything we did [referring to Pearson and Pressley] on comprehension instruction is being ignored!" Of course, Pearson was right. 1998 was a bad year for those of us who have worked hard to promote and improve comprehension strategies instruction in schools. Our work generally was being ignored by educators in 1998.

MOSAIC OF THOUGHT

With winter 1999 came some invitations to speak about reading instruction, mostly prompted by my book. It was heartening that there were a lot of questions about comprehension strategies from audiences at these talks. There was hope that someone remained interested in comprehension strategies instruction. Most intriguing, several members of one audience were emphatic that the summary of comprehension strategies instruction that I gave in my talk was identical to the perspective offered in a book by Ellin Oliver Keene and Susan Zimmermann (1997). Moreover, they described enthusiastically how the book was changing their teaching (and the teaching of others they knew). They claimed that in their classrooms, they now were teaching comprehension strategies.

I was intrigued enough by these assertions to buy and read a copy of Keene and Zimmermann's (1997) *Mosaic of Thought: Teaching Comprehension in a Reader's Workshop.* Some of the most important points in the book were the following:

- Reading is a very active process. Good readers question and challenge authors as they read. Sometimes the reader is confused by what is being read and makes efforts to resolve the confusions. The result of these efforts is a personal interpretation, which is affected by the reader's prior knowledge and experiences.

- Good readers use a relatively few thinking strategies consistently when they read (i.e., relating what is in text to their prior knowledge, figuring out the main ideas in text, questioning, constructing mental images of the meaning conveyed by text, making inferences beyond the information given in text, summarizing, seeking clarification when the meaning of text is confusing).

- Students' meaning making from text (i.e., understanding and memory) can be improved by teaching them to use the comprehension strategies used by good readers.

- The best way to teach comprehension strategies is to teach them one at a time, with a great deal of time devoted to each one. Teachers should model use of each strategy with a wide variety of texts. Students then should practice each strategy with a variety of texts, with the teacher encouraging student self-regulated use of the strategies by gradually releasing control of the strategies from the teacher to the student (Pearson & Gallagher, 1983).

- An important step in becoming a good teacher of comprehension strategies is to become a user of comprehension strategies. Thus teachers benefit from learning about comprehension strategies and attempting to use the strategies in their own reading. By learning to use and using the strategies, teachers become aware of the positive effects of using comprehension strategies.

- Comprehension strategies should be taught to students as they are immersed in the reading of excellent literature.

- Meaning of text can be socially constructed when readers of a text talk about it. Hence one mechanism for increasing active reading in children is to engage them in conversations about texts they are reading. Their interpretations of the particular texts read will be affected by such dialogue, and they will begin to learn how to engage texts actively themselves as they read them.

Keene and Zimmermann's (1997) book is mostly about the teaching of individual strategies, with whole chapters devoted to each of the comprehension strategies they believe are important (viz., relating to prior knowledge, identifying main ideas, questioning, mental imagery, making inferences, summarizing, and clarifying). There are many examples in the book of what happens when classroom teachers become comprehension strategies instructors.

In particular, there are many teacher–student and student–student dialogues included in the book. These dialogues illustrated instruction in using comprehension strategies, as well as the type of thinking that results when students do use strategies instruction. Comprehension strategies instruction as Keene and Zimmermann envision it is very active teaching, with teachers engaging students in using strategies to understand and interpret texts.

WHAT IS RIGHT WITH THE FRAMEWORK IN *MOSAIC OF THOUGHT*

There is much to admire in the Keene and Zimmermann text. In fact, most of their assumptions and their methods can be defended in light of substantial research on comprehension strategies.

Reading as an Active Process

Good readers are very active as they read, using a number of strategies as they proceed through text. The most revealing studies relative to this point used think-aloud methodology. Basically, readers were asked to verbalize their thought processes as they read. More than 40 such studies were included in a review of think-alouds during reading published by Pressley and Afflerbach (1995).

Before Reading   Before reading a text, the good reader has a goal (i.e., she or he knows what she or he wants to get out of the text). Often they overview a text before reading it, skimming to determine generally what is covered in the text. Based on such an overview, the good reader sometimes constructs a hypothesis about what the text says.

During Reading   Most good readers read text generally from front to back. They may skim some parts and concentrate intensely on others. Sometimes they repeat the reading of a section of text, perhaps making notes or pausing to reflect on parts of the text. Typically, they are especially alert to ideas that relate to their reading goal (i.e., information pertinent to what they want to find out). They check whether their tentative hypothesis about the meaning of text is borne out in the reading, typically changing hypotheses about the text meaning as new information is encountered and reflected on. The good reader is alert to the main ideas in a text, particularly main ideas that are relevant to the reader's goals or ones that are novel ideas. The good reader makes many inferences during reading, often conscious ones (e.g., inferring the meaning of a word encountered in the text based on context clues). These inferences often involve relating what is stated in text to the reader's prior knowledge. Sometimes the reader infers the author's intention (e.g., "The author wants me to think that . . ."). Part of this inference making is integrating ideas across different sections of text. The good reader's inferences often are interpretations of what is being read, paraphrases capturing the whole meaning of paragraphs or sections in a phrase or a sentence or two.

Throughout reading, the good reader is always monitoring, always aware of characteristics of the text (e.g., relevance to reading goal, whether reading is easy or difficult, whether the main ideas are being comprehended). The good reader monitors problems during reading, including loss of attention, words that are not known, or text that does not seem to make sense. Sometimes this awareness results in fix-up strategies being activated, such as rereading to seek clarification when text meaning is unclear.

Throughout reading, good readers also are evaluating the text. Thus, they are deciding whether they believe the information in the text or not. They decide whether they think the text is well written or poorly constructed. Good readers come to conclusions about whether the text is interesting enough to give to others. Such evaluations can be quite emotional, for example, as during a teary-eyed reading of a story about a heroic battle with a disease.

After Reading   On completion of a text, the good reader sometimes rereads selectively, sometimes consciously constructs a summary of what was in the text, and sometimes reflects on the text. Sometimes she or he thinks about how the information in the text might be used in the future.

Summary   Quite a bit goes on when good readers read. Does it make sense to conclude, as Keene and Zimmermann (1997) did, that skilled reading involves a relatively few strategic processes: relating to prior knowledge, identifying main ideas, questioning, mental imagery, making inferences, summarizing, and clarifying? In fact, all of the processes identified by Keene and Zimmermann (1997) were noted prominently in the Pressley and Afflerbach (1995) review of strategies reported by good readers as they read. Keene and Zimmermann's (1997) many admonitions that readers must learn to be aware when they read are consistent with the many reports of monitoring during reading by skilled readers. Moreover, the many evaluative interpretations of texts in the discussions reported by Keene and Zimmermann (1997) are very consistent with the portrait of skilled reading presented by Pressley and Afflerbach (1995). In particular, Keene and Zimmermann's emphasis on prior knowledge affecting understanding and interpretation of text also makes sense, with much of the monitoring, strategy use, and interpretation summarized in Pressley and Afflerbach (1995) clearly reflecting the extensive prior knowledge of very good readers.

In short, Keene and Zimmermann's (1997) conception of excellent reading is, in fact, consistent with the conception of skilled reading that emerges from studying the protocols of excellent reading analyzed by Pressley and Afflerbach (1995). Excellent reading does involve the strategies featured in Keene and Zimmermann's book, with lots and lots of monitoring of reading, and massive interpretation of what is read, with such interpretations often affected by the reader's prior knowledge.

Students Should Be Taught Strategies One at a Time

There is a great deal of evidence consistent with Keene and Zimmermann's (1997) assumption that students can be taught the strategies used by good readers and that when they are taught those strategies, their understanding and memory of texts read improves. Many experiments were conducted in the 1970s and 1980s of the following form: One group of students were taught to use some particular strategy while reading (e.g., imagery, summarization), with their reading compared with that of students who were not given such an instruction. In general, the students taught to use the comprehension strategy outperformed the students not given instruction; this result was obtained with a number of different strategies and with reading comprehension measured in a variety of ways.

Particularly relevant in this chapter directed at teaching in the upper elementary grades is that a number of individual strategies were validated as effective in improving comprehension in students in grades 4 through 8 (Pressley et al., 1989)—most prominently, the following:

- *Relating to prior knowledge*. Students were taught to compare their lives with situations in the text or to make predictions based on prior knowledge about what might happen in the text.

- *Mental imagery*. Students were taught to construct images in their heads consistent with the meanings conveyed in text.

- *Questioning*. Students were taught to develop questions pertaining to information represented in several different parts of the text. Students were also taught to evaluate their questions as to whether the questions covered important material and could be answered based on what was in the text.

- *Summarization*. Students are taught to find the big ideas in paragraphs and in longer passages by deleting trivial information. Sometimes students were taught to generate an outline of the passage.

That is, there is fairly definitive evidence that upper-grade elementary students can be taught to relate what they are reading to prior knowledge, to construct mental images of text content, to question themselves about ideas in text, and to summarize what has been read. I am less convinced, however, that we know how to teach upper elementary students to makes inferences when they are reading and to monitor their comprehension while they read.

With respect to making of inferences, there have been some successes in teaching children how to construct appropriate inferences when processing texts (Yuill & Oakhill, 1991). My reading of the literature, however, is that we are a long way from knowing how to teach children to make the many inferences they should make to get the most out of text. The challenge of teaching students to make inferences is obvious simply from considering the many types of inferences the good reader makes when processing text. Good readers infer all of the following (Pressley & Afflerbach, 1995): referents of pronouns; meanings of unknown vocabulary; subtle connotations in text; explanations for events described in text; examples of concepts explained in text; elaborations of ideas based on knowledge of the text or author or subject area; how ideas in a text relate to one's own opinions and theories; the author's purposes in writing the text; the author's assumptions about the world; the author's sources and strategies in writing the text; the text characters' intentions and characteristics; the nature of the world in which the written text takes place; and conclusions suggested by the text. There is high motivation to determine whether young readers can be taught to be highly inferential as they read, for skilled comprehension of text definitely depends on making inferences (Cain & Oakhill, 1998; Oakhill, Cain, & Yuill, 1998).

With respect to teaching children how to monitor their text comprehension, there also have been some limited successes (Elliott-Faust & Pressley, 1986; Ghatala, Levin, Pressley, & Goodwin, 1986; Lodico, Ghatala, Levin, Pressley, & Bell, 1983; Rao & Moely, 1989). However, even a very generous reading of the relevant studies does not permit the conclusion that we know how to teach children to do the many types of monitoring required during reading (Pressley & Afflerbach, 1995). Good readers can monitor all of the following: whether text is relevant to a current reading goal, the difficulty level of the text, the style of the text, the text's linguistic characteristics, the biases in a text, the relationship of parts of a text to larger themes in the text, the relationship of this text to other texts, when text is ambiguous, the relationship of the reader's background knowledge to the text, the tone of the text, and problems encountered in reading (e.g., loss of concentration, reading too quickly or too slowly, poorly written text, lack of background knowledge to understand text). Moreover, the skilled reader not only monitors but also shifts reading in reaction to what is monitored, and we are certainly a long way from knowing how best to teach readers to do such shifting. Shifting includes the following: attempting to figure out the meaning of a word detected as unknown; deciding whether to interpret text strictly or liberally; deciding whether to attend to or read carefully only certain parts of text that are most likely to be understood or most likely to be helpful; deciding to look up background material (e.g., a word in the dictionary) before continuing to read the text; attempting to pinpoint the parts of text that are confusing; and deciding to reread material that was not understood initially but that might be understood with more effort. There also are a few approaches to difficult text that good readers do not take, and monitoring plays an important role in stopping these behaviors from occurring; for example, as they read, good readers do not think about things other than the text, fall asleep, or simply give up on trying to understand the text. Unfortunately, however, we do not know how to teach weaker readers to monitor whether their attention is waning as they read.

In summary, Keene and Zimmermann's (1997) commitment to teach individual strategies one at a time can be defended by the many demonstrations of improved comprehension and memory for text when some individual strategic processes are taught. It remains unclear, however, whether it is possible to teach in the classroom all of the individual processes that Keene and Zimmermann favored in *Mosaic of Thought*. Both inference making and monitoring are very complicated processes, with only limited understanding at this point of how to develop these competencies through instruction.

WHAT IS WRONG WITH THE FRAMEWORK IN *MOSAIC OF THOUGHT*

Even though some of Keene and Zimmermann's (1997) assumptions are well supported by research, I was sometimes frustrated by their book.

Little about the Teaching Model

There is not much of a model of teaching specified in *Mosaic*. The authors do make reference to Pearson and Gallagher's (1983) gradual release of control approach to instruction, beginning with teacher modeling and continuing with increasingly greater control of processing by students. Even so, it is very difficult from the descriptions of teaching to envision how modeling occurs in actual classrooms or the many ways in which teachers can support student efforts to use strategies.

A prominent claim in the book is that comprehension strategies should take place in the context of a "readers' workshop," although the specifics of that approach also are not provided. It is clear that such a workshop approach includes student reading of and interaction over literature, but that is about all I could conclude from Keene and Zimmermann's (1997) book.

Little about Student Outcomes

There also is little information about how students read differently as a function of the strategy instruction. That is, it is not at all clear whether students became autonomously strategic readers as a function of the comprehension strategies instruction they received. That seemed to be the goal, for near the end of the book, one of the authors describes her own reading in these terms:

> As I read, I consciously and subconsciously use the strategies we've discussed in this book. I synthesize. I question. I infer. I create vivid sensory images. I relate the piece to my own experience. I tease out what I think is most important. I draw conclusions about what I think the key points of the passage are. Sometimes I use the strategies purposefully, other times they surface randomly. They are tools I use, sometimes effortlessly, sometimes purposefully to construct meaning. They intertwine and merge and I switch quickly among them, frequently using them simultaneously. They are the instruments which, as I become more familiar with them, gave me the ability to read more quickly. They are a means to an end. For proficient readers, they are second nature (Keene & Zimmermann, 1997, p. 216).

I wish Keene and Zimmermann had provided information about whether K–12 students were learning to read this way because of comprehension strategies instruction as they conceive of it and describe it in their book. There is a need for a lot of research on the Keene and Zimmermann (1997) approach and its effects on student reading.

Assumptions about Teachers' Reading

Despite the fact that Keene and Zimmermann (1997) insist that teachers using their approach learn to read differently than they did previously, I was frustrated during my reading of the text by the relative lack of attention by the authors to the changes in teachers' reading as a function of their becoming strategies instructors. An important research agenda should be to determine whether and how awareness of strategies increases as a function of learning to teach comprehension strategies to students and whether and how such increased awareness affects teaching *per se*.

The possibility that teachers can become strategic readers and aware of their own use of strategies is heartening. If that is so, then it should make it easier to sell teachers on the value of teaching comprehension strategies. This is critical, for if teachers do not buy into such comprehension strategies instructional models, it is unlikely that they will change their classroom teaching much in the direction of encouraging their students to use comprehension strategies. (This last assertion is discussed more fully later in this section.)

Teaching One Strategy at a Time

Keene and Zimmermann's (1997) focus on the teaching of individual strategies contrasts somewhat with other conceptions about how to teach comprehension strategies, including conceptions that define how comprehension strategies are taught when they are taught in American elementary schools. These conceptions begin with the recognition that multiple strategies are articulated by good readers as they read (e.g., Brown, Bransford, Ferrara, & Campione, 1983; Levin & Pressley, 1981), and hence it makes good sense to teach young readers to coordinate multiple strategies as they read.

For example, my colleagues and I studied classrooms that implemented comprehension strategies instruction (Brown & Coy-Ogan, 1993; El-Dinary, Pressley, & Schuder, 1992; Gaskins, Anderson, Pressley, Cunicelli, & Satlow, 1993; Pressley, El-Dinary, Gaskins, et al., 1992; Pressley, El-Dinary, Stein, Marks, & Brown, 1992; Pressley, Gaskins, Cunicelli, et al., 1991; Pressley, Gaskins, Wile, Cunicelli, & Sheridan, 1991; Pressley, Schuder, SAIL Faculty and Administration, Bergman, & El-Dinary, 1992). Consistently, we observed teaching of small repertoires of comprehension strategies, with students taught to articulate and coordinate strategies such as predicting from prior knowledge, relating to prior knowledge, generating images, seeking clarification, and summarizing. Although initially strategies were sometimes taught individually to acquaint students with a strategic process, typically such individual instruction yielded rather quickly to an emphasis on the repertoire of strategies and on learning to choose which strategy would be useful in a particular reading situation.

Consistent with the gradual release of responsibility approach favored by Keene and Zimmermann (1997), strategies typically were first modeled and explained, with student practice of the strategy (or repertoire) then following. Following the introduction of the strategies, students were coached as they attempted to use the strategies, particularly in the context of small group lessons. This was possible because students were encouraged during small group to model use of strategies for one another, thinking aloud as they read. Students did a lot of explaining to one another during these small group lessons, letting each other know how they were actively processing text. The students let one another know how useful the strategies were to them, reinforcing the teacher's instruction about how strategies improve understanding and memory of text. Although teacher modeling of strategies was reduced as students increased and improved their use of strategies, teachers continued to think aloud when they read to students, consistently modeling for them the flexible use of the repertoire of strategies being taught in the classroom.

Consistent as well with Keene and Zimmermann's (1997) emphasis on dialogue, the small group lessons my associates and I observed were filled with dialogue, and use of the strategies animated the discussions. That is, the discussions were filled with predictions about what might be in the stories, associations to the readings on the basis of prior knowledge, explanations of the images constructed during reading, commentaries about the parts of the text that were difficult to understand and alternative interpretations of such sections, and summaries of what readings were about. It was clear to us that strategies instruction is a powerful tool for stimulating rich conversations between students about the texts they are reading.

Eventually, my colleagues and I (Pressley, El-Dinary, Gaskins, et al., 1992) came to think of this type of instruction as transactional strategies instruction because the readers' transactions with text (i.e., interpretations) were so obvious as students applied strategies to text (Rosenblatt, 1978). We made the case that, as children practiced use of repertoires of comprehension strategies in small reading groups, they internalized the strategic processes, eventually using them on their own when reading.

There have been three published experimental evaluations of long-term transactional strategies instruction. Rachel Brown and I, in collaboration with Peggy Van Meter and Ted Schuder (Brown, Pressley, Van Meter, & Schuder, 1996), studied the effects of 1 year of transactional strategies instruction on weak grade 2 readers. Grade 2 readers who participated in classrooms that emphasized use of a small repertoire of comprehension strategies were compared with grade 2 readers in classrooms with conventional reading instruction. The particular strategies taught were predicting, questioning, seeking clarification, creating mental imagery, associating to ideas in text, and summarizing, with a strong emphasis on self-regulated use of these strategies. That is, it was emphasized that choosing an appropriate strategy was important and that different strategies apply in different situations. At the beginning of the year, the students in the two types of classrooms did not differ on standardized reading measures or on word attack measures. By the end of the year, striking differences on these measures favored the students in the transactional strategies instruction classrooms. Indeed, by the end of the year the students receiving transactional strategies instruction were more strategic as evidenced in their thinking aloud as they read and on measures of interpretive recall of text. The students who received a year of transactional strategies instruction were much better readers than control participants in the Brown et al. (1996) study.

Others besides my group, however, have also obtained positive results from long-term transactional instruction of repertoires of comprehension strategies. Cathy Collins Block (Collins, 1991) studied students in grades 5 and 6 as they received comprehension strategies instruction over a semester. The particular repertoire of strategies taught in her study included predicting, seeking clarification, looking for patterns and principles in ideas presented in text, analyzing decision making while reading, backward reasoning, mental imagery, summarizing, adapting and interpreting ideas in text, and negotiating interpretations of texts with others (i.e., discussing text with others, including how strategies are being applied in text). At the beginning of the study, the strategies-instructed students performed similarly to control participants on reading tasks, including standardized test measures. By the end of the 6 months of strategies instruction, the instructed students read much better than the control participants, including on standardized test measures.

Valerie Anderson (1992) provided 3 months of transactional strategies instruction to struggling readers in grades 6 through 11. Instruction was provided in small groups. The reading of students receiving strategies instruction was compared with the reading of other students who participated in small groups not receiving strategies instruction. By the end of the 3 months, strategies-instructed students were more willing to try challenging reading, more active while they read, and better able to interact with classmates to interpret texts read. After the instruction, the strategies-instructed students also outperformed control students on a standardized test of reading.

In summary, there is quite a bit of evidence that elementary, middle school, and secondary students benefit from instruction in the use of a small repertoire of reading comprehension strategies. In recent years especially, teaching of comprehension strategies has followed a common model, beginning with teacher modeling and explanation of strategies and continuing with student practice of strategies with the teacher then coaching students' use of strategies. Not only does such teaching work to increase reading comprehension but it does so by encouraging the kind of active reading done by proficient readers, as described earlier in this paper.

Teachers Are Motivated to Develop Strategic Readers and Be Comprehension Strategies Teachers

Keene and Zimmermann (1997) assume that most teachers will agree that students are too passive when they read. They also assume that teachers will agree that it is a good thing to stimulate use of strategies that encourage more active reading, strategies that encourage reading as good readers read. These assumptions may be too strong.

When my associates and I did our work on comprehension strategies instruction, we spent a great deal of time in classrooms of teachers who did it well. After all, we were interested in excellent comprehension strategies instruction. From time to time, however, we also observed teachers who were struggling with comprehension strategies instruction or were downright hostile toward it, for example, believing students were better off simply reading on their own. We also heard plenty of stories about teachers who tried comprehension strategies instruction and decided it was not for them or their students.

A particularly illuminating analysis was provided by Pamela Beard El-Dinary in her dissertation study (see Pressley & El-Dinary, 1997). She studied seven teachers as they attempted to become transactional strategies instruction teachers over the course of a school year. What became apparent early in the year was that learning to be a strategies instruction teacher was very challenging. For example, some of the teachers felt that transactional strategies instruction conflicted with their own beliefs about reading and teaching of reading. Some felt it conflicted with the whole-language methods they learned in their teacher education courses (i.e., strategies instruction seemed too teacher directed). Some teachers felt that comprehension strategies instruction and use of comprehension strategies during reading group took too much time, with the result that students were not reading nearly as many books and stories in reading groups. Also, there were teachers who had problems with the many interpretations emanating from reading group discussions that used the strategies: Some permitted any interpretation that emerged, regardless of whether it seemed consistent with the reading, and others seemed uncomfortable with anything except standard interpretations. By the end of the year of observations, only two of the seven teachers were committed comprehension strategies instruction teachers. El-Dinary's (1994) work made clear that comprehension strategies instruction, or at least the transactional strategies instructional approach, is not for every teacher.

Summary

In this section, I tried to place Keene and Zimmermann's (1997) book in the context of the larger comprehension strategies instructional literature. Compared with much of the work preceding it, *Mosaic of Thought* is relatively inattentive to details about how instruction should occur and how readers change as a function of the instruction they favor. More positively, I am certainly willing to accept as hypotheses that teaching individual strategies as Keene and Zimmermann (1997) conceived of it might improve teachers' comprehension processing and awareness of comprehension processes, might be a powerful approach to teaching of comprehension to elementary students, and might be an acceptable form of instruction for teachers. Indeed, I hope that all of these hypotheses will be supported as research on the model proceeds.

Even the most enthusiastic strategies instructionist, however, has to pause at the single-mindedness of Keene and Zimmermann (1997) with respect to comprehension: They advocate only for teaching of comprehension strategies. Thus, in the next section, I make the case that after a quarter of a century of research on comprehension strategies instruction, it is very clear that comprehension is not just about strategies and that instruction to improve comprehension should not be just about strategies.

WHAT SHOULD COMPREHENSION INSTRUCTION BE ABOUT?

There has been a great deal of work in recent decades establishing that comprehension depends very much on word-level skills and background knowledge, as well as on the processes stimulated by comprehension strategies instruction. Thus, as the century closes, it is well understood that if a child cannot decode a word, he or she will not comprehend the meaning intended by the word (Adams, 1990; Metsala & Ehri, 1998). Indeed, beyond accurate word recognition, if the child cannot decode words fluently, comprehension will be impaired (Breznitz, 1997a, 1997b; Gough & Tummer, 1986; LaBerge & Samuels, 1974; Tan & Nicholson, 1997). It is also well understood that comprehension depends on vocabulary, with good readers having more extensive vocabularies than weaker readers (e.g., Anderson & Freebody, 1981; Stanovich, 1986). When an elementary-level reader improves her or his vocabulary, reading comprehension improves (Beck, Perfetti, & McKeown, 1982; McKeown, Beck, Omanson, & Perfetti, 1983; McKeown, Beck, Omanson, & Pople, 1985).

Good readers also have extensive knowledge of the world that they relate to ideas in text in order to understand what they are reading (Anderson & Pearson, 1984). Making of inferences beyond the information given in text depends heavily on prior knowledge (Hayes-Roth & Thorndyke, 1979; Kintsch, 1988; van Dijk & Kintsch, 1983). Good readers use prior knowledge to make inferences required to understand a text (McKoon & Ratcliff, 1992), in contrast to weak readers who often make associations to prior knowledge that are only remotely related to ideas in the text (e.g., Williams, 1993).

There are a number of instructional recommendations (Pressley, 2000) that follow directly from the literature about word-level and prior knowledge contributions to comprehension:

- *Teach decoding skills.* Developing word recognition skills in the primary years pays off with comprehension gains in the upper elementary grades (e.g., Juel, 1988).

- *Encourage the development of sight words.* Sight words are recognized with less effort than words that must be decoded, freeing up cognitive capacity for comprehension (LaBerge & Samuels, 1974).

- *Teach vocabulary meanings.* Although more words are learned incidentally than through instruction (Sternberg, 1987), teaching of vocabulary often encountered in texts improves comprehension (Beck et al., 1982; McKeown et al., 1983; McKeown et al., 1985).

- *Encourage extensive reading.* Reading a great deal provides additional exposure to words, which affects fluency (LaBerge & Samuels, 1974). Reading increases young readers' vocabulary (e.g., Dickinson & Smith, 1994; Elley, 1989; Fleisher, Jenkins, & Pany, 1979; Pellegrini, Galda, Perlmutter, & Jones, 1994; Robbins & Ehri, 1994; Rosenhouse, Feitelson, Kita, & Goldstein, 1997; Valdez-Menchaca & Whitehurst, 1992; Whitehurst et al., 1988), as well as the knowledge of the world that mediates reading comprehension (Stanovich & Cunningham, 1993).

■ *Encourage students to relate prior knowledge to text.* (Anderson & Pearson, 1984; Levin & Pressley, 1981).

In short, there are multiple ways to improve comprehension, with all of them potentially affected by instruction. Although a good case can be made for teaching comprehension strategies to elementary students, it is most defensible to do so in the context of a reading program that includes teaching to promote word recognition skills, vocabulary knowledge, and extensive reading of books filled with the world knowledge that young readers need to acquire.

In *Mosaic of Thought*, Keene and Zimmermann (1997) argue for a reader's workshop approach, which should go far in promoting a great deal of reading, which in turn should affect fluency, vocabulary development, and construction of background knowledge. Thus it is possible that their call for adding comprehension strategies instruction to reading of literature is an effective approach to development of comprehension abilities. For myself, I would like to see some formal comparisons of the "strategies instruction plus reader's workshop" method recommended by Keene and Zimmermann (1997) with literature-based instruction filled with explicit teaching and encouragement of comprehension strategies, development of fluency, vocabulary learning, and coverage of critical world knowledge. That is, I do not think we have yet created and evaluated the best comprehension instruction possible based on what is known at the end of the 20th century about how to promote comprehension abilities. It seems to me that the time is ripe to do so.

REFERENCES

Adams, M. J. (1990). *Beginning to read.* Cambridge, MA: Harvard University Press.

Anderson, R. C., & Freebody, P. (1981). Vocabulary knowledge. In J. T. Guthrie (Ed.), *Comprehension and teaching: Research reviews* (pp. 77–117). Newark, DE: International Reading Association.

Anderson, R. C., & Pearson, P. D. (1984). A schema-theoretic view of basic processes in reading. In P. D. Pearson (Ed.), *Handbook of reading research* (pp. 255–291). New York: Longman.

Anderson, V. (1992). A teacher development project in transactional strategy instruction for teachers of severely reading-disabled adolescents. *Teaching and Teacher Education, 8,* 391–403.

Beck, I. L., Perfetti, C. A., & McKeown, M. G. (1982). Effects of long-term vocabulary instruction on lexical access and reading comprehension. *Journal of Educational Psychology, 74,* 506–521.

Breznitz, Z. (1997a). Effects of accelerated reading rate on memory for text among dyslexic readers. *Journal of Educational Psychology, 89,* 289–297.

Breznitz, Z. (1997b). Enhancing the reading of dyslexic children by reading acceleration and auditory masking. *Journal of Educational Psychology, 89,* 103–113.

Brown, A. L., Bransford, J. D., Ferrara, R. A., & Campione, J. C. (1983). Learning, remembering, and understanding. In J. H. Flavell & E. M. Markman (Eds.), *Handbook of child psychology: Vol. III. Cognitive development* (pp. 77–166). New York: Wiley.

Brown, R., & Coy-Ogan, L. (1993). The evolution of transactional strategies instruction in one teacher's classroom. *Elementary School Journal, 94*, 221–233.

Brown, R., Pressley, M., Van Meter, P., & Schuder, T. (1996). A quasi-experimental validation of transactional strategies instruction with low-achieving second grade readers. *Journal of Educational Psychology, 88*, 18–37.

Cain, K., & Oakhill, J. (1998). Comprehension skill and inference-making ability: Issues and causality. In C. Hulme & R. M. Joshi (Eds.), *Reading and spelling: Development and disorders* (pp. 329–342). London: Erlbaum.

Collins, C. (1991). Reading instruction that increases thinking abilities. *Journal of Reading, 34*, 510–516.

Dickinson, D. K., & Smith, M. W. (1994). Long-term effects of preschool teachers' book readings on low-income children's vocabulary and story comprehension. *Reading Research Quarterly, 29*, 104–122.

Durkin, D. (1978–1979). What classroom observation reveals about reading comprehension instruction. *Reading Research Quarterly, 14*, 481–533.

El-Dinary, P. B. (1994). *Teachers learning, adapting and implementing strategies-based instruction in reading.* Ann Arbor, MI: Dissertation Services (Order No. 9407625).

El-Dinary, P. B., Pressley, M., & Schuder, T. (1992). Teachers learning transactional strategies instruction. In C. K. Kinzer & D. J. Leu (Eds.), *Literacy research, theory, and practice: Views from many perspectives. 41st Yearbook of the National Reading Conference* (pp. 453–462). Chicago: National Reading Conference.

Elley, W. B. (1989). Vocabulary acquisition from listening to stories. *Reading Research Quarterly, 24*, 174–187.

Elliott-Faust, D. J., & Pressley, M. (1986). Self-controlled training of comparison strategies increase children's comprehension monitoring. *Journal of Educational Psychology, 78*, 27–32.

Fleisher, L., Jenkins, J., & Pany, D. (1979). Effects on poor readers' comprehension of training in rapid decoding. *Reading Research Quarterly, 15*, 30–48.

Gaskins, I. W., Anderson, R. C., Pressley, M., Cunicelli, E. A., & Satlow, E. (1993). Six teachers' dialogue during cognitive process instruction. *Elementary School Journal, 93*, 277–304.

Ghatala, E. S., Levin, J. R., Pressley, M., & Goodwin, D. (1986). A componential analysis of the effects of derived and supplied strategy-utility information on children's strategy selections. *Journal of Experimental Child Psychology, 22*, 199–216.

Gough, P. B., & Tunmer, W. E. (1986). Decoding, reading, and reading disability. *Remedial and Special Education, 7*, 6–10.

Hayes-Roth, B., & Thorndyke, P. W. (1979). Integration of knowledge from text. *Journal of Verbal Learning and Verbal Behavior, 18*, 91–108.

Juel, C. (1988). Learning to read and write: A longitudinal study of fifty-four children from first through fourth grade. *Journal of Educational Psychology, 80*, 437–447.

Keene, E. O., & Zimmermann, S. (1997). *Mosaic of thought: Teaching comprehension in a reader's workshop.* Portsmouth, NH: Heinemann.

Kintsch, W. (1988). The role of knowledge in discourse comprehension: A construction–integration model. *Psychological Review, 95*, 163–182.

LaBerge, D., & Samuels, S. J. (1974). Toward a theory of automatic information processing in reading. *Cognitive Psychology, 6*, 293–323.

Levin, J. R., & Pressley, M. (1981). Improving children's prose comprehension: Selected strategies that seem to succeed. In C. M. Santa & B. L. Hayes (Eds.), *Children's prose comprehension: Research and practice* (pp. 44–71). Newark, DE: International Reading Association.

Lodico, M. G., Ghatala, E. S., Levin, J. R., Pressley, M., & Bell, J. A. (1983). Effects of meta-memory training on children's use of effective learning strategies. *Journal of Experimental Child Psychology, 35*, 263–277.

McKeown, M. G., Beck, I. L., Omanson, R. C., & Perfetti, C. A. (1983). The effects of long-term vocabulary instruction on reading comprehension: A replication. *Journal of Reading Behavior, 15*, 3–18.

McKeown, M. G., Beck, I. L., Omanson, R. C., & Pople, M. T. (1985). Some effects of the nature and frequency of vocabulary instruction on the knowledge and use of words. *Reading Research Quarterly, 20,* 522–535.

McKoon, G., & Ratcliff, R. (1992). Inference during reading. *Psychological Review, 99,* 440–466.

Metsala, J., & Ehri, L. (Eds.). (1998). *Word recognition in beginning reading.* Mahwah, NJ: Erlbaum.

Oakhill, J., Cain, K., & Yuill, N. (1998). Individual differences in children's comprehension skill: Toward an integrated model. In C. Hulme & R. M. Joshi (Eds.), *Reading and spelling development and disorders* (pp. 343–367). London: Erlbaum.

Palincsar, A. S., & Brown, A. L. (1984). Reciprocal teaching of comprehension-fostering and monitoring activities. *Cognition and Instruction, 1,* 117–175.

Pearson, P. D., & Dole, J. A. (1987). Explicit comprehension instruction: A review of research and a new conceptualization of instruction. *Elementary School Journal, 88,* 151–165.

Pearson, P. D., & Fielding, L. (1991). Comprehension instruction. In R. Barr, M. L. Kamil, P. B. Mosenthal, & P. D. Pearson (Eds.), *Handbook of reading research* (Vol. 2, pp. 815–860). New York: Longman.

Pearson, P. D., & Gallagher, M. (1983). The instruction of reading comprehension. *Contemporary Educational Psychology, 8,* 317–344.

Pellegrini, A. D., Galda, L., Perlmutter, J., & Jones, I. (1994). *Joint reading between mothers and their Head Start children: Vocabulary development in two text formats* (Reading Research Report No. 13). Athens, GA, and College Park, MD: National Reading Research Center.

Pressley, G. M. (1976). Mental imagery helps eight-year-olds remember what they read. *Journal of Educational Psychology, 68,* 355–359.

Pressley, M. (1998). *Reading instruction that works: The case for balanced teaching.* New York: Guilford Press.

Pressley, M. (2000). What should comprehension instruction be the instruction of? In M. L. Kamil, P. B. Mosenthal, P. D. Pearson, & R. Barr (Eds.), *Handbook of reading research* (Vol. III, pp. 546–561). Mahwah, NJ: Erlbaum.

Pressley, M., & Afflerbach, P. (1995). *Verbal protocols of reading: The nature of constructively responsive reading.* Hillsdale, NJ: Erlbaum.

Pressley, M., & El-Dinary, P. B. (1997). What we know about translating comprehension strategies instruction research into practice. *Journal of Learning Disabilities, 30,* 486–488.

Pressley, M., El-Dinary, P. B., Gaskins, I., Schuder, T., Bergman, J., Almasi, L., & Brown, R. (1992). Beyond direct explanation: Transactional instruction of reading comprehension strategies. *Elementary School Journal, 92,* 511–554.

Pressley, M., El-Dinary, P. B., Stein, S., Marks, M. B., & Brown, R. (1992). Good strategy instruction is motivating and interesting. In A. Renninger, S. Hidi, & A. Krapp (Eds.), *The role of interest in learning and development* (pp. 333–358). Hillsdale, NJ: Erlbaum.

Pressley, M., Gaskins, I. W., Cunicelli, E. A., Bardick, N. J., Schaub-Matt, M., Lee, D. S., & Powell, N. (1991). Strategy instruction at Benchmark School: A faculty interview study. *Learning Disability Quarterly, 14,* 19–48.

Pressley, M., Gaskins, I. W., Wile, D., Cunicelli, E. A., & Sheridan, J. (1991). Teaching literacy strategies across the curriculum: A case study at Benchmark School. In S. McCormick & J. Zutell (Eds.), *40th Yearbook of the National Reading Conference* (pp. 219–228). Chicago: National Reading Conference.

Pressley, M., Johnson, C. J., Symons, S., McGoldrick, J. A., & Kurita, J. A. (1989). Strategies that improve children's memory and comprehension of text. *Elementary School Journal, 90,* 3–32.

Pressley, M., & McCormick, C. B. (1995). *Advanced educational psychology for educators, researchers, and policymakers.* New York: HarperCollins.

Pressley, M., Schuder, T., SAIL Faculty and Administration, Bergman, J. L., & El-Dinary, P. B. (1992). A researcher–educator collaborative interview study of transactional comprehension strategies instruction. *Journal of Educational Psychology, 84,* 231–246.

Pressley, M., Wharton-McDonald, R., Mistretta-Hampston, J. M., & Echevarria, M. (1998). The nature of literacy instruction in ten grade 4/5 classrooms in upstate New York. *Scientific Studies of Reading, 2,* 159–194.

Rao, N., & Moely, B. E. (1989). Producing memory strategy maintenance and generalization by explicit or implicit training of memory knowledge. *Journal of Experimental Child Psychology, 48,* 335–352.

Robbins, C., & Ehri, L. C. (1994). Reading storybooks to kindergartners helps them learn new vocabulary words. *Journal of Educational Psychology, 86,* 54–64.

Rosenblatt, L. M. (1978). *The reader, the text, the poem: The transactional theory of the literary work.* Carbondale: Southern Illinois University Press.

Rosenhouse, J., Feitelson, D., Kita, B., & Goldstein, Z. (1997). Interactive reading aloud to Israeli first graders: Its contribution to literacy development. *Reading Research Quarterly, 32,* 168–183.

Snow, C. E., Burns, M. S., & Griffin, P. (1998). *Preventing reading difficulties in young children.* Washington, DC: National Academy Press.

Stanovich, K. (1986). Matthew effects in reading: Some consequences of individual differences in the acquisition of literacy. *Reading Research Quarterly, 21,* 360–407.

Stanovich, K. E., & Cunningham, A. E. (1993). Where does knowledge come from? Specific associations between print exposure and information acquisition. *Journal of Educational Psychology, 85,* 211–229.

Sternberg, R. J. (1987). Most vocabulary is learned from context. In M. G. McKeown & M. E. Curtis (Eds.), *The nature of vocabulary acquisition* (pp. 89–105). Hillsdale, NJ: Erlbaum.

Tan, A., & Nicholson, T. (1997). Flashcards revisited: Training poor readers to read words faster improves their comprehension of text. *Journal of Educational Psychology, 89,* 276–288.

Valdez-Menchaca, M. C., & Whitehurst, G. J. (1992). Accelerating language development through picture book reading: A systematic extension to Mexican day care. *Developmental Psychology, 28,* 1106–1114.

van Dijk, T. A., & Kintsch, W. (1983). *Strategies of discourse comprehension.* New York: Academic Press.

Whitehurst, G. J., Falco, F. L., Lonigan, C. J., Fischel, J. E., DeBaryshe, B. D., Valdez-Menchaca, M. C., & Caulfield, M. (1988). Accelerating language development through picture book reading. *Developmental Psychology, 24,* 552–559.

Williams, J. P. (1993). Comprehension of students with and without learning disabilities: Identification of narrative themes and idiosyncratic text representations. *Journal of Educational Psychology, 85,* 631–441.

Yuill, N., & Oakhill, J. (1991). *Children's problems in reading comprehension.* Cambridge, England: Cambridge University Press.

INTEGRATING SOURCES

1. Would Pressley be likely to dispute any of the CIERA principles? If so, which ones and why?

2. The CIERA principles frequently include the phrase, "strategies and skills." How might Pressley react to this phrase?

3. Pressley identifies four strategies particularly useful in improving comprehension of children in grades 4–8. To which of the CIERA principles is each of these strategies most closely related?

CLASSROOM IMPLICATIONS

1. How realistic are the suggestions offered in these sources? Do they come close to describing what already happens in your classroom? In your school?

2. Can you think of additional principles, based on your experience, that might be added to those of CIERA?

3. Choose one comprehension strategy and describe how you might include it in a reading or content area lesson plan.

ANNOTATED BIBLIOGRAPHY

Block, C. C., & Pressley, M. (Eds.). (2000). *Comprehension instruction: Research-based best practices.* New York: Guilford.
   A collection of articles on various dimensions of comprehension instruction, all with a current research base.

Nagy, W. E. (1988). *Teaching vocabulary to improve reading comprehension.* Newark, DE: International Reading Association.
   Explores the link between vocabulary and comprehension and offers many research-based ideas for instruction.

Readence, J. E., Moore, D. W., & Rickelman, R. J. (2000). *Prereading activities for content area reading and learning* (3rd ed.). Newark, DE: International Reading Association.
   Excellent source of instructional activities designed to improve children's comprehension of nonfiction.

Southwest Educational Development Laboratory. *The cognitive foundations of learning to read: A framework.* Available on-line at: http://www.sedl.org/reading/framework/
   Presents a wealth of information about various components of reading, including comprehension. Instructional strategies are recommended as well.

YOU BECOME INVOLVED

1. Visit the CIERA Web site (www.ciera.org) and choose one of the archived articles. Read and critique it, relating it to the content of this chapter and to your own teaching assignment.

2. Examine the scope-and-sequence of the basal reader series used at your school. Contrast the comprehension strand with the suggestions made in these sources. Is there a close alignment? What, if anything, seems to be missing?

3. Reexamine the five issues we identified in the chapter overview. Now that you've read the selections, how has your thinking changed with respect to these issues? Or has it?

• • • • • ▬▬▬▬▬▬▬▬▬▬▬▬▬▬▬▬▬▬▬▬▬▬▬▬▬▬▬▬▬▬▬▬▬

CHAPTER SIX

ADOLESCENT LITERACY

*There are perhaps no days of our childhood we lived so fully as those we believe
we left without having lived them, than those we spent with a favorite book.*
—Marcel Proust (1910)

*Children don't read to find their identity, to free themselves from guilt, to quench
the thirst for rebellion or to get rid of alienation. They have no use for psychology.
They detest sociology. They still believe in God, the family, angels, devils, witches,
goblins, logic, clarity, punctuation, and other such obsolete stuff. . . . When a book
is boring, they yawn openly. They don't expect their writer to redeem humanity,
but leave adults to such childish illusions.*
—Isaac Bashevis Singer (1978)

Few would deny the existence of a widespread literacy problem among American adolescents. Consider these results from the 1998 National Assessment of Educational
Progress, a federally conducted periodic assessment:

- 23 percent of twelfth graders scored below the "Basic" level in reading (the level indicating "partial mastery of prerequisite knowledge and skills that are funda-mental for proficient work" at grade 12).
- 26 percent of eighth graders scored below the "Basic" level in reading.
- At grades 8 and 12, girls significantly outperformed boys.
- The average African American twelfth grader performed about as well as the average white eighth grader.
- At grades 8 and 12, less than 40 percent of students report discussing their stud-ies at home "almost every day."

In the Position Statement on Adolescent Literacy adopted by the International
Reading Association (IRA) in 2000, seven principles were advocated for fostering adolescents' growth as readers. Specifically, IRA's Commission on Adolescent Literacy
stated that adolescents deserve:

1. access to a wide variety of reading material that they can and want to read;
2. instruction that builds both the skill and desire to read increasingly complex materials;
3. assessment that shows them their strengths as well as their needs and that guides their teachers to design instruction that will best help them grow as readers;
4. expert teachers who model and provide explicit instruction in reading comprehension and study strategies across the curriculum;
5. reading specialists who assist individual students having difficulties learning how to read;
6. teachers who understand the complexities of individual adolescent readers, respect their differences, and respond to their characteristics; and
7. homes, communities and a nation that will support their efforts to achieve advanced levels of literacy and provide the support necessary for them to succeed.

Are these goals attainable in most schools? And, if they were to be attained, would they be sufficient to ensure that adolescent literacy would cease to be the problem it has become? The Commission's seven principles certainly provide grist for reconsidering the dilemma and our individual roles as teachers in contending with it. Carol Kirk, a veteran middle-grades teacher, applauded the statement in her March 2000 letter (*Journal of Adolescent and Adult Literacy*), but she raised an important question: "Why—given the clear need and rationale for adolescent literacy assessment, instruction, and support—has it been such a struggle over the years to develop and maintain strong reading programs for adolescents?" (p. 573). Many reasons might be offered, including:

- competing courses for limited blocks of time;
- general lack of financial resources;
- a dearth of effective remedial materials;
- an emphasis on beginning reading and early intervention;
- the faulty assumption that problems will be addressed by content specialists in the middle grades and high school; and
- the fatalistic conclusion that it is simply too late to adequately address the needs of struggling adolescent readers.

These reasons may help to explain the situation, but they do little to justify it. They may, however, assist you in framing for yourself this important cluster of issues.

AS YOU READ

The two selections included in this chapter represent cornerstones of current thinking about the problem of adolescent literacy. We begin with the forward-looking article of Elizabeth Moje and her colleagues, in which they examine the question of how changing literacy demands *beyond* school must occasion a reinspection of how we address adolescent literacy *within* school. The second piece is Donna Alvermann's review of effective instructional practices aimed at promoting adolescent literacy. This paper was commissioned by the National Reading Conference (NRC), a leading organization of reading researchers and teacher educators, and also appears on the NRC Web site at www.nrconline.org.

Consider the following questions as you read:

1. How does adolescent literacy differ from content area reading?
2. How can the literacy needs of struggling adolescents best be met?
3. What is critical literacy? Can and should it be fostered among adolescents?
4. What is your reaction to each of the "five statements" about adolescent literacy posed by Alvermann?

REFERENCES

Commission on Adolescent Literacy. (1999). *Adolescent literacy: A position statement for the Commission on Adolescent Literacy of the International Reading Association.* [On-line]. Available: http://www.reading.org/positions/adol_lit.html

Nation's Report Card: Reading. (2000). National Center for Educational Statistics, U.S. Department of Education. [On-line]. Available: http://nces.ed.gov/nationsreportcard/reading/

Reinventing Adolescent Literacy for New Times:

Perennial and Millennial Issues

ELIZABETH BIRR MOJE

JOSEPHINE PEYTON YOUNG

JOHN E. READENCE

DAVID W. MOORE

In the editorial that commenced their tenure as Editors of the *Journal of Adolescent & Adult Literacy*, Allan Luke and John Elkins (1998) called attention to unprecedented and disorienting changes in everyday literacy, and they proposed the need to reinvent literacy for new times. The 1999 position statement by the International Reading Association's Commission on Adolescent Literacy (Moore, Bean, Birdyshaw, & Rycik, 1999) contained these words calling for renewed attention to the literacy needs of adolescents:

> Adolescents entering the adult world in the 21st century will read and write more than at any other time in human history. They will need advanced levels of literacy to perform their jobs, run their households, act as citizens, and conduct their personal lives. They will need literacy to cope with the flood of information they will find everywhere they turn. They will need literacy to feed their imaginations so they can create the world of the future. In a complex and sometimes even dangerous world, their ability to read will be crucial. Continual instruction beyond the early grades is needed (p. 99).

Moje, E. B., Young, J. P., Readence, J. E., & Moore, D. W. (2000, Feb.). Reinvesting adolescent literacy for new times: Perennial and millennial issues. *Journal of Adult & Adolescent Literacy, 43* (5), 400–410.

160

These calls for action reaffirm beliefs that the reading, writing, and language development of youth beyond the primary grades deserves serious attention. A number of youth continue to struggle with basic processes of reading and writing beyond the third grade and require continued support in decoding, comprehending, and making meaning of the various texts they encounter in school and in their lives (Hiebert & Taylor, in press). For the many youth who have mastered the basic *processes* of reading and writing by the time they have reached fourth grade, there is still much to learn about the *practices* associated with literacy, especially the ones unique to different disciplines, texts, and situations (Gee & Green, 1998; Mosenthal, 1998). Additionally, the demands of a changing world necessitate the teaching and learning of specialized literacy practices. Luke and Elkins (1998) explained the necessity for such specialized practices as follows:

> [T]oday adolescence and adulthood involve the building of communities and identities in relation to changing textual and media landscapes. They involve finding a way forward in what is an increasingly volatile and uncertain job market, and negotiating a consumer society fraught with risk, where written and media texts are used to position, construct, sell, and define individuals at every turn and in virtually every domain of everyday life, in the shopping mall and the school, online, and face to face (pp. 6–7).

The need for a renewed focus on the literacy learning of adolescents seems clear. Nevertheless, a number of scholars have noted that in recent years state and federal funding for middle and high school reading programs has decreased, and funding for research on the literacy and language learning of middle and high school-aged students is minimal (Moore et al., 1999; Vacca, 1998).

Cognizant of these concerns, we four authors engaged in a public conversation—a point and counterpoint—at the 1999 convention of the International Reading Association (IRA) in San Diego, California, USA. Our conversation, which was sponsored by the International Reading Association's Commission on Adolescent Literacy, addressed instructional, policy, and research issues currently deserving attention. It centered around four questions:

- What does *adolescent literacy* signal that *content reading* and *secondary reading* do not?
- What constitutes best practices in adolescent literacy?
- How can we meet the needs of marginalized readers in new times?
- Should critical literacy be part of our classrooms?

In the following sections, we present our responses to these questions. We do so in hopes of promoting a public conversation that will contribute to the literacy and content learning needs of today's youth. We begin by examining the label *adolescent literacy* in a historical context, inquiring into what this term offers in contrast to terms used previously.

WHAT DOES *ADOLESCENT LITERACY* SIGNAL THAT *CONTENT READING* AND *SECONDARY READING* DO NOT?

Labels are words or phrases that people use to identify or describe the person, place, or thing under discussion or examination. Labels also carry with them the *baggage*, or connotations, that people ascribe to them. For instance, the phrase *middle school student* describes a student approaching adolescence and in transition between elementary school and high school. Yet, as Finders (1998/1999) has demonstrated, this label also carries with it some emotional baggage that limits how we define and think of middle school students. The following quote by one preservice teacher provides an example of this by characterizing all middle school students as having raging hormones that interfere with learning:

> You know how adolescents are. They are just plain out of control. It's a stressful time with hormones surging and all. You take a nice kid, and then puberty kicks in, and the kid becomes nothing but a bundle of raging hormones. They begin noticing the opposite sex, and they lose all ability to reason (p. 254).

Similarly, baggage comes with the terms *secondary reading* and *content reading* that limit how we think about literacy in middle and secondary schools. For example, secondary reading carries with it the notions of a lab setting, in which students who have not learned to read are cloistered, working on individual sets of grade-leveled materials supposedly designed to bring them up to grade level in their reading so they can be successful with their subject matter materials. This type of reading, unfortunately, has connotations of *remedial* reading, which limit its usefulness for the full range of adolescents' reading needs (Vacca, 1998).

Though the term *content reading* has existed since the days of William S. Gray and Arthur I. Gates, it gained prominence in the 1970s with the advent of the cognitive revolution in psychology and the publication of Hal Herber's (1970) text, *Teaching Reading in Content Areas*. However, this term, too, brings baggage with it. Associated with content reading is the slogan "every teacher a teacher of reading," coined by Gray in 1937 when he chaired the National Committee on Reading. This slogan has influenced many content teachers to turn off to reading instruction within their content areas because they prefer to act as content teachers, not reading teachers.

Common definitions of content reading focus on enabling students to cope with the special reading materials and tasks encountered during the study of school subjects. It is reading instruction that is confined to the in-school literacy of content materials and, as Vacca (1998) pointed out, necessarily becomes "one-dimensional if what counts as literacy is limited to reading and writing in academic contexts" (p. xv). Thus, in the cases of both secondary reading and content reading, instructional methods or materials might not match the literacy needs of adolescents.

The term *adolescent literacy* points to distinctive dimensions of the reading and writing of youth. With the September 1995 issue, the name of the *Journal of Reading* was changed to the *Journal of Adolescent & Adult Literacy* (JAAL) by the International Reading Association. In 1997 IRA also created the Commission on Adolescent Literacy to advise the organization on the policies related to literacy learning in adolescents' lives. Finally, as previously mentioned, Luke and Elkins (1998) have used the term in their call for a reinvention of literacy for new times, a way of focusing the readership on the question, "What does it mean to be an adolescent learning literacy as we approach the new millennium?"

The focus on adolescents takes the study of literacy beyond the constraints associated with secondary reading and content reading to a broad generative view. The publication *Reconceptualizing the Literacies in Adolescents' Lives* (Alvermann, Hinchman, Moore, Phelps, & Waff, 1998) for example, was guided by two principles learned from research that focused on adolescents: (a) adolescents want to be viewed as already possessing knowledge and skills and plans for the future, and (b) they want to participate in literacy practices suited to the ways they view their day-to-day lives. As a result of the various studies represented in this book, the editors and authors offered four themes for further research on adolescent literacy. First, adolescent literacy is more complex and sophisticated than what is traditionally considered in school-based literate activity. Adolescents have multiple literacies. Second, because adolescents have multiple literacies, they have multiple texts and an expanded notion of text; that is, they transcend adult-sanctioned notions of text forms. An expanded notion of what text is includes film, CD-ROM, the Internet, popular music, television, magazines, and newspapers, to name a few. Third, literacy plays an important role in the development of adolescents' individual and social identities. Readers act upon cues from what they read and how they perform in school to shape their emerging senses of self. Finally, adolescents need spaces in schools to explore and experiment with multiple literacies and to receive feedback from peers and adults. Schools advocating only school-sanctioned literacy do not currently provide such spaces.

Two recent publications epitomize this broad generative view of adolescent literacy. The first is a *JAAL* article published in the March 1999 issue by Tom Bean and his two adolescent daughters, Shannon and Kristen, entitled "Intergenerational Conversations and Two Adolescents' Multiple Literacies: Implications for Redefining Content Area Literacy" (Bean, Bean, & Bean, 1999). In this article Bean and his daughters described the multiple literacies the young women used over a 2-week period of time. In addition to their content textbooks, they used phones, pagers, cell phones, computers, electronic mail, the Internet, art, music, drama, film, video games, and digital aids of all types. Bean et al.'s point was simple: Being literate no longer means just learning to read and write traditional print texts; people need to be sociotechnically literate.

Similarly, in *Popular Culture in the Classroom: Teaching and Researching Critical Media Literacy*, Alvermann, Moon, and Hagood (1999) discussed the importance of increasing adolescents' awareness of the social, political, and economic messages coming at them from the popular media. The authors pointed out that these messages are largely ignored, and adolescents' desires to deal with them are not accommodated in formal classroom settings. This book provides model lessons incorporating media literacies in middle-level classrooms.

In sum, using the phrase *adolescent literacy* permits professionals to leave behind some of the baggage that secondary literacy and content literacy bring with them. It also highlights the role of the adolescent in the teaching and learning of literacy. However, we offer two cautionary points about this phrase. First, we do not wish the phrase *adolescent literacy* to become a new buzzword. We view the use of this phrase as a serious and sincere attempt to be positive and inclusive in teaching and researching with adolescents. Second, we recognize that simply focusing on adolescents will not address all issues involved in teaching and learning in secondary schools. Focusing on the secondary school as an institutional context and on the content areas as epistemological contexts in which adolescents learn and use literacy is just as important as is understanding how adolescents use literacy in their lives. Thus, we believe that teaching and researching with adolescents must continue to examine how the contexts of secondary schools and content areas shape how adolescents and their teachers use literacy to teach and learn.

WHAT CONSTITUTES BEST PRACTICES IN ADOLESCENT LITERACY?

Ecological ways of thinking emphasize relationships. An ecologist who takes up a plant thinks about how it relates with the surrounding soil, climate, wildlife, and so on. When planning possible interventions, ecologists keep in mind systems that embed living things. Thinking like an ecologist about best practices in adolescent literacy emphasizes how reading and writing relate with the world. Literacy events such as taking notes from a textbook or downloading information from the Internet are seen amid a web of prior instruction, social and economic opportunities, educational policies, personal decision making, and so on.

Ecological ways of thinking can help reinvent adolescent literacy for new times by shedding light on claims of best practice and what works (e.g., see Davidson & Koppenhaver, 1993; Mastropieri & Scruggs, 1997; Truscott & Watts-Taffe, 1998). To our way of thinking, any unqualified claim that an educational practice is effective is quite a bit like claiming that watering plants is effective: It depends. The value of watering plants depends on the circumstances. Similarly, the value of K–W–L, Reciprocal Teaching, Questioning the Author, sustained silent reading, study guides, and reading and writing workshops depends on how these fit the teaching-learning situation. Thus, we assert that the notion of best practice should be considered ecologically, focusing on relationships in particular settings.

One way to address best practices ecologically is to link specific promising practices with generally accepted principles of teaching and learning. For example, one of the general principles that IRA recently adopted to serve as touchstones for school programs is "Adolescents deserve access to a wide variety of materials that they can and want to read" (Moore et al., 1999, p. 101). This principle offers a base for deriving reader-friendly practices without sanctioning specific ones. For instance, commission members apparently knew that school-mandated sustained silent reading programs sometimes are counterproductive due to conflicting expectations and experiences among students, teachers, administrators, and community members. By expressing a general guiding principle regarding wide reading, members sought to generate relevant practices that fit local settings. Educators might derive from this principle the practice of school-mandated sustained silent reading, but they also might derive practices such as literature across the curriculum, book clubs, and book conferences. Linking practices with principles guides actions sensibly and is an ecologically sound way to handle claims of best practice and what works in adolescent literacy.

A second ecologically minded approach to best practices is to be critical consumers. Critical consumers situate recommendations, determining where they are coming from and where they would like us to go. Critical consumers continually question claims, analyzing, comparing, and evaluating what is said:

- Who says a practice is best; what is the philosophical orientation of the author?
- What is the basis for the claim; how is effectiveness determined?
- Who does the practice benefit; is it possible for everyone to gain all the time?
- When is the practice appropriate?
- What is the advantage of one over another?
- Do the authors address educators as professional decision makers or as assembly line workers?

A critical stance toward adolescent literacy recommendations is especially important because a teaching practice that seems effective for all ages might not be so. For instance, a noteworthy *1998 NAEP Reading Report Card* result is that U.S. fourth-grade students who read self-selected books in school on a daily basis averaged higher reading scores than those without such opportunities (National Assessment of Educational Progress, 1999). However, this outcome did not hold for students at Grades 8 and 12. This national-level finding complicates decisions regarding adolescent literacy programs and compels additional investigation.

Those involved with adolescent literacy deserve a closer look at daily self-selected reading in the upper grades—along with numerous other aspects of adolescent literacy—yet most well-funded literacy research involves children in the lower grades. Tremendous attention has been devoted to *Preventing Reading Difficulties in Young Children* (Snow, Burns, & Griffin, 1998), the National Academy of Science's compilation of research and policy recommendations that was the centerpiece of a reading summit in the U.S. Yet *Preventing Reading Difficulties* joins the earlier nationally sponsored reports of Adams's *Beginning to Read* (1990), the Center for the Study of Reading's *Becoming a Nation of Readers* (Anderson, Hiebert, Scott & Wilkinson, 1985) Chall's *Learning to Read: The Great Debate* (1983), and Bond and Dykstra's "The Cooperative Research Program in First Grade Reading Instruction" (1997) in ignoring adolescent readers. Additionally, the recently funded Center for the Improvement of

Early Reading Achievement (CIERA) concentrates on young children, although CIERA recently has initiated a strand of inquiry that examines reading achievement beyond the primary grades. Prominent programs for struggling readers such as Reading Recovery, Success for All, and the Kamehameha Project are for elementary-age children. We know of no comparably visible, well-documented, and well-supported efforts for adolescents.

It is important to realize that our profession tends to marginalize adolescent literacy. We educators need to keep our eyes open especially for adolescent literacy claims that are derived from work with young children. In brief, we need to be critical consumers, determining how well assertions about best practice fit our specific situations.

A final way an ecology of adolescent literacy helps consider assertions of best practice and what works involves interpersonal and personal dimensions. This perspective calls attention to the daily face-to-face interactions among individual adolescents, their teachers, and peers as they engage print; it addresses social–emotional climates. Directly addressing questions such as the following is important because adolescent literacy practices, such as literature discussion groups and study guides, play out differently in settings defined by the answers to these questions:

- Do classrooms display any passion for reading, writing, experiencing, and learning?
- Are expectations rigorous yet reasonable?
- Are individual learners' best interests foregrounded?
- Are reasons for teachers and learners committing themselves to literacy growth clear and convincing?
- Does a respectful and inviting community support self-expression?

Attention to the personal dimensions of literacy learning these questions address is crucial because they are wholly enmeshed with individuals' commitments and efforts. The most promising programs for struggling adolescent readers develop adolescents' personal resiliencies to factors limiting their academic success. These programs address literacy along with issues such as setting goals, resolving conflicts, staying within the law, and controlling alcohol and drugs. These programs enable teens to accommodate academic worlds with possible family, friendship, and community influences opposing the academy. They recognize potentially limiting forces such as work schedules and parenting responsibilities.

In sum, ecological ways of thinking can help reinvent adolescent literacy for ne times by leading educators to incorporate practices with principles, determine the fit of effectiveness claims with particular situations, and address interpersonal and personal dimensions of literacy. An ecological perspective promotes the assertion that adolescent literacy teaching and learning should be considered in a broad context.

HOW CAN THE NEEDS OF MARGINALIZED READERS BE MET IN NEW TIMES?

Marginalized readers are those who are not connected to literacy in classrooms and schools. Specifically, we identify as marginalized adolescents those who are not engaged in the reading and writing done in school; who have language or cultural practices different from those valued in school; or who are outsiders to the dominant group because of their race, class, gender, or sexual orientation.

The question of how to meet the needs of marginalized readers is an extremely important one not only for the present but also for the new times that are ahead. Our existing secondary literacy research does not fully address the demands of the diverse groups of students and communities educators serve. If we cannot address these new literacies and the increasing diversity that we encounter, then we may find that more and more students will struggle to be successful in school. The suggestions offered here are meant to reshape secondary classrooms to offer literacies that connect to students' lives and to reposition marginalized youth in classrooms and schools.

First, listen to and watch young people in a variety of spaces and contexts, looking for what they *can* do and for ways to bring that proficiency into the classroom. Often, kids who appear to struggle in the classroom are completely different people outside of the classroom. Youth who sit slumped in their desks and scowl when prompted to read or write are often fluent in other languages; can navigate cities with ease; can relate specific scientific information learned from television or from field trips; and can weave together cultural tales, classic children's literature, and colorful family stories. For example, as part of a year-long study of two English classrooms, Moje, Willes, & Fassio (in press) attended a number of students' out-of-school activities. One evening the teacher, Debra Willes, accompanied Moje to an African American dance and drumming troupe performance in which two of the students performed. Willes and Moje were stunned to see one of the students, Mark, a young man who was considered by many teachers at the school to have an attention deficit, perform with intense concentration throughout the entire event.

As a result of this experience, Willes and Moje began to think carefully about how the classroom was structured and whether the teaching practice was in part responsible for Mark's struggles. They did not turn to new strategies for addressing his struggles; instead, they asked questions about the strategies offered in the classroom. They asked, for example, why Mark had abandoned a story about African American drumming after only one draft. This experience with Mark, for example, allowed them to bring the specialized cultural and musical knowledge that Mark possessed into a subsequent class discussion in ways that showed Mark that others valued his experience and that allowed him to extend his knowledge. Thus, rather than only building students' prior knowledge so that they can comprehend the texts presented to them, educators can begin with adolescents' funds of knowledge (Moll, 1994; Velez-Ibanez, 1988). This requires, however, that educators expand their knowledge of students by spending time with adolescents outside of classrooms.

Interdisciplinary project-based pedagogies are another way to support the literacy learning of marginalized students. Projects engage young people in group-based inquiry about questions or problems of interest to them. Typical features of project-based curricula include (a) driving questions that encompass worthwhile and meaningful content anchored in real-world problems; (b) investigations and artifact creation that allow students to learn concepts, apply information, and represent knowledge; (c) collaboration among students, teachers, and others in the community; and (d) use of technological tools (Krajcik, Blumenfeld, Marx, Bass, & Fredricks, 1998). Such approaches provide opportunities for discourse and represent an excellent way to learn content, especially for kids who struggle with print or who are not engaged in school learning (Marx, Blumenfeld, Krajcik, & Soloway, 1997). Most project-based approaches also build in community-based research and the communication of what kids have learned to real audiences (Mercado, 1993; Roseberry & Warren, 1998).

Many people wonder whether such approaches will really teach young people, especially those who struggle with print, to read and write. This is a fair and important question. There is little in project-based pedagogy itself that specifically teaches reading and writing. Indeed, Krajcik et al. (1998) have raised questions about how to support students as they navigate project work, which is heavily dependent on multiple texts and on disciplinary and everyday discourse (see also Goldman, 1997). But as Guthrie et al. (1996) illustrated, content literacy strategies can be integrated into project-based approaches to support youth as they learn about new concepts and unfamiliar content (cf. Palincsar & Magnusson, in press). Thus, projects can provide a frame for content literacy strategies, a frame that allows young people to learn both learning strategies and content related to the authentic or essential questions that are of interest to them.

Interdisciplinary projects help to focus students and provide opportunities for young people who struggle with print to learn one concept in different ways (Hutchinson & Suhor, 1996). The student who does not understand a scientific concept when reading a scientific text may understand the concept if framed in literature or in the context of history. And acknowledging that each discipline has a unique set of social practices and accompanying discourses—ways of reading, writing, speaking, listening, believing, and acting—points to the usefulness for students to explore one concept from the perspective of different disciplines (Gee, 1996).

For example, Mark, the young man mentioned previously, could have engaged with a group of students in a cross-curricular project on music and history, a project that would have built on his existing knowledge, but also engaged him in new learning as he sought to answer questions about connections among the histories of various musical forms. With literacy strategies woven into the projects, Mark could have learned new content that built on his funds of knowledge, while also learning new skills to strengthen his reading and writing. Such a project could be integrated into music, history, mathematics (the mathematics of musical forms), science, English, art, and physical education courses. All students, and especially those who are at the margins in our classrooms, can benefit from opportunities to engage in deep, sustained research throughout the school day on questions of interest to them and their communities.

Our final recommendation is that we should draw from the texts adolescents value and offer them multiple forms of representation. Texts that young people choose, materials such as comic books or teen-zines, engage them (Alvermann et al., 1999). Many marginalized readers, especially those with learning disabilities, become so frustrated with their struggles to read that they give up or become resistant to reading traditional texts. But even marginalized readers and writers often read popular texts with fluency and enthusiasm. What's more, popular cultural and media texts are especially engaging with these readers and writers because they often include other kinds of representation (drawings, cartoons, comics, videos, icons). Students can also use alternative forms to represent their understandings of and meanings made from different content texts, which can enhance assessment of the knowledge that marginalized readers and writers construct from classroom work (cf. Eisner, 1994; Epstein, 1994). Mark, for example, was very interested in rap, jazz, and African drumming music. Such popular texts could bring Mark into the conversation and further develop his reading and writing skills.

Although we recommend using popular texts, it is important not to romanticize them. Such texts may be meaningful to students, but that does not mean that these texts should be invited uncritically into classrooms. Like print texts, these can be racist, classist, and sexist (cf. hooks, 1994), but that does not mean that teachers should avoid using them. We believe that even when texts, whether popular culture or classic texts, present images that reproduce negative stereotypes or practices the texts can be used productively, both to engage students and to raise questions about the way society works. The importance of questioning texts connects to the final issue raised in this commentary: the role of critical literacy in adolescents' classrooms and lives.

SHOULD CRITICAL LITERACY BE PART OF OUR CLASSROOMS?

During the last decade, the term *critical literacy* has had multiple meanings. Perhaps the common meaning implies the use of higher order thinking—mental operations that involve inferring, reasoning, and problem solving. Another use of the term *critical literacy* comes from Paulo Friere's (1970) work. He and his followers believed that literacy empowers people when it encourages them to actively question the social world and work toward social justice and equality. These two meanings inform our perspective on critical literacy. We also draw upon social linguistics (Fairclough, 1992; Gee, 1996) and critical perspectives such as feminist (Davies, 1993; Gilbert, 1997), critical (Apple, 1986), and poststructural (Foucault, 1975/1977; Luke, 1995/1996) theories.

Critical perspectives suggest a world of unequal power and resource distributions. Due, in part, to these unequal distributions, critical theorists reject the notion that objective and neutral productions and interpretations of texts are possible (Commeyras, 1994). Critical perspectives also assume that there is systematic privilege for certain groups of people based on their ethnicity, race, gender, and social class.

Based on these perspectives, critical literacy refers to an explicit awareness that the language of texts and readers' responses to texts are ideologically charged (Kempe, 1993). School texts are one means of enacting privilege. In other words, an author's language implicitly or explicitly produces certain meanings that tend to support particular social relations and institutions. Likewise, readers' responses to texts are informed by their past experiences as people of a particular gender, race, ethnicity, age, and social class. Critical literacy practices, therefore, involve the interrogation of texts to uncover the ideologies operating in them; they also involve the interrogation of the relationships among texts, readers, and the wider society in which ideologies are embedded (Fairclough, 1992; Freebody, Luke, & Gilbert, 1991).

The aim of critical literacy instruction is to enable readers to question texts and see how they provide selective versions of the world (Jongsma, 1991). Critical literacy activities examine how the language in spoken and written texts produces and reproduces race, ethnicity, social class, and gender positions. To illustrate how critical literacy practices can be used in adolescent classrooms we examine perspectives on gender and offer accompanying pedagogical practices.

Feminine and masculine practices are constructed in and through textual practices (Walkerdine, 1990). These practices become common sense and appear natural as they are constantly repeated (Butler, 1990; Gilbert, 1997; West & Zimmerman, 1987). Think for a moment: Are all boys naturally brave, athletic, and heroic? Are girls naturally more gentle and caring than boys? From a critical perspective, the answer to these questions is no; the language of texts often constructs femininity and masculinity in these rigid, stereotypical ways. Because these practices were constructed over time, they can be deconstructed.

Critical literacy opens up possibilities for adolescents to explore how their gender identities are defined by the language of texts and, in turn, how their constructions of gender influences their interpretations of texts. It provides a framework in which adolescents can explore the language that constructs and maintains dominant practices of femininity and masculinity; it makes visible the choices adolescents have for constructing their own gendered identities.

Specific critical literacy activities are necessary if readers are to become aware of how texts construct their gender identities in stereotypical ways (Gilbert, 1997). These activities range in purpose from recognizing sexist language in TV commercials or magazine advertisements; to noticing the inequitable representations of men and women in books or movies; to seeking to break down the stereotypic positioning of men and women (Gilbert, 1997); to determining whose version of reality is presented and whose is excluded (Lankshear & Knobel, 1997). Critical literacy activities might include close textual and linguistic analyses. For instance, one activity could be comparing the verbs selected to represent male and female athletes in newspaper articles. Articles about male athletes often contain more action verbs, while articles about female athletes contain more linking and passive verbs (Kempe, 1993). In this way, masculinity is constructed as more active than femininity. By comparing the verbs, students can identify how the author's word choice affects the way gender is constructed in texts.

Having students participate in critical literacy activities is not the same as forcing attitudinal change. Critical literacy activities are designed to make available space for students to consider multiple meanings and constructions of gender (Martino, 1995). Critical literacy activities can teach readers to resist "the power of print" (Janks, 1993, p. iii) and not to simply accept everything they read. Once they become aware of how texts manipulate them, adolescent students can become critical consumers and producers of text who challenge dominant meanings and realize that there is more than one way to read texts and their world. This is hard work, but it is work that could lead to a more fair and just world.

ON REINVENTING ADOLESCENT LITERACY FOR NEW TIMES

Our comments in the preceding sections are based on a deep respect for adolescents and on a conviction that their literacy needs for new times are complex and demanding. We are advocating a challenging, responsive literacy curriculum that puts adolescents first, yet one that pushes adolescents to learn new things, to have new experiences, and to read their worlds in new ways. This curriculum differs from the student-centered approaches often recommended because it urges adolescents to stretch their thinking beyond their immediate backgrounds and experiences while honoring those backgrounds and experiences.

Many teachers, teacher educators, and university researchers have expressed concerns that state and local literacy standards might limit them from facilitating the kind of challenging, responsive teaching and learning presented here. A concern over the potentially oppressive nature of standards is understandable because standards can easily become a way to deprofessionalize and control educational practice. But if standards are used as guides for instruction rather than assessments for outcomes, then they can be useful (Cunningham, 1999).

Consider, for example, how doctors, dentists, lawyers, and clinical psychologists use standards. They (not politicians) develop and approve professional guidelines for their actions. If an outcome of their practice is unfavorable but the standards of good practice are followed, then these professionals are not liable for malpractice. Because these professionals are held responsible for applying the appropriate standards of their practice, they devote considerable attention to constructing and reconstructing the practices and to developing their proficiencies with them so that, for example, doctors can be responsive to their patients and serve them as they prevent, diagnose, and address health issues. In the same way, educators can use state and national standards as guidelines rather than dicta for generating challenging, responsive literacy teaching for adolescents. We offer this analogy not to promote a medical model of educational practice, but rather to promote a *professional* model of practice.

Our conversations among the panelists and with the audience at the 1999 IRA convention pointed to the need for teachers and researchers who work with adolescents to take action, to become politically oriented and more vocal, as we engage in work with adolescent literacy. It is time for educators to take a strong stand about adolescent literacy and assume the lead in developing and implementing practices that respond to the ever-changing needs of adolescents in schools, and that prepare them to be active participants in the world.

REFERENCES

Adams, M. J. (1990). *Beginning to read. Thinking and learning about print.* Cambridge, MA: MIT Press.

Alvermann, D. E., Hinchman, K. A., Moore, D. W., Phelps, S. F., & Waff, D. R. (Eds.). (1998). *Reconceptualizing the literacies in adolescents' lives.* Hillsdale, NJ: Erlbaum.

Alvermann, D. E., Moon, J., & Hagood, M. (1999). *Popular culture in the classroom: Teaching and researching critical media literacy.* Newark, DE: International Reading Association/National Reading Conference.

Anderson, R. C., Hiebert, E., Scott, J. A., & Wilkinson, I. A. G. (1985). *Becoming a nation of readers: The report of the Commission on Reading.* Washington, DC: National Institute of Education.

Apple, M. (1986). *Teachers and texts: A political economy of class and gender.* London: Routledge.

Bean, T. W., Bean, S. K., & Bean, K. F. (1999). Intergenerational conversations and two adolescents' multiple literacies: Implications for redefining content area literacy. *Journal of Adolescent & Adult Literacy, 42,* 438–448.

Bond, G., & Dykstra, R. (1997). The cooperative research program in first grade reading instruction. *Reading Research Quarterly, 32,* 348–427. (Original work published 1967)

Butler, J. (1990). *Gender trouble: Feminism and the subversion of identity.* New York: Routledge.

Chall, J. (1983). *Learning to read: The great debate* (Rev. ed.). New York: McGraw Hill. (Original work published 1967)

Commeyras, M. (1994). Exploring critical thinking from a feminist standpoint: Limitations and potential. In C. K. Kinzer & D. J. Leu (Eds.), *Multidimensional aspects of literacy research, theory, and practice.* 43rd yearbook of the National Reading Conference (pp. 459–464). Chicago: National Reading Conference.

Cunningham, J. W. (1999). How can we achieve best practices in literacy instruction? In L. B. Gambrell, L. M. Morrow, S. B. Neuman, & M. Pressley (Eds.), *Best practices in literacy instruction* (pp. 34–45). New York: Guilford.

Davidson, J., & Koppenhaver, D. (1993). *Adolescent literacy: What works and why* (2nd ed.). New York: Garland.

Davies, B. (1993). *Shards of glass: Children reading and writing beyond gendered identities.* Cresskill, NJ: Hampton Press.

Eisner, E. W. (1994). *Cognition and curriculum reconsidered* (2nd ed.). New York: Teachers College Press.

Epstein, T. L. (1994). Sometimes a shining moment: High school students' representations of history through the arts. *Social Education, 58,* 136–141.

Fairclough, N. (1992). *Critical language awareness.* London: Longman.

Finders, M. J. (1998/1999). Raging hormones: Stories of adolescence and implications for teacher preparation. *Journal of Adolescent & Adult Literacy, 42,* 252–263.

Freebody, P., Luke, A., & Gilbert, P. (1991) Reading positions and practices in the classroom. *Curriculum Inquiry, 21,* 435–457.

Freire, P. (1970). *Pedagogy of the oppressed.* New York: Seabury Press.

Foucault, M. (1977). *Discipline & punish: The birth of a prison.* (A. Sheridan, Trans.). New York: Vintage. (Original work published 1975)

Gee, J. P. (1996). *Social linguistics and literacies: Ideology in discourses* (2nd ed.). Bristol, PA: Taylor & Francis.

Gee, J. P., & Green, J. L. (1998). Discourse analysis, learning, and social practice: A methodological study. In P. D. Pearson & A. Iran-Nejad (Eds.), *Review of research in education* (Vol. 23, pp. 119–170). Washington, DC: American Educational Research Association.

Gilbert, P. (1997). Discourses on gender and literacy. In S. Muspratt, A. Luke, & P. Freebody (Eds.), *Constructing critical literacies* (pp. 69–75). Cresskill, NJ: Hampton Press.

Goldman, S. R. (1997). Learning from text: Reflections on the past and suggestions for the future. *Discourse Processes, 23,* 357–398.

Gray, W. S. (1937). The nature and organization of basic instruction in reading. In G. M. Whipple (Ed.), *The teaching of reading: A second report.* 36th yearbook of the National Society for the Study of Education, Part I (pp. 65–131). Bloomington, IN: Public School Publication Company.

Guthrie, J. T., van Meter, P., McCann, A. D., Wigfield, A., Bennett, L., Poundstone, C. C., Rice, M. E., Faibisch, F. M., Hunt, B., & Mitchell, A. M. (1996). Growth of literacy engagement: Changes in motivations and strategies during concept-oriented reading instruction. *Reading Research Quarterly, 31,* 306–343.

Herber, H. L. (1970). *Teaching reading in content areas.* Englewood Cliffs, NJ: Prentice-Hall.

Hiebert, E. H., & Taylor, B. M. (in press). Beginning reading instruction: Research on early interventions. In M. Kamil, P. Mosenthal, P. D. Pearson, & R. Barr (Eds.), *Handbook of reading research: Volume III.* New York: Longman.

hooks, b. (1994). *Outlaw culture: resisting representations.* New York: Routledge.

Hutchinson, J., & Suhor, C. (1996). The jazz and poetry connection: A performance guide for teachers and students. *English Journal, 85,* 80–85.

Janks, H. (1993). *Language and power.* Johannesburg, South Africa: Hodder & Stoughton.

Jongsma, K. S. (1991). Critical literacy: Questions and answers. *The Reading Teacher, 44,* 518–519.

Kempe, A. (1993). No single meaning: Empowering students to construct socially critical readings of the text. *The Australian Journal of Language and Literacy, 16,* 307–322.

Krajcik, J., Blumenfeld, P. C., Marx, R. W., Bass, K. M., & Fredricks, J. (1998). Inquiry in project-based science classrooms: Initial attempts by middle school students. *The Journal of the Learning Sciences, 7,* 313–350.

Lankshear, C., & Knobel, M. (1997). Critical literacy and active citizenship. In S. Muspratt, A. Luke, & P. Freebody (Eds.), *Constructing critical literacies: Teaching and learning textual practice* (pp. 95–124). Cresskill, NJ: Hampton Press.

Luke, A. (1995/1996). Text and discourse in education: An introduction to critical discourse analysis. In M. W. Apple (Ed.), *Review of research in education* (Vol. 21, pp. 3–48). Washington, DC: American Educational Research Association.

Luke, A., & Elkins, J. (1998). Reinventing literacy in "new times." *Journal of Adolescent &Adult Literacy, 42,* 4–7.

Martino, W. (1995). Deconstructing masculinity in the English classroom: A site for reconstituting gendered subjectivity. *Gender and Education, 7,* 205–220.

Marx, R. W., Blumenfeld, P. C., Krajcik, J. S., & Soloway, E. (1997). Enacting project-based science. *The Elementary School Journal, 97,* 341–358.

Mastropieri, M. A., & Scruggs, T. E. (1997). Best practices in promoting reading comprehension in students with learning disabilities 1976–1996. *Remedial and Special Education, 18,* 197–213.

Mercado, C. (1993). Researching research: A classroom-based student-teacher-researchers collaborative project. In A. Ambert & M. Alvarez (Eds.), *Puerto Rican children on the mainland: Interdisciplinary perspectives* (pp. 167–192). New York: Garland.

Moje, E. B., Willes, D. J., & Fassio, K. (in press). Constructing and negotiating literacy in a writer's workshop: Literacy teaching and learning in the seventh-grade. In E. B. Moje & D. G. O'Brien (Eds.), *Constructions of literacy: Studies of literacy teaching and learning in secondary classrooms and schools.* Mahwah, NJ: Erlbaum.

Moll, L. C. (1994). Literacy research in community and classrooms: A sociocultural approach. In R. B. Ruddell, M. R. Ruddell, & H. Singer (Eds.), *Theoretical models and processes of reading* (4th ed., pp. 179–207). Newark, DE: International Reading Association.

Moore, D. W., Bean, T. W., Birdyshaw, D., & Rycik, J. A. (1999). Adolescent literacy: A position statement. *Journal of Adolescent & Adult Literacy, 43*, 97–112.

Mosenthal, P. P. (1998). Reframing the problems of adolescence and adolescent literacy: A dilemma-management perspective. In D. E. Alvermann, K. A. Hinchman, D. W. Moore, S. F. Phelps, & D. R. Waff (Eds.), *Reconceptualizing the literacies in adolescents' lives* (pp. 325–352). Hillsdale, NJ: Erlbaum.

National Assessment of Educational Progress. (1999). *NAEP 1998 reading report card for the nation* [Online]. Available: http://www.ed.gov/NCES/NAEP [1999, March].

Palincsar, A. S., & Magnusson, S. J. (in press). The interplay of first-hand and text-based investigations to model and support the development of scientific knowledge and reasoning. In D. Klahr & S. Carver (Eds.), *Cognition and instruction: 25 years of progress.* Mahwah, NJ: Erlbaum.

Rosebery, A. S., & Warren, B. (1988). *Boats, balloons, and classroom video: Science teaching as inquiry.* Portsmouth, NH: Heinemann.

Snow, C. E., Burns, M. S., & Griffin, P. (Eds.). (1998). *Preventing reading difficulties in young children.* Washington, DC: National Academy Press.

Truscott, D. M., & Watts-Taffe, S. (1998). Literacy instruction for second-language learners: A study of best practices. In T. Shanahan & F. V. Rodriguez-Brown (Eds.), *National Reading Conference yearbook 47* (pp. 242–252). Chicago: National Reading Conference.

Vacca, R. T. (1998). Foreword. In D. E. Alvermann, K. A. Hinchman, D. W. Moore, S. F. Phelps, & D. R. Waff (Eds.), *Reconceptualizing the literacies in adolescents' lives* (pp. xv–xvi). Hillsdale, NJ: Erlbaum.

Velez-Ibanez, C. G. (1988). Networks of exchange among Mexicans in the U.S. and Mexico: Local level mediating responses to national and international transformations. *Urban Anthropology, 17*, 27–51.

Walkerdine, V. (1990). *Schoolgirl fictions.* London: Verso.

West, C., & Zimmerman, D. (1987). Doing gender. *Gender and Society, 1*, 125–151.

Effective Literacy Instruction for Adolescents

DONNA E. ALVERMANN

EXECUTIVE SUMMARY

The National Reading Conference (NRC) recognizes the importance of continuing literacy instruction beyond the elementary grades, especially for students at the middle and high school level. In commissioning this paper on *Effective Literacy Instruction for Adolescents*, the NRC acknowledges the complexities of reading in relation to writing and oral language in an array of 21st century media environments, of which print is a part. The term *adolescent literacy*, broader in scope than secondary reading, is also more inclusive of what young people count as texts (e.g., textbooks, digital texts, hypertexts). Many adolescents of the Net Generation find their own reasons for becoming literate—reasons that go beyond reading to acquire school knowledge of academic texts. This is not to say that academic literacy is unimportant; rather, it is to emphasize the need to address the implications of youth's multiple literacies for classroom instruction. The following statements represent NRC's position on keeping adolescents' interests and needs in mind when designing effective literacy instruction at the middle and high school level.

- Adolescents' perceptions of how competent they are as readers and writers, generally speaking, will affect how motivated they are to learn in their subject area classes (e.g., the sciences, social studies, mathematics, and literature). Thus, if academic literacy instruction is to be effective, it must address issues of self-efficacy and engagement.

- Adolescents respond to the literacy demands of their subject area classes when they have appropriate background knowledge and strategies for reading a variety of texts. Effective instruction develops students' abilities to comprehend, discuss, study, and write about multiple forms of text (print, visual, and oral) by taking into account what they are capable of doing as everyday users of language and literacy.

■ Adolescents who struggle to read in subject area classrooms deserve instruction that is developmentally, culturally, and linguistically responsive to their needs. To be effective, such instruction must be embedded in the regular curriculum and address differences in their abilities to read, write, and communicate orally as strengths, not as deficits.

■ Adolescents' interests in the Internet, hypermedia, and various interactive communication technologies (e.g., chat rooms where people can take on various identities unbeknown to others) suggest the need to teach youth to read with a critical eye toward how writers, illustrators, and the like represent people and their ideas—in short, how individuals who create texts make those texts work. At the same time, it suggests teaching adolescents that all texts, including their textbooks, routinely promote or silence particular views.

■ Adolescents' evolving expertise in navigating routine school literacy tasks suggests the need to involve them in higher level thinking about what they read and write than is currently possible within a transmission model of teaching, with its emphasis on skill and drill, teacher-centered instruction, and passive learning. Effective alternatives to this model include participatory approaches that actively engage students in their own learning (individually and in small groups) and that treat texts as tools for learning rather than as repositories of information to be memorized (and then all too quickly forgotten).

EFFECTIVE LITERACY INSTRUCTION FOR ADOLESCENTS

More often than not in the United States, newspaper headlines and feature stories on national television networks focus on early literacy instruction and the so-called reading wars between advocates of direct skills instruction and those who favor more holistic approaches to teaching young children to read print text. As a result, adolescents and their specialized needs for literacy instruction at the middle and high school level often go unnoticed by policy makers and the general public. This is indeed unfortunate. Although the neglect of older readers might signal that all is well in the area of adolescent literacy instruction, such is not the case. Despite the work of conscientious teachers, reading supervisors, curriculum coordinators, and principals in middle schools and high schools across the country, young people's literacy skills are not keeping pace with societal demands of living in an information age that changes rapidly and shows no sign of slowing.

Equally demanding of adolescents and their teachers are the higher standards for reading achievement set as a consequence of policies enacted during the previous two decades of school reform. Although data collected on trends in reading achievement for 13-year-olds and 17-year-olds show that achievement levels have not declined between 1971 and 1999 (in fact, the average score for 13-year-olds was higher than that in 1971) (U.S. Department of Education, 2000), the percentages of students in grades 8 and 12 who are performing at or above the *basic* level (e.g., comprehending primarily factual information) are 74 and 77 percent, respectively. In grade 8, fewer than 3 percent of the students can analyze and extend information, which is required for reading at an *advanced* level. In grade 12, fewer than 6 percent of the students can read at an *advanced* level (U.S. Department of Education, 1999a). The percentages are similar for achievement levels in writing for students in grades 8 and 12 (U.S. Department of Education, 1999b). Simply put, *basic* level literacy is insufficient in today's world where both reading and writing tasks required of adolescents are continuing to increase in complexity and difficulty. As argued in the International Reading Association's position statement on adolescent literacy, "adolescents deserve instruction that builds both the skill and desire to read increasingly complex materials" (Moore, Bean, Birdyshaw, & Rycik, 1999, p. 5)

Literacy and reading, though related, are neither synonymous nor unambiguous terms. Typically reading is subsumed by literacy, with the latter term used to refer to reading, writing, and other modes of symbolic communication that are often valued differently by people living in different social and economic structures and holding different political views. Simply broadening the definition, however, does not alleviate the ambiguity; nor does it adequately describe the terms in question. Reading is too complex a process to refer to it simply as decoding alphabetic print or making meaning of text. To read critically, one must go beyond asking "What does this text mean?" to asking "How does it come to have a particular meaning (and not some other)?" Similarly, literacy is more than school literacy. The privileging of one form of literacy (academic literacy) over multiple other forms (e.g., computer, visual, graphic, and scientific literacies) has been criticized for ignoring the fact that different texts and social contexts (reading for whom, with what purpose) require different reading skills (Barton, Hamilton, & Ivanic, 2000; Gee, 1996; Street, 1995).

Effective literacy instruction for adolescents acknowledges that all uses of written language (e.g., studying a biology text, interpreting an online weather map, and reading an Appalachian Trail guide) occur in specific places and times as part of broader societal practices (e.g., formal schooling, searching the Internet, and hiking). Typically it is the case that book reading is privileged in middle and high school classrooms. This privileging elevates the importance and value of academic reading but tells teachers little about their students' everyday uses of language and literacy. Effective instruction builds on elements of both formal and informal literacies. It does so by taking into account students' interests and needs while at the same time attending to the challenges of living in an information-based economy during a time when the bar has been raised significantly for literacy achievement.

The situation grows considerably more tense, however, when the general public becomes convinced that a literacy crisis exists or is imminent. Worried that educators are not holding up their end of the bargain, parents and policy makers are understandably quick to respond. Among other things, a search begins for the "best" way to teach adolescents to read and study the print-based texts their teachers assign. Unfortunately, what starts out as a quest for better instruction sometimes ends up looking more like a search for the proverbial "skills-in-a-box solution" (Schoenbach, Greenleaf, Cziko, & Hurwitz, 1999, p. 7). Teachers are wary of quick fixes and the twin notion that one-size-instruction fits all. Moreover, they sense that such approaches fail to take into account the multiple literacies young people living in the 21st century already possess or are in need of developing.

The remaining sections of this paper offer a situated view of effective literacy instruction for adolescents in the middle and high school grades. Specifically, five statements grounded in current literacy research and school-based inquiry precede more fully developed descriptions of the warrants for each claim. Although the resulting descriptions are but snapshots of the research available on any given topic, their aim is to focus attention on the varied literacy interests and needs of older readers in relation to what is known about effective literacy instruction for adolescents.

Self-Efficacy and Engagement

Adolescents' perceptions of how competent they are as readers and writers, generally speaking, will affect how motivated they are to learn in their subject area classes (e.g., the sciences, social studies, mathematics, and literature). Thus, if academic literacy instruction is to be effective, it must address issues of self-efficacy and engagement.

The potency of one's beliefs about the self is phenomenal. In adolescence as in earlier and later life, it is the belief in the self (or lack of such belief) that makes a difference in how competent a person feels. Although the terms *self-concept* and *self-efficacy* are sometimes used interchangeably in the research literature, they actually refer to different constructs. For example, an adolescent may have a good self-concept of herself as a reader, but her answer "Not very" to the question "How confident are you that you can comprehend a primary source on the Battle of Gettysburg?" would indicate low self-efficacy for that particular task. A statement of self-concept is domain specific, whereas self-efficacy is task specific. Moreover, the two constructs need not relate to one another. For instance, an adolescent boy may feel highly efficacious in American Literature class yet experience few if any positive feelings of self-worth, partially due to the fact he may not value excelling in this subject area (Pajares, 1996).

Perceptions of self-efficacy are central to most theories of motivation, and the research bears out the hypothesized connections. For example, providing adolescents who are experiencing reading difficulties with clear goals for a comprehension task and then giving feedback on the progress they are making can lead to increased self-efficacy and greater use of comprehension strategies (Schunk & Rice, 1993). As well, creating technology environments that heighten students' motivation to become independent readers and writers can increase their sense of competency (Kamil, Intrator, & Kim, 2000). The research is less clear, however, on the shifts that occur in students' motivation to read over time. Although decreases in intrinsic reading motivation have been noted as children move from the elementary grades to middle school, explanations vary as to the cause, with a number of researchers attributing the decline to differences in instructional practices (Eccles, Wigfield, & Schiefele, 1998; Oldfather & McLaughlin, 1993).

In an extensive review of how instruction influences students' reading engagement and academic performance, Guthrie and Wigfield (2000) concluded that various instructional practices, while important, do not directly impact student outcomes (e.g., time spent reading independently, achievement on standardized tests, performance assessments, and beliefs about reading). Instead, the level of student engagement (including its sustainability over time) is the mediating factor, or avenue, through which classroom instruction influences student outcomes. Guthrie and Wigfield's conception of the engagement model of reading calls for instruction that fosters: student motivation (including self-efficacy and goal setting); strategy use (e.g., using prior knowledge, self-monitoring for breaks in comprehension, and analyzing new vocabulary); growth in conceptual knowledge (e.g., reading tradebooks to supplement textbook information, viewing videos, and hands-on experiences); and social interaction (e.g., collaborating with peers on a science project, and discussing an Internet search with the teacher).

Other research on effective literacy instruction has shown that teachers contribute to adolescents' sense of competence and self-worth when they are able to convince them that they care about them as individuals and want them to learn (Dillon, 1989). It is also the case that teachers' perceptions of students' motivations to learn influence how hard they are willing to work to instill in them a sense of competence and self-worth. For example, Patrick Finn (1999), an educator born into a working-class Irish Catholic family on the south side of Chicago, has devoted a lifetime to exploring teachers' perceptions of working-class adolescents and what those perceptions mean in terms of the education students receive. According to Finn, there are two kinds of education in the United States: "First, there is empowering education, which leads to powerful literacy, the kind of literacy that leads to positions of power and authority. Second, there is domesticating education, which leads to functional literacy, or literacy that makes a person productive and dependable, but not troublesome" (pp. ix–x). Students also seem aware of distinctions in the quality of education offered them, and some are speaking out, as in the case of one young woman who was overheard telling a roomful of high school teachers:

> We know we aren't very well educated. We know there are things we should know by now that we don't. But we're not stupid; most of us are really smart. You just need to show us, break it down for us, work with us and expect us to do it (Schoenbach et al., 1999, p. 10).

Thus, by all accounts, it is the strength of one's belief in the ability of the self to tackle a particular task that affects whether or not (and how well) the task will be performed. The young woman speaking to the roomful of high school teachers perceived that she and others in her same situation were capable of learning if teachers were willing to work with them and hold their feet to the fire, so to speak. Although attending to issues of self-efficacy is certainly a start in the right direction, it takes a sustained level of student engagement and teacher support over a long period of time to meet the demands of subject matter learning.

Demands of Academic Literacy

Adolescents respond to the literacy demands of their subject area classes when they have appropriate background knowledge and strategies for reading a variety of texts.

Effective instruction develops students' abilities to comprehend, discuss, study, and write about multiple forms of text (print, visual, and oral) by taking into account what they are capable of doing as everyday users of language and literacy.

The expectation that effective literacy instruction should address the demands that various subject area classes place on adolescents is fueled by the perceived need to develop students' abilities to comprehend and think critically about multiple forms of text related to the school curriculum. Tied to this perception of academic literacy is the research finding that comprehension is indeed a complex process—one that should not be left to chance for its development. Members of the National Reading Panel (NRP) (2000) concluded that seven types of comprehension strategies met their strict criteria for effectiveness in an evidence-based assessment of the experimental and quasi-experimental research on reading. The panel's findings, which were based primarily on research conducted in grades 3–8, suggest that the following strategies are effective ways of teaching comprehension in the middle grades, and possibly beyond:

- *Comprehension monitoring*—knowing when understanding falters or breaks down and which "fix-up" strategies to apply (e.g., rereading, reasoning the matter through, and using cues from the sentence/paragraph's organizational structure).
- *Cooperative learning*—engaging with peers in problem-solving activities or to share ideas through peer-led discussions.
- *Using graphic and semantic organizers (including story maps)*—representing ideas by combining words, symbols, and lines to organize information.
- *Answering questions*—providing responses to teachers' questions and receiving feedback on responses.
- *Generating questions*—asking questions of one's self to understand various aspects of a text.
- *Using text structure*—developing an awareness of how a writer organizes information to assist readers in recalling the content of a selection.
- *Summarizing*—integrating ideas and generalizing information across one or more texts.

The importance of vocabulary knowledge to subject matter comprehension has been recognized since the 1920s (Whipple, 1925). Although the NRP reported research trends that suggest vocabulary instruction does facilitate comprehension, it drew no conclusions as to the most effective method or combination of methods, partly due to the large number of variables represented and the small number of studies that met the panel's criteria for analysis. Among the trends cited were those that found using computer-assisted vocabulary instruction was more effective than traditional methods; listening to others read was a way of enhancing students' incidental vocabulary knowledge; and preteaching vocabulary in assigned materials facilitated comprehension.

Caution needs to be taken generally in interpreting the NRP's findings. The report did not include research on second language reading and reading to learn in subject-specific areas. Nor did it include studies using qualitative research designs, the absence of which severely limits what can be known about the contexts in which instruction occurred. Moreover, six of the seven comprehension strategies considered effective were ones that teachers would use if they believe the reading process typically consists of students working individually to extract information from print texts. This rather narrow view of comprehension instruction risks disenfranchising students who may learn better in more socially interactive settings or whose literacies (e.g., visual and computer) span a broader range than those typically emphasized in school literacy.

In addition to providing strategy instruction, effective teachers ensure that students have adequate background information and relevant hands-on experience as ways of preparing them to read a textbook, view a video, or listen to a tape on content particular to their subject areas (Alexander & Jetton, 2000). Effective teachers look for ways to integrate reading and writing as often as possible because they know that each process reinforces the other and can lead to improved comprehension and retention of subject area content (Tierney & Shanahan, 1991). They also make room for student-generated visual, oral, and written texts in an effort to provide adolescents with opportunities to weave their own experiences, feelings, and interests into various learning activities. Through hypermedia projects, peer-led discussions and journal writing, adolescents find ways to make textbook reading and studying less "dry" or boring. At the same time, teachers learn from student-generated texts about adolescents' everyday literacies and the competencies they exhibit when reading, talking, and writing about things that matter to them (Knobel, 1999; Wade & Moje, 2000).

In recapping what is involved in meeting the literacy demands of subject area learning, it is useful to emphasize the centrality of teaching students to comprehend and think critically about different kinds of print and nonprint texts, including those that are student generated, visual, oral, or digital in nature. Providing instruction in vocabulary development and in one or more of the comprehension strategies found to be effective by the National Reading Panel is one way of meeting the demands of academic literacy, but it is not foolproof. Too little is known yet about the efficacy of these strategies when used with second language readers or with students whose literacies do not dovetail with those stressed in academic settings.

Struggling Readers and Their Needs

Adolescents who struggle to read in subject area classrooms deserve instruction that is developmentally, culturally, and linguistically responsive to their needs. To be effective, such instruction must be embedded in the regular curriculum and address differences in their abilities to read, write, and communicate orally as strengths, not as deficits.

The *struggling reader* label is a contested term and one that means different things to different people. It is sometimes used to refer to youth with clinically diagnosed reading disabilities as well as to those who are English language learners (ELLs), "at-risk," underachieving, unmotivated, disenchanted, or generally unsuccessful in school literacy tasks that involve print-based texts. As such, these labels tell very little about the reader, though they do suggest ways of thinking about culture and adolescents, who, for whatever reason, are thought to be achieving below their "full potential" as readers. The research on struggling readers covers a broad spectrum and varies in specificity according to the perceived reasons behind the struggle. For example, reviews of research that take into account individuals with clinically diagnosed reading disabilities (Shaywitz et al., 2000) focus on the cognitive basis for the struggle. Reviews of second language reading, on the other hand, encompass a much wider view of the reasons behind the struggle. In fact, the difficulties ELLs experience are often spread over a vast array of sociocultural, motivational, and linguistic factors that vary with the population being studied (Bernhardt, 2000; Jiménez, Garcia, & Pearson, 1996). These same factors are often manifested in the difficulties monolingual adolescents experience when a reading problem is present.

One framework through which to examine literacy instruction for struggling adolescent readers is known as the culture-*as*-disability perspective. This perspective finds support in the writings of anthropologists McDermott and Varenne (1995) and a group of interdisciplinary scholars with an interest in literacy who call themselves the New London Group (1996). Proponents of this perspective argue that skills instruction for adolescents who struggle with reading is necessary but insufficient. What is needed, they say, is greater access to teachers who understand that the manner in which schools promote certain normative ways of reading texts is, in effect, disabling some of the very students deemed most in need of help. Viewed from the culture-*as*-disability perspective, society (for the problem does not lie solely with schools) is seen as *making* struggling readers out of some adolescents who for any number of reasons have turned their backs on school literacy. This perspective assumes that all cultures, as historically evolved ways of doing life, teach people about what is worth working for, how to succeed, and who will fall short. To McDermott and Varenne's (1995) way of thinking, "cultures offer a wealth of positions for human beings to inhabit" (p. 336). Each position requires certain things. For example, to inhabit the position of "good reader" (or "struggling reader"), a person must possess certain abilities that are verifiable and recognizable to others who occupy that same position or who have the authority to fill it. McDermott and Varenne challenge us to consider the possibility that culture arranges for certain types of students to take up the position of struggling reader by institutionalizing a set of school-related tasks on which they will be measured and found to come up short. In their words,

> It takes a whole culture of people producing idealizations of what everyone should be and a system of measures for identifying those who fall short for us to forget that we collectively produce our disabilities and the discomforts that conventionally accompany them. (McDermott & Varenne, 1995, p. 337)

The instructional implications of the culture-*as*-disability perspective are considerable. For example, when teachers conceive of adolescents who struggle with subject area reading assignments as being part of the same cloth from which good readers come, they may begin to question what they had assumed to be stable (though arbitrary) sets of literacy tasks. They may observe the struggling readers in their classes with new eyes, as Elizabeth Moje and her colleagues (Moje, Willes, & Fassio, 2001) did. They may look for reading and writing proficiencies that qualify under a different set of literacy tasks (e.g., Moje et al. adapted the way they had structured writing workshops to be more inclusive of students who had previously avoided sharing time).

Teachers may also begin to question the fairly common practice of allowing struggling readers to rely on them, rather than on the assigned texts, as a source of information. Often it is a matter of simply expecting struggling readers to use their texts and then supporting them in their attempts to do so. For example, in research conducted as part of the Strategic Literacy Network, Ruth Schoenbach and her colleagues (Schoenbach et al., 1999) found that teachers who had earlier shelved their course textbooks in despair of students ever reading them were able to reintroduce the texts once students were taught comprehension strategies and gained greater confidence in themselves as readers.

Culturally responsive instruction also extends English language learners' opportunities to learn by connecting home, community, and school literacy practices. The importance of building on students' home language and culture has been documented repeatedly in the literature. For example, a cultural modeling approach to teaching has been shown to be effective in motivating underachieving African American high school students to read book-length novels and engage in fairly sophisticated levels of literary analysis. This approach, which built on students' cultural knowledge and personal experiences, fostered an intellectual community in the classroom that sustained interest in reading and discussing texts over an entire school year (Lee, 2001).

Similarly, a series of carefully documented studies, known collectively as the "cultural funds of knowledge project," have shown that Latino/a students are motivated to engage in school literacy tasks when the gap between school and the home/community environment is bridged. Teachers in this project double as ethnographers. They visit the working-class homes of their students' families for the purpose of tapping into cultural and linguistic resources that can be used to make their classroom literacy instruction more relevant. In addition to documenting as false the various and sundry claims about working-class, language minority homes providing little in the way of background knowledge and experiences that is useful for literacy development in a second language, teachers leave the project with positive shifts in attitude and considerable information with which to revamp their instruction (García, 2000; Moll & González, 1994). Because culturally responsive instruction need not match home, community and school literacies in grid-like precision, teachers come away with what Au (2000) described as a heightened sensitivity of the need to connect *patterns* of participation and home/community values with the regular curriculum. Although teachers need not be "insiders" in a particular culture to engage in culturally responsive instruction (Au, 2000; Ladson-Billings, 1994), they can learn about that culture, respect its values, and view differences in students' literacies as strengths, not deficits.

To argue for culturally responsive instruction, then, is to call for teaching that takes into account everyday, patterned interfaces between home/community and school literacy practices. This kind of teaching taps into struggling readers' funds of knowledge, encourages them to use their textbooks and other texts as sources of information, and supports such usage through strategy instruction. In short, engaging in culturally responsive literacy instruction is an important hedge against losing the race while attempting to reach struggling readers through a skills-only approach to teaching.

Critical Literacy

Adolescents' interests in the Internet, hypermedia, and various interactive communication technologies (e.g., chat rooms where people can take on various identities unbeknown to others) suggest the need to teach youth to read with a critical eye toward how writers, illustrators, and the like represent people and their ideas—in short, how individuals who create texts make those texts work. At the same time, it suggests teaching adolescents that all texts, including their textbooks, routinely promote or silence particular views.

The Internet figures prominently in the lives of American adolescents, sometimes referred to as the Net Generation (Tapscott, 1998). According to a phone survey of 754 teenagers and 754 of their parents reported by Pew Internet and American Life Project in conjunction with a week-long online discussion group study conducted by the research firm Greenfield Online (Lenhart, Rainie, & Lewis, 2001), 17 million youths between the ages of 12 and 17 use the Internet. This number represents 73% of the young people in that age bracket. Moreover, close to 13 million adolescents use instant messaging (with one-quarter of that number saying that they pretend to be different people when online). The idea that literacy is reinventing itself through new digital technologies (Luke & Elkins, 1998) has enormous implications for teachers at the middle and high school level, as does the fact that these new technologies are fundamentally and irreversibly affecting how ideas get represented in texts and communicated (de Castell, 1996).

Everyday literacy practices are changing at an unprecedented pace, and speculation as to the impact of interactive communication technologies and multimedia on current conceptions of reading and writing is evident on many fronts. At the center of much of the discussion is the perceived need to develop adolescents' critical awareness of how all texts (print, visual, and oral) position them as readers and viewers within different social, cultural, and historical contexts. This is not a call for the type of critical literacy instruction that would have students searching for the villains or heroes in their texts, for the oppressors or emancipators amongst us, and the general labeling of oppositional categories such as "us" and "them" (Morgan, 1997). As Morgan pointed out, doing away with these overly simplistic categories would give teachers and students alike the opportunity to "develop a different view of how people may act, provisionally, at a particular time and within particular conditions" (p. 26). For teachers, the implications of this perspective on critical literacy might translate instructionally into purposes such as these:

- To motivate students to explore the assumptions that authors/video artists/web page designers/cartoonists, and so on may have been operating under when constructing their messages.
- To facilitate students' thinking about the decisions computer users in chat rooms make (and why) when it comes to choice of words, content, topics included (or excluded), and interests served.
- To encourage multiple readings of the same text from different perspectives (e.g., an ecology text on water resources read from the perspectives of a scientist,

a swimmer, a shrimp boat captain, a homeowner, a Greenpeace activist, and a politician).

Working within a hypermedia environment, however, teachers might need to vary their instructional purposes to accommodate its special qualities. The term *hypermedia*, which is an amalgam of *hypertext* and *multimedia* (Semali & Pailliotet, 1999), refers to the links that readers simultaneously make between computer windows and a mix of media texts, such as sounds, images, words, movies, and the like. Jay Bolter (1991), a literacy expert in hypertext applications, observed that above all else, this medium challenges the notion that any single text represents an author's complete, separate, or unique expression. Taking Bolter's observation into account when teaching for critical literacy awareness with hypertext could conceivably lead to addressing questions such as the following:

- Are hypertext readings privileged in ways that traditional (linear) readings are not? For example, do hypertexts allow readers to make multiple interpretations of what they read with greater ease than do traditional texts? If so, what might be the consequences of this privileging? What kind of reader would stand to benefit? Who might fail to benefit?

- How does hypertext create opportunities for readers to manipulate information in ways that are unavailable to them in print-based media? What are the trade-offs in working within such an environment?

The extent to which the Internet, hypermedia, and other new technologies effectively support literacy teaching and learning in classrooms is unknown. There is little empirical research on the topic generally, and even less that applies specifically to instruction at the middle and high school level (Kamil, Intrator, & Kim, 2000; National Reading Panel, 2000). A related issue is the paucity of available research sites given that so few schools have integrated the new technologies into their curricula (Leu, 2000). Still, from the work that has been done (and synthesized by Kamil et al., 2000; Leu, 2000), there is promising evidence of the effectiveness of literacy instruction that integrates print and visual texts (e.g., hypermedia, hypertext, the Internet, and interactive CD-ROMS). This is especially the case among populations of second-language readers. There is also evidence that adolescents are making valuable reading-writing connections in their bid to communicate in a computer-mediated world (e.g., Beach & Bruce, in press; Beach & Lundell, 1998; Horney & Anderson-Inman, 1994).

Moreover, researchers working within a qualitative paradigm have found patterns in their data to suggest that adolescents who appear most "at risk" of failure in the academic literacy arena are sometimes the most adept at (and interested in) understanding how media texts work, and in particular, how meaning gets produced and consumed. For example, O'Brien (1998, 2001) found in a 4-year study of working-class adolescents deemed "at risk" of dropping out of high school that students were quite successful in producing their own electronic texts, such as multimedia documentaries, and critiquing media violence using multiple forms of visual texts. Working alongside the students and their teachers in what came to be called the Jeff Literacy Lab, O'Brien observed that when printed texts were not privileged over other forms of literacy, the students appeared capable and literate. This finding is similar to one that Alvermann and her colleagues (Alvermann, 2001; Alvermann et al., 2000) reported based on an after-school study of 30 adolescents who participated in a 15-week Media Club project. Although the participants had scored in the lowest quartile on a standardized reading achievement test, they capably demonstrated their critical awareness of how a variety of popular media texts represent people, ideas, and events. They also engaged in literacy practices of their own choosing (what they called their "freedom activities"). These activities included, among other things, searching the Internet for song lyrics, reading Japanese animé online, e-mailing knowledgeable others to obtain information on favorite rap groups, and producing hair and fashion magazines. Activities such as these, along with numerous other examples in *Intermediality: The Teachers' Handbook of Critical Media Literacy* (Semali & Pailliotet, 1999), point to young people's interest in working with diverse symbol systems within various media and digital environments.

Without critical literacy instruction that is sensitive to youth's and adults' needs, however, little may be gained from venturing into these environments. For example, in a study of two girls' out-of-school instant messaging (IM) practices, Lewis and Fabbo (2000) documented the girls' intricate manipulations of friends and social situations as the two adolescents simultaneously went about constructing their own identities, seemingly with little critical awareness for how the chat/IM technology might be manipulating them and their literacy practices. Adults who worry about young people's identity constructions vis-à-vis the new technologies would do well to examine the parallels and disjunctures between their own such constructions and those of adolescents (Hagood, Stevens, & Reinking, in press; Lewis & Finders, in press). For in doing so, they may come to understand better the futility of asking young people to critique the very texts they find most pleasurable. For such a request, as Luke (1997) has adroitly noted, would likely "cue a critical response which can often be an outright lie. . .[because while youth] are quick to talk a good anti-sexist, anti-racist, pro-equity game. . .what they write in the essay or what they tell us in classroom discussion is no measure of what goes on in their heads" (p. 43).

In sum, adolescents of the Net Generation often find their own reasons for becoming literate—reasons that go beyond reading to acquire school knowledge or mastery of academic texts. This is not to say that academic literacy is unimportant; rather, it is to emphasize the need to address the implications of youth's multiple literacies for classroom instruction, especially in regard to reading and writing with a critical eye.

Participatory Approaches to Instruction

Adolescents' evolving expertise in navigating routine school literacy tasks suggests the need to involve them in higher level thinking about what they read and write than is currently possible within a transmission model of teaching, with its emphasis on skill and drill, teacher-centered instruction, and passive learning. Effective alternatives to this model include participatory approaches that actively engage students in their own learning (individually and in small groups) and that treat texts as tools for learning rather than as repositories of information to be memorized (and then all too quickly forgotten).

The teacher-centered transmission model of instruction is common to most subject area classrooms in the United States (Bean, 2000; Wade & Moje, 2000). Although it is often impugned for its lock-step approach to literacy learning and for emphasizing subject matter coverage (with little depth) over more authentic activities for engaging adolescents in learning academic content, the widespread use of this model at the high school level (and to a lesser extent at the middle school level) suggests reasons for its existence. One frequently cited justification for its use is the need to address pressures coming from outside the classroom, such as accountability in meeting curriculum standards and preparing students for statewide assessments. However, pressures within the classroom to maintain order, regulate socialization patterns, and meet the constraints of time and resource availability also contribute to the transmission model's longstanding use among subject area teachers (Alvermann & Moore, 1991; Hinchman & Zalewski, 1996).

Participatory approaches to literacy instruction are no less concerned with content mastery than is the transmission model. However, rather than emphasize the teacher's role in transmitting facts and concepts (often through lecturing), participatory approaches support adolescents' academic literacy development by incorporating classroom structures that promote peer interaction (e.g., peer-led literature discussions and reading/writing workshops) and interaction with a more knowledgeable other (e.g., scaffolded instruction whereby a teacher supports student learning and then gradually withdraws that support as students show they are capable of assuming more responsibility for their own learning). Reading apprenticeship is an example of scaffolded instruction. Its primary goal is to show adolescents "what goes on behind the curtain of expert reading" (Schoenbach et al., 1999, p. 21) by demystifying the comprehension process. Central to this approach is what is known as the "metacognitive" conversation, which is an ongoing interactive discussion between teachers and students about personal reading goals, problem-solving strategies for making sense of text, and the resources available for building knowledge beyond the text.

A distinguishing feature between participatory approaches to classroom instruction and the transmission model of teaching is the role of the text in students' learning. In transmission classrooms, texts (like teachers) are viewed as dispensers of knowledge, whereas in participatory classrooms, students use texts as *tools* for learning and constructing new knowledge. The range of texts used in these different classrooms also varies. In transmission classrooms, subject matter textbooks are often the *de facto* curriculum; in participatory classrooms, a mix of textbooks, magazines, student-generated texts, hypermedia productions, visuals, and so on are used to support and extend the curriculum (Wade & Moje, 2000).

Differences also exist that are not so readily recognized between these two approaches to instruction. Researchers who have conducted studies of actual classroom practice maintain that it is rarely the case that one can draw definitive lines separating participatory from transmission model classrooms. For example, as Pearson

(1999) has noted, teaching approaches that seem theoretically opposed, or contradictory on the surface, often support one another in actual classroom practice. A case in point—repeated several times over in the studies Moore (1996) reviewed on contexts for literacy instruction at the middle and high school level—is the finding that teachers' knowledge and beliefs about the goals that should drive literacy instruction, plus the availability of resources, influence how a particular approach is used. Thus, a participatory approach such as peer-led discussion did not necessarily look the same in different teachers' classrooms. Neither did a more teacher transmission-like discussion look the same across classrooms. In fact, often the two types of discussion were used to support one another in the same classroom over a period of time. What mattered in each instance was a teacher's knowledge and beliefs about the goals of a particular approach and the resources available to support those goals.

Adolescents' beliefs and knowledge about different approaches to literacy instruction also vary with the context. In a multi-case study of adolescents' perceptions of classroom discussion at five sites across the United States (Alvermann et al., 1996), students in classrooms favoring mostly the transmission model of literacy instruction held strong views about their role as learners. In those rooms, discussions often reflected the teacher's emphasis on learning facts and covering the content rather than on students interacting with each other to construct new knowledge based on those facts. When students believed a topic was meaningless or a task unchallenging, they did not comply with the teacher's instructions to discuss the text in small groups. In their view, the topic and/or task did not merit a collaborative effort. Rather than discuss the topic as a group, students often divided it into smaller parts, with each one working independently on his or her part to produce a written response—very much like they would do had the task required them to answer questions at the end of a chapter. On the other hand, when a group of seventh graders engaged in a classroom project that required them to use several software authoring tools to construct their own hypermedia documents for a poetry unit, discussions flowed (Myers, Hammett, & McKillop, 2000). Seated around computers, they debated how, when, and why to bring together various kinds of texts (e.g., graphics, sounds, video excerpts, and electronic text); they made suggestions that would improve each other's work; and they (rather than the teacher) decided the criteria for effectively communicating their ideas.

The differences reflected here are about much more than the two approaches to literacy instruction just discussed might suggest. They echo a larger debate in the field of education, and increasingly the public sector as well. Briefly, this debate centers on the degree to which teacher-centered instruction is superior (or inferior) to more student-centered instruction. The question most often raised is whether or not participatory approaches that engage youth in project-based learning "will really teach young people, especially those who struggle with print, to read and write" (Moje, Young, Readence, & Moore, 2000, pp. 9–10). It is a fair and important question, as Moje et al. noted, especially given that project-based instruction, such as software authoring of hypermedia documents, rarely focuses specifically on teaching reading and writing. In part, the answer to that question rests with how much one believes that meaningful content learning displaces literacy teaching. It would be false to claim that there are no tradeoffs. For example, project-based learning that motivates students to use their literacy skills to solve real-world problems is of little value if such skills are unavailable or at a level of development insufficient for completing a project. On the other hand, adolescents who possess the requisite literacy skills for learning content area material may not apply those skills if they are bored or unmotivated by teacher-centered instruction. Of course, nowhere is it written that one approach must prevail at the expense of the other.

SUMMARY

Effective literacy instruction for adolescents must take into account a host of factors, including students' perceptions of their competencies as readers and writers, their level of motivation and background knowledge, and their interests. To be effective, such instruction must be embedded in the regular curriculum and make use of multiple forms of texts read for multiple purposes in a variety of learning situations. Because many adolescents of the Net Generation will find their own reasons for becoming literate—reasons that go beyond reading to acquire school knowledge or mastery of academic texts—it is important that teachers create sufficient opportunities for students to engage actively in meaningful subject matter projects that both extend and elaborate on the literacy practices they already own and value.

REFERENCES

Alexander, P. A., & Jetton, T. L. (2000). Learning from text: A multidimensional and developmental perspective. In M. L. Kamil, P. B. Mosenthal, P. D. Pearson, & R. Barr (Eds.), *Handbook of reading research* (Vol. 3, pp. 285–310). Mahwah, NJ: Erlbaum.

Alvermann, D. E. (2001). Reading adolescents' reading identities: Looking back to see ahead. *Journal of Adolescent & Adult Literacy, 44,* 676–690.

Alvermann, D. E., Hagood, M. C., Heron, A. H., Hughes, P., Williams, K. B., & Jun, Y. (2000). *After-school media clubs for reluctant adolescent readers.* Final report of grant #199900278 submitted to the Spencer Foundation. [On-line]. Available: http://www.spencer.org

Alvermann, D. E., & Moore, D. W. (1991). Secondary school reading. In R. Barr, M. L. Kamil, P. B. Mosenthal, & P. D. Pearson (Eds.), *Handbook of reading research* (Vol. 2, pp. 951–983). New York: Longman.

Alvermann, D. E., Young, J. P., Weaver, D., Hinchman, K. A., Moore, D. W., Phelps, S. F., Thrash, E. C., & Zalewski, P. (1996). Middle and high school students' perceptions of how they experience text-based discussions: A multicase study. *Reading Research Quarterly, 31,* 244–267.

Au, K. H. (2000). A multicultural perspective on policies for improving literacy achievement: Equity and excellence. In M. L. Kamil, P. B. Mosenthal, P. D. Pearson, & R. Barr (Eds.), *Handbook of reading research* (Vol. 3, pp. 835–851). Mahwah, NJ: Erlbaum.

Barton, D., Hamilton, M., & Ivanic, R. (Eds.) (2000). *Situated literacies.* New York: Routledge.

Beach, R., & Bruce, B. (in press). Using digital tools to foster critical inquiry. In D. E. Alvermann (Ed.), *Adolescents and literacies in a digital world.* New York: Peter Lang.

Beach, R., & Lundell, D. (1998). Early adolescents' use of computer-mediated communication in writing and reading. In D. Reinking, M. McKenna, L. Labbo, & R. Kieffer (Eds.), *Handbook of literacy and technology: Transformations in a post-typographic world* (pp. 323–341). Mahwah, NJ: Erlbaum.

Bean, T. W. (2000). Reading in the content areas: Social constructivist dimensions. In M. L. Kamil, P. B. Mosenthal, P. D. Pearson, & R. Barr (Eds.), *Handbook of reading research* (Vol. 3, pp. 629–654). Mahwah, NJ: Erlbaum.

Bernhardt, E. (2000). Second-language reading as a case study of reading scholarship in the 20th century. In M. L. Kamil, P. B. Mosenthal, P. D. Pearson, & R. Barr (Eds.), *Handbook of reading research* (Vol. 3, pp. 793–811). Mahwah, NJ: Erlbaum.

Bolter, J. D. (1991). *Writing space: The computer, hypertext, and the history of writing.* Hillsdale, NJ: Erlbaum.

de Castell, S. (1996). On finding one's place in the text: Literacy as a technology of self-formation. In W. F. Pinar (Ed.), *Contemporary curriculum discourses: Twenty years of JCT* (pp. 398–411). New York: Peter Lang.

Dillon, D. R. (1989). Showing them that I want them to learn and that I care about who they are: A microethnography of the social organization of a secondary low-track English classroom. *American Educational Research Journal, 26,* 227–259.

Eccles, J. S., Wigfield, A., & Schiefele, U. (1998). Motivation to succeed. In N. Eisenberg (Vol. Ed.), *Handbook of child psychology: Vol. 3, Social, emotional and personality development* (5th ed., pp. 1017–1095). New York: Wiley.

Finn, P. J. (1999). *Literacy with an attitude: Educating working-class children in their own self-interest.* Albany: State University of New York Press.

Garcia, G. E. (2000). Bilingual children's reading. In M. L. Kamil, P. B. Mosenthal, P. D. Pearson, & R. Barr (Eds.), *Handbook of reading research* (Vol. 3, pp. 813–834). Mahwah, NJ: Erlbaum.

Gee, J. P. (1996). *Social linguistics and literacies: Ideology in Discourses* (2nd ed.). London: Taylor & Francis.

Guthrie, J. T., & Wigfield, A. (2000). Engagement and motivation in reading. In M. L. Kamil, P. B. Mosenthal, P. D. Pearson, & R. Barr (Eds.), *Handbook of reading research* (Vol. 3, pp. 403–422). Mahwah, NJ: Erlbaum.

Hagood, M. C., Stevens, L. P., & Reinking, D. (in press). What do *they* have to teach *us*? Talkin' 'cross generations! In D. E. Alvermann (Ed.), *Adolescents and literacies in a digital world.* New York: Peter Lang.

Hinchman, K. A., & Zalewski, P. (1996). Reading for success in a tenth-grade global-studies class: A qualitative study. *Journal of Literacy Research, 28,* 91–106.

Homey, M. A., & Anderson-Inman, L. (1994). The electrotext project: Hypertext reading patterns of middle school students. *Journal of Educational Multimedia and Hypermedia, 3,* 71–91.

Jiménez, R. T., Garcia, G. E., & Pearson, P. D. (1996). The reading strategies of bilingual Latino/a students who are successful English readers: Opportunities and obstacles. *Reading Research Quarterly, 31,* 90–112.

Kamil, M. L., Intrator, S. M., & Kim, H. S. (2000). The effects of other technologies on literacy and literacy learning. In M. L. Kamil, P. B. Mosenthal, P. D. Pearson, & R. Barr (Eds.), *Handbook of reading research* (Vol. 3, pp. 771–788). Mahwah, NJ: Erlbaum.

Knobel, M. (1999). *Everyday literacies.* New York: Peter Lang.

Ladson-Billings, G. (1994). *The dreamkeepers: Successful teachers of African American children.* San Francisco: Jossey-Bass.

Lenhart, A., Rainie, L., & Lewis, O. (2001, June 20). *Teenage life online.* (Available at: http://www.pewinternet.org/reports/toc.asp?Report=36)

Lee, C. D. (2001). Is October Brown Chinese? A cultural modeling activity system for underachieving students. *American Educational Research Journal, 38,* 97–141.

Leu, D. J., Jr. (2000). Literacy and technology: Deictic consequences for literacy education in an information age. In M. L. Kamil, P. B. Mosenthal, P. D. Pearson, & R. Barr (Eds.), *Handbook of reading research* (Vol. 3, pp. 743–770). Mahwah, NJ: Erlbaum.

Lewis, C., & Fabbo, B. (2000). But will it work in the heartland? A response and illustration. *Journal of Adolescent & Adult Literacy, 43,* 462–469.

Lewis, C., & Finders, M. (in press). Implied adolescents and implied teachers: A generation gap for new times. In D. E. Alvermann (Ed.), *Adolescents and literacies in a digital world.* New York: Peter Lang.

Luke, A., & Elkins, J. (1998). Reinventing literacy in "New Times." *Journal of Adolescent & Adult Literacy, 42*, 4–7.

Luke, C. (1997). Media literacy and cultural studies. In S. Muspratt, A. Luke, & P. Freebody (Eds.), *Constructing critical literacies: Teaching and learning textual practice* (pp. 19–49). Cresskill, NJ: Hampton Press.

McDermott, R., & Varenne, H. (1995). Culture *as* disability. *Anthropology & Education Quarterly, 26*, 324–348.

Moje, E. B., Willes, D. J., & Fassio, K. (2001). Constructing and negotiating literacy in a seventh-grade writer's workshop. In E. B. Moje & D. G. O'Brien (Eds.), *Constructions of literacy: Studies of teaching and learning in and out of secondary schools* (pp. 193–212). Mahwah, NJ: Erlbaum.

Moje, E. B., Young, J. P., Readence, J. E., & Moore, D. W. (2000). Reinventing adolescent literacy for new times: Perennial and millennial issues. *Journal of Adolescent & Adult Literacy, 43*, 400–410.

Moll, L. C., & González, N. (1994). Critical issues: Lessons from research with language-minority children. *JRB: A Journal of Literacy, 26*, 439–456.

Moore, D. W. (1996). Contexts for literacy in secondary schools. In D. J. Leu, C. K. Kinzer, & K. A. Hinchman (Eds.), *Literacies for the 21st century: Research and practice* (45th Yearbook of the National Reading Conference, pp. 15–46). Chicago: National Reading Conference.

Moore, D. W., Bean, T. W., Birdyshaw, D., & Rycik, J. A. (1999). *Adolescent literacy: A position statement.* Newark, DE: International Reading Association.

Morgan, W. (1997). *Critical literacy in the classroom.* New York: Routledge.

Myers, J., Hammett, R., & McKillop, A. M. (2000). Connecting, exploring, and exposing the self in hypermedia projects. In M. A. Gallego &. S. Hollingsworth (Eds.), *What counts as literacy: Challenging the school standard* (pp. 85–105). New York: Teachers College Press.

National Reading Panel. (2000). *Report of the National Reading Panel.* Washington, DC: National Institute of Child Health and Human Development.

New London Group. (1996). A pedagogy of multiliteracies: Designing social futures. *Harvard Educational Review, 66*, 60–92.

O'Brien, D. G. (1998). Multiple literacies in a high-school program for "at-risk" adolescents. In D. E. Alvermann, K. A. Hinchman, D. W. Moore, S. F. Phels, & D. R. Waff (Eds.), *Reconceptualizing the literacies in adolescents' lives* (pp. 27–49). Mahwah, NJ: Erlbaum.

O'Brien, D. G. (2001, June). "At-risk" adolescents: Redefining competence through the multiliteracies of intermediality, visual arts, and representation. *Reading Online, 4*(11). Available: http://www.readingonline.org/newliteracies/lit_index.asp?

Oldfather, P., & McLaughlin, H. J. (1993). Gaining and losing voice: A longitudinal study of students' continuing impulse to learn across elementary and middle school contexts. *Research in Middle Level Education, 3*, 1–25.

Pajares, F. (1996). Self-efficacy beliefs in academic settings. *Review of Educational Research, 66*, 543–578.

Pearson, P. D. (1999). Foreword. In R. Schoenbach, C. Greenleaf, C. Cziko, & L. Hurwitz, *Reading for understanding* (pp. xi–xiii). San Francisco: Jossey-Bass.

Schoenbach, R., Greenleaf, C., Cziko, C., & Hurwitz, L. (1999). *Reading for understanding.* San Francisco: Jossey-Bass.

Schunk, D. H., & Rice, J. M. (1993). Strategy fading and progress feedback: Effects on self-efficacy and comprehension among students receiving remedial reading services. *Journal of Special Education, 27*, 257–276.

Semali, L., & Pailliotet, A. W. (1999). *Intermediality.* Boulder, CO: Westview.

Shaywitz, B. A., Pugh, K. R., Jenner, A. R., Fulbright, R. K., Fletcher, J. M., Gore, J. C., & Shaywitz, S. E. (2000). The neurobiology of reading and reading disability (dyslexia). In M. L. Kamil, P. B. Mosenthal, P. D. Pearson, & R. Barr (Eds.), *Handbook of reading research* (Vol. 3, pp. 229–249). Mahwah, NJ: Erlbaum.

Tapscott, D. (1998). *Growing up digital: The rise of the net generation.* New York: McGraw-Hill.

Tierney, R. J., & Shanahan, T. (1991). Research on the reading-writing relationship: Interactions, transactions, and outcomes. In R. Barr, M. L. Kamil, P. B. Mosenthal, & P. D. Pearson (Eds.), *Handbook of reading research* (Vol. 2, pp. 246–280). New York: Longman.

Street, B. V. (1995). *Social literacies: Critical approaches to literacy in development. ethnography. and educa-tion.* New York: Longman.

U.S. Department of Education. (1999a). *The NAEP 1998 reading report card for the nation and the states.* (NCES 1999-500, by P. L. Donahue, K. E. Voelkl, J. R. Campbell, and J. Mazzeo). Washington, DC: Office of Educational Research and Improvement. National Center for Education Statistics. Available: http://nces.ed.gov/nationsreportcard/pubs/main1998/1999500.asp

U.S. Department of Education. (1999b). *The NAEP 1998 writing report card for the nation and the states.* (NCES 1999-462, by E. A. Greenwald, H. R. Persky, J. R. Campbell, and J. Mazzeo). Washington, DC: Office of Educational Research and Improvement. National Center for Education Statistics. Available: http://nces.ed.gov/nationsreportcard/pubs/main1999/1999462.asp

U.S. Department of Education. (2000). *NAEP 1999 trends in academic progress: Three decades of student performance* (NCES 2000-469, by J. R. Campbell, C. M. Hombo, and J. Mazzeo). Washington, DC: Office of Educational Research and Improvement and National Center for Education Statistics. Available: http://nces.ed.gov/nationsreportcard/reading/trendsnational.asp

Wade, S. E., & Moje, E. B. (2000). The role of text in classroom learning. In M. L. Kamil, P. B. Mosenthal, P. D. Pearson, & R. Barr (Eds.), *Handbook of reading research* (Vol. 3, pp. 609–627). Mahwah, NJ: Erlbaum.

Whipple, G. (Ed.). (1925). *The twenty-fourth yearbook of the National Society for the Study of Education: Report of the National Committee on Reading.* Bloomington, IL: Public School Publishing Company.

INTEGRATING SOURCES

1. Choose any one of Alvermann's "five statements." How might Moje et al. react to it?

2. Moje and her colleagues complain that too little research has been conducted in the area of adolescent literacy. Their article appeared before the findings of the National Reading Panel were announced. Alvermann refers to these findings and presents many others as well. Do you believe that more research is needed? If so, along what lines should it be conducted?

3. Alvermann differentiates the transmission model from the participatory model of instruction. Which would Moje and her colleagues favor? What evidence tells you so?

CLASSROOM IMPLICATIONS

1. What role do the transmission model and the participatory model of instruction have in your own teaching? Is there room for both?

2. What advice can you now offer teachers of preadolescents (PreK-5) to help minimize the literacy problems later faced by adolescents?

3. What can be done to contend with the complications of diversity as they relate to the literacy growth of adolescents? Is diversity among students necessarily a concern or can it be a strength?

ANNOTATED BIBLIOGRAPHY

Brooks, M. (2001). Surviving the journey: Literature meets life. *ALAN Review, 28*, 64–65.
Discusses the positive role of adolescent literature in dealing with various social issues facing young people today.

Cartedge, G., & Kiarie, M. W. (2001). Learning social skills through literature for children and adolescents. *Teaching Exceptional Children, 34*, 40–47.
Encourages the learning of various types of positive social skills through a variety of classroom activities, using different types of adolescent literature materials.

Galda, L., & Beach, R. (2001). Theory and research into practice: Response to literature as a cultural activity. *Reading Research Quarterly, 36*, 64–73.
Reviews various ways in which the classroom teacher can effectively use adolescent literature as a means to *encourage* students to respond to their own cultural experiences in a positive manner.

George, M. A. (2001). What's the big idea? Integrating young adult literature in the middle school. *English Journal, 90*, 74–81.
Describes how three middle school teachers were able to integrate various forms of adolescent literature into the traditional curriculum.

Giorgis, C., & Johnson, N. J. (2001). The language of story. *Reading Teacher, 54*, 824–834.
Illustrates the meaning of the term *language of story* through the use of a variety of genres such as poetry, chapter books, picture books, and novels.

Kaywell, J. F. (2001). Preparing teachers to teach young adult literature. *English Education, 33*, 323–327.
Presents information on the preparation of preservice teachers in the area of the teaching of adolescent literature, based on guidelines developed by the National Council of Teachers of English.

Mitchell, D. (2001). Young adult literature and the English teacher. *English Journal, 90*, 23–25.
Explains how one teacher was able, through various personal experiences with a variety of adolescent literature books, to increase student involvement in effective reading activities.

Murphy, E. (2001). In search of literature for the twenty-first century. *English Education, 90*, 110–115.
Describes one teacher's development of a year-long adolescent literature curriculum based on current books dealing with issues appropriate to this age group.

Randale, K. D. (2001). Let it be hope. *English Journal, 90*, 125–130.
Encourages English and language teachers to select reading material that is not overly dark and depressing and, instead, use adolescent literature that reflects a theme of hope and encouragement.

Vasquez, V., Comber, B., & Nixon, H. (2001). Social worlds of adolescents living on the fringe. *Journal of Adolescent & Adult Literacy, 45*, 170–173.
Explores literature considered appropriate for those students who are experiencing social and educational problems of various types, and how the reading of adolescent literature can help some of these students.

YOU BECOME INVOLVED

The problem of adolescent literacy is complex and has stubbornly resisted numerous initiatives designed to alleviate it.

1. Were you to design a program for a single school, what would it look like? Specifically, what role (if any) would you assign to the following?
   a. remedial classes and reading specialists
   b. teacher inservice
   c. parent involvement
   d. technology applications
2. Explore Don Leu's collection of useful on-line sources and see if they broaden and refine your views on the problem: http://www.literacy.uconn.edu/adolit.htm

CHAPTER SEVEN

• • • • • ▬▬▬▬▬▬▬▬▬▬▬▬▬▬▬▬▬▬▬▬▬▬▬▬▬▬▬▬

WRITING

Composition is, for the most part, effort of slow diligence and steady perseverance, to which the mind is dragged by necessity or resolution.

—Samuel Johnson (1759)

I have just found out what makes a piece of writing good . . . it is making the sentences talk to each other as two or more speakers do in a drama. The dullness of writing is due to its being, much of it, too much like the too long monologues and soliloquies in drama.

—Robert Frost (1936)

. . . the classroom environment should reflect a living example of written language put to purposeful ends.

—Jo Ann Vacca et al. (2003)

CHANGES AND ISSUES IN WRITING

Few areas of literacy instruction have undergone more sweeping changes over the past 25 years than writing. Several important trends have characterized this period and have led to a transformation in the way educators have come to view the role of writing.

1. *Emphasis on process.* Insights into the approaches used by skilled writers have led to a refocusing of instruction from the final product to the process through which it was produced. Consequently, *process writing* instruction is now an everyday activity in many classrooms and at virtually every grade level. While authorities differ slightly on the nature of the stages, there is general agreement that they include the following: (1) drafting, (2) revising, (3) editing, (4) proofing, and (5) publishing. Nancie Atwell's approach to the "writers' workshop" has become

a popular means of facilitating children as they move through various stages of the writing process, but there are other viable approaches as well.

2. *Emphasis on learning.* It is now undisputed that writing can cause knowledge to become organized and coherent. Writing is for this reason now recognized as a means of reinforcing and extending learning (Myers, 1984) The phrases, *writing to learn* and *writing across the curriculum*, are testaments to its usefulness as a learning tool.

3. *Emphasis on reading.* The *reading–writing connection* has emerged as one of the more important insights of the twentieth century. Reading and writing are now viewed not as opposite processes, but as complementary activities. In particular, an early emphasis on writing facilitates learning to read (e.g., Adams, 1990). Through the years, important approaches to beginning reading instruction have made writing a central component. These include Montessori's techniques and the language experience approach. The success of a writing emphasis on the reading development of some children led Patricia Cunningham to make writing one of the "four blocks" in her own highly popular approach to language arts instruction (see Cunningham & Allington, 1999).

4. *Emphasis on word processing.* Word processing software is now firmly established in the workplace and is increasingly evident in classrooms. As David Reinking (1995) has put it, the most relevant instructional question will soon become not *whether* to incorporate word processing but *how* to incorporate it. Still, hardware limitations have meant that word processing, as an integral part of writing instruction, is a trend that is still in its early stages, particularly in elementary schools.

These trends, which together suggest a heightened interest in writing instruction, have given rise to a host of issues. The following list captures some of the more important controversies, though other issues could undoubtedly be added. Those that follow underscore just how difficult these issues tend to be.

1. *Time.* Granted, writing can help young children learn to read and can assist other children in organizing and solidifying what they learn. But writing takes time. What is the proper balance between classroom time devoted to writing activities and to other means of engaging learners? And what about the teacher's time? Given that children's writing must be *read*, how much writing can feasibly be assigned and evaluated?

2. *Attitudes.* Many children lack a natural inclination to engage in writing. In fact, studies suggest a steady worsening of attitudes toward writing into the secondary years (Kear, Coffman, & McKenna, 1997). Good writing is, after all, nearly always taxing, as our rather startling quotation from Samuel Johnson, one of the most gifted writers of the eighteenth century, clearly indicates. How can teachers effectively motivate their students to engage in meaningful writing?

3. *Assessment.* Evaluating writing is anything but straightforward. Rubric systems, consisting of descriptive rating scales devoted to various aspects of writing are now used extensively and help make the process systematic. However, many questions remain. What is the proper balance between assessing mechanics and content? How can the sensibilities of developing writers be spared the inhibiting effects of candid criticisms?

4. *Electronic transformation.* Word processing has already drastically altered the landscape of writing instruction, and changes are still under way. The use of spelling and grammar checkers, for example, can heavily support a student who is deficient in the mechanics of writing. Will the assessment of writing mechanics be permanently distorted by the use of these devices? As such devices become increasingly part of the preferred method of writing, both at home and in the workplace, does it matter that an individual's mechanical deficiencies may be remedied by their continual use? Moreover, such support extends well beyond mechanics. Access to a variety of electronic sources, such as encyclopedias and Internet documents, now makes copying and pasting from a variety of sources a simple matter. At what point do documents constructed in this way amount to plagiarism? For that matter, will plagiarism continue to have any real meaning in an electronic future? (For a provocative view that our traditional notions of plagiarism must give way, see Reinking [1996].) Finally, writing in electronic environments makes options available that have no place in traditional writing. For example, incorporating animation and hypertextual links to other documents are changing what it means to write. How must writing instruction change to accommodate these options?

AS YOU READ

Both of these articles trace aspects of writing instruction over a broad span of years. Michael Moore wrote his article specifically for this volume, and in it he traces various movements across the latter half of the twentieth century and up to the present. Sharon Sicinski Skeans focuses more specifically on the reading–writing connection. These questions should focus your reading:

1. What were the major trends in writing research, writing instruction, and writing assessment?
2. What future projections seem likely in these areas?
3. How did the reading–writing connection begin and how did it develop?
4. How does a think-link chart work? In what ways does it take advantage of the reading–writing connection?

REFERENCES

Adams, M. J. (1990). *Beginning to read: Thinking and learning about print.* Cambridge, MA: MIT Press.

Cunningham, P. M., & Allington, R. L. (1999). *Classrooms that work: They can all read and write* (2nd ed.). New York: Longman.

Johnson, S. (1759, January 6). *The Adventurer, No. 38.* In W. J. Bate, J. M. Bullitt, & L. F. Powell (Eds.), *The Yale edition of the works of Samuel Johnson. Volume II, The Idler and the Adventurer.* New Haven and London: Yale University Press.

Kear, D. J., Coffman, G. A., & McKenna, M. C. (1997, December). *Students' attitudes toward writing: A national survey.* Paper presented at the meeting of the National Reading Conference, Scottsdale, AZ.

Myers, J. W. (1984). *Writing to learn across the curriculum.* Bloomington, IN: Phi Delta Kappa.

Reinking, D. (1995). Reading and writing with computers: Literacy research in a post-typographic world. In K. A. Hinchman, D. J. Leu, & C. K. Kinzer (Eds.), *Perspectives on literacy research and practice: Forty-fourth yearbook of the National Reading Conference* (pp. 17–33). Chicago: National Reading Conference.

Reinking, D. (1996). Reclaiming a scholarly ethic: Deconstructing "intellectual property" in a post-typographic world. In D. J. Leu, C. K. Kinzer, & K. A. Hinchman (Eds.), *Literacies for the 21st century: Research and practice: Forty-fifth yearbook of the National Reading Conference* (pp. 461–470). Chicago: National Reading Conference.

Issues and Trends in Writing Instruction

MICHAEL T. MOORE

Those of us who lived through the early days of writing process/composition theory all have our own particular stories. We see this history through the lens of the contexts of our situations. As an English and reading teacher in the early seventies, it is amazing today to consider how inadequately prepared I was to teach writing. I can think of no course that even mentioned the teaching of writing in my undergraduate teacher preparation education. In retrospect, we intuited how to teach writing from our own university writing experiences. All of us had written reams of compositions and all of us had received each one back hideously scarred with red, and with each subsequent rewrite (when there were rewrites), there seemed to be less red. We were journeymen or apprentices. I learned about comma splices and fused sentences by making them as a freshman writer and having my errors pointed out to me along with an appropriate penance. As we grew adept in determining what was expected of us, we became better academic writers as evidenced by our only mildly scarred papers. The lessons we learned in red were the lessons that we passed along to our students when we became teachers. As a beginning classroom teacher I had no idea that I would live through a paradigm shift that would substantially change the way we conceptualize and teach writing. When I think back now, I am amazed at what we didn't know as a field when I started teaching, but what we now take for granted and that is part of every teacher education program. I didn't know about process, free writing, topic choice, multiple perspectives, multiple drafts, the effect of audience, the many ways writing could be assessed (holistic evaluation, primary trait scoring, the effect of audience on writing, peer editing, and portfolio assessment), the effect of topic on writing, or even the many kinds of writing that could exist in school. Little did I know of the trends that I would see develop from this shift in emphasis. The study of process over product would spawn the writing process movement, the Bay Area and National Writing Projects, workshop approaches to teaching writing, a reappraisal of revision in writing, and a new focus on assessing writing.

The first inkling that I had that change was in the wind for writing instruction (I assumed that writing was what students did to produce themes that were designed to answer our probing literary inquiries) was when I joined the National Council of Teachers of English in 1973 and read an article in the *English Journal* on journal

Printed here with the permission of the author.

writing and its implications for multiple drafts. This was the first time I had ever considered another form of writing that was not a formal essay. This was the same year that I became a graduate student and would remain a graduate student for the next eleven years. During this time I became a writing teacher at the middle school, high school, and college levels as well as a writing researcher.

A BRIEF HISTORY OF WRITING RESEARCH

Until the 1960s, the acknowledged view of teaching students to write stemmed from a "formalist" view of literature from the "New Critics." This group, including Robert Penn Warren, John Crowe Ransom, Allen Tate, and others, held that the meaning of a text could only be determined by a close reading. The text was the point of emphasis, not the writer or the circumstances of the text. Everything we needed to construct meaning was in a given text. This view wended its way from literary critics to college classrooms and soon to public school English curricula. Thus, writing for students meant that the text or written product was subject to the same kind of close reading of any text. Texts were subject to rigid structural guidelines in the four traditional modes of discourse: description, narration, exposition, and argument (Young, 1978).

This model for studying grammar grew from the "classical" model for schools. This model held that the importance of an education was to train one's memory and one's reasoning ability (Applebee, 1974). English itself held little interest as a subject, but grammar had two things going for it. Students had to learn rules and their practical application. Grammar became great preparation for college but not necessarily a college subject. Interestingly enough, 1874 marked the first time composition became a prescribed course at a university (Harvard), and English study as a discipline in our public schools marks its own beginnings in 1958 with funds from the Ford Foundation and righteous curricular squabbling from both the Modern Language Association and the National Council of Teachers of English (Applebee, 1974).

As a field matures, a worldview emerges from a collection of research studies, and this becomes the dominant view. Paradigm shifts occur when the previous stance is no longer tenable. A paradigm shift in the teaching of writing began in the early sixties. In 1963 Braddock, Lloyd-Jones, and Schoer, writing in *Research in Written Composition*, identified a list of 504 studies (two of these dealt with process), but no "worldview" emerged from this research as there was in literature study. What existed prior to 1962 was what Young (1978) called a concern with the composed product, the analysis of discourse, a general preoccupation with the essay form and the term paper. These studies, reviewed by Braddock et al. (1963), focused on curricula, textbook making, rhetoric, teaching by television, writing vocabulary, handwriting, typewriting, among others. Thus, North (1987) dates the birth of modern Composition (with a capital *C*), to 1963 and Braddock's, Lloyd Jones' and Schoer's review of written composition research to date. In the next ten years a distinct shift in stance would be very apparent in Janet Emig's *The Composing Process of Twelfth Graders*, James Moffett's *Teaching the Universe of Discourse*, Donald Murray's *A Writer Teaches Writing*, Peter Elbow's *Writing Without Teachers*, and Ken Macrorie's *Telling Writing*.

Also in this time period, NCTE began plans for the bulletin soon to become the journal, *Research in the Teaching of English*, to be edited by Richard Braddock and N. S. Blount. This new journal became a forum for composition research (Gere, 1985). Cooper and O'Dell (1978) in *Research on Composing: Points of Departure*, their sequel to *Research in Written Composition*, asked researchers to begin to consider new methodologies to examine not methodology and product but of composition first. Cooper and O'dell challenged researchers to examine writing competence, categorizing diverse pieces of discourse, successful writing practices, observations of competent writing teachers, cross-disciplinary approaches to studying writing, and what new methods or procedures would best be suited for studying these questions.

Kuhn (1970) calls a "paradigm" a system of widely held beliefs, values, or supporting elements that form a discipline or a worldview. In *The Structure of Scientific Revolutions*, Kuhn (1996) called into question the standard view of science. This new view critically examined previous approaches and encouraged new interpretations of previous research and new research that would consider new approaches. By 1973, writing research now had the theoretical underpinnings to explode in several new directions, most notably in process and assessment. Cooper & O'dell's challenge clearly signaled the end of the previous paradigm and the ushering in of a new paradigm in teaching writing.

WRITING AS A PROCESS

I, personally, have always dated the beginning of the process writing approach at 1971 with the publication of Janet Emig's dissertation, *The Composing Process of Twelfth Graders*. North (1987) called it "the single most influential piece of Researcher inquiry—and maybe *any* kind of inquiry—in Composition's short history" (p. 197). Emig's study was a venture away from product examination and a focus on how writers actually wrote. Emig's study spawned a plethora of similar studies that looked at college writers, children learning to write, the causes of writing failure, and the role of the teacher, as well as a number of other studies where the focus was the writer. Emig's study also served to condemn public school writing instruction, which she called "a neurotic activity" (p. 99). She wittily observes further,

> A species of extensive writing that recurs so frequently in student accounts that it deserves special mention is the five-paragraph theme, consisting of one paragraph of introduction . . . three of expansion and example . . . and one of conclusion. This mode is so indigenously American that it might be called the Fifty-Star Theme. In fact, the reader might imagine behind this and the next three paragraphs Kate Smith singing "God Bless America" or the piccolo obligato from "The Stars and Stripes Forever" (p. 97).

I encountered Emig's work in 1973 as a graduate student and first-year middle grades teacher. She described the writing process as both "laminated and recursive" and said that there was a "blending" among identifiable writing behaviors she had observed of "planning, starting, stopping" and so on. Over the next thirty years, composition research on process would flourish to the extent that now most universities support composition studies as its own discipline. Writing research is published regularly in both liberal arts and education venues. The Bay Area, then later The National Writing Project, were partially funded by the federal government. Writing across the curriculum as a movement has been with us almost as long as research on composing. However, old habits die hard, and although "process" is known to most teachers, a regular observer of schools might note that a thirty-year lag continues to exist between research and practice (Burhans, 1983). One does not have to travel far to find that the five-paragraph theme is alive and well, and indeed flourishing, in our nation's schools.

One of the earliest process-writing gurus on the scene was Donald Murray, and I was especially influenced by *A Writer Teaches Writing* (1968). Although this book has undergone at least three editions, I have always found his first edition to clearly conceptualize what we mean by process. Murray later crystallized the process as "Collect, Plan, Develop" (Murray, 1985), but it is in his description of the writer's seven skills that I began to understand what Emig was referring to as a "recursive process." Murray's Seven Skills were: [a writer] "discovers a subject, senses an audience, searches for specifics, creates a design, writes, develops a critical eye, and rewrites" (pp. 2–12). Although missing from subsequent editions, these seven skills became the way I understood process to work and what it might mean for a new teacher. The term *recursive* means that we are not quite sure when anything is happening. A writer might be developing a topic at any time, including when he/she is developing a critical eye or editing. Editing itself might be occurring as the writer is discovering a topic or sensing an audience. The purpose of instruction shifted from teacher to student. The implications for instruction were that writing was about student choice. Students wrote to clarify and understand their own thinking. Writing no longer was formal only and personal and narrative forms of writing were encouraged. Multiple drafts became part of the process and we kept student writing in writing portfolios, a device borrowed from artists.

James Moffett published *Teaching the Universe of Discourse* in 1968 and, with B. J. Wagner, *A Student Centered Language Arts Curriculum, Grades K–13: A Handbook for Teachers* in 1983. Moffett proposed a highly interactive curriculum that stressed drama, writing for different audiences, peer review, and editing and adaptation over formal writing assessment. Moffett also wrote about the reading–writing connection. Moffett observed the "role of the teacher, then, is to teach the students to teach each other" (p. 196). Moffett put his theory into practice by publishing the highly controversial "Interaction" series through Houghton Mifflin. This series was an integrative curriculum that promoted trade books using real literature and students responding to literature through a process approach. This series actually led to rioting in Kanawha County, West Virginia. This account is chronicled by Moffett (1989) in *Storm in the Mountains: A Case Study of Censorship, Conflict, and Consciousness.*

Today, the writing process is characterized as events (not always agreed upon) that involve talking, reading, planning, idea generating, detail generating, collaborating, drafting, editing, reenvisioning, proofing, sharing, publishing, responding, and revisiting. Students choose their own subjects, they become part of a community of writers, they write to explore, they have something to say to us and to each other, and they publish what they write. Standard Five in the IRA/NCTE *Standards for the English Language Arts* (1996) reads: "Students employ a wide range of strategies as they write and use different writing process elements appropriately to communicate with different audiences for a variety of purposes. Unfortunately, in too many writing classrooms the emphasis is still on the product and on each student's achieving one purpose only: to learn to write academically acceptable exposition." Traditions die hard in education.

OUTGROWTHS OF THE WRITING PROCESS MOVEMENT: THE BAY AREA WRITING PROJECT AND THE NATIONAL WRITING PROJECT

Tracing its roots directly to the outgrowth of writing/composition theory was the 1974 inception of the Bay Area Writing Project (Bay Area Writing Project Web site) in the Graduate School of the University of California at Berkeley. The Bay Area Writing Project would later become the flagship site of the National Writing Project. Writing projects abound and are firmly entrenched as summer institutes in most states. A teacher-teaching-teachers model is used, in collaboration with a university writing program. The Bay Area Project's stated goals are:

- To improve student writing abilities by improving the teaching and learning of writing in Bay Area schools.
- To provide professional development programs for classroom teachers.
- To expand the professional roles of teachers.
- To increase the academic achievement of the Bay Area's diverse student population (Bay Area Writing Project Web site).

The Bay Area Project, like the National Writing Project, embraces the following principles:

- Writing is fundamental to learning in all disciplines.
- Writing deserves constant attention from kindergarten through university.
- Teachers are the key to educational change.
- The best teacher of teachers is another teacher.
- Effective literacy programs are inclusive, reaching all teachers in order to reach all students.
- Universities and schools accomplish more in partnership.
- Exemplary teachers of writing write and use writing themselves.
- Excellent professional development is an ongoing process. (Bay Area Writing Project Web site)

Each year close to 4,000 teachers participate in the Bay Area Project alone. Different sites set their own programs, but among the areas of focus are: process, theory, workshop approaches, writing across the curriculum, emergent writing, publishing student writing, and coaching models for teaching writing, among other strategies. At each project, teachers learn to teach writing by first becoming writers themselves. Teachers become immersed in all aspects of the process and become convinced (as they will soon convince their own students) that they are real writers with all the rights and privileges thereof.

WRITING ACROSS THE CURRICULUM/ WRITING IN THE DISCIPLINES

The WAC/WID movement is a broadly based pedagogical practice that grew from the process movement. Most WAC/WID programs began in the 1980s as an outgrowth of the writing process movement and were started on university campuses across the country. Although not as widely based in public schools, WAC/WID programs hold the premise that writing is important in all academic areas, not just composition classes. Additionally, students use writing as a bridge from what is known to what one expects to learn, and writing is a means of making sense of a discipline. Most sites urge that all courses include a writing component, but a popular model is one in which a number of courses are designated by the university as writing-intensive courses. Thus, students know in advance that writing will be an important aspect of the course. Often, writing-intensive courses are listed as such on student transcripts.

WORKSHOP APPROACH

An outgrowth of both writing projects and whole language in the early eighties was the implementation of the Writers' Workshop approach. Since writing projects saw it as their job to convince teachers that they were real writers, teachers next had to convince their students that they also were real writers. Writing and reading workshops grew out of the concept of writing retreats, where writers worked on their own materials and came together to share, discuss, criticize, and edit. The person who captured teachers' imaginations on how writing workshops could be organized for instruction was Nancie Atwell in the eighties (Atwell, 1987). Atwell showed teachers that workshops could be highly organized and could function smoothly. Atwell describes her approach to the workshop as having principles that serve to inform both teaching and learning:

1. Writers need regular chunks of time—time to think, write, confer, read, change their minds, and write some more.

2. Writers need their own topics. Right from the first day of kindergarten, students should use writing as a way to think about and give shape to their own ideas and concerns.

3. Writers need response. Helpful response comes during—not after—the composing. It comes from the writer's peers and from the teacher, who consistently models the kinds of restatements and questions that help writers reflect on the content of their own writing.

4. Writers learn mechanics from context, from teachers who address errors as they occur within individual pieces of writing, where these rules and forms will have meaning.

5. Children need to know adults who write. We need to write, share our writing with our students, and demonstrate what experienced writers do in the process of composing, letting our students see our own drafts in all their messiness and tentativeness.

6. Writers need to read. They need access to a wide-ranging variety of texts, prose and poetry, fiction and non-fiction.

7. Writing teachers need to take responsibility for their writing and teaching. We must seek out professional resources that reflect the far-reaching conclusions of recent research into children's writing. And we must become writers and researchers, observing and learning from our own and our students' writing (Atwell, 1987, pp. 17–18).

Atwell showed teachers how to respond to student writing in a workshop format, negotiate grading and how to implement instruction through "writing mini-lessons." She clearly articulated the roles of teacher and student. As a student, you knew what you were supposed to do on a daily basis and how to go about doing it. Teachers also let students know what they themselves were responsible for and allowed students to hold them responsible for their obligations in the workshop. Atwell's book, now in its second edition, remains very popular with whole language teachers and graduates of writing projects.

TRENDS IN WRITING ASSESSMENT

Writing assessment has largely followed the same trends as reading assessment. As reading assessment shifted from a focus solely on the text to a focus on how students read, much the same has happened in writing. Previously, writing assessment was purely textual analysis. Basically, teachers focused on errors, how many and how often. Writing assessment has shifted to interpretation and process. One element of this shift has been from sentence-level correctness to revision as reformulation (Hull, 1985). In *Errors and Expectations: A Guide for the Teacher of Basic Writing*, Mina Shaughnessy (1977) wrote: "Errors count but not as much as most English teachers think" (p. 120). Error analysis now serves as an analytical tool that helps teachers to understand student thinking and to help students develop strategies that lead to better writing. Unfortunately, errors still count. Formal assessment in all aspects of education is growing and writing assessment in many states focuses solely on grammatical accountability. For writing, this debate focuses on direct and indirect assessment. Proponents of indirect assessment view writing as a means of communicating ideas while proponents of direct assessment view writing as the construction of meaning (Williamson, 1993). In fact, it is only in recent years that formal testing of writing has moved from a multiple-choice examination to a holistic evaluation of students' actual writing.

Holistic Assessment

Perhaps the most common form of informal assessment is holistic scoring. Many state competency tests and college placement tests in writing favor an open topic structure. These tend to produce more errors in student papers (see Smith et al., 1985) and thus tend to make it easier for evaluators to place students. Basically, in holistic evaluation, two readers rate each paper on a four- or five-point scale (most use a four-point scale because differences are easier to resolve). If the raters are in agreement, then a third rater is not needed. If raters are not in agreement then a third rater is used to resolve disagreements. Another way of conducting holistic evaluation is to have three readers read each student essay and then to average their ratings. In a holistic evaluation, where readers have been trained, error is one of several factors that influence raters. Other factors might include format, content, vocabulary, and spelling. However, since the mid-seventies, holistic evaluation has attempted—through carefully posed topics, scoring guides, and sample papers for raters to use for uniformity, and attention to reliability and validity—to rate student papers for placement and minimum competency as accurately as possible. The downside of holistic evaluation is its prohibitive cost both in time and money, especially in large-scale assessment.

Portfolio Assessment

Portfolio advocates make a strong case for using portfolios in large-scale assessment. They argue that a portfolio is much more reliable as a measure of growth and ability. It really is not accurate to call portfolios a means of assessment. Portfolios are a means of collection. Some sort of holistic evaluation would probably have to be done on the content of the portfolios. Questions must be decided on what to include in portfolios as well as to determine the purpose of the portfolio in the first place.

Primary Trait Guides

Another form of writing assessment is the use of primary trait scoring guides. A primary trait guide focuses specifically on a few key aspects of student writing. A primary trait guide might focus on error and especially particular types of errors. Another guide might focus on paragraph patterns or topic sentences. Although generally viewed as unsuitable for large-scale assessment, primary trait guides are very useful in classroom settings, especially those advocating a workshop format.

ISSUES IN WRITING ASSESSMENT

The current political climate for assessment means that large-scale writing assessment will continue. The shift from using multiple-choice measures to evaluating student-produced essays has turned the corner. Even the venerable SAT exam has begun to use a writing sample, and "trickle-down" pressure to high school and middle grades teachers to focus more of their attention on writing is predicted. However, issues of reliability and validity will persist. Work by Smith (1993) has questioned exactly what the difference is between a 3 and a 4 on a 4-point scale or especially between a 2 and 3, given that whatever the difference is, it might mean that a student should be placed in a remedial program or, in extreme circumstances, should not be permitted to graduate from high school. The emerging focus on writing is likely to bring about healthy debate over assessment issues such as these.

CONCLUSION

Nothing these days is more a political hot button than literacy in general and "readin' and 'ritin' " in particular. Interest in writing will doubtless not flag any time soon. To be sure, the focus on the product and on students' ability to produce academic writing will remain in the forefront of educational reform. Clearly, process is part of this reform, as is writing for real audiences and writing for personal understanding. How process and product will play out in this era of high stakes assessment is anyone's guess. More importantly, though, the lesson learned over the last thirty years is that writers get better at writing by writing. Good teachers find ways of motivating students to do their best writing by paying careful attention to *both* process and product. Surprisingly, technology has not had the effect one would have imagined on writing. Surely computers have made writing easier to edit and revise. Teachers can take far less time to edit students' papers, and publishing no longer relies on justifiers and professional publishers. It is the rare school where students do not have access to word processors for at least final drafts. However, we may all have been born with an instinct for oral language development, but, alas, like most everything else, writing and reading must be taught and learned.

REFERENCES

Applebee, A. N. (1974). *Tradition and reform in the teaching of English: A history.* Urbana, IL: NCTE.

Atwell, N. (1987). *In the middle: Writing, reading and learning with adolescents.* Portsmouth, NH: Boynton Cook/Heinemann.

Braddock, R., Lloyd-Jones, R., & Schoer, L. (1963). *Research in Written Composition.* Champaign, IL: NCTE.

Bay Area Writing Project. Retrieved June 24, 2002, from http://bawpblogs.org

Burhans, C. S. (1983). The teaching of writing and the knowledge gap. *College English, 45,* 639–656.

Cooper, C. R., & O'dell, L. (1978). *Research on composing: Points of departure.* Urbana, IL: NCTE.

Elbow, P. (1973). *Writing without teachers.* New York: Oxford University Press.

Emig, J. (1971). *The composing processes of twelfth graders.* Urbana, IL: NCTE.

Gere, A. (1985). Empirical research in composition. In B. W. McClelland & T. R. Donovan (Eds.), *Perspectives on research and scholarship in composition* (pp. 116–124). New York: MLA.

Kuhn, T. S. (1970) *The structure of scientific revolutions.* (2nd ed.; Foundations of Unity of Science Series, Vol. 2, No. 2). Chicago: University of Chicago Press.

Kuhn, T. S. (1996). *The structure of scientific revolutions.* (3rd Ed.). Chicago: University of Chicago Press.

Macrorie, K. (1970). *Telling writing.* Rochelle Park, NJ: Hayden.

Moffett, J. (1968). *Teaching the universe of discourse: A Theory of discourse: A rationale for English teaching used in a student-centered language arts curriculum.* Boston: Houghton Mifflin.

Moffett, J. (1989). *Storm in the mountains: A case study of censorship, conflict, and consciousness.* Carbondale: IL: Southern Illinois University Press.

Moffett, J., & Wagner, B. J. (1983). *Student-centered language arts and reading, K–13: A handbook for teachers.* (3rd Ed.). Boston: Houghton Mifflin.

Murray, D. M. (1968). *A writer teaches writing: A practical method of teaching composition.* Boston: Houghton Mifflin.

Murray, D. M. (1975). *A writer teaches writing.* (2nd Ed.). Boston: Houghton Mifflin.

North, S. M. (1987). *The making of knowledge in composition: Portrait of an emerging field.* Upper Montclair, NJ: Boynton/Cook.

Shaughnessy, M. (1977). *Errors and expectations: A guide for the teacher of basic writing.* New York: Oxford University Press.

Smith, W. L., Hull, G. A., Land, R. E., Moore, M. T., Ball, C., Dunham, D. E., Hickey, L. S., & Ruzich, C. W. (1985). Some effects of varying the structure of the topic on college students' writing. *Written Communication, 2,* 73–89.

Smith, W. L. (1993). Assessing the reliability and adequacy of using holistic scoring of essays as a college composition placement technique. In M. M. Williamson & B. A. Huot (Eds.), *Validating holistic scoring for writing assessment* (pp. 142–205). Cresskill, NJ: Hampton Press.

Standards for the English language arts. (1996). Urbana, IL: IRA/NCTE.

Williamson, M. M. (1993). An introduction to holistic scoring: The social, historical and theoretical context for writing assessment. In M. M. Williamson & B. A. Huot (Eds.), *Validating holistic scoring for writing assessment* (pp. 1–44). Cresskill, NJ: Hampton Press.

Young, R. E. (1978). Paradigms and problems: Needed research in rhetorical invention. In C. R. Cooper & L. O'dell (Eds.), *Research on composing: Points of departure* (pp. 29–48). Urbana, IL: NCTE.

Reading . . . with Pen in Hand!

SHARON SICINSKI SKEANS

The voice you hear when you read silently is not silent; it is a speaking-out-loud voice in your head: it is spoken, *a voice is* saying *it as you read. It's the writer's words, of course, in a literary sense his or her "voice" but the sound of that voice is the sound of* your *voice. Not the sound your friends know or the sound of a tape played back, but your voice caught in the dark cathedral of your skull, your voice heard by an internal ear informed by internal abstracts and what you know by feeling, having felt. It is your voice saying, for example, the word "barn" that the writer wrote but the "barn" you say is a barn you know or knew.*

The voice in your head, speaking as you read, never says anything neutrally— some people hated the barn they knew, some people love the barn they know so you hear the word loaded and a sensory constellation is lit: horse-gnawed stalls, hayloft, black heat tape wrapping a water pipe, a slippery spilled chirrr *of oats from a split sack, the bony, filthy haunches of cows . . . And "barn" is only a noun—no verb or subject has entered into the sentence yet! The voice you hear when you read to yourself is the clearest voice: you speak it speaking to you.*

—Thomas Lux (1997)

One of the most crucial lessons English teachers can teach their students is the ability to hear the "speaking-out-loud voice" in their heads while reading. When students can do this, they have experienced interacting with text. They are *active* readers. They mentally engage with text by connecting what they already know to what they encounter as readers. Equally important, active readers self-monitor their comprehension throughout the reading process by reflecting on what they understand and by asking themselves questions to clarify misunderstandings. So how can teachers facilitate this internal dialogue? One way is to use writing as a tool while directly teaching comprehension strategies. This reading-writing connection can be done not only *before* and *after,* but also *during* the reading of a selection.

Reprinted by permission of the author. This article originally appeared in *English Journal, 89* (2000), 69–72.

A HISTORICAL OVERVIEW OF THE
READING-WRITING CONNECTION

Experts in the field have advocated the integration of reading and writing since the turn of the century. Ohmann cites the report of the 1892 Conference of Ten, sponsored by the National Education Association, which proclaimed as its primary goals the facilitating of students' ability to comprehend the thoughts of others and to give expression to their own thoughts. According to Ohmann, these goals "should never be disassociated in the mind of the teacher and their mutual dependence should be constantly present in the minds of the pupils." Ohmann sadly comments that these goals, although still paramount, were yet unrealized in the late 1980s (11–26).

Clifford gives a historical perspective on the cyclical relationship between reading and writing. Although the National Council of Teachers of English has advocated an integrated language arts approach since 1935, circumstances have prevented its universal acceptance in the classroom. With the 1950s and 1960s came society's expectation that the ability to read and exhibit correct usage would lead to social and economic success. The post-Sputnik era perpetuated fragmentation with its return to a traditional, tripartite curriculum of language, literature, and composition. The concept of developmental reading was coined, which resulted in the creation of reading courses separate from English and the teaching of writing. Textbook publishers continued to market separate books for reading, composition, spelling, and handwriting. Reading research dominated studies, while writing was viewed as only a supplemental activity at best. Even reading specialists broke away from NCTE in 1955 and formed the International Reading Association. Clifford concludes, "Instructional atomism probably reached its peak . . . during the craze in the 1970s for behavioral objectives" (7).

By the early 1970s, researchers began to reexamine links between reading and writing. The separate, yet seminal, works of Kenneth Goodman and Janet Emig suggested that reading and writing should be conceptualized as processes. Advances in cognitive psychology further supported this perspective in the 1980s, which posited the theory of constructivism. Both comprehending and composing were viewed as text production processes. Both reader and writer were active participants in the making or construction of meaning as they interacted with text.

During the last two decades, most English teachers have embraced writing as a process. Activities that connect reading and writing, namely the literary essay as an *after* reading assignment, are commonplace (e.g., Was Brutus or Caesar a tragic hero? Describe a day in the life of an Elizabethan playgoer. Discuss Twain's symbolism for the river. Write your own "modest proposal" about a societal ill.).

Some teachers have even discovered the power of writing as a *before* reading activity. Freewrites and quickwrites not only build background knowledge and focus readers on the content of the reading selection, but they also provide teachers with diagnostic information about students' prior knowledge of topics (e.g., Write about a time when a group of your friends, led by your best friend, hurt your feelings. Freewrite for five minutes discussing everything that comes to mind when you hear the word "Puritan."). Although writing activities *before* and *after* reading are important, teachers need to be reminded of the power of writing activities *during* reading because of the transactional relationship between reading and writing. Tierney describes the interfacing of these two processes:

> Writers consider their readers as they compose text—they consider the transactions in which readers are likely to engage. At the same time, writers act as their own readers— they read and review what they have written as if they (the writers) assumed they were their own audiences (what Donald Murray has called inner readers). Readers, as they comprehend text, respond reflexively and actively to what writers are trying to get them to think, or do. These readers use knowledge of the world and the text cues to compose meaning: they recognize that these cues to meaning making are provided by an author who is trying to get them to think or do something (4).

FROM THEORY TO PRACTICE

To build on the transactional nature of the reading-writing connection, classroom practices should involve the act of writing to scaffold and support the teaching of specific comprehension strategies. Written comments manifest students' mental text production and provide diagnostic clues for teachers as to key behaviors of active readers, namely the making of personal connections and the ability to self-monitor comprehension. One *during* reading activity that requires writing and facilitates comprehension is the think-link chart.

A pseudonym for James Hoffman's language chart, the think-link chart assists students in self-monitoring their understanding of text and encourages them to make personal connections with what they are reading. (See Figure 7.1)

After the teacher introduces a reading selection to the whole class and facilitates appropriate prereading strategies and activities, students are assigned a portion or chunk of text to read silently. This chunk could be the first scene of a play, the first chapter of a novel, or the first few paragraphs of a nonfiction selection. While students are reading, the teacher enters a model statement under each column of the think-link chart that is either sketched on the chalkboard or posted on butcher or easel chart paper on the wall. As students complete their silent reading, they are invited to add

OBSERVATIONS I noticed . . .	**WONDERINGS** I wonder . . .	**CONNECTIONS** This reminds me of . . .

FIGURE 7.1

their own original comments and to initial each statement. The end product: a visual representation of the mental processing that occurred *during* the student's reading. The teacher can then lead the class in a discussion of entries under each column.

Typical responses under the "observations" column include both literal and inferential comprehension statements; under the "wonderings" column, questions, confusions, and vocabulary needing clarification; and under the "connections" column, links to similar experiences, related ideas about content, as well as recollections of television shows, movies, song lyrics, and literature with common themes and elements. During class discussion, the teacher can focus on the "wonderings" column before assigning the next chunk of text to be read silently by individual students. This reading-writing cycle can continue throughout the reading of the selection. The visual display before the entire class can then, with subsequent selections, become a think-link chart in individual students' response logs. Finally, once students are cognizant of these *during* reading strategies, they can resort to a simple checkmark, question mark, and exclamation mark in the margins of texts while reading.

FINAL COMMENTS

The think-link chart directly and explicitly teaches students how to mentally engage with text *during* reading. Furthermore, it graphically demonstrates the unique interaction and transaction of each reader with text. During metacognitive debriefing sessions, students can be made aware that what goes on in one person's mind may be similar to or totally different from that of another person who is reading the same text. Prior knowledge and experience tempers understanding. This realization and the awareness of making links to one's thinking foster students' ability to self-monitor their comprehension.

Additionally, the think-link chart activity addresses Fielding and Pearson's criteria for teacher-directed instruction of comprehension strategies:

(1) Authenticity of strategies. Selected strategies should be authentic, or those used by actual readers. The think-link chart does address the active reading strategy of connecting what is already known to what is being read, and of self-monitoring of comprehension.

(2) Demonstration and Guided Practice. Teachers should model the strategies and monitor student practice before gradually releasing support, allowing students to perform the strategies independently. The think-link procedures described above do replicate the gradual release of responsibility model advocated by Vygotsky, Pearson and Gallagher, and Graves and Graves.

(3) Authenticity of texts. Authentic texts, rather than contrived texts or workbook passages, should be used. The think-link activity can be done with any reading material, whether it is selected by the teacher or required by the school's curriculum. No artificially designed materials need be purchased or developed. Furthermore, since students formulate their own questions in the "wonderings" column, which good readers do to propel their reading, no prepared set of comprehension questions need be developed, typed, and duplicated (65).

If proficient readers make personal connections and self-monitor their comprehension, the think-link chart is a valid classroom activity that teaches these mental processes *during* reading. The physical act of writing serves as a vehicle in this learning, which strengthens the reading-writing connection. In *Reading/Writing Connections: Learning from Research*, Irwin and Doyle suggest that traditional instruction of the past focused on only teacher-directed activities, which teach reading and writing strategies as ends in themselves. These editors advance the concept of "new literacy" for use in classrooms of the twenty-first century as defined by Willinsky:

> The New Literacy consists of those strategies in the teaching of reading and writing which attempt to shift the control of literacy from the teacher to the students: literacy is promoted in such programs as a social process with language that can from the very beginning extend the students' range of meaning and connection (ix–x).

The think-link chart, requiring reading with pen in hand, is one such strategy-building activity. Long after the chart is discarded, the "speaking-out-loud voice" in students' minds remains.

WORKS CITED

Clifford, Geraldine. *A Sisyphean Task: Historical Perspectives on the Relationship between Writing and Reading Instruction.* Berkeley: University of California Center for the Study of Writing, 1987.

Emig, Janet. *The Composing Processes of Twelfth Graders.* Urbana: NCTE, 1971.

Fielding, Linda, and P. David Pearson. "Reading Comprehension: What Works." *Educational Leadership* 51. 2 (1994): 62–68.

Goodman, Kenneth. "Psycholinguistic Universals in the Reading Process." *Psycholinguistics and Reading.* Ed. Frank Smith. New York: Holt, 1973.

Graves, Michael, and Bonnie Graves. *Scaffolding Reading Experiences: Designs for Student Success.* Norwood, MA: Christopher-Gordon, 1994.

Hoffman, James. "Language to Literacy." Texas Regional Educational Service Center IV, Houston. 18 Oct. 1996.

Irwin, Judith, and Mary Anne Doyle. *Reading/Writing Connections: Learning from Research.* Newark: International Reading Association, 1992.

Lux, Thomas. "The Voice You Hear When You Read Silently." *The New Yorker* 14 July 1997: 77.

Ohmann, Richard. "Reading and Writing, Work and Leisure." *Only Connect: Uniting Reading and Writing.* Ed. Thomas Newkirk. Upper Montclair, NJ: Boynton/Cook, 1986. 11–26.

Pearson, P. David, and M. C. Gallagher. "The Instruction of Reading Comprehension." *Contemporary Educational Psychology* 8 (1983): 317–44.

Tierney, Robert. "Writer-Reader Transactions: Defining the Dimensions of Negotiation." *Forum: Essays on Theory and Practice in the Teaching of Writing.* Ed. Patricia Stock. Upper Montclair, NJ: Boynton/Cook, 1983. 4.

Vygotsky, Lev. *Thought and Language.* Cambridge: MIT Press, 1962.

Willinsky, J. *The New Literacy: Redefining Reading and Writing in the Schools.* New York: Routledge, 1990.

INTEGRATING SOURCES

1. Complete the four time lines below by capturing key developments in writing instruction.

WRITING RESEARCH	50s	60s	70s	80s	90s

WRITING PROCESS	50s	60s	70s	80s	90s

WRITING ASSESSMENT	50s	60s	70s	80s	90s

READING– WRITING CONNECTION	50s	60s	70s	80s	90s

2. What conclusions can you draw by contrasting the long-term trends revealed by the time lines?

CLASSROOM IMPLICATIONS

1. What types of writing assessment do you use? Have you tried some of the alternatives mentioned by Moore?

2. What questions would you like to see writing research address?

3. Could a think-link chart be used at your grade level or teaching assignment? Would adaptations be necessary?

4. What other instructional approaches can you suggest to harness the reading–writing connection?

ANNOTATED BIBLIOGRAPHY

Adams-Boateng, A. (2001). Second graders' use of journal writing and its effect on reading comprehension. (ERIC Reproduction Service No. ED450409).
> Describes an extensive writing project in second grade that encouraged the development of various types of comprehension and other language-related skills.

Atwell, N. (1998). *In the middle. New understandings about writing, reading, and learning* (2nd ed.) Portsmouth, NH: Boynton/Cook, Heinemann.
> The second edition of Atwell's acclaimed book provides ideas and a rationale for process writing instruction, writers' workshop, and other current approaches. Lots of ideas for teachers at a range of levels (not just middle school).

Cohle, D. M., & Towle, W. (2001). Connecting reading and writing in the intermediate grades: A workshop approach. (ERIC Reproduction Service No. ED451484).
> Discusses a workshop approach to the writing process that emphasized the fact that this aspect of the language process was more than just a school subject but should be taught as a lifelong skill.

Graham, L. (2001). From Tyrannosaurus to Pokemon: Autonomy in the teaching of writing. *Reading, 35*, 18–26.
> Presents information on a series of case studies of children who were given the opportunity to experience a wide range of personal writing activities that were largely self-selected by the individual student.

Graves, D. H. (1994). *A fresh look at writing.* Portsmouth, NH: Heinemann.
> Graves places his views on writing in historical perspective as he provides innumerable suggestions for teachers who wish to employ a process approach.

Hatton, S. C., & Ladd, P. M. (2002). Teaching idea development: A standards-based critical-thinking approach to writing. (ERIC Reproduction Service No. ED458580).
> Emphasizes the importance of critical thinking in the content area classroom through the use of various types of reading and writing activities. Literacy skills such as description, comparison and contrast, cause and effect, dialogue, anecdotes, and vignettes are described in detail.

Novelli, J. (2001). Writing workshop. *Instructor, 111*, 67–68, 70.
> Suggests various ways in which classroom teachers can effectively use writers' workshop in their literacy instruction. Specific suggestions as to how mini-lessons can incorporate the principal aspects of the writing process are also included.

Strickland, D., Ganske, K., & Monroe, J. K. (2002). *Supporting struggling readers and writers: Strategies for classroom intervention 3–6.* Newark, DE: International Reading Association.
> Presents information on how classroom teachers, school administrators, and staff can effectively help those students in grades 3–6 who are having various types of literacy difficulties. Specific program activities are described that can be used both at the school level as well as in individual classrooms and with specific students.

Van Horn, L. (2001). Reading and writing essays about objects of personal significance. *Language Arts, 78*, 273–278.
> Describes how the personal writing of students can be significantly enhanced through the use of a variety of personal objects of different types.

YOU BECOME INVOLVED

1. Inventory your own focus on writing. Review lesson plans over the span of a week and determine how much time you have apportioned to writing. Do the results surprise you? Are you satisfied?

2. Interview a sample of your students about what they like most and least about writing. Do the results agree with your predictions?

3. Visit the Web site of the National Center for the Study of Writing and Literacy. Even though the mission of the Center is over, the site still houses information concerning research findings. http://www-gse.berkeley.edu/research/NCSWL/ csw.homepage.html

CHAPTER EIGHT

READING ASSESSMENT

Let us now take liberty to exercise himself in any English book till he can perfectly read in any place of a book that is offered him; and when he can do this, I adjudge him fit to enter into a Grammar *Schoole, but not before.*

—C. H. (1659)

Because the [reading] instruments of diagnosis have not been perfected, the limitation of each instrument must be thoroughly understood.

—William D. Sheldon (1960)

The heart of education reform is accountability. The heart of making sure every child learns and no child is left behind is accountability. Because how do you know if you don't measure?

—President George W. Bush (2001)

Reading assessment today is both an important educational as well as political topic (Benson, 2001; Donahue, et al. 2000; Strickland, 2000; Sweet, 2000). Not only is there concern about the more traditional roles of assessment in measuring students' reading performance but there is also the increased use of tests to evaluate teacher performance in the classroom. Issues such as high-stakes testing, teacher licensure, and school evaluation are important agenda items today at the local, state, and national levels (Bush, 2001).

Historically, students' assessment data have been used for making instructional decisions such as student placement, class grouping, materials selection, and so on. In addition, assessment procedures have been used to measure literacy program effectiveness and to track student achievement over time. More recently, school districts and government leaders have utilized assessment results to support various types of school reform, most notably in the areas of teacher accountability and curricular change.

STATE AND NATIONAL READING ASSESSMENT INITIATIVES

Perhaps the most dramatic recent development in assessment is the increasingly wide use of state and national testing programs (Donahue, et al., 2000; Linton, 2000; Stofflet, Fenton, & Straugh, 2001; Wellstone, 2000). While the intent of these assessment initiatives is to measure large groups of students on specific skills such as ability levels in reading comprehension for all third graders in a state, this ideal has not consistently been met. Often the results of state tests have been used to compare and contrast the academic achievements of school districts and specific schools, as well as the teaching expertise of individual teachers (Cheng, 2000; Spritzler, 2000).

The various uses of state and national assessment results are both an educational and political issue: educational, in that these measures give a general picture of the achievement level of large groups of students and, thus, provide guidance for the planning of statewide curriculum evaluation and suggested changes in current practices; political, in that many decisions are made based on these test results, which most would agree are clearly inappropriate. For instance, as noted above, to measure individual teacher practices related to a state test is clearly inappropriate, yet major decisions are often made on the basis of these results, for example, teachers' salaries, continued approval of teachers' licenses, and even faculty salaries (Howe, 2000; Huber & Moore, 2000; Kohn, 2000).

Closely related to the issue of state and national assessment is the establishment of academic standards. For instance, a set of standards for evaluating teacher knowledge and practice in reading has been developed (IRA, 1994, 1999). The roles and responsibilities of various literacy providers are defined in these standards with regard to professional training as well as instructional practices. With the development of standards comes concern over how they will be used, once established. The basic dilemma is, simply: Should these standards be used only to measure existing practices, or are they designed to drive the curriculum through the establishment of goals and objectives that must be met by all school districts? Currently this is still an open and unresolved issue.

ADMINISTRATIVE VERSUS INSTRUCTIONAL USES OF ASSESSMENT RESULTS

The need for accurate, current, and essential information about students' academic progress is a critical need for both classroom teachers and administrators. Traditionally, this information has been provided by various types of standardized assessment measures. The results from these tests have increasingly been subject to criticism from many who say they do not accurately measure actual student performance or knowledge of a specific academic area.

The uses of this test data are fundamentally different for administrators and teachers. Whereas the former group is interested in assessment results as a way of measuring total curriculum development and the effectiveness of large groups of students, teachers are most concerned with the academic growth of their classes as well as individual student growth. This exemplifies the dichotomies related to reading assessment (McMillan, 2000).

PROCESS VERSUS PRODUCT ASSESSMENT

Any test designed to measure a child's ability in a given area at a given time is primarily concerned with the *product* of learning. On the other hand, measures such as observation and miscue analysis, designed to provide information about the processes of reading, tend to be more qualitative in nature. Quantitative product measures include standardized tests but also tests devised to measure the mastery of specific skills. Whether a teacher's practice is better informed by specific-skill product tests or by continuously compiled process measures will depend largely on the teacher's instructional philosophy. Much of the controversy in this area is a direct result of conflicting literacy materials and the type of assessment being used.

TRADITIONAL VERSUS PROGRESSIVE STANDARDIZED COMPREHENSION FORMATS

Traditionally, standardized tests of reading comprehension have relied on short passages followed by a combination of literal and inferential comprehension questions. Sometimes, the troublesome task of composing good questions has been circumvented by using a multiple-choice cloze format, which requires the reader to choose the best word for completing sentences. These approaches have been challenged in recent years on several grounds. First, they fail to assess a student's ability to integrate information across large samples of text. Second, they fail to account for prior knowledge. Present-day initiatives to bring comprehension test formats into line with reading theory have led to longer selections (for example, entire short stories) and to the use of questions that draw on information located at more than one point in the selection. Whether such test reforms can satisfy critics is inevitably related to a question that is essentially political: What should be expected of students in terms of comprehension?

CONSTRUCTIVE VERSUS RECONSTRUCTED ASSESSMENT OF READING

If you believe that comprehension is discerning what an author has intended to convey, then you have taken a reconstructive view. That is, you probably see the goal of the reader to be "reconstructing" the author's meaning that has been encoded in printed language. You might also have little objection to using traditional assessment formats to determine which students have been successful in their effort to reconstruct meaning. On the other hand, you may view the reading process as a "transaction" between what a reader *wishes* to derive from a text and what the text offers the reader. A reader's personal desires, cultural background, language distinctions, and so forth will all determine what is actually "constructed" from a given reading experience. If you take this view, then a traditional comprehension assessment may have serious short-comings in that it will have been constructed by someone removed from the immediate learning environment, who has specific ideas about what meaning a reader should derive, which answers to questions are "correct," and so on.

SITUATED VERSUS DECONTEXTUALIZED ASSESSMENT

Standardized tests, and for that matter other types of paper-and-pencil tests, may produce misleading results because they require students to apply skills in artificial, contrived settings. Critics of such measures have argued that it is more valid to observe how students perform "authentic" tasks undertaken for reasons the students value. That is to say, the assessment should be situated within the learning context (Young, 1997). This view has great appeal but poses serious logistical problems. It might prove especially difficult to use truly situated assessment for administrative purposes given the lack of uniformity among the techniques used by various teachers (Purcell-Gates, 1998). One of the outcomes of the drive toward situated assessment has been the development of portfolios. These provide collections of records of performance during authentic tasks. Whether the benefits of portfolios outweigh their inherent disadvantages (e.g., size, subjectivity, lack of uniformity, etc.) is a decision that individual teachers must ultimately make (Sustein & Lovell, 2000).

AS YOU READ

The articles in this section present a variety of views on reading assessment. The position statement on *High-Stakes Assessments in Reading* (1999) from the International Reading Association presents the views of this national organization on the current use of this type of reading assessment. While Hoffman, Assaf, & Paris (2001) provide a discussion of high-stakes testing in Texas, they also note that developments in this state have national implications as well.

1. What do you believe should be the primary role(s) of reading assessment in an effective classroom reading program?
2. Are performance or standardized reading tests better suited to the ongoing needs of classroom teachers? Students? School administrators? State and national educational administrators?

REFERENCES

Benson, C. (2001). *America's children: Key national indicators of well-being.* (ERIC Reproduction Service No. ED 455036).

Bush, G. W. (2001). *No child left behind.* (ERIC Reproduction Service No. ED 447608).

Cheng, L. (2000). *Washback or backwash: A review of the impact of testing on teaching and learning.* (ERIC Reproduction Service No. ED442280).

Donahue, P., et al. (2000). *The nation's report card: Fourth-grade reading, 2000.* (ERIC Reproduction Service No. ED447473).

Hoffman, J. V., Assaf, L. C., & Paris, S. G. (2001). High-stakes testing in reading: Today in Texas, tomorrow? *Reading Teacher, 54,* 482–492.

Howe, H. (2000). High-stakes trouble. *American School Board Journal, 187,* 58–59.

Huber, R. A., & Moore, C. J. (2000). Educational reform through high-stakes testing—don't go there. *Science Educator, 9,* 7–13.

International Reading Association. (1994). *Standards for the assessment of reading and writing.* Newark, DE: Author.

International Reading Association. (1999). *High-stakes assessments in reading.* Newark, DE: Author.

International Reading Association. (1999). *Standards for literacy professionals and paraprofessionals.* Newark, DE: Author.

Kohn, A. (2000). *The case against standardized testing: Raising the scores, ruining the schools.* (ERIC Reproduction Service No. ED446126).

Linton, T. H. (2000). *High-stakes testing in Texas: An analysis of the impact of including special education students in the Texas Academic Indicator System.* (ERIC Reproduction Service No. ED440109).

McMillan, J. H. (2000). *Basic assessment concepts for teachers and administrators.* (ERIC Reproduction Service No. ED447201).

Purcell-Gates, V., et al. (1998). *U.S. adult literacy program practice: A typology across dimensions of life-contextualized/decontextualized and dialogic/monologic.* (ERIC Reproduction Service No. ED423451).

Spritzler, J. (2000). Students, parents, and teachers, "Take this test and shove it!" *Paths of learning: Options for families & communities, 3,* 46–47.

Stofflet, F., Fenton, R., & Straugh, T. (2001). *Construct and predictive validity of the Alaska state high school graduation qualifying examination: First administration.* (ERIC Reproduction Service No. ED 453257).

Strickland, K. (2000). *Making assessment elementary.* Portsmouth, NH: Heinemann.

Sunstein, B. S., & Lovell, J. H. (2000). *The portfolio standard: How students can show us what they know and are able to do.* Portsmouth, NH: Heinemann.

Sweet, A. P. (2000). *Proven principles for teaching reading.* Washington, DC: National Education Association.

Wellstone, P. D. (2000). High-stakes tests: A harsh agenda for America's children. *Education revolution, 29,* 31–35.

Young, M. F. (1997). The unit of analysis for situated assessment. *Instructional Science, 25,* 133–150.

High-Stakes Assessments in Reading:

A Position Statement

INTERNATIONAL READING ASSOCIATION

The Board of Directors of the International Reading Association is opposed to high-stakes testing. High-stakes testing means that one test is used to make important decisions about students, teachers, and schools. In a high-stakes testing situation, if students score high on a single test they could be placed in honors classes or a gifted program. On the other hand, if students score low on a high-stakes test, it could mean that they will be rejected by a particular college, and it could affect their teacher's salary and the rating of the school district as compared with others where the same test was given.

In the United States in recent years there has been an increase in policymakers' and educators' reliance on high-stakes testing in which single test scores are used to make important educational decisions. The International Reading Association is deeply concerned about this trend. The Board of Directors offers this position statement as a call for the evaluation of the impact of current types and levels of testing on teaching quality, student motivation, educational policymaking, and the public's perception of the quality of schooling. Our central concern is that testing has become a means of controlling instruction as opposed to a way of gathering information to help students become better readers. To guide educators who must use tests as a key element in the information base used to make decisions about the progress of individual children and the quality of instructional programs, we offer this position in the form of a question-and-answer dialogue. This format is intended to ensure that important conceptual, practical, and ethical issues are considered by those responsible for designing and implementing testing programs.

International Reading Association. (1999). *High-stakes assessments in reading.* (A position statement of the International Reading Association.) Published in *The Reading Teacher,* 53, 3(November 1999): 257–263, and reprinted with permission. All rights reserved. Available at: www.reading.org

WHAT DOES THE TERM *HIGH-STAKES TESTING* MEAN?

High-stakes testing means that the consequences for good (high) or poor (low) performance on a test are substantial. In other words, some very important decisions, such as promotion or retention, entrance into an educational institution, teacher salary, or a school district's autonomy depend on a single test score.

High-stakes tests have been a part of education for some time. Perhaps the most conspicuous form of high-stakes testing, historically speaking, was in the British educational system. National exams in England and in other countries that adopted the British system separated students into different educational tracks. In the United States, tests such as the Medical College Admission Test and Law School Admission Test, as well as professional certification examinations (for example, state bar examinations, medical board examinations, state teacher examinations) all represent high-stakes tests.

The meaning of high stakes can be confusing at times. Tests that have no specific decision tied to them can become high stakes to teachers and school administrators when they must face public pressure after scores are made public. In other cases, a low-stakes state test can be transformed into a high-stakes test at a school district level if a local school board decides to make educational or personnel decisions based on the test results.

WHY ARE WE CONCERNED WITH HIGH-STAKES TESTING?

Although high-stakes testing has been and probably will continue to be part of the educational landscape, there has been an increase in such testing in recent years, particularly at the state level. More children are being tested at younger ages, and states and local school districts are using these tests to make a greater variety of important decisions than ever before. Increased frustration with lack of achievement has led to a greater reliance on testing. In response to these frustrations many states have adopted educational standards and assessments of those standards. The logic is that tests of standards accompanied by a reward and penalty structure will improve children's achievement. In too many cases the assessment is a single multiple-choice test, which would be considered high stakes and would not yield enough information to make an important instructional decision.

IS TESTING AN IMPORTANT PART OF GOOD EDUCATIONAL DESIGN?

Yes, testing students' skills and knowledge is certainly an important part of education, but it is only one type of educational assessment. Assessment involves the systematic and purposeful collection of data to inform actions. From the viewpoint of educators, the primary purpose of assessment is to help students by providing information about how instruction can be improved.

Assessment has an important role to play in decision making beyond the classroom level, however. Administrators, school board members, policymakers, and parents make significant decisions that impact students. The needs of many audiences must be considered in building a quality assessment plan.

Testing is a form of assessment that involves the systematic sampling of behavior under controlled conditions. Testing can provide quick reliable data on student performance. Single tests might be used to make decisions that do not have major long-term consequences, or used to supplement other forms of assessment such as focused interviews, classroom observations and anecdotal records, analysis of work samples, and work inventories.

Different kinds of assessment produce different kinds of information. If a teacher needs to know whether a student can read a particular textbook, there are many sources of information available to her. She can consult districtwide achievement tests in reading, estimate the level of the textbook, determine what score a student would need to read the textbook effectively, and then make a decision. However, it might be simpler for the teacher to ask the student to read a section of the text and then talk with the student about the text. This would probably be faster and more accurate than looking up test scores and conducting studies to see what kind of a test score is needed to comprehend the textbook. In general, teachers need information specific to the content and strategies they are teaching, and they can best get that information through assessments built around their daily educational tasks.

The public and policymakers have different needs from teachers. In general they need to know whether the school, school district, and state are effectively educating the students in their charge. For this purpose they need to collect information about many students and they need to know how those students stand in relation to other students across the United States or in relation to some specific standards set by the state. For these purposes, standardized norm-referenced or criterion-referenced tests are efficient and can give a broad picture of achievement on certain kinds of tasks. These kinds of tests are used most commonly for high-stakes decisions regarding schools and school districts.

WHY DOES USING TESTS FOR HIGH-STAKES DECISIONS CAUSE PROBLEMS?

There are several possible problematic outcomes of high-stakes testing. These include making bad decisions, narrowing the curriculum, focusing exclusively on certain segments of students, losing instructional time, and moving decision making to central authorities and away from local personnel.

Tests are imperfect. Basing important decisions on limited and imperfect information can lead to bad decisions—decisions that can do harm to students and teachers and that sometimes have unfortunate legal and economic consequences for the schools. Decision makers reduce the chance of making a bad decision by seeking information from multiple sources. However, the information from norm-referenced and criterion-referenced tests is inexpensive to collect, easy to aggregate, and usually is highly reliable; for those reasons it is tempting to try to use this information alone to make major decisions.

Another problem is that high-stakes tests have a tendency to narrow the curriculum and inflate the importance of the test. Schools should address a broad range of student learning needs, not just the subjects or parts of subject areas covered on a particular test. As the consequences for low performance are raised, teachers feel pressured to raise scores at all costs. This means they will focus their efforts on activities that they think will improve the single important score. Time spent focusing on those activities will come from other activities in the curriculum and will consequently narrow the curriculum. Most state assessments tend to focus on reading, writing, and mathematics. Too much attention to these basic subjects will marginalize the fine arts, physical education, social studies, and the sciences.

Narrowing of the curriculum is most likely to occur in high-poverty schools that tend to have the lowest test scores. Compared to students in schools in affluent communities, students in high-poverty schools receive teaching with a greater emphasis in lower level skills, and they have limited access to instruction focusing on higher level thinking. A recent survey in one state that uses high-stakes assessments found that 75% of classroom teachers surveyed thought the state assessment had a negative impact on their teaching (Hoffman et al., in press).

Another way that educators sometimes respond to test pressure is to focus their attention on particular students. Sometimes this means that only low-performing readers get the instructional resources they need, and those doing only slightly better are ignored. Sometimes there is an attempt to raise test scores by focusing instructional initiatives on those students scoring just below cut-off points, and ignoring those both above or far below cutoff points. And sometimes schools place children in expensive special education programs they do not need, discourage particular children from attending school on testing days, or encourage low-achieving students to drop out of school altogether, all in the name of getting higher test scores.

The loss of instructional time also is a negative result of high-stakes tests. The time for preparing for and taking tests is time taken away from basic instruction. The consequences of lost instructional time, particularly for low-performing students, are too great for information that can be gathered more efficiently.

Finally, we are concerned that instructional decision making in high-stakes testing situations is diverted from local teachers and is concentrated in a central authority far away from the school. The further decision making is removed from the local level of implementation, the less adaptive the system becomes to individual needs. High-stakes assessment shifts decisions from teachers and principals to bureaucrats and politicians and consequently may diminish the quality of educational services provided to students.

DO TEST SCORES IMPROVE WHEN HIGH-STAKES ASSESSMENT IS MANDATED?

Test scores in the states with high-stakes assessment plans have often shown improvement. This could be because high-stakes pressure and competition lead teachers to teach reading more effectively. An alternative interpretation is that gains in test scores are the result of "teaching to the test" even when reading does not improve. Analyses of national reading scores do not show the substantial gains claimed by state reading assessments. Studies of norm-referenced tests in states with sustained patterns of growth in state skill assessments (for example, Texas and Kentucky) show no comparable patterns of gain. Although Texas showed steady improvement on state tests, its National Assessment of Educational Progress (NAEP) reading scores are not among the highest, and the scores did not show significant improvement between 1992 and 1998 (U.S. Department of Education, 1999). This may be the result of high-stakes assessments that tend to narrow the curriculum and emphasize only parts of what students need to learn to become successful readers.

WHY DON'T WE JUST END HIGH-STAKES ASSESSMENT?

It is unlikely that states using these assessments will abandon them. Indeed, the most likely scenario is for an increasing number of states to develop and adopt similar assessment plans. Tests can be useful for making state-level educational decisions, and they provide the public with at least a partial understanding of how well schools are doing. Less positively, politicians, bureaucrats, and test publishers have discovered that they can influence classroom instruction through the use of high-stakes tests. Tests allow these outside parties to take control away from local educational authorities without assuming the responsibilities of educating the students.

IS THERE A WAY TO HELP STATES MONITOR STUDENT SUCCESS IN THE CURRICULUM?

If the intent of state assessments is to measure how well students are learning the outcomes identified in the state curriculum framework, then one way students' success can be monitored is by following the NAEP model with selective sampling across student populations and across content areas on a systematic basis. This model monitors achievement without encouraging high-stakes testing. The tests are directed toward particular grade levels and are not given every year. A sampling procedure is used so very few students actually participate in testing. NAEP is designed to give a report card on general achievement levels in the basic subject areas over time.

Many aspects of the NAEP assessment in reading are commendable. The NAEP sampling strategy has been useful in keeping efficiency high and maintaining a focus on the questions that the national assessment is designed to address. Sampling also has provided NAEP with an opportunity to experiment with a wide variety of testing formats and conditions. Such a strategy would avoid most of the problems associated with teaching to the test. This type of plan would reflect sound principles of instructional design and assessment.

In the book *High Stakes: Testing for Tracking, Promotion, and Graduation* (Heubert & Hauser, 1999), the following basic principles for test use are presented:

- The important thing about a test is not its validity in general, but its validity when used for a specific purpose. Thus tests that are valid for influencing classroom practice, "leading" the curriculum, or holding schools accountable are not appropriate for making high-stakes decisions about individual student mastery unless the curriculum, the teaching, and the tests are aligned.

- Tests are not perfect. Test questions are a sample of possible questions that could be asked in a given area. Moreover, a test score is not an exact measure of a student's knowledge or skills. A student's score can be expected to vary across different versions of a test—within a margin of error determined by the reliability of the test—as a function of the particular sample of questions asked and/or transitory factors, such as the student's health on the day of the test. Thus, no single test score can be considered a definitive measure of a student's knowledge.

- An educational decision that will have a major impact on a test taker should not be made solely or automatically on the basis of a single test score. Other relevant information about the student's knowledge and skills should also be taken into account.

- Neither a test score nor any other kind of information can justify a bad decision. Research shows that students are typically hurt by a simple retention and repetition of a grade in school without remedial and other instructional support services. In the absence of effective services better tests will not lead to better educational outcomes (p. 3).

State testing programs should respect these basic principles.

WHAT ARE THE RECOMMENDATIONS OF THE INTERNATIONAL READING ASSOCIATION REGARDING HIGH-STAKES READING ASSESSMENTS?

In framing our recommendations the Association would like to stress two points. First, we recognize accountability is a necessary part of education. Concerns over high-stakes tests should not be interpreted as fear of or disregard for professional accountability. Second, the intent in this position statement is not to blame policymakers for the current dilemma with high-stakes testing.

Our recommendations begin with a consideration of teachers and their responsibility to create rich assessment environments in their classrooms and schools. Next, we suggest that researchers must continue to investigate how assessment can better serve our educational goals. Third, we stress the importance of parents and community members in bringing balance to the assessment design. Finally, we offer recommendations to policymakers for developing a plan of action.

Recommendations to teachers:

- Construct more systematic and rigorous assessments for classrooms, so that external audiences will gain confidence in the measures that are being used and their inherent value to inform decisions.

- Take responsibility to educate parents, community members, and policymakers about the forms of classroom-based assessment, used in addition to standardized tests, that can improve instruction and benefit students learning to read.

- Understand the difference between ethical and unethical practices when teaching to the test. It is ethical to familiarize students with the format of the test so they are familiar with the types of questions and responses required. Spending time on this type of instruction is helpful to all and can be supportive of the regular curriculum. It is not ethical to devote substantial instructional time teaching to the test, and it is not ethical to focus instructional time on particular students who are most likely to raise test scores while ignoring groups unlikely to improve.

- Inform parents and the public about tests and their results.

- Resist the temptation to take actions to improve test scores that are not based on the idea of teaching students to read better.

Recommendations to researchers:

- Conduct ongoing evaluations of high-stakes tests. These studies should include but not be limited to teacher use of results, impact on the curriculum focus, time in testing and test preparation, the costs of the test (both direct and hidden), parent and community communication, and effects on teacher and student motivations. There are few data on the impact of tests on instruction. Good baseline data and follow-up studies will help in monitoring the situation. These studies should not be left to those who design, develop, and implement tests; they should be conducted by independent researchers.

- Find ways to link performance assessment alternatives to questions that external audiences must address on a regular basis. Researchers must continue to offer demonstrations of ways that data from performance assessments can be aggregated meaningfully. This strategy will allow them to build trustworthy informal assessments.

Recommendations to parents, parent groups, and child advocacy groups:

- Be vigilant regarding the costs of high-stakes tests on students. Parents must ask questions about what tests are doing to their children and their schools. They cannot simply accept the "we're just holding the school accountable" response as satisfactory. They must consider cost, time, alternative methods, and emotional impact on students as a result of these tests.

- Lobby for the development of classroom-based forms of assessment that provide useful, understandable information, improve instruction, and help children become better readers.

Recommendations to policymakers:

- Design an assessment plan that is considerate of the complexity of reading, learning to read, and the teaching of reading. A strong assessment plan is the best ally of teachers and administrators because it supports good instructional decision making and good instructional design. Consider the features of good assessment as outlined in *Standards for Assessment of Reading and Writing* (International Reading Association & National Council of Teachers of English, 1994) in designing an assessment plan. Be aware of the pressures to use tests to make high-stakes decisions.

- When decisions about students must be made that involve high-stakes outcomes (e.g., graduation, matriculation, awards), rely on multiple measures rather than just performance on a single test. The experiences in England with high-stakes assessment have been instructive. England has moved to an assessment system that values teacher informal assessments, ongoing performance assessments, portfolios, teacher recommendations, and standardized testing. The triangulation of data sources leads to more valid decision making.

- Use sampling strategies when assessments do not involve decisions related to the performance of individual students (e.g., program evaluation). Sampling is less intrusive, less costly, and just as reliable as full-scale assessment plans. Sampling strategies also provide an opportunity to design alternate forms and types of assessments. Such a variety of assessments encourages careful inspection of issues of validity and reliability.

- Do not use incentives, resources, money, or recognition of test scores to reward or punish schools or teachers. Neither the awards (e.g., blue ribbon schools) nor the punishing labels (e.g., low-performing schools) are in the interest of students or teachers. The consequences of achieving or not achieving in schools are real enough. Well-intentioned efforts to recognize achievement often become disincentives to those who need the most help.

- Do not attempt to manipulate instruction through assessments. In other words, do not initiate, design, or implement high-stakes tests when the primary goal is to affect instructional practices. Ask the question, "Is the primary goal of the assessment to collect data that will be used to make better decisions that impact the individual students taking the test?" If the answer is "no," high-stakes tests are inappropriate.

The pattern of testing as the preferred tool to manipulate teaching continues to expand. We call on educators, policymakers, community leaders, and parents to take a common-sense look at the testing in schools today. Visit classrooms. Talk to teachers. Listen to teachers talk about the curriculum and the decisions they are making. Talk to the teachers about the kinds of assessments they use in the classroom and how they use collected data. To be opposed to large-scale, high-stakes testing is not to be opposed to assessment or accountability. It is to affirm the necessity of aligning our purposes and goals with our methods.

REFERENCES

Heubert, J. P., & Hauser, R. M. (1999). *High stakes: Testing for tracking, promotion, and graduation.* Washington, DC: National Academy Press.

Hoffman, J., Paris, S., Patterson, E. U., Pennington, J., & Assaf, L. C. (in press). High-stakes assessment in the language arts: The piper plays, the players dance, but who pays the price? In J. Flood, J. M. Jensen, D. Lapp. & J. Squire (Eds.), *Handbook of research on teaching the English language arts* (2nd ed.).

International Reading Association & National Council of Teachers of English. (1994). *Standards for the assessment of reading and writing.* Newark, DE: International Reading Association; Urbana, IL: National Council of Teachers of English.

U.S. Department of Education. (1999). *The NAEP 1998 reading report card for the nation and the states* (NCES 1999-459). Washington, DC: Author.

High-Stakes Testing in Reading:

Today in Texas, Tomorrow?

JAMES V. HOFFMAN

LORI CZOP ASSAF

SCOTT G. PARIS

State-mandated achievement testing has grown at an exponential rate over the past 2 decades. Prior to 1980 fewer than a dozen states in the USA required mandated standardized testing for students, but in 2000 nearly every state used high-stakes testing. Accountability through testing, for students, teachers, and administrators, is the key leverage point for policymakers seeking to promote educational reform. Policies surrounding educational testing have become political spectacles and struggles for both publicity and control (Smith, Heinecke, & Noble, 1999–2000). State-mandated standardized tests have become the centerpiece for standards-based reform and are "high stakes" because they are often used to make decisions about tracking, promotion, and graduation of students (Heubert & Hauser, 1999). Centralized control is achieved through explicit educational standards (e.g., state curriculum frameworks, performance standards), and standardized tests that allow comparisons of students' relative performance. Educators, caught between standards and tests, are left to "align" classroom practices to meet the demands that surround them. Policymakers, and the public to this point, have judged the impact of educational reform efforts through a comparison of outcomes (i.e., changes in test scores) over time. Despite cautions and caveats from testing experts, high-stakes tests have become the public benchmark of educational quality (Linn, 2000).

This design for educational reform is conceptually elegant and seductive to those who embrace rational planning models. Many of the "results" reported by the media to date suggest positive effects for this model of change. But is this the whole

Reprinted by permission of the authors. Originally published in *The Reading Teacher*, *54*, 5(February 2001): 484–492.

story of reform? We think not. How much of the "success" is an illusion that masks an intrusion of testing into good teaching. We think a lot. We are concerned about the hidden costs of standards-based reform efforts on teachers, on the curriculum, and on teacher education. We are concerned about the negative impact on students, especially low-achieving and minority students, who may be retained in grade or denied high school promotion because of poor test performance. In an effort to explore these issues, we conducted a survey of a selected group of educators in one state—Texas. We chose Texas because the accountability system and the standards-based reform effort there have been recognized as "a model" for other states to follow. Indeed, the press has dubbed the reform of education through accountability and high-stakes testing as the "Texas Miracle" (Haney, 2000). We begin with a brief history of the testing movement in Texas and then report the findings from our study. We conclude with suggestions to minimize the negative impact of high-stakes testing on students and teachers.

TAAS IN TEXAS

What began in the era of minimum basic-skills testing as TABS (Texas Assessment of Basic Skills) has expanded over the past 25 years to become one of the most highly touted state education accountability systems in the United States. The main part of this accountability system is the TAAS (Texas Assessment of Academic Skills). This criterion-referenced test focuses, for the most part, on the areas of reading, writing, and mathematics and is linked directly to the state-prescribed curriculum. The TAAS test is set within a broader set of indices that feed into the total accountability system. For example, districts also monitor such factors as dropout rates, the proportion of students assigned to special education, and graduation rates. Changes in TAAS performance are examined carefully in relation to patterns on this broader set of accountability measures. These other measures are used as checks to determine if any positive changes in test performance are the result of higher levels of student learning or the result of some other factors (e.g., high levels of exemption for low-performing students). In recent years, TAAS has been expanded to include more students, more grade levels, and more subject areas. Currently, the test is administered annually in the spring to all students in Grades 3 through 8 in reading and mathematics. Students in Grades 4, 8, and 10 are tested in writing. Grade 8 students also take tests in science and social studies.

As the amount of testing has increased, so have the consequences associated with student performance on TAAS. For students, high school graduation is dependent on successful performance on TAAS. For schools and districts, accreditation is dependent in large part on TAAS performance. For principals and teachers, performance ratings and merit raises are influenced by TAAS performance of their students. The state requires the reporting of TAAS data to individual schools with school improvement plans developed in consideration of student performance patterns. The high-stakes consequences were intended to increase the quality of both teaching and learning. It is important to recognize that the identification of the "achievement problem," as well as the identification of a solution through rigorous testing, were both politically inspired and imposed on educators (Berliner & Biddle, 1997).

TAAS scores increased consistently during the last decade across all areas tested and at every grade level. For example, the proportion of students passing TAAS rose from 55% in 1994 to 74% in 1997. Further, the "gap" in performance between minority students and white students has narrowed. Only 32% of the African American students passed the tests in 1994 as compared with 56% in 1997. The passing rates for Hispanics rose from 41% to 62% in the same period. Scores rose again in 1998 with an overall passing rate of 78%. Scores for African American students rose to 63% and for Mexican American students to 68% (Texas Education Agency, 1999). In the future, TAAS may be extended into the primary grades and included as part of high school course examinations. Perhaps the most controversial proposal is to use TAAS performance as a requirement for grade-level promotion.

The apparent success of the TAAS has attracted national attention and figured prominently in Texas Governor George W. Bush's presidential campaign. Because the TAAS model of testing and accountability may be adopted by states, it is important to examine it critically. A comprehensive review of the TAAS was conducted by Haney (2000), a testing expert who was also an expert witness in a lawsuit against the TAAS. Haney concluded that claims about Texas education have been greatly exaggerated because of five fundamental problems with the TAAS. First, the TAAS has continuing adverse effects on African American and Hispanic American students. Compared with Caucasian students, minority students have significantly lower passing rates on the TAAS; they are more likely to be retained in grade; and they are less likely to graduate from high school. Second, the use of TAAS tests to control high school graduation is contrary to professional standards regarding the use of test scores.

Third, Haney (2000) argued that the passing score set on the TAAS is arbitrary and results in racial discrimination. He conducted a small study in which randomly selected adults were asked to examine the TAAS data and set the passing scores in a way that would maximize the differences between racial groups. Their passing scores were virtually identical to the scores set by the Texas Education Authority (TEA) leading to the conclusion that the passing scores were discriminatory, whether intended or not. Fourth, analyses of the psychometric data on the TAAS, and comparisons with the National Assessment of Educational Progress (NAEP) test results, cast doubt on the validity of the TAAS test scores. The apparent increases in TAAS scores are due to factors such as teaching to the test, higher retention and dropout rates for minority students, and exemption of minority students by increased placement in special education. Fifth, there are more appropriate ways to use TAAS scores, such as in sliding combination with high school grades, that would increase the validity and decrease the negative impact of TAAS scores. The judge who presided over the TAAS lawsuit was not persuaded that these problems invalidate the TAAS. He concluded that the TAAS does have discriminatory consequences for black and Hispanic students but is not illegal because it is educationally necessary (*GI Forum Image De Tejas v. Texas Education Agency*, 87 F. Supp. 667 [W.E. Tex. 2000]).

TEACHERS RESPOND TO TAAS

While the legal and political implications of the TAAS attract headlines, teachers are left to implement instruction aligned with the TAAS. What is happening at the classroom level in response to the expansion of TAAS and the pressure to perform well on tests? In an effort to explore this issue, we conducted a survey of a selected group of teachers in Texas that focused on TAAS and its effects. Our primary goal was to examine the ways in which TAAS affects teachers, students, and instruction from the perspective of the professional educators in classrooms and schools who are most affected by TAAS. Our goal is to reveal some of the ways in which the pressures of high-stakes assessments may threaten or compromise excellence in teaching.

THE PARTICIPANTS

All of the participants in this survey were members of the Texas State Reading Association (TSRA), an affiliate of the International Reading Association. The membership of this organization includes classroom teachers, reading specialists, curriculum supervisors, and others in leadership positions. Most of the members hold advanced degrees with a specialization in reading and extensive teaching experience. The complete membership mailing list, containing approximately 4,000 names, was obtained from TSRA headquarters. Using a random selection process, 500 individuals were initially identified (20% of the total membership) and sent survey questionnaires with self-addressed and stamped return envelopes. No incentives were offered to respond. After 3 weeks, a reminder letter was sent out to those who had not responded. Additional surveys, using the random selection process, were mailed until a total of 200 usable surveys were returned. In all, 750 surveys were sent out. The 200 surveys in the sample represent an overall return rate of 27% from 5% of the total membership. No biases were detected in the response rates based on geographical areas of the state. However, the sample is a select group of educators in Texas with both expertise and experience in the teaching of reading. The sample also includes many teachers who work primarily with students in circumstances of poverty. It may be that teachers who cared most about their profession or who felt most affected by the TAAS were more likely to respond to the survey, but there is no reason to believe that the views of these 200 educators are not representative of Texas teachers.

In general, survey respondents were older and more experienced than average classroom teachers in Texas. Sixty-six percent of the sample were over the age of 30, and 33% were between the ages of 40 and 60. Likewise, 63% had more than 10 years of classroom experience and 29% had more than 20 years' experience. This is not surprising given that our selection process focused on teachers with an active affiliation with a professional organization. It is also not surprising that most respondents worked in elementary schools (78%) that have predominantly minority students (81%) and serve low-income communities (72%) where the need for reading specialists is greatest and the funding sources for reading specialists most available. Only 16% of the respondents reported working in schools where the passing rate was over 90% on TAAS. The majority of those responding (51%) were working in schools with a past passing rate for students between 70% and 90%, and 32% were working in schools where the overall passing rate was less than 70%.

THE SURVEY

The survey consisted of 113 items about the following topics: demographic information (12 items); general attitudes of the respondent (20 items); perceived attitudes of others (22 items); test preparation and administration practices (27 items); uses of scores (16 items); effects of the TAAS on students (11 items); and overall impressions about TAAS testing (5 items). Many of the items included in the survey were exact duplicates or slightly modified versions of items that appeared on the Urdan and Paris (1994) survey of teachers in Michigan and the Nolen, Haladyna, and Haas (1989) survey of teachers in Arizona. All of the items about attitudes focused directly on TAAS testing. The majority of items about attitudes required responses on a five-point scale: 1 = Strongly Disagree, 2 = Disagree, 3 = Agree, 4 = Strongly Agree, and 5 = Don't Know. All "5" responses were treated as missing data and ignored in calculating the average responses. The last five items contained an invitation for extended responses.

THE FINDINGS

The data from the 200 returned surveys were entered into a data file for item-level analyses. Subsequently, some composite scores were constructed combining items from sections of the questionnaire (e.g., general attitudes). Items were combined based on a priori decisions about face validity rather than factor analyses of the data. In the reporting of findings that follows, we will refer to data from individual items as well as combined items. Composite scores are reported using means and standard deviations, and individual items are reported using categories of responses and percentages. Lower mean scores indicate greater disagreement with the proposition in the item; higher mean scores indicate greater agreement. The qualitative analysis of comments on the final section of the survey focused on common themes among the responses. More than 80% of the respondents offered additional comments on the five items, and their comments reveal the depth of teachers' feelings regarding TAAS testing.

General attitudes and perceptions of others. To examine teachers' general attitudes about the TAAS, we created a composite score from the following four items.

- Better TAAS tests will make teachers do a better job. (M = 1.8; SD = .75)
- TAAS motivates students to learn. (M = 1.6; SD = .71)
- TAAS scores are good measures of teachers' effectiveness. (M = 1.6; SD = .68)
- TAAS test scores provide good comparisons of the quality of school from different districts. (M = 1.9; SD = .76)

Each item was asked in order to assess teachers' perceptions of the political intentions of the TAAS test. The average rating on the composite variable for these four items was 1.7, a rating between Strongly Disagree and Disagree, which suggests that teachers disagree with many of the underlying intentions of the TAAS.

Another composite variable was created with items related to the validity of TAAS as a measure of student learning. The four variables included in this analysis follow.

- TAAS tests accurately measure achievement for minority students. (M = 1.6; SD = .73)
- TAAS test scores accurately measure achievement for limited English-speaking students. (M = 1.5; SD =.64)
- Students' TAAS scores reflect what students have learned in school during the past year. (M = 1.8; SD = .75)
- Students' TAAS scores reflect the cumulative knowledge that students have learned during their years in school. (M = 2.1; SD = .84)

The average rating on the composite variable for these four items was also 1.7, suggesting that teachers challenge the basic validity of the test, especially for minority students and ESL speakers who are the majority of students in Texas public schools.

Contrast these general attitudes and beliefs regarding TAAS with the perception of the respondents that administrators believe TAAS performance is an accurate indicator of student achievement (M = 3.1) and the quality of teaching (M = 3.3). Also, contrast this with the perception of the respondents that parents feel TAAS reflects the quality of schooling (M = 2.8). The gaping disparity between the perceptions of teachers and their estimates of administrators' and parents' attitudes suggests an uncomfortable dissonance in attitudes about the TAAS. Although we cannot determine whether the perceptions of the respondents regarding administrators' and parents' attitudes are accurate or not, the overwhelming majority of the respondents question the assumptions, intentions, and validity of the TAAS test but believe that parents and administrators do not share their views.

A final composite variable for this section was constructed to capture additional stances toward TAAS that explore some extreme positions. This variable consisted of responses to the following four items.

- TAAS should be eliminated. (M = 2.8; SD = .97)
- TAAS tests take too much time from the regular curriculum. (M = 3.2; SD =.89)
- TAAS tests are overemphasized by administrators. (M = 3.5; SD = .74)
- TAAS testing is not worth the time and money spent on it. (M = 3.0; SD = .91)

The average rating on the composite variable for these four items was 3.0 (Agree), again reflecting a strong negative attitude toward TAAS.

Preparation and administration of the TAAS. The questions in this section of the survey focused on the amount of time and attention that teachers devote to preparing students to take the TAAS and the kinds of strategies teachers use to prepare students to take the test. Nearly all of the respondents indicated that preparation for TAAS begins more than a month before testing. Comments from respondents suggested that preparation occurs across the entire academic year reaching its peak in the months just before TAAS is administered. The responses reveal an average of 8 to 10 hours per week spent in TAAS preparation activities. TAAS preparation is required by principals, and the majority of respondents reported that principals encourage more time than is currently devoted. Direct preparation is only one point of impact on the curriculum. Respondents reported that teachers almost always plan their curriculum for the year to emphasize those areas that will be tested on TAAS. Although some reformers may regard this planning as a positive outcome, many teachers consider it to have a negative impact on the curriculum and their instructional effectiveness.

The line between what is acceptable and what is not acceptable in standardized test preparation and administration is not always clearly delineated. Respondents were asked to rate the frequency with which teachers in their schools engaged in various testing practices related to TAAS using the following scale: 1 = Never, 2 = Sometimes, 3 = Often, and 4 = Always. The actions of teachers described in Table 8.1 are arranged from commonly accepted as appropriate to those that could be questioned. Although only some of these practices fall clearly into a "cheating" category, many approach an unethical stance toward testing. All are capable of affecting test performance. Haladyna, Nolen, and Haas (1991) referred to such practices on a continuum of "test pollution" because they have the potential to enhance, when present, the scores of students in unethical ways. Such practices raise test scores without actually changing students' underlying knowledge or achievement so they give the spurious impression of educational improvement.

Haladyna et al. (1991) argued that as pressures increase to raise test scores, unethical testing practices will occur more often. Our data support this hypothesis. All of the practices noted in Table 8.1 were reported with greater frequency in schools that had a history of low TAAS performance. For example, the practice of rewarding students for doing well occurred at a reported mean level of 3.4 (Often +) in the schools with a history of low TAAS scores; whereas the practice was reported at a mean level of 1.9 (Sometimes –) in the schools with a history of high performance. In the

TABLE 8.1   Reported practices related to test prepartion and administration

PRACTICES	MEANS
Demonstrate how to mark the answer sheet correctly.	3.2
Give general tips on how to take tests.	3.4
Tell students how important it is to do well on the test.	3.7
Use commercial test-preparation materials.	3.4
Have students practice with tests from previous years.	3.4
Encourage student attendance.	3.7
Reduce stress and anxiety by teaching relaxation.	2.4
Teach test-taking skills.	3.5
Teach or review topics that will be on the test.	3.5
Give students hints about answers.	1.2
Point out mismarked items to students.	1.3
Give some students extra time to finish.	2.6
Provide instruction during the test.	1.2
Allow students breaks for fatigue or stress.	3.0
Directly point out to students correct responses.	1.1
Change students' answers once they have been recorded.	1.1
Award prizes to students who do well/pass the test.	2.4

lowest performing schools, the most blatant forms of "cheating" were reported at higher levels than in the schools with a history of high performance. The practices included giving hints about answers ($M = 1.7$), pointing out mismarked items ($M = 1.7$), providing instruction during the test ($M = 1.5$), and directly pointing out correct responses ($M = 1.5$). Although the frequency of these unethical practices is low even in the low-performing schools, the rates are consistent with previous findings (e.g., Haas, Haladyna, & Nolen, 1989; Nolen et al., 1989). The total combination of practices creates a disturbing scenario of teachers succumbing to pressures to raise test scores at any cost and the TAAS scores being contaminated by factors unrelated to students' abilities.

Effects on students.   The items included in this section of the survey explored the impact of the TAAS on students and were borrowed directly from the surveys used in the Arizona and Michigan research cited earlier. The findings suggest the same patterns for TAAS as with other standardized tests. The data from our survey are displayed in Table 8.2. According to teachers, many students experience headaches and stomachaches while taking the TAAS. A surprising number are anxious, irritable, or aggressive. The data are troubling because discomfort and illness during the TAAS undermine students' test performance, further polluting the scores and decreasing their validity. It seems likely that low-scoring students would be the ones most negatively affected, which puts at-risk students in more jeopardy during TAAS testing. We did not explore directly the effects of TAAS on student motivation or self-concept,

TABLE 8.2   Effects of TAAS testing on students

BEHAVIOR	REPORTED FREQUENCY			
	NEVER %	SOMETIMES %	OFTEN %	ALWAYS %
Truancy	40	52	5	3
Upset stomach	7	53	32	8
Vomiting	18	53	21	8
Crying	22	60	13	5
Irritability	12	50	30	8
Increased aggression	22	43	28	7
Wetting or soiling themselves	74	23	3	0
Headaches	8	45	33	14
Refusing to take test	53	37	7	3
Increased misconduct	29	42	23	6
Freezing up	12	54	25	9

although the negative effects of standardized tests, in particular on low-performing and minority students, have been clearly demonstrated (Paris, Lawton, Turner, & Roth, 1991).

Uses of TAAS.   Two composite variables were created to summarize the uses of TAAS results. The first variable focused on how teachers use TAAS results by combining responses on the following items:

- To make decisions about curricula. (M = 3.2; SD = .74)
- To measure school or classroom effectiveness. (M = 3.1; SD = .76)
- To make decisions about how to group students. (M = 2.7; SD =.92)
- To identify students for remedial programs. (M = 3.0; SD =.86)
- To predict future performance. (M = 2.8; SD =.76)
- To diagnose learning problems for specific students. (M = 2.4; SD = .90)
- To assign students to low-track and basic classes. (M = 2.3; SD = 1.0)

Each of these items had been rated separately on a scale of 1 = Never, 2 = Sometimes, 3 = Often, and 4 = Always. The mean response for the composite variable for these seven items was 2.8 (*SD* = .62) suggesting that TAAS results are often used in these ways.

The second composite variable focused on the uses of TAAS results by school principals. Here we combined responses on the following items:

- To help teachers improve their instruction. (*M* = 2.8; *SD* = .86)
- To identify strengths and weaknesses of the curriculum. (*M* = 3.0; *SD* = .75)
- To evaluate teacher effectiveness. (*M* = 3.0; *SD* =.80)
- To evaluate school effectiveness. (*M* = 3.3; *SD* =.73)
- To evaluate the effectiveness of new programs. (*M* = 2.9; *SD* =.82)
- To recognize outstanding student or teacher performance. (*M* = 2.8; *SD* = .98)

The mean for the composite variable for these six items was 3.0 (*SD* = .60) suggesting that TAAS results are often used in these ways. None of the uses described in this section are surprising. What is a matter of concern is the extreme if not sole reliance on TAAS results as the data source in guiding planning, decisions, and actions.

Overall impressions on TAAS. This final section of the survey included five questions and teachers' comments about each topic. We provide the questions and responses below.

1. The results from TAAS testing over the past several years seem to indicate that scores are on the rise. Do you think this rise in test scores reflects increased learning and higher quality teaching?

Yes = 27% No = 50% Not Sure = 23%

Half of the respondents did not believe that the increases in TAAS scores were the result of higher levels of student learning. Their comments suggest that they believed the higher scores were the direct result of teaching to the test.

"Teaching to the test and test-taking strategies."

"Teaching to the format of the test."

"Students know how to take the test because we practice ad nauseam."

"Teachers are spending the school day teaching to the test."

Awareness of the objectives as well as better training and test practice materials were also given credit.

"We have better training on how to prepare students."

"We know what to expect on the test."

Many believed that TAAS is incapable of tapping the higher level learning that is taking place in schools.

"TAAS does not require higher level thinking and does not allow for it."

Some teachers even suggested that the test is getting easier.

"I think the tests are easier to make the legislators look better."

Some teachers raised the explanation of cheating.

"There are a lot of teachers and administrators who know how to 'cheat' and get higher scores from kids . . . they don't want their school to score bad, so they cheat."

The results from the NAEP (Donahue, Voelkl, Campbell, & Mazzeo, 1999), as well as the results of the TEAs own national comparison study (Texas Education Agency, 1997), suggested that the improved scores in the area of reading are restricted to the TAAS test and that these increases are not reflected on the performance of Texas students on nationally standardized tests. Apparently, many respondents felt the same way because they indicated that the increases in test scores might be due to artificial causes such as teaching to the test, rather than increasing children's reading abilities.

2. It has been suggested that the areas not tested directly on the TAAS (e.g., fine arts) and other areas not tested at certain grade levels (e.g., science at the fourth-grade level) receive less and less attention in the curriculum. What do you feel about this assertion?

Very True = 49% Somewhat True = 36% Somewhat False = 8% Totally False = 7%

The responses related to the second item indicate that there is considerable curriculum displacement due to TAAS because 85% of the teachers replied that "if it's not being tested, it's not being taught." These findings are consistent with those of Darling-Hammond and Wise (1985) who found that tested content was taught at the expense of untested content.

"We were told by administration if it isn't tested don't spend the bulk of your time teaching it."

"We hardly teach social studies and science."

"There is no time to teach these subject areas because of TAAS."

"At our school, third- and fourth-grade teachers are told not to teach social studies and science until March (after TAAS)."

"The test has become the curriculum."

"The principal told us not to be teaching social studies and science."

"We only teach TAAS. The rest is just fluff. My social studies and science grades come from TAAS reading passages. Everything must be done in TAAS format."

3. It has also been suggested that the emphasis on TAAS is forcing some of the best teachers to leave teaching because of the restraints the tests place on decision making and the pressures placed on them and their students. Do you agree or disagree?

Strongly Agree = 42% Somewhat Agree = 43% Disagree = 11 % Strongly Disagree = 4%

The third item explored the consequences of high-stakes testing on teachers. Although teachers may not value the TAAS as much as parents and administrators, they are expected to teach to the TAAS and raise test scores. This leads to frustration and a desire to escape the pressures of the TAAS. Eighty-five percent of the teachers expressed agreement with the statement that some of the best teachers are leaving the field because of the TAAS.

"People do not want to work in this type of environment."

"I know of a great many (who are leaving), and I am also."

Some teachers described efforts to flee TAAS pressure without dropping out of teaching altogether.

"I used to teach fourth grade, but now I teach first grade. I just don't want the pressure."

"This is why I teach in a specialization area where TAAS is not tested."

"It has dramatically shifted the purpose of teaching. We are 'required' to teach to the TAAS. I became a teacher to teach children."

4. TAAS is being recommended as the basis for making promotion decisions about students in some schools. What is your view regarding this policy?

Strongly Agree = 4% Somewhat Agree = 30% Disagree = 36% Strongly Disagree = 30%

The use of TAAS as a requirement for high school graduation is a reality. The proposals for using TAAS to control grade-level advancement are widespread. A substantial majority (66%) of the respondents opposed the use of TAAS scores to make decisions about grade-level advancement.

"If you have a poor instrument, then you will always make poor decisions."

"TAAS + promotions = bull—."

Many commented on the logistical nightmare that would be created by such a policy.

"Fourth grade will be huge. In my class alone I suspect 40% to fail."

Some expressed general dissatisfaction with retention as a solution to anything.

"Retention doesn't work and research has shown this! We should be considering other areas to help, not the same old things that didn't work before."

Most of those responding, including those who seem to favor the use of TAAS in promotion decisions, suggest that multiple factors should be considered.

"I think it could support the decision on promotion, but it should not be the sole source for this decision."

"TAAS should be a factor in promotion decisions but not the sole criterion."

5. Do the informal assessments you currently make in your classroom provide you with a sufficient basis for good instructional decision making, or do TAAS results help you?

Informal assessments are sufficient = 43% TAAS helps some = 52% TAAS helps a lot = 5%

This notion of multiple measures was confirmed by the respondents' answers. Many favored a combination of measures.

DISCUSSION

The findings from this study are consistent with research on the negative effects of "high-stakes" assessments. (e.g., Airasian, 1988; Madaus, 1988; Meisels, 1989; Paris, 1998; Shepard & Dougherty, 1991). The findings from this study are also consistent with two other studies of the TAAS. In one study, Gordon and Reese (1997) surveyed 100 Texas teachers (who were apparently graduate students in their program) about the impact of TAAS on teachers and students. Twenty individuals were also interviewed. Respondents reported that preparation for the TAAS was the main activity for months before the test and that there was a de-emphasis on teaching content that was not related to the TAAS. Of the 20 interviewed, 19 teachers felt that the TAAS was not an appropriate tool for evaluating students or teachers. Teachers reported that the TAAS was culturally biased and had deleterious impact on at-risk students. A second study conducted by Haney (2000) involved two surveys of secondary teachers in Texas. He summarized four similarities among the surveys administered in his study, the survey reported in this paper, and the Gordon and Reese (1997) study. All the similarities undermine effective teaching and learning.

1. Texas schools are devoting a huge amount of time and energy preparing students specifically for the TAAS.
2. Emphasis on TAAS is hurting more than helping teaching and learning in Texas.
3. Emphasis on TAAS is particularly harmful to at-risk students.
4. Emphasis on TAAS contributes to retention in grade and dropping out of school.

This study confirms the negative impact on teachers and students in Texas. The respondents to this survey, experts in reading and close to the classroom, reported that the TAAS does not measure what it purports, is unfair to minority students, is affecting instruction in negative ways, is leading both students and teachers to "drop out," and is being used in ways that are invalid. These educators would argue that the triumph of the Texas accountability system touted by politicians, bureaucrats, and test publishers should be challenged. The extensions of TAAS into more subject areas and into earlier grade levels are disturbing. More disturbing is the prospect that many state policy-makers regard the TAAS as successful and want to expand the use of TAAS results for teacher evaluation and student promotion.

TODAY IN TEXAS, TOMORROW?

The impact of Texas on textbooks, curriculum, and assessment across the U.S. is enormous and continues to expand. The Texas state curriculum, The Texas Essential Knowledge and Skills, is used to guide commercial textbook development and may become the de facto reading curriculum for a large part of the U.S. As pubic recognition of the TAAS increases, it is likely to be emulated by other states too. When tests drive instruction, teachers become increasingly responsive to the demands of the tests and less considerate of the needs of the students in their classrooms. Instruction that conforms to high-stakes tests in content and format will become more patterned and predictable and less responsive and adaptive. Teachers and students deserve better, and the respondents to our survey recognize this. Our survey forms were filled with comments that revealed frustration, anger, and helplessness with respect to TAAS testing.

> "I am very sad that education has stooped to the low level of measuring performance with standardized testing and Texas has taken it even lower with their TAAS. We know what works in education—we just seem to ignore the research and keep on banging our heads against the 'TAAS wall' and 'retention walls'."

> "Please support teachers more than ever. Our children are hurting more than ever. If there was ever a time to change, it is now. Give teachers back their classrooms. Let them teach and spend quality time with their students. They need us."

> "I think TAAS is the biggest joke in Texas. I have never seen such an injustice."

> "I believe that TAAS interferes with the very nature of our job. The pressure from administrators to increase campus scores leaves teachers little time for real instruction. My heart breaks to see so many teachers 'just surviving.' I believe that our solution is just to support each other because the public has no real concept of the situation."

> "TAAS is ruining education in Texas! Help!"

WHAT CAN BE DONE?

If we were totally fatalistic about the future of reading assessment, we would not have conducted this study, nor would we be writing this article. We believe there are actions to be taken within Texas and the U.S. to stem the tide of high-stakes assessments. As part of a profession of concerned reading educators, we suggest the following steps.

Provide data.   Statistical claims regarding high-stakes assessments typically use data provided by those who control its design, administration, and data analysis. We are in desperate need of independent research that provides a critical analysis of the effects of high-stakes assessments on stakeholders from a variety of perspectives. Parents, teachers, and students should be surveyed about the high-stakes tests given by their districts.

Compare.   There are a number of other states that have taken other paths to ensure educational accountability that are based on sound principles of assessment without the high-stakes pressure of TAAS. We need careful examination and comparison of the alternatives. Fair-Test (http://fairtest.org) offers a good example for how this kind of principled analysis can be conducted (Neill, 1999).

Advocate.   Both individually and collectively, we must advocate for reasonable assessment of students in schools. The International Reading Association (1999) has taken a bold stance toward high-stakes assessment. Other national, state, and local organizations need to act similarly. We believe it is particularly important that student advocacy groups and parent groups become more active in voicing their concerns.

Challenge.   The Mexican-American Legal Defense and Educational Fund (MALDEF) has taken the lead in challenging the TAAS test and its use as a graduation requirement in Texas as racially discriminatory. Despite a complex and lengthy court battle, the MALDEF suit was not successful. More challenges should be made, and the current efforts supported.

Explore alternatives.   No one is opposed to accountability in education. We must demonstrate that the goals of accountability can be achieved through alternative testing. For example, states and districts could use a NAEP model in which only some sampled students are tested. This removes the onus of an individual score for students or teachers yet still provides an estimate of achievement by district or state. When high-stakes decisions are required about promotion, retention or graduation of students, or the quality of teaching, multiple measures should be used.

Don't be seduced.   Silence prevails in educational circles with respect to TAAS-type testing because it is viewed as a necessary evil to achieve other goals. Recent pay raises for teachers in Texas have been negotiated in the context of accepting, if not embracing, high-stakes assessment. The words of the president of the National Education Association speak to this.

> [Our] colleagues in Texas . . . are dealing positively and creatively with standards-based instruction . . . I repeat, high standards and high stakes tests are here to stay. They have thrust us into a brave new world. By all means, let us be brave and affirmative in shaping this new world in the best interests of the children we serve (Chase, 1999).

Similarly, some minority leaders have been silent on high-stakes testing because low performance is seen as a way of increasing the flow of money to needy schools. These are indefensible positions in the light of the negative effects of such tests on education.

It is easy to get discouraged by the TAAS frenzy and the political steamrollers of standards and testing. The political and economic forces supporting the movement are formidable. TAAS is approaching a hundred-million-dollar-a-year industry in direct costs alone (Brooks, 1998). Teaching to TAAS is far easier than teaching to students. Every good teacher who drops out opens a space for someone who might be more vulnerable to the pressures of high-stakes testing. We urge teachers to stay the course. Be creatively compliant and selectively defiant as it fits the learning needs of your students. As leaders in reading and literacy education, we have an important role to play in the appropriate use of high-stakes assessment. Our professional colleagues, the voices of those responding in our survey, are crying out for assistance and guidance. Their pleas are not just about themselves and their situation but the plight of the students they serve. Will we remain silent?

REFERENCES

Airasian, P. W. (1988). Symbolic validation: The case of state-mandated, high-stakes testing. *Educational Evaluation and Policy Analysis, 10,* 301–313.

Berliner, D. C., & Biddle, B. J. (1997). *The manufactured crisis: Myths, fraud, and the attack on America's public schools.* White Plains, NY: Longman.

Brooks, P. A. (1998, December 16). Lawmaker proposes more frequent TAAS testing. *Austin American Statesman,* p. B5.

Chase, B. (1999). Don't get mad. Get ready! *NEA Today, 17*(6), 2.

Darling-Hammond, L., & Wise, A. (1985). Beyond standardization: State standards and school improvement. *The Elementary School Journal, 85,* 315–336.

Donahue, P. L., Voelkl, K. E., Campbell, J. R., & Mazzeo, J. (1999). *NAEP 1998 reading: Report card for the nation and states.* Washington, DC: U.S. Department of Education.

Gordon, S. P., & Reese, M. (1997). High stakes testing: Worth the price? *Journal of School Leadership, 7,* 345–368.

Haas, N. S., Haladyna, T. M, & Nolen, S. B. (1989). *Standardized testing in Arizona: Interviews and written comments from teachers and administrators* (Tech. Rep. No. 89-3). Phoenix, AZ: Arizona State University, West Campus.

Haladyna, T., Nolen, S. B., & Haas, N. S. (1991). Raising standardized achievement test scores and the origins of test pollution. *Educational Researcher, 20*(5), 2–7.

Haney. W. (2000, April). *The myth of the Texas miracle in education.* Paper presented at the annual meeting of the American Educational Research Association, New Orleans, LA.

Heubert, J. P., & Hauser, R. M. (1999). *High stakes. Testing for tracking, promotion, and graduation.* A report of the National Research Council, Washington, DC: National Academy Press.

International Reading Association. (1999). *High-stakes testing in reading. A position paper.* Newark, DE: International Reading Association.

Linn, R. L. (2000). Assessments and accountability. *Educational Researcher, 29*(2), 4–15.

Madaus, G. F. (1988). The influence of testing on curriculum. In L. N. Tanner (Ed.), *Critical issues in curriculum: 87th yearbook of the National Society for the Study of Education* (pp. 83–121). Chicago: University of Chicago Press.

Meisels, S. J. (1989). High stakes testing in kindergarten. *Educational Leadership, 46,* 16–22.

Neill, M. (1999). Is high-stakes testing fair? *NEA Today, 17*(6), 6.

Nolen, S. B., Haladyna, T. M., & Haas, N. S. (1989). *A survey of Arizona teachers and school administrators on the uses and effects of standardized achievement testing* (Tech. Rep. No. 89-2). Phoenix, AZ: Arizona State University, West Campus.

Paris, S. G. (1998). Why learner-centered assessment is better than high-stakes testing. In N. Lambert & B. McCombs (Eds.), *Issues in school reform: A sampler of psychological perspectives on learner-centered schools* (pp. 189–209). Washington, DC: American Psychological Association.

Paris, S. G., Lawton, T. A., Turner, J. C., & Roth, J. L. (1991). A developmental perspective on standardized achievement testing. *Educational Researcher, 20,* 12–20.

Shepard, L. A., & Dougherty, K. C. (1991). *Effects of high-stakes testing on instruction.* Paper presented at the annual meeting of the American Educational Research Association, Chicago. (ERIC Document Reproduction Service No. ED 337 468)

Smith, M. L., Heinecke, W., & Noble, A. J. (1999–2000). State assessment becomes political spectacle: Parts I–VIII. *Teachers College Record.* Available at: www.tcrecord.org. ID Number 10454.

Texas Education Agency. (1997). *Texas Student Assessment Program: Student performance results 1995–1996.* Austin, TX: Author.

Urdan, T. C., & Paris, S. G. (1994). Teachers' perceptions of standardized achievement tests. *Educational Policy, 8*(2), 137–156.

CLASSROOM IMPLICATIONS

1. How can classroom teachers effectively use reading assessment results in their teaching? Suggest some specific problems that must be overcome in this area as well as appropriate solutions.

2. Describe what you believe is an effective classroom program of reading assessment. What types of tests would you use, including both formal and informal reading assessment procedures? How would you use the results of these reading tests in designing both your total reading curriculum as well as working with individual students?

ANNOTATED BIBLIOGRAPHY

Colorado reads! Implementing the Colorado basic literacy act: Thoughtful and practical responses. (ERIC Reproduction Service No. ED448427).

  State-published book suggesting ways in which teachers can prepare their students for the Colorado Student Assessment Program as well as effectively use the results of this test instrument in their daily classroom instruction efforts.

Dunn, E. (2000). *Appropriate reading assessment: Are we on the right track?* (ERIC Reproduction Service No. ED44840).

  Questions whether standardized assessment is the best form of measurement that can be used to determine current student performance in the area of reading. Suggests that a more balanced approach to testing would provide a better view of actual reading ability.

Engelhard, G. (2001). Historical views of the influences of measurement and reading theories on the assessment of reading. *Journal of Applied Measurement, 2,* 1–26.

  Discusses a conceptual framework for reviewing reading assessment in relation to prominent measurement theories of the twentieth century.

Morrow. J. (2001). Undermining standards. *Phi Delta Kappan, 82,* 52–59.

  Argues that high-stakes tests threaten to undermine national standards by forcing decisions that will encourage undesirable educational practices.

Perry, A. (2000). Coaching for a reading test? Yes, it is possible and necessary. *Reading Improvement, 37,* 19–25.

  Encourages classroom teachers to provide their students with appropriate information on how to best prepare for various types of literacy assessment.

The adverse effect of high-stakes testing on minority students: Evidence from 100 years of test data. (2001). (ERIC Reproduction Service No. ED450183).

  Describes the negative impact of high-stakes testing on educational decisions related to minority students. This research was based on an historical review of past assessment data.

Tierney, R., et al. (2000). Snippets: How will literacy be assessed in the next millennium? *Reading Research Quarterly, 35,* 244–250.

  Presents the views of four prominent educators as to the future of literacy assessment, noting important trends such as high-stakes testing, large-scale assessment, and, hopefully, increased emphasis on classroom-based testing.

Villaire, T. (2001). High-stakes testing: Is it fair to test students? *Our Children, 26,* 5–7.

  Discusses the question of whether it is fair to all students to have major educational decisions made strictly on the basis of high-stakes testing.

Willis, A. (2000). Political acts: Literacy learning and teaching. *Reading Research Quarterly, 35,* 72–88.

  Notes the importance of politics as it affects various aspects of literacy instruction and teaching, including various forms of assessment.

Zigo, D. (2001). Constructing firebreaks against high-stakes testing. *English Education, 33,* 214–232.

  Suggests that effective language teachers use other teaching techniques rather than high-stakes testing to measure student performance. These include rich classroom discussion, reading from a variety of texts, student-centered writing assignments, and metacognitive awareness of one's reading and writing strategies.

YOU BECOME INVOLVED

1. Almost all school districts have policies related to the administration of school tests and the use of the results of these instruments. If you are not aware of these procedures, locate and read the current policies on assessment, particularly as it relates to the area of literacy. What are your feelings about these regulations? If you are not comfortable with them, how might you change these policies?

2. What are your general feelings about the many issues related to the current assessment of literacy abilities in relation to your own personal classroom instructional program.

• • • • •

CHAPTER NINE

TECHNOLOGY

[Reading researchers] . . . succeeded in photographing upon a moving plate a beam of light reflected from the eye at different angles during its movement from one fixation point to another, thus permitting a computation of the rate of movement.

—Edmund Huey (1924)

. . . experimental evidence reveals that the pacing of eye movements by means of elaborate devices [reading machines] is not necessary to improve speed of reading. In fact, there is no adequate evidence that training of eye movements as such improves reading.

—Miles Tinker (1952)

Like it or not, technology is here to stay. The range of applications in classrooms continues to grow, and some of them could scarcely have been envisioned a few short years ago. This change has been accelerated by the fact that hardware is consistently becoming faster, smaller, cheaper, and more powerful. Together these trends have created a number of issues that educators must address. The list that follows includes some of the more salient. We pose them as questions.

1. How can the "digital divide" be bridged so that economically disadvantaged youngsters have adequate access to technology?
2. How has technology changed the nature of literacy and helped to transform it into "literacies"?
3. How must reading and writing instruction change so that children can become proficient at reading and writing in electronic environments?
4. How can teacher educators better prepare preservice teachers to use the new technologies effectively?
5. How can schools meet the daunting cost of technology in order to bring it to all children and to keep it current?
6. How can inservice teachers be trained in effective new applications?
7. How can the Internet best be utilized to improve instruction?

In a position statement adopted in December of 2001, the International Reading Association addressed some of these questions and articulated its stance on information and communication technology (ICT). In it, IRA affirmed that students have a right to:

- teachers who are skilled in the effective use of ICT for teaching and learning;
- a literacy curriculum that integrates the new literacies of ICT into instructional programs;
- instruction that develops the critical literacies essential to effective information use;
- assessment practices in literacy that include reading on the Internet and writing using word-processing software;
- opportunities to learn safe and responsible use of information and communication technologies; and
- equal access to ICT.

Realizing these rights is a complex matter, of course. It will not happen quickly, but without teachers who are cognizant of the issues and who embrace in their classrooms what the workplace has made irreversible, it will not happen at all. (Download the entire position statement by visiting http://www.reading.org/positions/technology.html)

AS YOU READ

The following article summarizes some of the principal ways in which technology is being applied in classrooms to foster literacy growth. It appeared in a volume devoted to research-based best practices in a number of areas of literacy education, and we believe it adheres to that high standard. A number of applications are described, mostly in the context of classroom scenarios, and as you read we encourage you to focus on these questions.

1. What are some of the ways technology can be used effectively with beginning readers?
2. How does conventional literacy differ from electronic literacy?
3. In what ways can teachers introduce technology into the social environment of the classroom?
4. How is process writing facilitated by word-processing software?
5. What are some of the ways in which computers can assist struggling readers?

Effective Use of Technology in Literacy Instruction

MICHAEL C. McKENNA

LINDA D. LABBO

DAVID REINKING

In this article, we

- examine research-based classroom practice using technology;
- describe how the instructional use of technology relates to learning theory;
- dispel myths concerning technology use by young children;
- suggest how best practice can (and must) successfully embrace technology; and
- identify activities for self-reflection and planning.

The advent of computer technology presents literacy educators with an ever-expanding array of possible applications. Some, like utilities for producing materials and maintaining records, are used behind the scenes. These have obvious value in terms of convenience, flexibility, and time saved. Other applications entail student use of computers in classroom settings. Such uses continue to be proposed and employed by creative teachers, and research into their effectiveness has steadily accumulated. In this chapter we explore some of the major classroom applications shown to be effective to date, applications that offer the brightest promise to literacy teachers.

COMPUTER APPLICATIONS
WITH BEGINNING READERS

It is now commonplace to see students in the upper elementary grades and higher using classroom-based computers productively for a variety of applications. It is far less common, in our experience, to observe primary-grade children similarly engaged, and work products on display in schools rarely involve computer applications (Labbo, Montero, & Eakle, 2001). What accounts for the reluctance of many primary teachers to embrace computer technology as a means of fostering the literacy growth of their students? We believe that two popular myths play a role in constraining their thinking.

Myth One: Computers Are Too Hard for Young Children to Use

According to this myth, the basic operation of a computer is too difficult for most children in kindergarten and grade one to master. While computers are sophisticated machines, to be sure, and while some applications require considerable expertise, a range of available software invites their use by the very young. Granted, a certain level of fine motor development is needed for tasks such as the operation of a mouse, but our experience is that this level has been reached by most children in early kindergarten. Indeed, in some cases fine motor skills needed for computer use develop before the corresponding skills needed for conventional literacy tasks. For example, it is far simpler for children at this age to create a letter of the alphabet by pressing a key than by moving a pencil. While this first myth might have been plausible during the advent of microcomputers in the early 1980s, there is no longer a defensible reason for deferring technology use until the upper elementary grades. Seymour Papert, in his book *The Children's Machine*, (1993) employs the metaphor of a virus invading the body in order to describe how teachers and schools sometimes react to the "invasion" of microcomputers. They are often relegated to labs and the corners of classrooms, places where they can least interfere with conventional operations. We suspect that some teachers may rely on Myth One in order to avoid integrating technology into their early literacy instruction.

Myth Two: You Must Be Able to Read to Read with a Computer

The limited reading skills of K-1 students, as this myth implies, prevent any meaningful interaction with text displayed on a computer. To be sure, the need to decode unfamiliar words might indeed prohibit successful reading on the part of many beginners. This is true, however, only if their decoding is not supported by the software. If it is displayed on screen in a static way, as it would appear in a book, then of course there would be little chance of independent reading. On the other hand, when electronic text is supported by digitized pronunciations available on a point-and-click basis, then children are presented with a tool that is unavailable to them in print environments. Pronunciation support has the potential to erase the difference between a child's frustration and independent reading levels (McKenna, 1998). In effect, such support makes it possible for a child to read materials at or near the listening level, with minimal teacher assistance. In our studies at the National Reading Research Center, we found that children learned a substantial number of new sight words through incidental exposure while reading electronic books equipped with pronunciation support. The only prerequisite was that certain emergent literacy skills (alphabet recognition, left–right orientation, and knowledge about word boundaries) must have been attained.

These two myths can be summarized in a single, dismissive statement: Young children lack the skills to use computers, and even if they possessed them, they couldn't read what they see on the screen. Hopefully, we have begun to dispel these myths. The following classroom scenarios further suggest how best practice in beginning reading instruction must now embrace the integration of technology.

Scenarios from Two Effective Classrooms

The scenarios that follow illustrate the range of effective computer applications that are possible with beginning readers. This first set of scenarios provides insights into a classroom community of kindergarten children who are as comfortable with reading and writing on a computer screen as they are with reading and writing on paper. When the children work at the computer with another child or with an adult, they have occasions for socially constructing concepts about print (e.g., directionality, speech-to-word match), gaining insights into functions and forms of literacy, composing with a word-processing program, and even enhancing their social status with their classmates. In part because the centrally located computer adjoins other areas of high activity, the computer is part of the classroom culture (Haughland, 1992). The second set of scenarios explores the uses of electronic text in a first-grade classroom. Here, children find that they can "read" material that far exceeds their decoding ability because of the support the computer offers them.

Ms. Martin's Kindergarten Class.   It is 9:20 A.M. on a cold October morning in Ms. Martin's kindergarten and the room is filled with the sounds of children working at various centers. Patrick and Dartrell sit side by side in the computer center, which adjoins the sociodramatic play center and the classroom library. They are contemplating a color monitor that displays information about bats (see Figure 9.1). Earlier, during rug time, the boys had listened to their teacher introduce the unit for the week,

FIGURE 9.1   Patrick and Dartrell Learn about Bats

"Creatures that Fly in the Night Sky." After listening to the text on the screen read aloud to them, the boys decide how to interact with the computer to receive additional information, in this instance an audio rereading of a definition, pronunciations of words that are highlighted in blue, digital drawings that will pop up in boxes over the text, or various sound effects. They confer briefly and click on an illustration that also provides the sound of a feeding bat. As Kelly, a classmate, walks by the computer, she stops, looks at the screen, and asks them a question.

Kelly: How did you do that? Get that up there [*on screen*]?

Patrick: All you do is . . . Wait. [*closes the application*]. Like Ms. Martin did. All you do is . . . this [*demonstrates how to click the mouse and get access to the CD*].

Kelly: You're so smart, Patrick. You should be in college.

Word of Patrick's expertise quickly spreads throughout the classroom and soon other children ask him for a demonstration of how this application works from the CD inserted in the CD-ROM drive of the computer. Patrick's computer ability seems to enhance his social standing with several of his peers, who seek him out for the first time as a reading partner during buddy reading.

At 9:50 A.M., Aerial and Jasmine sit in the computer center and compare a story-book version to an electronic book version of *Stella Luna* (Cannon, 1993). As a "page" of the text is highlighted and read aloud on the computer screen, Aerial points her finger at the corresponding text on a page in the book. Jasmine delights in using the mouse to click on a screen illustration of one of the main characters, a lost baby bat's mother. The girls watch the animation of the mother bat flying over trees, calling, and looking for her baby, who is lost but safely snuggled in a nest with baby birds. Later, when the girls use a Stella Luna bat puppet and a bird puppet to retell the story in the sociodramatic play center, they are joined by three other children, who serve as an audience. The story innovation they enact is filled with plot twists, melancholy dialogue, humorous events, and voices that sound a great deal like the characters from the electronic book.

At 1:30 P.M. during afternoon center time, JaMaris brings an informational book about bats and the Stella Luna puppet with him. He props the book on a small, book-size easel that has been placed beside the computer monitor and holds the puppet on his lap. He has decided to contribute to a class book of collected stories on bats. His assignment is to draw and write something about bats using *KidPix2* (Hickman, 1992). As he begins, he is joined for a few minutes by his teacher, who crouches by his side.

Ms. Martin: So, what's your story going to be about?

JaMaris: It's gonna be a story about a really cool bat named Spidey and his super powers.

Ms. Martin: OK. So how do you want to begin? With "Once upon a time"?

JaMaris: No . . . my name first (*selects the keyboard function and types in the letters of his name using the hunt-and-peck method*) . . . and I want to draw Spidey.

Ms. Martin: That's not a bad idea. If you draw it, that bat, you might get some good story ideas. So, what does this old bat look like—like Stella Luna?

JaMaris: Sorta like this one but with big green eyes (*pointing to the photograph of a bat on the book cover*). How do I get green?

Ms. Martin: Remember how I showed you the other day, during rug time? (*Before leaving the computer center Ms. Martin demonstrates how to access the color option from the program's menu.*)

JaMaris uses electronic artist tools to draw a bat with big green eyes, large fangs, and a crooked "B" on the chest (see Figure 9.2). He then writes a two-line story that consists of strings of letters and a word copied from the book cover. He makes two printouts. One is placed in a folder of children's stories that will be bound into a class book, and the other goes into his backpack so he can show it to his mother.

A classroom visitor, witnessing the children's computer work, might assume that they are all remarkably gifted or that they come from affluent homes, where they have daily access to computers. However, quite the reverse is true. None of the six children mentioned in the above vignettes has a computer at home, all qualify for free or reduced-price lunches, and all are of average or below-average literacy ability. The primary reason that the children are adept at using technology is because their teacher consistently plans inviting, enriching, and appropriate computer-related experiences. In Ms. Martin's classroom, computer-related learning is meaningful and purposeful.

Mr. Saunders' First-Grade Class.   Our second set of scenarios explores the uses of electronic text in Mr. Saunders' first-grade classroom. Here, children find that they can "read" material that far exceeds their decoding ability because of the support the computer offers them. By October, Mr. Saunders' first graders already represent a wide range of literacy development. Most of them know the alphabet and have mastered basic concepts about print. Some have begun to acquire a store of sight words and a few have become accomplished decoders. One or two already read with relative proficiency while others will challenge his resourcefulness as a teacher.

FIGURE 9.2   JaMaris's Bat Story

Mr. Saunders makes use of well-designed decoding software, such as *Reading Mansion*, that embodies research underlying effective instructional practice (see Fox & Mitchell, 2000; McKenna, 2002). However, he also makes a point of engaging the children with electronic text. He does so by using his four computers as centers, giving the children a variety of experiences that complement conventional print-based activities. He uses electronic text in two basic ways.

Sometimes he presents a commercially prepared electronic book, such as one of the Living Books developed by Broderbund. Since these contain hidden seek-and-find features that he regards as engaging but distracting (see Labbo & Kuhn, 2000), he allows the children first to explore the book thoroughly in a spirit of play. Later, they return to the book in a "read only" manner. Mr. Saunders has learned from experience that he cannot rely on the computer to engage the children and lead the way to productive results. Clear expectations must be communicated and careful monitoring must follow (Labbo, Sprague, Montero, & Font, 2000). He therefore makes his expectations clear, namely that a child visiting the center will read every word of the book even if it is necessary to click on all of the words. Because there is no built-in comprehension follow-up, Mr. Saunders tries to engage his young center visitors in a brief postreading discussion focusing on inferential and critical questions that provoke thinking while ensuring that they have read the book.

All of the books have paper versions, and Mr. Saunders calls his students' attention to them on his bookshelf, though he stops short of situating the print versions near the computers as Ms. Martin does. Many of the children choose one of these books during self-selected reading time, and the books provide an opportunity for repeated reading after an initial supported reading via computer. Mr. Saunders occasionally asks the children which version they prefer, and nearly all of them indicate that they like the computer versions better. All but Sarah, that is, who complains that the mouse "makes my hand sweat."

The second way in which Mr. Saunders makes electronic text available to his students is through brief passages that he composes himself. He uses a text-to-speech program called *Write Out Loud*, produced by Don Johnston, Inc. The software automatically provides pronunciations for any of the words Mr. Saunders has written. As with the commercially prepared books, all the children need to do is point to a troublesome word and then click to hear it pronounced.

One morning, as Jarrell visits the computer, he discovers to one side a copy of Mr. Saunders' class roster. On the screen is the following paragraph:

Find your name on the list beside the computer. Count the number of letters in your first name. Write this number next to your name. Then go back to your seat.

It has taken Mr. Saunders only a minute or two to compose and enter this paragraph. Note that this particular paragraph combines a built-in comprehension check and also a timely math link. Some of these first graders take far longer than others to accomplish the task and return to their seats. This is because they must access a greater number of pronunciations in order to interpret the message. Nevertheless, most of the children are eventually able to accomplish the task successfully. A few of them need his help, and he monitors the center while he works with children elsewhere in the room.

Mr. Saunders occasionally varies the use of *Write Out Loud* by entering a brief passage from a trade book they have studied. He then follows it with a brief question that he later uses to ground a short discussion at the end of center time. He sometimes uses stories the students themselves have written, after receiving their permission to share and also after making a few touch-ups with respect to spelling and syntax. For example:

Toby's Story

My favorite food is chocolate. I love to eat it at Easter and Halloween. I also like it at other times. It is my favorite food.

To monitor his students' comprehension of stories like Toby's, Mr. Saunders does not ask for critical reactions to the writing but concentrates rather on whether they remembered what Toby's favorite food was, whether they shared his opinion, and so forth. Mr. Saunders has found that posting student work for others to read is a highly popular activity, one that would have been impossible without the support offered through technology. These applications by a resourceful teacher are representative of a wide variety of effective strategies for implementing electronic text in classroom-based computer centers (for others, see Labbo, 2000).

BROADENING THE CONCEPT OF LITERACY

Although we still have much to learn about effective technology and literacy instruction in primary classrooms, research over the last decade (e.g., see Fatorous, 1995; Labbo, 1996) provides insights into how to plan appropriate computer-related learning experiences that foster young children's literacy development. In this chapter we draw upon relevant research and underlying sociocognitive theory (Vygotsky, 1978) to offer suggestions for establishing a classroom environment that promotes demonstration, collaboration, and other forms of social interaction. We do so by describing how teachers can use technology to support children's conventional literacy development and the development of what has been called "electronic literacy" (Reinking, 1994).

Conventional literacy development refers to language arts processes of listening, speaking, reading, and writing that are related to traditional typographic features of linear text, such as print, illustrations, and graphics. Electronic literacy development expands conventional literacy to include digital and multimedia materials with these fundamental processes. Others have referred to this expanded view of literacy in other ways. For example, Flood, Heath, and Lapp (1997) refer to the "visual and communicative arts," and the Vanderbilt Learning and Technology Group refers to "representational literacy," which includes a variety of new media that can be integrated with conventional texts to create meaning. (For a range of perspectives on the notion of multiple literacies and how to address them in classroom settings, see Richards and McKenna, in press). Conventional approaches to literacy instruction are being revisited and modified accordingly. Labbo, Eakle, & Montero (2002), for example, have successfully adapted the language experience approach to include multimedia as well as text.

INTEGRATING TECHNOLOGY INTO THE SOCIAL ENVIRONMENT OF THE CLASSROOM

The evidence is clear that the social environment of the classroom will always play a central role in determining how a computer is used by children in schools (see Kamil, Kim, & Intrator, 2000; Leu, 2000). It is our belief that if computers are to adequately support both the conventional and electronic literacy development of children, then computer-related activities must be woven into the fabric of daily classroom routines through planned activities in areas such as (1) teacher interactive demonstration, (2) thematic integration and innovation, (3) diverse collaboration, and (4) addressing special needs.

Teacher Interactive Demonstration

Our research (Labbo, Phillips, & Murray, 1995/1996) suggests that integration of technology can be achieved when teachers demonstrate the use of a classroom computer during whole-group and small-group lessons; however, the makeup of the demonstrations should not consist only of the teacher explaining or modeling the use of a computer. Rather, demonstrations should combine teacher modeling with opportunities for children to become involved. For example, Mr. Saunders uses a projector to demonstrate how to point and click on the words in electronic text to hear them pronounced. He asks one or more of the children to assist him in this demonstration. Teachers can also solicit children's input during demonstrations of how to use the computer to maintain a calendar of events, to compose and print out notes to parents, to write and print out individual copies of the morning message and daily news, to make lists of things to do, and to create signs for classroom events. By socially negotiating the form, content, and context of the demonstrations, teachers can help children create a rich schema for employing technology in ways that quite naturally involve many literacy-related activities. Thus, the perspective we advocate implies much more than perfunctory uses of technology that place computers outside the mainstream of literacy activities in classrooms.

For example, from a sociocognitive perspective, we posit that children who observe and interact with teachers during whole- and small-group technology demonstrations will internalize relevant vocabulary, develop approaches to problem solving, and encounter action schemes—all enabling them to use the computer as a tool for thinking, learning, and communicating. As Papert (1980) suggests, children will use a computer in ways that they see the adults in their lives make use of computers. Adult modeling of literacy activities is a major factor in children's acquisition of conventional literacy. It is no less so in the acquisition of electronic, or digital, literacy.

Other benefits of interactive demonstrations are evident when young children dictate personal news to add to the morning message, watch their words typed on the screen, and thereby have opportunities to become aware of graphophonemic aspects of print. Additionally, when each child receives an individual printout of the morning message and is invited to circle words, letters, or letter-sounds he or she recognizes, he or she then has an opportunity to enrich or refine his or her conventional literacy knowledge.

Thematic Integration and Innovation

Creative teachers who put a classroom computer to its best use seem to consistently discover natural connections between curricular themes, learning objectives, and innovative uses of technology. The scenarios given earlier in this chapter provide concrete instances of four guidelines that we have discovered to be instrumental in designing technology-related units, such as "Creatures that Fly in the Night Sky":

1. Collect, display, and demonstrate themed children's books and software related to the theme.
2. Design computer-based learning center activities connected to the theme.
3. Enhance sociodramatic play that connects the theme and computer-based activities.
4. Provide occasions for celebrating children's computer experiences and products.

First, collections of thematically related children's books and software are displayed, shared, and discussed. Just as books are selected to provide a variety of genres and perspectives on a theme, software can be selected to provide various types of literacy experiences related to the theme. Appropriate software for young children should be easy to open, easy to use, highly interactive, responsive to student choices, and ideally related to the other forms of classroom literacy experiences and skill instruction.

Some of the materials for Ms. Martin's unit consist of several fictional and informational books, two puppets with a puppet staging area, and three software programs that are displayed on a bookshelf close to the computer center. Her daily routine includes a shared reading of one of the books or a shared viewing of one of the software applications. On one day, she reads aloud the book *Stella Luna* (Cannon, 1993). Children discuss the story plot, the characters, and ways that the author of this fictional story helps us explore our feelings about bats.

On another day she conducts a shared viewing of the CD-ROM, *My First Incredible Amazing Dictionary* (1995). Ms. Martin has a large monitor that allows her to display the computer output to all of her students. Much as a big book is recommended for sharing stories and concepts about print with a large group of children, a large monitor or a projector is recommended for shared viewing of software. Ms. Martin's shared viewing consists of the following steps:

- She begins by briefly introducing the title and general purpose of the software and then stating a specific purpose for interacting with the program. In our example, her purpose is to find definitions and see illustrations related to unit topics. This activity helps her students understand that different software has different purposes and must be approached strategically, depending on one's intentions. In other words, the decisions made before using the software will depend upon the intent. In this instance, the teacher shows how to access definitions through an alphabet index or a search-and-find function. Mr. Saunders encourages a somewhat different purpose—to read for pleasure and understanding while decoding all of the words—and he makes his purpose clear to the children.

- Next, Ms. Martin reads or clicks on audio messages and animation that appear on the screen. While navigating through the program, the teacher briefly explains how selecting particular options helps to meet the previously stated goal of learning more about vocabulary related to the unit. While navigating through the program, children may be invited to take turns operating the software or offering opinions about the importance of various types of information included in the program. This activity allows children to develop strategies for making decisions while using the program on their own later.

- Last, after a shared viewing, Ms. Martin encourages the children to critically discuss the information, presentation of the content, and the operation of the program itself. This activity helps students develop the ability to critically analyze the software. It also helps students develop the ability to take a critical stance in using digital material just as we hope they will in using conventional printed materials. Mr. Saunders likewise engages his students in brief discussions, and one of his motives is to monitor their comprehension.

Second, center activities include computer-related options aimed at accomplishing various literacy objectives. Ms. Martin's students all worked in the same computer center on the same day, yet they all selected different activities. By providing them with choices, Ms. Martin's children learn how to select an activity that they find interesting and meaningful. They are also given occasions for making sense of topics across various classroom activities that include computer explorations. When children bring objects with them to the computer center, they may use the objects to inspire stories and illustrations, to focus them on the topic, and to help them acquire information from different sources. As Schwartz (1985) has pointed out, three-dimensional objects such as a stuffed animal or a book may help young children connect to a similar two-dimensional object they see on the computer screen.

For example, after hearing Ms. Martin read the story of Stella Luna, Aerial and Jasmine interact in what we have called a "screen and book read along" (Labbo & Ash, 1998) in the computer center. That is, children connect the audio, text, and animation of the screen with the print and illustration of the book by turning the virtual pages on the screen and the real pages in the book simultaneously. They point to words in the book as they are read on the screen. Whether children choose to listen to an electronic book, echo read, or chorally read, our research suggests that the listening version of an electronic story can help young children develop a sense of story, extend their vocabulary, increase knowledge of words, and enrich concepts about print (McKenna 1998).

In Mr. Saunders' class, when beginning readers click on unfamiliar words and hear them pronounced, they make substantial gains in sight word acquisition, provided they can already name letters and can recognize word boundaries (McKenna & Watkins, 1994, 1995, 1996). We have obtained the same results with older, struggling readers (McKenna, Cowart, & Watkins, 1997; McKenna & Shaffield, 2002).

Third, sociodramatic or dramatic play is related to the unit theme and to the use of technology. In Ms. Martin's room, the sociodramatic play center was transformed into a puppet theater equipped with puppets related to the characters in the books and software. Reenacting and often extending the story through dramatic puppet play gives children additional occasions for trying out characterizations, reinforcing story structure, and reliving story plots.

When sociodramatic play centers are enriched with literacy props, including a computer or even a cardboard model of a computer, children gain insights into the role of technology and literacy in various cultural and workplace settings (see Neuman & Roskos, 1992; Labbo & Ash, 1998). For example, if a unit theme focuses on various ways to travel, the sociodramatic play center may be transformed into an imaginary travel agency. Children may make tickets, timetables, maps, travel posters, destination booklets, and passports to use in their play scenarios. The office may be set up with a cardboard model of a computer, available at local office supply stores, a play telephone, notepads, nameplates on desks, credit card facsimiles, and brochures. An interview with a travel agent or a field trip to a travel agency can help children understand how the office works, the role of literacy in the work that takes place there, what types of conversational discourse are appropriate in that setting, and how computers are an integral part of the environment. By playing in the center, children have opportunities to enrich their schemata about workplace forms and functions of literacy.

Mr. Saunders employs a different approach to play, encouraging his students to explore the hidden features of e-books. They do so with partners and delight in taking turns with the mouse. This use of play is not sociodramatic, to be sure, but it is certainly social and affords an enjoyable opportunity for students to learn from one another in concert.

Fourth, children's computer experiences and work are celebrated. When children learn how to use a computer to accomplish their communicative tasks, teachers can invite them to demonstrate and explain their newfound knowledge to their classmates. Collections of students' theme-related work may be bound into a class book, exhibited as artwork, or displayed in a computer presentation such as an electronic slide show. As is the case with printed materials, celebrating accomplishments and finished products involving digital materials enhances motivation and engagement. One example is Mr. Saunders' use of text-to-speech software to allow his students' written work to be shared with one another. Doing so apprises the children at an early age that reading and writing are reciprocal processes in which literate people engage for meaningful purposes.

Another example involves our work with students in the upper elementary grades. We found that involving teachers and students in creating multimedia book reviews on the computer had far greater benefits for reading and writing than did conventional book reports. Students were much more engaged in creating the multimedia book reviews, and we found that their use of technology to respond to their reading involved them in a much richer socially interactive process. We found that these benefits were derived partly from the fact that, unlike conventional book reports, the multimedia book reviews were stored in a searchable database that was easily accessible to other students looking for books to read and to parents who visited the school at various times (including a school technology fair). Inevitably, too, students' interactions about the books they were reading took place incidentally in the context of celebrating their accomplishments in mastering the technology. For example, when one student eagerly explained to another student, who was an equally avid listener, how he had added sound effects to his book review, the other student incidentally discovered an interest in the book that was the subject of the review. This example also illustrates how celebrating accomplishments in one medium can enhance involvement in another medium.

Our work (Reinking & Watkins, 2000) suggests that when teachers make children's multimedia book reports accessible through a networked framework that is authored and presented on hypertext, students electronically share book titles, exchange information about authors, and consider various responses to books. Additionally, children can make intertextual links, or electronic connective paths, between information in their own book reports that is related to information in the reports of their classmates. Having easy access and tools to make such links gives students a capability to manage the exchange of information that is unique to an electronic environment.

DIVERSE OPPORTUNITIES FOR COLLABORATION

Children who collaborate while working on the computer have opportunities to construct conventional and electronic literacy knowledge. Traditional writing processes employing traditional paper-and-pencil tools are enhanced by the malleable screen, the keyboard, and the cutting and pasting tools of technology. Additionally, Internet and E-mail interactions foster unique forms for students' socially constructed learning experiences.

For example, a process writing approach to composition, such as writing workshop, can be enhanced by computer-based collaborations. When children brainstorm, write drafts, revise, edit, and publish with a word-processing program, they can focus more on managing and organizing their ideas and less on tedious or mechanical aspects of writing (Jones, 1994). When writing is supported by a word-processing program, the computer may be viewed as an interactive partner in the writing process. Such a view is especially warranted when a child's communicative intentions involve multimedia, such as audio and video. Creating high-quality final drafts is also facilitated by desktop publishing capabilities such as formatting text, incorporating graphics, and selecting typefaces. Wild and Braid (1996) note that collaborative or cooperative computer-related word-processing experiences foster children's cognitively oriented talk that is focused on the task of writing.

We believe that it is crucial for teachers to provide enough time for children to be able to compose on the computer and not just type in a handwritten draft so they can print out their work. To reap the benefits of technology, and indeed to prepare children to use the tools of contemporary writing, word-processing must be integrated into all phases of the writing process. Students may keep an electronic file of their work, such as a reflective journal, topic ideas, responses to books, works in an early draft stage, works to be edited or spell-checked, or works to be read and responded to by a peer. In these instances, the computer is used as an organizer, a manager, and an electronic writing folder similar to a conventional portfolio. However, unlike a conventional portfolio, an electronic one reinforces the idea that electronic writing is never a final product. Each electronic file awaits future modification.

Paired keyboarding occurs when one child who has knowledge about computer operations and the Internet works with another child who is less knowledgeable about accessing information from the Internet. Peters (1996) suggests that such interactions extend the less-able partner's zone of proximal development, enabling the child to internalize strategies for successful explorations. Leu and Leu (2000) have argued for a project approach to Internet use, both because of its collaborative nature and because expertise can be shared among students. When students reach the middle grades, projects of all kinds present teachers with highly motivating possibilities (Miller, in press), and linking projects in various ways to technology seems especially promising.

Other effective collaborations involve a form of electronic pen pals. Garner and Gillingham (1998) explain how students use E-mail to communicate effectively with students in various geographic regions. Beach and Lundell (1998) report that shy students become more interactive and even develop on-line personalities when they exchange messages through electronic communication systems.

SPECIAL POPULATIONS

Technology can support the literacy learning needs of various types of learners who may be mainstreamed into the classroom. Students at all grade levels who struggle with reading and writing may benefit from particular computer applications. Nonfluent readers, reluctant readers, or children for whom English is a second language may also benefit from features of software. We believe that teachers should approach the use of technology with special populations by following the guidelines we have outlined. Namely, through teacher interactive demonstrations, thematic integration and innovation of software and books, and diverse collaboration.

Supporting Struggling Readers and Writers with Computers

Many children who struggle with learning to read and write in elementary schools may benefit from various types of support that are available in electronic text formats. Traditional instructional and tutorial approaches for readers experiencing difficulty have been based on a determination of a child's strengths and weaknesses. From this traditional perspective, a teacher or a tutor decides how to support the struggling reader by presenting materials, introducing skills, and managing reading practice at a slower pace than that of the regular classroom (Walmsley & Allington, 1995). Once struggling readers have become familiar with unique features of electronic hypertexts through interactive teacher or peer demonstrations, they may be allowed to self-select the type of support they believe is the most beneficial, thereby allowing them to maintain a pace similar to that of the regular classroom.

How readers use supported text will vary with their developmental level. Emergent readers, for example, will gain more from accessing the full listening version of a text than from more advanced resources. Children like those in Mr. Saunders' class, who are functioning within the decoding stage, can be expected to rely heavily on digitized pronunciations. Those who are approaching fluency will have greater recourse to glossary entries, prose simplifications, digitized video clips, and the like as they endeavor to acquire content from expository text (Anderson-Inman & Horney, 1998). At this stage, their comprehension will also benefit from accessing linked resources, such as graphic organizers, databases, or electronic encyclopedias. Since the efficacy of these resources is based on aligning software use with a child's stage of reading development, it is important that assessment be aimed at precisely determining that stage so that a teacher is able to guide the child toward the most appropriate use of such resources (McKenna, Reinking, Labbo, & Kieffer, 1999; Reinking, Labbo, & McKenna, 2000).

For example, a small proportion of struggling middle-grade readers still require extensive decoding support if they are to read successfully. Determining this need and then providing electronic text equipped with support in the form of digitized pronunciations available on demand can dramatically affect their performance. The two applications Mr. Saunders uses in grade one (commercial e-books and teacher-constructed electronic text) have been successfully employed with students in the middle grades who continue to experience difficulties. Hasselbring (1999) provided Don Johnston's *Start-to-Finish* electronic books to this struggling, older population and reported significantly improved comprehension and motivation. McKenna and Shaffield (2002) used *Write Out Loud* to create tailored texts (including scanned textbook passages) for a similar sample of students and observed increased confidence and success due to the support the students received.

A future abundance of supported text will bring both drawbacks and advantages for the struggling reader. Surely one of the challenges of electronic literacy is the need to develop the ability to strategically navigate through hypertext environments in order to achieve specific purposes. Even when the hypertextual elements are limited to a few helpful resources, the effect of so many choices can appear labyrinthine to a struggling reader. On the positive side, students will be able to read text independently that would have frustrated them without the built-in support of what McKenna (1998) has called "electronic scaffolding" (p. 47). Indeed, the very notion of the instructional reading level will have to be reexamined in electronic environments since many struggling readers will be able to read at or near their listening levels (McKenna, Reinking, & Labbo, 1997). Mr. Saunders takes full advantage of this potential in his first-grade classroom computer center, where beginning readers successfully negotiate books written well beyond their decoding ability.

Supporting Nonfluent, Reluctant, or LEP Readers and Writers with Computers

Children who are nonfluent or reluctant readers may benefit from repeated or echo readings of text that is digitally read aloud. While reading to learn new information, a struggling reader may find it useful to compose and record summaries of passages on an electronic clipboard. Burns (1996) notes that multimedia technology can be used to facilitate the English language acquisition of non-native speakers. Multimedia resources accommodate the needs of students with limited English proficiency (LEP) as they progress in second language proficiency and gain specific content area knowledge. Some electronic, interactive books have the option of listening to the story in Spanish or another language. More research about the effectiveness of such programs on children's acquisition of a second language, and their understanding of specific reading passage content, is needed.

Finally, speech synthesizer software offers some promising directions for supporting the spelling development of young LEP or nonfluent writers. Shilling (1997) introduced the use of a basic word-processing program and an external speech synthesis unit that gave the children studied a choice of listening to a word they had attempted to spell on the screen, listening to the entire text that they had typed on the screen, or not using speech synthesis at all. Findings suggest that before children consistently benefit from synethsizer software they need to have acquired some basic concepts about print, phonemic awareness, and a notion of the alphabetic principle. As the capabilities of speech synthesizer software improves, continued research in this area is warranted.

IMPLICATIONS FOR FUTURE RESEARCH AND PRACTICE

We hope it is clear in this chapter that digital forms of reading and writing not only can be, but must be, integrated into the mainstream of literacy instruction for children in the elementary school. Establishing a program of best practices in literacy instruction today means acknowledging that literacy is no longer a monolithic concept defined by print, pages, and books. Attention to conventional uses of written language centered in a world of print must be balanced by attention to how digital technologies are increasingly moving toward the center of what it means to be literate. Teachers, even those who teach young children at the earliest stages of literacy development, must begin to initiate their students into the use of digital forms of expression with a vigor equal to that they have dedicated to more traditional printed forms.

We would be the first to admit that this is no easy task. To integrate technology into their teaching, teachers must confront many challenges on multiple levels. Not the least of the challenges many teachers face is coming to terms with their own predisposition to favor printed materials, sometimes accompanied by a devaluation of digital reading and writing as inferior. It is hard for some teachers to consider, let alone accept, that emerging forms of electronic reading and writing may be as informative, pedagogically useful, and aesthetically pleasing as more familiar printed forms. To consider that electronic forms of text may in some instances even be superior is undoubtedly more difficult.

A reluctance to embrace technology is often sustained by insecurities over using computer technology. It is not trivial to note that today, for the first time in the modern era, teachers have an obligation to prepare children to become literate in ways in which the teachers themselves might not be fully literate. This situation is created by the juggernaut of change that has occurred in the lifetimes of many teachers who are witnessing the digital revolution but who themselves have to some degree been left in its wake. It is hard enough to think about preparing children for the fuzzy future of literacy in a post-typographic world. It is even harder to prepare children for a world in which our print-based literacy skills are less central, let alone for a world that may negate some of our most cherished assumptions about literacy.

Beyond these conceptual issues is a host of practical obstacles that teachers must often overcome. While the base of computer hardware in schools is generally seen as adequate, many schools do not have the physical or administrative infrastructure needed to use their computers effectively (Morra, 1995). For example, computers are of little use if there is not adequate wiring in places where teachers and students need to use them. Neither are they useful if there is no opportunity for teachers to learn how to use them and to become familiar with software and how it might be integrated into instruction. Neither are they useful when there are no established instructional niches in the curriculum and school day for computer use, especially in the language arts, at least beyond word-processing. Moreover, there are logistical problems involved in bringing students and new technologies together in time and space. This challenge is often faced by teachers who have only one or two computers in their classrooms or who can only have access to a computer lab for an hour or two a week.

So, how are teachers to cope in achieving balance between a focus on conventional literacy and electronic literacy? We have found some commonalities among teachers who have successfully achieved this balance, especially among those who do not gravitate naturally to technology. Most teachers have been realistic about the obstacles they face in using technology and realistic about expectations given these obstacles. Often they have found a single computer-based activity or application that connects powerfully with their own teaching and with their personal conceptions of literacy. They may have found it at a conference, in a university course, or through a colleague; but it is something they find hard to imagine teaching without, once they have discovered it. It may be a simple program addressing in some new way a problematic reading skill, or it may be a more open-ended and sophisticated application involving the Internet. For many teachers, finding such an application stimulates them to confront the challenges of using technology in their teaching. For them, it serves as a gateway to seeking more balance between conventional and digital literacies.

We recommend that teachers who wish to integrate technology into their literacy teaching consider several ideal criteria aimed at transcending perfunctory uses of computers. If technology is used to advance their goals of conventional print-based literacy, software applications should, at a minimum, be consistent with what the teacher knows and believes to be true about reading instruction (Miller & Burnett, 1987). Ideally, use should be made of the unique capabilities of the computer to go beyond conventional materials, addressing some problematic area of literacy that would benefit from a new approach.

Different criteria are relevant if technology is used more to initiate students and teachers into the world of digital literacy. First, like other literacy activities, technology-related activities should ideally involve authentic and personally meaningful communication. Electronic worksheets are, in the long run, no more meaningful and useful to students' development than are printed ones. Using the computer to enable a kindergarten child to read more texts independently is more worthwhile, as is enabling third-grade children to use E-mail to correspond with other children and adults around the country. Another ideal criterion is that the activity will allow teachers and students to compare and contrast electronic and digital forms of reading and writing. For example, how is an electronic storybook different from a printed one? What are the advantages and limitations of a multimedia encyclopedia over a printed one? How is E-mail similar to or different from sending a letter mailed at the post office? Finally, computer-based activities that increase literacy in the digital domain should allow students to develop functional strategies for reading and writing electronic texts. For example, when might it be appropriate to seek out the pronunciation or definition of a word while reading? How are key words used efficiently to locate information in a computer database?

As Bruce and Hogan (1998) point out, technologies that are truly integrated into daily life are invisible. Fully integrated technologies blend into the environment by virtue of their repeated and natural use. No one views stairs leading from one floor to another as a complicated technology—except someone who is confined to a wheelchair. Integrating computer-based activities into literacy instruction in schools has a long way to go before new technologies are completely unremarkable. Nonetheless, teachers who choose not to wait until digital reading and writing are so widely used as to be scarcely noticed are laying the groundwork for the day when computer technology will be as fundamental to literacy as print technology is today.

DISCUSSION AND ACTIVITIES

Successful integration of computer technology into your own instruction begins with self-assessment. Consider the following lists of hardware and classroom applications. Check the equipment you have available to you and that you feel competent to use (C) or that is available but that you are not comfortable using (A). Then mark the applications that you regularly employ (R), that are not germane to your assignment or grade level (NA), or that you rarely or never employ but that (on the basis of what you have learned from this chapter) may prove useful to you in the future (F).

HARDWARE
___ One or more classroom-based microcomputers
___ High-speed Internet access in your classroom

___ Scanner
___ Digital camera
___ Zip and CD drives
___ Camcorder

APPLICATIONS
___ Integrated Learning System (i.e., a comprehensive, prescriptive software package)
___ Decoding software that conforms to best practice research
___ Comprehension software that stresses higher-order thinking as well as literal
___ Vocabulary reinforcement software
___ Electronic books
___ Text-to-speech software
___ Sofware for emerging literates that conforms to theory
___ Word-processing software
___ Kid-friendly desktop publishing software with multimedia capabilities

Now look again at the hardware you have marked with an "A" and the applications you have marked with an "F." Consider the following questions.

1. Where might you look for useful information that would enhance your expertise?
2. With which of your colleagues might you collaborate to learn more?
3. When would be a convenient time to begin?
4. How might you record your experiences with new applications in order to learn from them and refine your future practice?

Taking stock of what you know and what you might attempt with the tools you have is an important first step, but it is a purely academic exercise unless you act on the results. We encourage you to take the next step and believe it will broaden your practice if you do.

REFERENCES

Anderson-Inman, L., & Horney, M. A. (1998). Transforming text for at-risk readers. In D. Reinking, M. C. McKenna, L. D. Labbo, & R. D. Kieffer (Eds.), *Handbook of literacy and technology: Transformations in a post-typographic world* (pp. 15–43). Mahwah, NJ: Lawrence Erlbaum.

Beach, & Lundell (1998). Early adolescents' use of computer-mediated communication in writing and reading. In D. Reinking, L. D. Labbo, M. C. McKenna, & R. D. Kieffer (Eds.), *Handbook of literacy and technology: Transformations in a post-typographic world* (pp. 93–112). Mahwah, NJ: Lawrence Erlbaum.

Bruce, B. C., & Hogan, M. P. (1998). The disappearance of technology: Toward an ecological model of literacy. In D. Reinking, L. D. Labbo, M. C. McKenna, & R. D. Kieffer (Eds.), *Handbook of literacy and technology: Transformations in a post-typographic world* (pp. 269–281). Mahwah, NJ: Lawrence Erlbaum.

Burns, D. (1996, March). Technology in the ESL classroom. *Technology & Learning*, 50–52.

Fatorous, C. (1995). Young children using computers: Planning appropriate learning experiences. *Australian Journal of Early Childhood, 29*(2), 1–6.

Flood, J., Heath, S. B., & Lapp, D. (Eds.). (1997). *Handbook of research on teaching literacy through the communicative and visual arts.* New York: MacMillan.

Fox, B. J., & Mitchell, M. J. (2000). Using technology to support word recognition, spelling, and vocabulary acquisition. In S. B. Wepner, W. J. Valmont, & R. Thurlow (Eds.), *Linking literacy and technology: A guide for K-8 classrooms* (pp. 42–75). Newark, DE: International Reading Association.

Garner, R., & Gillingham, M. G. (1998). The Internet in the classroom: Is it the end of transmission-oriented pedagogy? In D. Reinking, L. D. Labbo, M. C. McKenna, & R. D. Kieffer (Eds.), *Handbook of literacy and technology: Transformations in a post-typographic world* (pp. 221–231). Mahwah, NJ: Lawrence Erlbaum.

Hasselbring, T. (1999, May). *The computer doesn't embarrass me.* Paper presented at the meeting of the International Reading Association, San Diego.

Haughland, S. W. (1992). The effect of computer software on preschool children's developmental gains. *Journal of Computing in Childhood Education, 3,* 15–29.

Hickman, C. (1992). *KidPix2, Version 2.* Novato, CA: Broderbund Software.

Jones, I. (1994). The effect of a word processor on the written composition of second-grade pupils. *Computers in the Schools, 11*(2), 43–54.

Kamil, M. L., Kim, H., & Intrator, S. (2000). Effects of other technologies on literacy and literacy learning. In M. L. Kamil, P. B. Mosenthal, P. D. Pearson, R. Barr (Eds.), *Handbook of reading research* (Vol. 3, pp. 773–791). Mahwah, NJ: Lawrence Erlbaum.

Labbo, L. D. (1996). A semiotic analysis of young children's symbol making in a classroom computer center. *Reading Research Quarterly, 31,* 356–385.

Labbo, L. D. (2000). 12 things young children can do with a talking book in a classroom computer center. *Reading Teacher, 53,* 542–546.

Labbo, L. D., & Ash, G. E. (1998). Supporting young children's computer-related literacy development in classroom centers. In S. Neuman & K. Roskos (Eds.), *Children achieving: Instructional practices in early literacy* (pp. 180–197). Newark, DE: International Reading Association.

Labbo, L. D., Eakle, A. J., & Montero, M. K. (2002, May). Digital Language Experience Approach: Using digital photographs and software as a Language Experience Approach innovation. *Reading Online, 5*(8). Available: http://www.readingonline.org/electronic/elec_index.asp?HREF=labbo2/index.html

Labbo, L. D., & Kuhn, M. R. (2000). Weaving chains of affect and cognition: A young child's understanding of CD-ROM talking books. *Journal of Literacy Research, 32,* 187–210.

Labbo, L. D., Montero, M. K., & Eakle, A. J. (2001, October). Learning how to read what's displayed on school hallway walls—and what's not. *Reading Online, 5*(3). Available: http://www.readingonline.org/newliteracies/lit_index.asp?HREF=labbo/index.htmI

Labbo, L. D., Phillips, M., & Murray, B. (1995/1996). "Writing to Read": From inheritance to innovation and invitation. *Reading Teacher, 49*(4), 314–321.

Labbo, L. D., & Sprague, L., with Montero, K., & Font, G. (2000, July). Connecting a computer center to themes, literature, and kindergartners' literacy needs. *Reading Online, 4.* Available: http://www.readingonline.org/default.asp

Leu, D. J. (2000). Literacy and technology: Deictic consequences for literacy education in an information age. In M. L. Kamil, P. B. Mosenthal, P. D. Pearson, R. Barr (Eds.), *Handbook of reading research* (Vol. 3, pp. 745–772). Mahwah, NJ: Lawrence Erlbaum.

Leu, D. J., & Leu, D. D. (2000). *Teaching with the Internet: Lessons from the classroom* (3rd ed.). Norwood, MA: Christopher-Gordon.

McKenna, M. C. (1998). Electronic texts and the transformation of beginning reading. In D. Reinking, M. C. McKenna, L. D. Labbo, & R. D. Kieffer (Eds.), *Handbook of literacy and technology: Transformations in a post-typographic world* (pp. 45–59). Mahwah, NJ: Lawrence Erlbaum.

McKenna, M. C. (2002). Phonics software for a new millennium. *Reading and Writing Quarterly, 18,* 93–96.

McKenna, M. C., Cowart, E., & Watkins, J. W. (1997, December). *Effects of talking books on the reading growth of problem readers in second grade.* Paper presented at the meeting of the National Reading Conference, Scottsdale, AZ.

McKenna, M. C., Reinking, D., & Labbo, L. D. (1997). Using talking books with reading-disabled students. *Reading and Writing Quarterly, 13,* 185–190.

McKenna, M. C., Reinking, D., Labbo, L. D., & Kieffer, R. D. (1999). The electronic transformation of literacy and its implications for the struggling reader. *Reading and Writing Quarterly, 15,* 111–126.

McKenna, M. C. & Shaffield, M. L. (2002, May). *Creating electronic books and documents for poor decoders.* Paper to be presented at the meeting of the International Reading Association, San Francisco.

McKenna, M. C., & Watkins, J. H. (1994, December). *Computer-mediated books for beginning readers.* Paper presented at the meeting of the National Reading Conference, San Diego.

McKenna, M. C., & Watkins, J. H. (1995, November). *Effects of computer-mediated books on the development of beginning readers.* Paper presented at the meeting of the National Reading Conference, New Orleans.

McKenna, M. C. & Watkins, J. H. (1996, December). *The effects of computer-mediated trade books on sight word acquisition and the development of phonics ability.* Paper presented at the meeting of the National Reading Conference, Charleston, SC.

Miller, L., & Burnett, J. D. (1987). Using computers as an integral aspect of elementary language arts instruction: Paradoxes, problems, and promise. In D. Reinking (Ed.), *Reading and computers: Issues for theory and practice* (pp. 178–191). New York: Teachers College Press.

Miller, S. D. (in press). How high- and low-challenge tasks affect motivation and learning: Implications for struggling learners. *Reading and Writing Quarterly.*

Morra, L. G. (1995, April). *America's schools not designed or equipped for the 21st century.* Testimony before the Subcommittee on Labor, Health and Human Services. Education and Related Agencies Committee on Appropriations. U.S. Senate. Washington, DC: U.S. General Accounting Office, ERIC Document ED 381 153.

My first incredible amazing dictionary (CD-ROM). (1995). New York: Dorling Kindersley Multimedia.

Neuman, S. B., & Roskos, K. (1992). Literacy objects as cultural tools: Effects on children's literacy behaviors in play. *Reading Research Quarterly, 27,* 202–225.

Papert, S. (1980). *Mindstorms.* New York: Basic Books.

Papert, S. (1993). *The children's machine: Rethinking school in the age of the computer.* New York: Basic Books.

Peters, J. M. (1996). Paired keyboards as a tool of Internet exploration of 3rd grade students. *Journal of Educational Computing Research, 14,* 229–242.

Reading mansion [Computer software]. (1998). Scotts Valley, CA: Great Wave Software.

Reinking, D. (1994). *Electronic literacy.* (Perspectives in Reading Research No. 4, National Reading Research Center). Athens: University of Georgia.

Reinking, D., Labbo, L. D., & McKenna, M. C. (2000). From assimilation to accommodation: A developmental framework for integrating digital technologies into literacy research and instruction. *Journal of Reading Research, 23,* 110–122.

Reinking, D., & Watkins, J. (2000). A formative experiment investigating the use of multimedia book reviews to increase elementary students' independent reading. *Reading Research Quarterly, 35,* 384–419.

Richards, J. C., & McKenna, M. C. (Eds.). (in press). *Teaching for multiple literacies: Cases and commentaries from K-6 classrooms.* Hillsdale, NJ: Lawrence Erlbaum.

Schwartz, S. (1985). Microcomputers and young children: An exploratory study. In *Issues for educators: A monograph series.* Flushing, NY: School of Education, Queens College, City College of New York.

Shilling, W. (1997). Young children using computers to make discoveries about written language. *Early Childhood Education Journal, 24,* 253–259.

Vygotsky, L. (1978). *Mind in society: The development of higher psychological processes.* Cambridge, MA: Harvard University Press.

Walmsley, S. A., & Allington, R. L. (1995). Redefining and reforming instructional support programs for at-risk students. In R. L. Allington & S. A. Walmsley (Eds.), *No quick fix: Rethinking literacy programs in America's elementary schools* (pp. 19–44). Newark, DE, and New York: International Reading Association and Teachers College Press.

Wild, M., & Braid, P. (1996). Children's talk in cooperative groups. *Journal of Computer Assisted Learning, 12,* 216–321.

CLASSROOM IMPLICATIONS

1. Were one or more of the applications described in the article unfamiliar to you? How might you go about trying these strategies in your classroom? What adaptations do you think you might need to make?

2. Can you think of ways to *combine* any of the applications described to form novel approaches? (For example, text-to-speech software might be combined with E-mail.) What other combinations might you suggest?

3. Can you think of effective technology applications *not* described in the article? List them and compare your list with those of your colleagues.

ANNOTATED BIBLIOGRAPHY

Baker, E. A. (2001). The nature of literacy in a technology-rich, fourth-grade classroom. *Reading Research and Instruction, 40,* 153–179.
Reports a five-month study of how technology was used in a fourth-grade classroom. Offers many insights about effective applications.

Bennett, K. B. (2001). *Using technology and creative reading activities to increase pleasure reading among high school students in resource classes.* (ERIC Reproduction Service No. ED454507).
Describes a literacy effort that, thorough the extensive use of various forms of technology, encouraged high school students to read widely for pleasure.

Castellani, J. (2001). Emerging reading and writing strategies using technology. *Teaching Exceptional Children, 33,* 60–67.
Discusses specific literacy teaching strategies for using computers to encourage various reading and writing activities with those students having language disabilities.

Chenoweth, K. (2001). Keeping score. *School Library Journal, 47,* 48–51.
Examines the use of Accelerated Reader and Reading Counts, two computer-based reading programs, and the reactions of school librarians to the use of these literacy efforts.

Ferguson, I. (2001). *Building background knowledge to improve reading comprehension through the use of technology.* (ERIC Reproduction Service No. ED454504).
Describes the extensive use of various forms of technology in helping low-income students increase their comprehension of reading materials of different types. Of particular note were the improved comfort levels experienced by the students after the use of technology in this program of instruction.

Hammerberg, D. D. (2001). Reading and writing "hypertextually": Children's literature, technology, and early writing instruction. *Language Arts, 78,* 207–216.
Discusses the use of hypertext as a means of encouraging young children in their early writing experiences, especially as this relates to response to various types of literature.

Kreul, M. (2001). New tools for teaching and learning: Connecting literacy and technology in a second-grade classroom. *Reading Research and Instruction, 40,* 225–232.
Describes how the author changed literacy instruction through the use of a variety of technology-related projects. Of particular importance was the use of the Internet in these new instructional practices.

Leu, D. J. (2000). Literacy and technology: Deictic consequences for literacy education in an information age. In M. L. Kamil, P. B. Mosenthal, P. D. Pearson, R. Barr (Eds.), *Handbook of reading research* (Vol. 3, pp. 745–772). Mahwah, NJ: Lawrence Erlbaum.
Comprehensive, forward-looking review of research concerning technology applications in literacy education.

Nichols, W. D., Wood, K. D., & Rickelman, R. (2001). Using technology to engage students in reading and writing: Research into practice. *Middle School Journal, 32,* 45–50.
Suggests that various forms of technology can enhance middle-school students' interest in reading in different content areas of instruction.

Poftak, A. (2001). Getting a read on E-books. *Technology and Learning, 21,* 22–24, 26, 28, 30–31, 34, 36.
Discusses the use of electronic books (E-books) in the classroom literacy program. Notes the advantages and disadvantages of this form of literacy technology.

Reinking, D., McKenna, M. C., Labbo, L. D., & Kieffer, R. D. (Eds.). (1998). *Handbook of literacy and technology: Transformations in a post-typographic world.* Mahwah, NJ: Lawrence Erlbaum.
Collection of articles by key researchers interested in technology applications. Each article contains an extensive research review.

Shakeshaft, C., Mann, D., Becker, J., & Sweeney, K. (2002). Choosing the right technology. *School Administrator, 59,* 34–37.
Provides information on how to evaluate and select various types of technology to be used in literacy instruction.

Wepner, S. B., Valmont, W. J., & Thurlow, R. (2000). *Linking literacy and technology: A guide for K-8 classrooms.* Newark, DE: International Reading Association.
Superb collection of articles describing effective applications in the major dimensions of literacy education (word recognition, comprehension, etc.).

YOU BECOME INVOLVED

1. In the section entitled "Discussion and Activities," a self-survey of hardware and software is presented. You may not have actually completed the survey as you read it, but we encourage you to do so now.

2. Now take time to answer the four questions posed at the end of the activity about future applications you might consider.

3. Visit the Web site of the National Reading Conference (www.nrconline.org) and access the extensive, annotated list of hot-linked literacy sites you find there. Then visit those sites that relate to your teaching assignment (or that simply interest you) and judge whether they can help you. Bookmark them before you forget!

4. Return to the list of seven issues identified at the beginning of this chapter. Choose one or more of them and, in a small-group session with your colleagues, discuss possible ways of addressing them.

CHAPTER TEN

SCIENTIFICALLY-BASED READING RESEARCH

There is something fascinating about science. One gets such wholesale returns of conjecture out of such a trifling investment of fact.

—Mark Twain (1873)

Our research continues to converge on the following findings. Good readers are phonemically aware and understand the alphabetic principle and can apply these skills to the development and application of phonics skills when reading words, and can accomplish these applications in a fluent and accurate manner. Given the ability to rapidly and automatically decode and recognize words, good readers bring strong vocabularies and good syntactic and grammatical skills to the reading comprehension process, and actively relate what is being read to their own background knowledge via a variety of strategies.

—Reid Lyon (2002)

What is scientifically-based reading research (SBRR), and what implications does it have for instruction? These are important questions for both pedagogical and political reasons. The Reading Excellence Act has awarded billions of dollars in funding for K-3 reading education, but only for schools willing to embrace SBRR. The more recent Reading First initiative carries with it a similar mandate. Are these schools compromising their professional integrity in order to obtain funding? To answer that question, we must examine the nature of SBRR-based, or "evidence-based," practice.

When an instructional practice is grounded in SBRR, it has been statistically compared with alternative approaches and found to be superior. Usually this means that experimental and control groups received different teaching methods under regulated conditions. Ideally, the practice in question has been validated in this way not just once but in a variety of settings, with different groups of children and different teachers. To a teacher shopping for an effective new approach to try, an SBRR-based method of this kind is assumed to have a higher probability of success because of its impressive track record.

The word *effective* has special meaning in terms of SBRR. An effective approach is one that produces a desirable *effect*, a change in children's learning that can be observed and measured. Some research designs, including experiments and quasi-experiments, are conducted to determine whether an effect has resulted and, if so, how extensive it has been.

Research of this nature is considered the cornerstone of SBRR-based practice. Other approaches to research, such as correlational and descriptive studies and qualitative investigations, are useful for answering other important questions, but they cannot be used to identify whether a particular effect has resulted from an instructional practice. This is not to say that such research is outside the realm of science. However, experiments and quasi-experiments go to the heart of the scientific method, developed by Sir Francis Bacon to identify causal relationships. ("If I use teaching method A, I can cause learning effect B.")

The International Reading Association, in its 2002 position statement, opted for the term *evidence-based research*, which is open to a far greater range of studies. Such research has these characteristics:

- Objective— data would be identified and interpreted similarly by any evaluator
- Valid—data adequately represent the tasks that children need to accomplish to be successful readers
- Reliable—data will remain essentially unchanged if collected on a different day or by a different person
- Systematic—data were collected according to a rigorous design of either experimentation or observation
- Refereed—data have been approved for publication by a panel of independent reviewers.

A narrower, "Baconian" view was adopted by the National Reading Panel, a fifteen-member group charged by Congress with the task of reviewing existing research on effective reading instruction and of producing a summary of what the research indicates. The Panel first identified over 100,000 research studies reported since 1966 and then applied strict criteria to the results. Only experimental and quasi-experimental studies, involving control groups, were considered. The Panel was especially interested in teaching methods that have been validated in numerous studies. Using such strict criteria yielded few surprises. The Panel concluded, for example, that the best K-3 programs have six important dimensions:

1. Phonemic awareness
2. Phonics
3. Fluency
4. Vocabulary
5. Construction of meaning from text (comprehension) and
6. Motivation

More specifically, they found that instructional approaches like graphic organizers, student-generated questions, and the use of both large and small groups are likely to yield good results. Indeed, any teacher who takes the trouble to read the voluminous *Report of the Subgroups*, may wonder that it occasioned any controversy.

Tim Shanahan, a member of the Panel, responded with surprise to the negative reaction of some educators to the NRP report. In an interview published in *Reading Today* (June/July 2000), he said, "I am perplexed that anyone would be particularly concerned about a report that makes sense of research findings in a public and systematic manner. I am personally much more concerned about all of the claims that are made in our field with little or no empirical proof " (p. 4). "It is not a report of opinions or a consensus of experts," Shanahan went on to say, "but an objective and rule-based analysis of what the research findings actually have been" (p. 4).

Nevertheless, critics have found portions of the report and the process by which it was produced disturbing. Some of the principal criticisms can be summarized as follows:

- Quantitative methods are always flawed in some way, and, besides, they attempt to quantify elements that resist quantification.
- The Panel avoided some of the really pressing issues in reading education, such as "reading wars," which have pitted decoding and whole-language advocates against one another.
- The selection criteria employed by the Panel were so strict that large bodies of credible evidence were ignored.
- Practices validated by the Panel may still not work well for individual teachers or in particular settings.
- There is a danger that the Panel's findings may be adopted in a mindless, rote fashion.

REFERENCES

International Reading Association. (2002). *What is evidence-based reading instruction?* Position Statement. [On-line]. Available: http://www.reading.org/positions/evidence_based.html

National Reading Panel. (2000). *Report of the subgroups.* Washington, DC: U.S. Department of Education. [On-line]. Available: http://www.nationalreadingpanel.org/

Shanahan, T. (2000). Interview in "National Reading Panel report: Work praised, but distortion fears persist." *Reading Today, 17*(6), 1, 4.

AS YOU READ

The selection that follows is the text of an address delivered by Michael Pressley to the 2001 meeting of the National Reading Conference. Pressley was the recipient of the Oscar Causey Award for his career contributions to reading research, and he took the opportunity to examine the issue of scientific research. We believe you will find his remarks accessible, enlightening, and balanced. As you read them, keep these questions in mind:

1. How does Pressley's view of good research differ from that of the National Reading Panel? Or does it?

2. What is Pressley's view of the position taken by Joanne Yatvin, who was the lone dissenter on the Panel and whose comments were published in an addendum?

What I Have Learned Up Until Now about Research Methods in Reading Education

MICHAEL PRESSLEY

Earlier this year, I was commissioned to write a paper by the National Reading Conference (Pressley, in press) that was critical of the National Reading Panel (2000). I argued that the Panel relied too much on experiments and meta-analyses. I argued there that there was much, much more about reading instruction that enjoys at least some scientific validation than the Panel admitted in their report.

Since the NRC-commissioned paper appeared, many inquiries have come my way about methodology in reading research. Thus, I offer here the few conclusions about methods that seem incontrovertible to me.

This is a decidedly autobiographical tour of methods. I will discuss some of my previous studies and reflect with you how I feel about those contributions now, emphasizing what doing the studies and the reactions to the studies have taught me about reading education research. I make the conservative case that there are good reasons to rely on a very few methods that we have known since our schooldays.

CONCLUSION 1: EXPERIMENTS ARE THE BEST WAY TO UNDERSTAND WHETHER A RELATIONSHIP IS A CAUSE-AND-EFFECT RELATIONSHIP

A major message in my undergraduate education in psychology at Northwestern University was that true experiments provide more certain understanding of causal relationships than other types of investigations. By the end of my junior year in college, I had internalized Campbell and Stanley's (1966) classic monograph on experimental and quasi-experimental designs. Nothing that has happened since then has undermined my confidence in excellent experimentation as a means to reveal causality. And, yes, I have seen all of those structural equation, causal modeling studies, and frankly, I've never once been compelled by the causal arguments coming out of the whirling cloud of endogenous and exogenous variables and relationships. Oh, maybe once or twice, but only after a lot of doubts!

I have no problem whatsoever with the National Reading Panel weighing the experimental work heavily with respect to causal conclusions. A major problem that I did have, however, was that the Panel excluded all other scientific approaches (or almost all of them), a point I will take up later in this talk.

Many Replications of an Experimental Manipulation

The Panel favored cause-and-effect relations replicated in many, many experiments, for many, many experiments are needed to do a meta-analysis, the summary procedure favored by the National Reading Panel. For example, the National Reading Panel located 52 studies establishing that phonemic awareness instruction increases reading performance. With so many replications, I believe it!

As the editor of the *Journal of Educational Psychology*, I am very aware that most recent phonemic awareness training studies submitted to the journal in recent years have not been getting accepted. Even though I always seek reviews of these studies from individuals who are sympathetic to phonemic awareness instruction, usually, they tell me not to publish the paper. I get this recommendation even when the study is technically very sound. The explanation for the recommendation usually boils down to the study not providing enough of a scientific advance to justify its publication. With respect to experimentation related to phonemic awareness instruction, current work, and most of the work of the past few years, has been fine tuning.

Those most interested in phonemic awareness can think of many good theoretical reasons to continue experimentation on phonemic awareness instruction. For me the problem is that I can think of so many other problems in reading instruction that need study. I have difficulty justifying continued expenditure of resources on experimental evaluation of phonemic awareness interventions when so much is known about this issue already relative to other issues that need illumination. Sadly, from my point of view, both a meta-message and a direct message of the National Reading Panel report was that there is a need for a good deal more experimental evaluation of phonemic awareness instruction.

Some contextualists in the audience undoubtedly are seething right now, with their position being that the effectiveness of instruction very much depends on the contextual specifics, on characteristics of the child, teacher, and setting. It also depends on the "how" of teaching, from grouping practices, to motivation, to whether technology is used, to the extent of parental involvement. The only way we get a window on interactions between phonemic awareness interventions and contexts is by doing many, many studies.

That said, I am old enough to have seen many, many times what is occurring with respect to phonemic awareness instruction research. The central phenomenon, that phonemic awareness can be trained with positive effects on reading, is easily replicable, with this replicability encouraging additional replications. Because obtaining a significant difference in a study increases the likelihood of publishability, a surefire significant difference will be studied even after demonstrations of the difference are no longer significantly novel, inspiring many to produce replications across different students and contexts. Yes, there are some contextualist wrinkles that have fallen out of the flood of phonemic awareness research, as for example, that simpler forms of phonemic awareness instruction seem to be more powerful. Is such a small advance in understanding important enough to be putting so many research resources into the additional experimental evaluation of phonemic awareness instruction? I am struck by those negative reviews I have read as the editor of the *Journal of Educational Psychology*. The evaluations of phonemic awareness instruction coming at this point do not seem to be valued much, even by those who have published this kind of work in the past. I respect greatly those who can do experiments well. After all, I spent several decades of my professional career doing almost nothing except experiments! I would urge those of you who are committed to experimentation as an analytic strategy not to focus exclusively on topics already studied well, such as phonemic awareness instruction, but to think harder about whether there might be other issues in reading education research that would benefit more from your talents. In my view, you have an ethical obligation to beginning readers and their teachers to apply your considerable talents elsewhere.

Interpreting One or a Very Few Experiments

Emphasizing many, many replications sends the message that if there is only one demonstration of an effect or only a few replications, then the effect should not be taken seriously. The problem is that there are some very important reading interventions so complicated that their study is very difficult. Hence, at best, only a few well-done studies are likely. One such example is long-term instruction of repertoires of comprehension strategies.

Some of you may recall the quasi-experimental evaluation of transactional comprehension strategies instruction that Rachel Brown, several others, and I published in 1996 (Brown, Pressley, Van Meter, & Schuder, 1996). It involved comparison of students in five classrooms with students in five other classrooms. The classrooms varied with respect to whether transactional comprehension strategies teaching occurred in the class. I am grateful that the National Reading Panel and others have responded so favorably to the study. A frequent question I receive from admirers is, "When will you do a follow up?" A variation is, "Why don't you replicate the study with. . .?"

The answer is that no follow up or replication is planned. I simply do not have the resources to do such a study. More than a year of ethnographic observations and interview studies preceded the Brown et al. (1996) investigation, informing the research team about the nature of the instruction as well as its probable effects. It took almost a school year to identify classrooms that could be matched well so that the comparison of interest (transactional strategies instruction present versus absent) could be made as cleanly as possible. Data collection took a full year. Then, it took a year to analyze the data and write them up. From beginning the study to journal submission, Brown et al. (1996) was about a four year venture!

By my count, there are three well-done studies of something like transactional strategies instruction (see also Anderson, 1992; Collins, 1991). There are so few studies because they are so difficult to do, so very resource intensive. I believe that all of you can think of other problems that might get studied in one or a very few well-controlled studies but never could be studied in 50 or more experiments. As a profession, we are often going to have to make decisions based on a very few comparisons simply because often we cannot afford many, many comparisons.

One characteristic of an excellent scholar in a field is that she or he can recognize single studies that are pointing the field in a direction that is worthwhile. If you examine any excellent review chapter or integrative scholarly book in reading, what you will find is that good scholars quite often draw conclusions based on one or a very few studies. And the really, really good scholars recognize the value of great studies before others do! Let me give you an example of what I mean.

In 2001, everyone knows what comprehension monitoring is. It was not always so. I know exactly when I found out what it was—October 1978. There was a conference at the University of Wisconsin–Madison on communications skills. John Flavell sent me his paper to read. In it, he talked about comprehension monitoring as Ellen Markman (e.g., 1979) had been studying it. Markman had figured out that when children do not understand something, often they do not understand that they do not understand it! I had learned from my graduate school association with Flavell to pay attention when he flagged a study as important, for he was often right. As for the importance of Markman's discovery, the rest is not only history but well known history, with many studies of comprehension monitoring following on the heels of Markman's pioneering work. My point here, however, is that John Flavell did not need 50 replications to recognize the importance of the Markman study. He filtered Markman's research outcome through his deep understanding of children's thinking, based on years of experience reading the cognitive development literature and interacting with children over cognitive tasks. People well grounded in phenomena can often separate the single studies that are wheat from the many others that are chaff. We need to remember this when claims are being made that conclusions should only be drawn after there are many, many replications of a phenomenon. This is just not how cutting-edge scientists think much of the time. Rather, excellent scientists are the ones who can figure out which of the single experiments offered are ones that deserve much more attention.

CONCLUSION 2: CORRELATIONAL STUDIES ARE VERY, VERY IMPORTANT

We all have heard the put-down, "It's only a correlational outcome—impossible to know the cause and effect." Of course, it is a mistake to make a causal argument based on correlational data. That in no way reduces the importance of correlational studies. Indeed, correlational studies are absolutely essential in the development of causal hypotheses.

In 1975, Benton Underwood argued that correlational studies are a crucible for experimental work: Correlations point to potential causal relationships. Perhaps, more importantly, he emphasized that in the absence of a correlation, there would be no point in expending resources to do experiments to test a causal theory, for if correlation does not imply causation, causation certainly implies correlation. So, to return to an example considered earlier in this talk, think again about phonemic awareness: Children high in phonemic awareness during the kindergarten years are better readers during the elementary years (e.g., Juel, 1988). That correlation went far in motivating many experimental tests of the effects of phonemic awareness instruction on reading. Yes, there had been a few prominent instructional experiments targeting phonemic awareness before Juel's work, but Juel's research created quite a stir among reading researchers with respect to the phonemic awareness issue. Correlational studies can stimulate experimental tests.

Moreover, once more experiments were completed, understanding why phonemic awareness instruction worked has increased because of correlational data. For example, I am particularly impressed with the work of Jamie Metsala (1999) that permits the conclusion that phonemic awareness is a natural byproduct of extensive vocabulary development, which is a byproduct of extensive language exposure. In outline, the claim is that when children learn more words, there are more opportunities to compare the sounds in them (e.g., to note that *cat* and *bat* are similar except for one sound). When children lack phonemic awareness at age 5, it seems likely it is because they have not had as rich language experiences as children who naturally develop phonemic awareness. This work serves to highlight that it is not one simple language competency that must be considered in struggling beginning readers but multiple interpenetrating language competencies. The many correlations between early language experiences and competencies and later reading (Scarborough, 2001) strongly suggest that skilled reading is rooted in a complicated sociolinguistic world. Phonemic awareness instruction alone cannot make up for lack of rich language exposure over years of preschool, and sadly, for many children, language exposure is anything but rich and deep during the preschool years (Hart & Risley, 1995).

We could never have figured out why phonemic awareness instruction is so important for some children for them to learn to read without the correlational work, and we would not be aware today of the importance of early language experience to literacy success in school without the many correlational studies establishing linkages between early childhood language and literacy success in school. It is a mistake to write about scientific understandings about reading and exclude correlational data, as the National Reading Panel did for the most part.

Some of the best scientific thinkers I have ever encountered, including Benton Underwood (1975) and Lee J. Cronbach (1957), argued emphatically for the use of correlational and experimental evidence together as absolutely necessary to understand causal relations in the complex natural world. Of course, many members of this audience remember Rosenshine and Furst's (1973) call for correlational instructional research to identify hypotheses about teaching that would inform us about the types of instruction that can cause achievement gains in school. Many of you also are aware of experiments like Anderson, Evertson, and Brophy's (1979) study that evaluated the effects of instruction that was loaded with components known to be correlated with reading achievement. We have known for a long time that reading education scientists should not be rushing toward the conduct of only true experiments, but rather should be designing research programs that marry and intermix correlational and experimental methods to maximize understanding of reading and the reading education processes.

CONCLUSION 3: QUASI-EXPERIMENTS ARE SOMETIMES THE *BEST* WE CAN DO

The true experiment is a high ideal for producing cause and effect conclusions. Sometimes, however, it is not the best approach.

Recall again the study of transactional strategies instruction that Rachel Brown, Ted Schuder, Peggy Van Meter, and I did, that I described earlier (Brown et al., 1996). That was a quasi-experiment, with students in five classrooms experiencing transactional strategies instruction and students in five classrooms who did not. The five transactional strategies instruction teachers had been teaching that way for a few years and were committed to it; the five control teachers were committed to other approaches, mostly variations on whole language.

I definitely heard from critics of the study that it would have been better to assign teachers randomly to condition, having half teach with transactional strategies instruction and the other half continue as they typically taught. The problem, however, is that it takes time to learn how to be a transactional-strategies-instruction teacher, and only some teachers who try the approach become committed to it (Pressley & El-Dinary, 1997). Had we randomly assigned teachers to the instructional condition, we would have had an anemic version of transactional strategies instruction in at least some of the intervention classrooms, and we would have been asking what effect lack of commitment had on the outcome of the study. What made Brown et al. (1996) credible was that we very carefully matched classrooms before the study began, so that the participants were very, very comparable at the outset of the study.

There are many reading education interventions that require lengthy teacher preparation and great teacher commitment. When such interventions are studied, every effort must be made to study a good version of it carried out by people committed to the treatment. As a field, we need to think just as hard about how to do excellent quasi-experiments as we do about how to do excellent experiments. This brings me to my next point.

CONCLUSION 4: RESEARCH IS NEVER PERFECT, BUT WHY WE SHOULD TRY TO MAKE IT BETTER

More than a decade ago now, Linda Lysynchuk, Hsaio D'Ailly, Michael Smith, Heather Cake, and I published an analysis that caused a stir among some NRC regulars (Lysynchuk, Pressley, D'Ailly, Smith, & Cake, 1989). We analyzed comprehension strategies instructional studies with respect to their methodological strengths and weaknesses, generally evaluating how well the studies met classic internal and external validity criteria (Bracht & Glass, 1968; Campbell & Stanley, 1966). One reaction I experienced was from those who felt that it was outrageous that my student colleagues and I would attempt to impose these traditional standards on research, that the field had moved away from them. A second reaction was that my colleagues and I had succeeded in documenting that reading education research was very bad indeed, with not a single study of comprehension strategies instruction identified that did not fall short on at least several important criteria. A third reaction was that the Lysynchuk et al. (1989) analysis was completely unnecessary, for anyone who had ever sat with a group of graduate students discussing any study knew that every study can be criticized on methodological grounds!

Well, the graduate students were right! Since my colleagues and I published the 1989 paper, there have been several other similar methodological analyses done, and always, the results have been the same (Almasi, Palmer, Gambrell, & Pressley, 1994; Ridgeway, Dunston, & Qian, 1993; Troia, 1999). Every study falls short on at least a few criteria, with at least some published studies falling short on many criteria.

The methodological analysis of phonemic awareness training studies carried out by Gary Troia (1999) especially caught the eye of the National Reading Panel. What the Panel discovered in extending Troia's analysis was that the greatest effects of phonemic awareness instruction occurred in studies with the fewest methodological problems. Intuitively, this makes sense: Methodological errors should, if anything, increase unreliability of measurements. In general, the lower the reliability of measurements, the greater the error variance, and this reduces effect sizes. The lesson here is that anyone interested in demonstrating that a reading intervention has an effect does well to invest the resources to do a study well, that is, to do one with as few methodological compromises as possible.

I remain puzzled by those who claim that the traditional internal and external validity criteria are out of date. As an editor, I can tell you that concerns about internal and external validity are often mentioned in reviews of studies used to determine their publishability. Those of you who do qualitative work know that issues of credibility are very similar to quantitative internal and external validity concerns (Lincoln & Guba, 1985), with establishing the credibility of a qualitative study and the conclusions offered essential if the study is to be taken seriously by the scholarly community. If we carry out research that is methodologically better, we increase the likelihood of illuminating the effects of reading interventions. We, as reading researchers, need to renew our commitments to methodologically excellent work for our own sakes, the sakes of educators we wish to inform, and the sakes of children whose education may be affected by decisions based on this science of reading instruction that is the focus of our professional lives.

CONCLUSION 5: QUALITATIVE RESEARCH IS SCIENCE, TOO!

As you know, for the past decade, I have done more grounded theory analysis than anything else. Why did I abandon my previous career as an experimenter to do grounded theory? It started as a search for better hypotheses about reading comprehension strategies instruction than were driving the field in the late 1980s.

I had been interested in comprehension strategies instruction since graduate school. Back in those days, I did work establishing when and how instructions to create mental images affect children's comprehension of text. I decided in the late 1980s to get back into comprehension strategies instruction, with the inaugural study of this rebirth being an experimental evaluation of reciprocal teaching (Lysynchuk, Pressley, & Vye, 1990). As I was doing this study, I was reviewing and reflecting on the entire comprehension strategies instruction literature (Pressley, Johnson, Symons, McGoldrick, & Kurita, 1989). I was also visiting settings where comprehension strategies instruction seemed to be done well in that the educators doing it could point to evidence that it was improving their students' reading. Those visits led to significant reflection about how truly challenging comprehension strategies instruction is to do (Pressley, Goodchild, Fleet, Zajchowski, & Evans, 1989). It also led to an important insight: The way comprehension strategies instruction was occurring in the schools I visited did not look like reciprocal teaching or any of the instruction that researchers had been studying in true experiments. Yes, the comprehension processes that were validated in true experiments, for example, questioning, mental imagery, summarization, were included in the repertoires of strategies elementary students were being taught, but the teaching was much more complex compared to any instruction evaluated in the extant literature.

I knew that I needed to do something other than quantitative experimentation to understand the comprehension strategies instruction I had begun to see in the late 1980s, but I did not know what. With a move to the University of Maryland in summer 1989, something happened that changed my life. The first week of school in fall 1989, Pamela El-Dinary showed up at my office door. She had completed a master's degree emphasizing qualitative methods at the University of Georgia and now was going to do doctoral study at College Park. This was not an ordinary first meeting with a graduate student. Pam let me know in no uncertain terms that my work would be better if it got more qualitative. Somewhat to her surprise, I agreed with her, and thus began a collaboration that in the years ahead would do much to illuminate the nature of comprehension strategies instruction.

The grounded theory work with Pam and others allowed Rachel Brown and me to design the comparative study described earlier. Why was the Brown et al. (1996) study received so favorably, including by the National Reading Panel? I think it was because every aspect of the study was informed by the grounded theory work that had preceded it. Hence, the treatment that was evaluated really was something that was happening in real schools, not something invented by an experimenter and dropped into a school for a few weeks so that a comparative study could be done. The grounded theory work also permitted identification of dependent variables that captured a wide range of effects produced by the instruction and a rich theoretical description of comprehension strategies instruction (Pressley et al., 1992). Those years of sitting in classrooms and interviewing teachers who had carried out transactional strategies instruction paid off in the design of the quasi-experiment.

I am proud that throughout the transactional strategies instruction research, educators, and especially teachers doing comprehension strategies instruction, were co-investigators, although sometimes I almost drove them crazy. For example, after I did some observations at Benchmark School, Irene Gaskins and her colleagues participated in an ethnographic interview I designed. The interview questions were inspired by what I had seen in the Benchmark classrooms. They also were somewhat open-ended, to make certain the teachers' thinking was tapped as completely as possible.

That posed no problem with the inexperienced teachers at Benchmark, those just learning to teach comprehension strategies instruction. Their interviews took about a half hour. With Benchmark's many experienced teachers, however, there was one difficulty: They had so much to say. Some interviews lasted over five hours, filled with informative insights about comprehension strategies instruction. The publication resulting from that study (Pressley et al., 1991) still seems to me to be one of the very most informative about comprehension strategies instruction. I do not think anyone is well served when a process intended to inform the nation about scientifically validated instruction ignores the kind of rich interview data that was collected at Benchmark or the many observations we made to understand comprehension strategies instruction done well.

Throughout my career, I have believed that good scientists need to report themselves regularly with respect to the problems they study. After about a half dozen years of studying comprehension strategies instruction, it seemed to me that it was time to move on. With Ruth Wharton-McDonald, who was then a graduate student at SUNY-Albany, I initiated a series of grounded theory studies to illuminate the nature of excellent primary-level literacy instruction, instruction that engages children and results in better reading and writing than is often observed in primary-level classrooms. As many of you know, there is now quite a bit of that research produced by my colleagues and me (Bogner, Raphael, & Pressley, in press; Dolezal, Mohan, Pressley, & Vincent, 2001; Pressley, Allington, Wharton-McDonald, Block, & Morrow, 2001; Pressley et al., 2001; Snow et al., 1991; Wharton-McDonald, Pressley, & Hampston, 1998).

As you know as well, the principal reason for doing grounded theory research is to develop hypotheses. I am happy to report that my colleagues and I have succeeded in doing that. Recently, Alysia Roehrig, Kate Bohn, Sara Dolezal, and Lindsey Mohan have been especially active in helping me to pull together all that we have hypothesized (see Pressley et al., in press) into what I call, "The Big Hypothesis" about effective beginning literacy instruction. The big hypothesis is that effective primary-level literacy classrooms differ from less effective classrooms in three ways:

(1) Effective elementary classrooms do much to motivate their students. Indeed, effective teachers saturate the school day with motivation (see Bogner et al., in press).

(2) Effective primary-level teachers are such effective classroom managers that the management is hardly noticeable. There is just little need for overt discipline.

(3) Effective primary-level teachers use a huge variety of curriculum and instruction approaches, matching teaching to curriculum demands and student needs. There is a great deal of instruction, especially engaging instruction, occurring in highly effective classrooms compared to less effective ones.

I want to emphasize as I present The Big Hypothesis that all three elements have always been present in the engaging and effective primary-level classrooms my colleagues and I have studied. Engaging primary-level classrooms are exceptionally impressive places, where all the children are working away and learning, almost every minute of every school day.

I am hoping that in the next few years we can study "The Big Hypothesis" in a quasi-experiment, evaluating the many advantages produced by such instruction. Such a quasi-experiment will be very, very hard to do. It will never be replicated 50 times over.

Until that study can be done, what should we do? Our grounded theory work relating teaching approaches to engagement and literacy outcomes provides plenty of reason to encourage teachers to be more like the very engaging primary-level teachers that we have studied. By doing so, I think we will also gain insights into whether teachers can change to be more like the most engaging of primary-level teachers. Alysia Roehrig is now doing a dissertation in which she is attempting to shift the teaching of beginning teachers in the directions specified in The Big Hypothesis. Based on a preliminary study, the answer is that only some teachers can make progress even when given extensive support. Of course, this is also what El-Dinary and I found with respect to transactional comprehension strategies instruction, that only some teachers could learn how to do it even when they are given extensive support (see Pressley & El-Dinary, 1997).

CONCLUDING REFLECTIONS

Scientific information about reading instruction comes in various forms. Excellent programs of research, in my view, use a variety of methodological approaches. There are important roles in science for experiments, correlational studies, and qualitative investigations. Although I think that the National Reading Panel did a great job with some of their subtasks, for example, evaluating the experimental literatures relating to phonemic awareness, phonics, comprehension, and teacher education, I think the ground rules by which the entire enterprise was conducted were wrong—simply too narrow for even a very conservative scientist such as myself.

My view is that the science we should be most thinking about is not the work that has been studied to the point of diminishing returns. Rather, we should be focusing our attention on emerging hypotheses that might dramatically transform our thinking about how reading education could and should occur. That is why I am spending so much time thinking about The Big Hypothesis. That position has not been studied yet in even one true experiment or quasi-experiment. Nonetheless, it is pointing to the possibility that reading education should be done entirely differently than occurs in the vast majority of primary-level classrooms. If we are to find out whether The Big Hypothesis is valid, we need to be getting to work on it rather than expending great resources on reports that simply summarize a small part of the previous reading research, research that is already reasonably well understood and appreciated by many in the reading education community. The work summarized in the *Report of the National Reading Panel* was very, very good work. For the most part, however, it is just not where the scientific edge is moving at present.

School-based folks need to spend time studying that edge as well, for they have a role in advancing the science, too. Remember those teachers I observed who were doing more complete comprehension strategies instruction than was being studied by the experimentalists at the time. Those educators had taken the starting point defined by the scientific cutting edge and created a new cutting edge. And please notice that my colleagues and I found The Big Hypothesis in primary-grades classrooms, we did not put it there. The great beginning literacy educators we were privileged to observe had pulled together the various bits and pieces of instruction validated in basic educational research and created something quite a bit bigger than anything evaluated by educational scientists to date. My colleagues looked at their creation and derived The Big Hypothesis from their work. Good educational scientists spend their time with good educators, just as good educators think about the cutting edge of educational science. As a result, good educational scientists and good educators become better educational scientists and educators together.

REFERENCES

Almasi, J. F., Palmer, B. M., Gambrell, L. B., & Pressley, M. (1994). Toward disciplined inquiry: A methodological analysis of whole-language research. *Educational Psychologist, 29*, 193–202.

Anderson, L., Evertson, C., & Brophy, J. (1979). An experimental study of effective teaching in first-grade reading groups. *Elementary School Journal, 79*, 193–223.

Anderson, V. (1992). A teacher development project in transactional strategy instruction for teachers of severely reading-disabled adolescents. *Teaching & Teacher Education, 8*, 391–403.

Bogner, K., Raphael, L. M., & Pressley, M. (2002). How grade-1 teachers motivate literate activity by their students. *Scientific Studies of Reading, 6*, 135–165.

Bracht, G. H., & Glass, G. V. (1968). The external validity of experiments. *American Educational Research Journal, 5*, 437–474.

Brown, R., Pressley, M., Van Meter, P., & Schuder, T. (1996). A quasi-experimental validation of transactional strategies instruction with low-achieving second grade readers. *Journal of Educational Psychology, 88*, 18–37.

Campbell, D. T., & Stanley, J. C. (1966). *Experimental and quasi-experimental designs for research.* Chicago: Rand-McNally.

Collins, C. (1991). Reading instruction that increases thinking abilities. *Journal of Reading, 34*, 510–516.

Cronbach, L. J. (1957). The two disciplines of scientific psychology. *American Psychologist, 12*, 671–684.

Dolezal, S., Mohan, L., Pressley, M., & Vincent, M. (in press). *How do grade-3 teachers motivate academic engagement in their students? Elementary School Journal.*

Hart, B., & Risley, T. R. (1995). *Meaningful differences in the everyday experience of young American children.* Baltimore: Brookes.

Juel, C. (1988). Learning to read and write: A longitudinal study of 54 children from first through fourth grades. *Journal of Educational Psychology, 80*, 417–447.

Lincoln, Y. S., & Guba, E. G. (1985). *Naturalistic inquiry.* Beverly Hills: Sage.

Lysynchuk, L. M., Pressley, M., D'Ailly, H., Smith, M., & Cake, H. (1989). A methodological analysis of experimental evaluations of comprehension strategy instruction. *Reading Research Quarterly, 24*, 458–470.

Lysynchuk, L. M., Pressley, M., & Vye, N. J. (1990). Reciprocal teaching improves standardized reading comprehension performance in poor grade-school comprehenders. *Elementary School Journal, 90*, 469–484.

Markman, E. M. (1979). Realizing that you don't understand: Elementary school children's awareness of inconsistencies. *Child Development, 50,* 643–655.

Metsala, J. L. (1999). Young children's phonological awareness and nonword repetition as a function of vocabulary development. *Journal of Educational Psychology, 91,* 3–19.

National Reading Panel (2000). *Teaching children to read: An evidence-based assessment of the scientific research literature on reading and its implications for reading instruction: Reports of the subgroups.* Washington DC: National Institute of Child Health and Development.

Pressley, M. (in press). Effective beginning reading instruction: A paper commissioned by the National Reading Conference. *Journal of Literacy Research.*

Pressley, M., Allington, R., Wharton-McDonald, R., Block, C. C., & Morrow, L. M. (2001). *Learning to read: Lessons from exemplary first grades.* New York: Guilford.

Pressley, M., & El-Dinary, P. B. (1997). What we know about translating comprehension strategies instruction research into practice. *Journal of Learning Disabilities, 30,* 486–488.

Pressley, M., El-Dinary, P. B., Gaskins, I., Schuder, T., Bergman, J. L, Almasi, J., & Brown, R. (1992). Beyond direct explanation: Traditional instruction of reading comprehension strategies. *Elementary School Journal, 92,* 511–554.

Pressley, M., Gaskins, I. W., Cunicelli, E. A., Bardick, N. J., Schaub-Matt, M., Lee, D. S., & Powell, N. (1991). Strategy instruction at Benchmark School: A faculty interview study. *Learning Disability Quarterly, 14,* 19–48.

Pressley, M., Goodchild, F., Fleet, J., Zajchowski, R., & Evans, E. D. (1989). The challenges of classroom strategy instruction. *Elementary School Journal, 89,* 301–342.

Pressley, M., Johnson, C. J., Symons, S., McGoldrick, J. A., & Kurita, J. A. (1989). Strategies that improve memory and comprehension of what is read. *Elementary School Journal, 90,* 3–32.

Pressley, M., Roehrig, A., Raphael, L., Dolezal, S., Bohn, K., Mohan, L., et al. (in press). Teaching processes in elementary and secondary education. In W. Reyonlds & G. E. Miller (Eds.) *Comprehensive handbook of psychology* (Vol. 7): *Educational Psychology.* New York: John Wiley & Sons.

Pressley, M., Wharton-McDonald, R., Allington, R., Block, C. C., Morrow, L., Tracey, D., et al. (2001). A study of effective grade-1 literacy instruction. *Scientific Studies of Reading, 5,* 35–58.

Ridgeway, V. G., Dunston, P. J., & Qian, G. (1993). A methodological analysis of teaching and learning strategy research at the secondary school level. *Reading Research Quarterly, 28,* 335–349.

Rosenshine, B., & Furst, N. (1973). The use of direct observation to study teaching. In R. M. W. Travers (Ed.), *Second handbook of research on teaching* (pp. 122–183). New York: Longman.

Scarborough, H. S. (2001). Connecting early language and literacy to later reading (dis)abilities: Evidence, theory, and practice. In S. B. Neuman & D. K. Dickinson (Eds.), *Handbook of early literacy research.* New York: Guilford.

Troia, G. A. (1999). Phonological awareness intervention research: A critical review of the experimental methodology. *Reading Research Quarterly, 34,* 28–52.

Underwood, B. J. (1975). Individual differences as a crucible in theory construction. *American Psychologist, 30,* 128–134.

Wharton-McDonald, R., Pressley, M., & Hampston, J. M. (1998). Outstanding literacy instruction in first grade: Teacher practices and student achievement. *Elementary School Journal, 99,* 101–128.

CLASSROOM IMPLICATIONS

1. Should preservice teachers be trained in SBRR? If so, should their training be limited to SBRR?

2. Should teachers be evaluated by administrators who use observation instruments developed around SBRR-based instructional methods? Have you had experience with such approaches?

3. Are there important reading-related outcomes that seem inaccessible to the quantitative research methods used by the Panel? If so, can you name a few?

ANNOTATED BIBLIOGRAPHY

National Reading Panel. (2000). *Report of the subgroups*. Washington, DC: U.S. Department of Education. [On-line]. Available: http://www.nationalreadingpanel.org/
   The full text of the report, including the method and criteria employed by the Panel. This is a must read before defensible judgments can be reached. Note that the Web site also features additional materials.

Snow, C. E., Burns, M. S., Griffin, P. (1998). *Preventing reading difficulties in young children*. Washington, DC: National Research Council.
   Summarizes scientific studies as they apply to young children (especially preK and younger) and to parenting programs. Instrumental in programs developed through the Reading Excellence Act.

U.S. Department of Education. *Scientifically based research*. [On-line]. Available: http://www.ed.gov/offices/OESE/esea/research/
   A collection of links to sites affording information about SBRR.

Yatvin, J. (2002). Babes in the woods: The wanderings of the National Reading Panel. *Phi Delta Kappan*, [On-line]. Available: http://www.pdkintl.org/kappan/k0201yat.htm
   A critique of how the NRP was selected, how it conducted its research review and produced its report. Presents an "insider's" view of one of the panelists.

YOU BECOME INVOLVED

1. Return to the list of five criticisms of the NRP report (listed previously). Choose one of them and write a brief response to it.

2. We have constructed a T-chart, with the five criticisms listed in the left-hand column. Complete the chart by writing possible counters that the NRP might have suggested in the right-hand column. You might not agree with all of the counterarguments, but the experience may be broadening.

CRITICISM OF THE NRP REPORT	POSSIBLE COUNTERARGUMENTS
Quantitative methods are always flawed in some way, and, besides, they attempt to quantify elements that resist quantification.	
The Panel avoided some of the really pressing issues in reading education, such as "reading wars," which pitted decoding and whole-language advocates against one another.	
The selection criteria employed by the Panel were so strict that large bodies of credible evidence were ignored.	
Practices validated by the Panel may still not work well for individual teachers or in particular settings.	
There is a danger that the Panel's findings may be adopted in a mindless, rote fashion.	

INDEX